To Jack

Best wishes

L. Muhmmad

Praise for
For Crying Out Loud: From Open Outcry to the Electronic Screen

"Anyone who cares how economic institutions grow great will be fascinated by Leo Melamed's tale of the creation of the CME Group and the crises weathered and solved over three combative decades. The Chicago markets Melamed invented, led, tinkered with, expanded, and defended have come through the recent unpleasantness without a scratch."

  —MARTIN MAYER
   Guest scholar of the Brookings Institution

For Crying Out Loud

From Open Outcry to the Electronic Screen

LEO MELAMED

WILEY

John Wiley & Sons, Inc.

For general information on our other products and services or for technical support,
please contact our Customer Care Department within the United States at
(800) 762-2974, outside the United States at (317) 572-3993 or fax (317) 572-4002.

Wiley also publishes its books in a variety of electronic formats. Some content that
appears in print may not be available in electronic books. For more information about
Wiley products, visit our web site at www.wiley.com.

Library of Congress Cataloging-in-Publication Data

Melamed, Leo.
    For crying out loud : from open outcry to the electronic screen / Leo Melamed.
      p. cm.
    Includes bibliographical references and index.
    ISBN 978-0-470-22943-9 (cloth)
  1. Chicago Mercantile Exchange–History.
  2. Commodity exchanges–Illinois–Chicago–History.   I. Title.
    HG6049.M45 2009
    332.64'40973—dc22

                                           2009013312

Printed in the United States of America

10 9 8 7 6 5 4 3 2 1

I dedicate this book to all the traders and brokers in the world, especially to those in Chicago who were part of this history.

Contents

Foreword

Since its founding in 1898 as the Butter & Egg Board, the Chicago Mercantile Exchange has been on the ascendancy, arguably one of the greatest American business success stories of the last century. But the last decade, between 1998 and 2008, represents an era of unparalleled transformation, innovation, dynamism, and growth at CME, now CME Group. CME became the first U.S. exchange to demutualize and the first to complete an initial public offering and become a publicly traded company. CME established itself as the global leader in electronic trading in all financial and commodity products, effectively managing through a combination of skill, vision, and magic what no one thought possible: the transformation from "open-outcry" trading on the floor of the exchange to trading electronically 24 hours a day, 7 days a week in more than 85 countries around the world. Throughout this decade, CME established itself as one of the most important financial institutions in the world, recognized as the leading provider of electronic trading services and liquidity through its Globex platform; as the undisputed leader in clearing, settlement, and risk management services through the CME Clearing House; and as the largest and most effective consolidator in global exchange markets with nearly $20 billion with its acquisitions of the Chicago Board of Trade and the New York Mercantile Exchange.

- In 1998, average daily volumes were less than 1 million contracts; today they are more than 10 times that number.
- In 1998, 95 percent of transactions were completed manually through the open-outcry system of trading; today more than 83 percent of transactions are completed electronically.
- Average response times in CME Group's electronically traded products improved from 2.5 seconds (2,500 milliseconds) in 1998 to less than 10 milliseconds by 2008.
- In the first quarter of 2003, our first as a publicly traded company, our quarterly net income was a mere $26 million; in 2008, the first-quarter net income was $284 million.

The CME's $11 billion acquisition of the Chicago Board of Trade (CBOT) was a key turning point in our history, solidifying Chicago's position as the global center of futures and options markets and extending CME into the highly complementary Treasury and commodity futures markets. Together, CME could now offer Eurodollar short-term interest rate and Treasury futures contracts as well as wheat, corn, soybean, cattle and hog futures, and options contracts, side by side on the CME Globex electronic trading platform. The CME/CBOT combinations also significantly increased our leadership in the area of clearing, settlement, and risk management, making us the largest global derivatives clearinghouse, with more than $100 billion in collateral, a financial safeguards system worth more than $7 billion, and producing hundreds of millions of dollars in capital and margin efficiency for CME Group customers.

Not resting on our laurels, our CME/CBOT megadeal was closely followed by CME Group's $9 billion acquisition of the New York Mercantile Exchange, one of the world's most profitable and fastest-growing exchanges, on August 22, 2008. This important transaction further advanced our strength in global financial markets by bringing us into the important energy, metals, and over-the-counter swaps clearing businesses. Today, we offer the broadest array of deeply liquid contracts across every major tradable asset class—far more than any other exchange in the world. In 2007, we facilitated the trading of more than 2.2 billion futures and options contracts having a notional value in excess of $1 quadrillion.

Our rapid organic growth combined with our successful mergers and acquisitions strategy was accompanied by significant new global expansion efforts. In recent years, we became the single largest shareholder in the BM&F/Bovespa exchange in Brazil and the Dubai Mercantile Exchange, establishing ourselves in both Latin America and the Middle East. We also entered into important new partnerships in China, Japan, South Korea, and Malaysia, cementing our long-term future by positioning CME Group to take advantage of the rapid growth and development of risk transfer and financial markets in emerging market economies of great significance.

Finally, we stand on the precipice of another momentous sea change of opportunity: the vast over-the-counter derivatives markets. As of the time of this writing, our world's financial markets have crashed in a way that could not have been imagined. For the first time in 30 years, governments, regulators, investment banks, and market participants recognize the value and importance of greater transparency and central counterparty clearing services—long the hallmarks of our three exchanges and CME Group. Today, we are witnessing explosive growth in Clearport, our over-the-counter clearing facility for oil and gas swaps, and we are expanding to include the clearing of interest rate swaps, foreign exchange options, agricultural and metals swaps, and credit default swaps. Like the transformation of floor-based open-outcry markets to global electronic trading systems, this new arena will further transform our business and take us into whole new realms of financial markets activity.

This book is a history of the last 10 years of unparalleled accomplishment at CME Group, told by Leo Melamed, one of the great innovators in financial markets and the guiding hand of CME for much of the last 45 years.

CRAIG DONOHUE
Chief Executive Officer
CME Group

Preface

On Friday, September 12, 2008—the last weekday before the 158-year-old legendary investment bank, Lehman Brothers, filed for bankruptcy—its total of open customer and house positions at the Chicago Mercantile Exchange (CME Group) exceeded $1.1 billion. (That translates to a notional value in excess of $1.1 trillion, a number so large it is nearly impossible to fathom.) And yet bankruptcy and the attendant turmoil notwithstanding, all positions were fully paid for on the CME books—no defaults, no failures, no federal bailouts. That's right! In the midst of the unprecedented global financial meltdown, as marquee names of finance, no matter of what stripe, age, or financial strength, trembled or failed, the CME performed its operational functions without a hitch or disruption. It was without doubt one of the finest hours in its 100-year plus history.

It begs the question: How did it come to pass that during the current unprecedented global meltdown—when giants such as Goldman Sachs, Merrill Lynch, Bank of America, and American International Group, to name but a few, needed government bailouts to stay alive; when so much on Wall Street went wrong—the Chicago Mercantile Exchange (the Merc) was the poster child for what went right? How did the "House that Pork Bellies Built"—35 years earlier a secondary backwater Chicago futures market strictly for agricultural products—become the colossal global powerhouse of futures and options in three decades? There are a number of answers to these questions, but they begin and end with CME's willingness and talent to innovate.

Leadership, operational wherewithal, technological know-how, the ability to attract quality personnel, and the courage to experiment were its key drivers—coupled, to be sure, with a measure of good luck. Without question, the launch of the International Monetary Market division (IMM) in 1971, for trading of financial futures, was central to CME's success. By good fortune, it could not have been timed more perfectly. On August 15, 1971, when President Richard Nixon dropped the U.S. dollar convertibility to gold, it led to an irreversible breakdown of the system of fixed exchange rates, initiated the modern era of globalization, and provided the rationale for the launch of financial futures. What followed was an era of financial turmoil that until the present time has rarely been equaled in modern history.

Indeed, one could not have ordained a more perfect backdrop for the creation of a new financial futures exchange designed to help manage the risk of currency and interest rate price movement than what actually happened. It gave the Merc the first-mover advantage in an eventuality that spectacularly changed the course and history of futures markets. Starting from a second-rate "meats" futures market—cattle, hogs, pork bellies—by the end of the twentieth century the CME had evolved into a global enterprise with 98 percent of its product line dealing in financial contracts. It became the CME Group by merging with the Chicago Board of Trade (CBOT) in July 2007 and with the New York Mercantile Exchange (NYMEX) in August 2008, thus becoming the largest futures market in the world.

The Merc, of course, inherited its operational model from the founders of the Butter & Egg Board in 1898. However, it is doubtful that any of those founding fathers would see anything they recognized in the operating systems of today. At the very nucleus of its structure stands the CME Clearing House, the world's largest futures clearing organization, clearing nearly 90 percent of all futures and options traded in the United States. Risk management and financial surveillance are its two primary functions. It is designed to provide the highest level of safety and the early detection of unsound financial practices on the part of any clearing members. The CME Clearing House, functioning as the central counterparty (CCP) to each trade, has ultimate accountability for credit risk management of trading counterparties. At the core of its safeguards lie several risk management procedures that are fundamental to its success and dramatically distinguish exchange-traded futures from over-the-counter (OTC) derivatives. These include a performance bond or "margin" deposit; a "no-debt system" that performs a twice daily mark-to-market procedure to ensure that market losses do not accumulate; and SPAN, a standard portfolio analysis of risk developed in 1988 to effectively assess risk on an overall portfolio basis. In its 110-year history, no clearing member has ever defaulted and no customer has ever lost funds due to counterparty failure.

The Clearing House system's aggregate financial resources are today over $100 billion, including its $8 billion guaranty fund. In 2008, it handled 3.3 billion contracts with a notional value of $1.2 quadrillion. The financial integrity of the CME Clearing House is currently under the watchful eye of its president, Ms. Kim Taylor. The clearing system has weathered every disaster that has come its way, be it the 1976 Mexican peso devaluation, the Drexel Burnham Lambert failure, the crisis brought about by September 11, the Enron debacle, the Gulf War, Hurricane Katrina, or the most recent global financial crisis.

A primary hallmark of CME's success is Globex, its electronic transaction system. Globex enabled the Exchange to evolve from the antiquated open-outcry transaction architecture to one that is at the cutting edge of present-day electronic automation. It extended the Merc's pits to every nook and cranny of the financial world with live access from more than 80 countries. Its technological evolution is nearly incomprehensible, the stuff of science fiction. At its launch in 1992, Globex was capable of a maximum of 10 trades per second, a response time of 1.3 seconds, and quote dissemination in 150 milliseconds. By 2008, Globex's inbound record peak (on July 16, 2008) hit 23,513 messages per second, with 20,870 orders per second and 2,643 mass quotes per second—astonishing even for a system that is today the premier global electronic platform for futures and options.

Moreover, not only are there electronic Globex pits everywhere in the world, the nature and makeup of the traders who man them has been dramatically altered. Computers, no longer acting within the structure of their classical capability, have gained artificial intelligence and assumed a significant role in directing the actions of the traders themselves. Hugely successful proprietary trading enterprises have sprung up in all parts of the globe with jealously guarded algorithms (trading programs) that have achieved a new generation of analytics. These programs, operating at unimaginable speeds, apply advanced mathematical models in order to capture countless sophisticated trading strategies based on price correlations and associations between markets that were never before possible. It has forever changed the definition of a "trader."

The number of transactions generated as a result of Globex technology tells much of the story: In 1971, before the introduction of financial futures, the CME's average daily volume (ADV) was 12,774 transactions. The total annual volume amounted to just over 3 million contracts. After the birth of the IMM, the Merc's volume began to grow dynamically. Two decades later, on the eve of Globex, the CME had reached an impressive ADV of 427,000 contracts, with an annual total of over 108 million transactions. Still, as the CME entered the twenty-first century, there was only so much volume the open-outcry system could engender, leveling off with an ADV of under a million contracts per day. Beginning in 2001, however, as Globex materially advanced its capabilities, the Merc's ADV began to skyrocket—going ballistic after the Eurodollar contract went electronic. In 2008, the CME Group ADV reached nearly 13 million contracts, with a total volume of just under 2 billion transactions.

The CME revenue story is identical—becoming one of the great stories of Wall Street after it went public. At the outset of my chairmanship in 1969, the Merc's annual revenue was under $4 million. Two decades after the launch of financial contracts, revenues had reached an impressive $124 million. But even that was chump change when compared to what occurred after Globex matured. Last year, in 2008, the Merc's revenue—not including the CBOT or NYMEX—was well over $1 billion. To state the obvious, Globex represented the means that would transport the Chicago

Mercantile Exchange to the pinnacle of the global marketplace. In 2002, the Merc's electronic platform provided the credibility and investor attraction to successfully launch an initial public offering and subsequently acted as the irresistible magnet to draw into its fold the CBOT and NYMEX.

Today, the Merc's product line arguably offers coverage for the entire spectrum of business risk: equities, energy, notes and bonds, Eurodollars, commodities, foreign exchange, metals, and weather. The Exchange is currently poised to provide an industry-leading CCP solution for clearing of credit default swaps (CDS) and other OTC derivatives. Its users include the largest and most sophisticated financial institutions in the world—domestic and international banks and investment banks, public and private pension funds, index funds, mutual funds, hedge funds, investment companies, energy providers, asset and liability managers, mortgage companies, swap dealers, insurance companies, corporate entities, proprietary trading firms, and individuals.

In a word, the old Butter & Egg Board has evolved into a global colossus for the management of risk: The CME Group.

*   *   *

For Crying Out Loud is the informal history of the Chicago Mercantile Exchange between 1996 and 2006, during which time the Exchange was successfully transformed from a market operating within an age-old open-outcry trading framework into a technologically cutting-edge electronic trading system and from a tight-knit, not-for-profit entity owned and run by its members into a widely traded public corporation. While by no means a complete history of the CME during this period, it highlights the critical events, significant personalities, and cliff-hanging twists and turns that were instrumental or involved in this very difficult but enormously successful metamorphosis.

The author's purpose in writing these memoirs is twofold. First, it provides the reader with an inside look at a major American enterprise throughout a fascinating, make-or-break historical time period during which Globex, the CME's phenomenal electronic trading system overcame its adversaries, matured, and proved absolutely critical to the CME's success. Second, it underscores for every business endeavor the preeminent necessity of innovation coupled with a determination to overcome the inevitable forces of the status quo.

The opinions expressed in this book are solely those of the author and are not intended to represent the opinions of the CME Group, its officers or board of directors.

The book is divided into three parts. Part I, "Battling the Tyranny of the Status Quo," is comprised of 10 chapters written from the author's vantage point as the CME's prime mover throughout this period and picks up the Merc's history beginning in 1996, where the author's initial memoirs, *Escape to the Futures* (John Wiley & Sons, 1996), left off. Some of these chapters include original documents or exhibits that are referenced and are relevant to the history discussed.

Part II, "Messenger from the Futures," is comprised of essays written by the author during the time period depicted. Some of these essays have been published previously and in some instances include minor revisions to correct language and reduce redundancy. The author's selection of writings for this book was based on one or more of these criteria:

- *The essay was of particular relevance to the history being discussed:* Tomorrow's Technological Tidal Wave (11); Wakeup Call (12); CME Fred Arditti Award (27); CME: The House that Innovation Built (32); The Law of Selective Gravity (33); The Gray Swan (34)
- *The essay offers a more comprehensive examination of the particular theme under discussion or of general significance to futures markets:* Panel on the Stock Market Crash of 1987 (15); Chicago Futures in the Twenty-First Century (19); Transformation of Futures Exchanges (22); Our Middle Name (23); CME Center for Innovation (24); Math Is in Our Futures (28)
- *The essay provides a window into other geographical centers where issues pertaining to futures markets were also under consideration:* The Need for Futures Markets in an Emerging World Economy (14); Preface to the Japanese Translation of *Escape to the Futures* (16); Buy a Call on the Snake (21); Remarks at the Celebration of the Chinese-Language Publication of *Escape to the Futures* (25)
- *The essay gives unique insight to the background or philosophical makeup of the author:* Reminiscences of a Refugee (13); Pain, Progress, and Promise (17); There Are No Jews in Bialystok (18); Merton Miller, 1923–2000 (20); Knowledge Tag (26); If It's Good Enough for Milton (29); Education: The Only Thing that Never Fails (30); The Boy of Steel (31)

LEO MELAMED

April 28, 2009

Acknowledgments

The phenomenal successes of the Chicago Mercantile Exchange during the era I was privileged to lead the institution was achieved in concomitance with the efforts and contributions of countless members and colleagues who stood with me in leadership roles. Indeed, throughout the years of my officialdom, I was fortunate to have some highly talented people as top advisors who served in my "Inner Council" and upon whom I heavily depended for counsel. Among those of note in the early years were Barry Lind and Brian Monieson; in subsequent years, Fred Arditti, Henry Jarecki, Les Rosenthal, and Bill Shepard were added to the team. In addition, of special significance during the course of those many years were the CME chairmen with whom I shared the leadership stage, namely: Michael Weinberg Jr., Jack Sandner, John Geldermann, Larry Rosenberg, Brian Monieson, Scott Gordon, and presently Terry Duffy. Last but certainly not least were the CME presidents and CEOs who provided ideas, guidance, and continuity: Everett B. Harris, Clayton Yeutter, William Brodsky, Rick Kilcollin, and our current CEO, Craig Donohue.

Similarly, in writing this book, I relied heavily on the advice and ideas of a host of associates, some of whom I must single out: first and foremost, CME chairman Terry Duffy, CME CEO Craig Donohue, CME president Phupinder Gill, and former CBOT chairman Charlie Carey. While over a stretch of time, memories can fade and often events are remembered differently by different people, I tried to check my facts and remembrances in as many ways as was possible. Toward this purpose, I owe a debt of gratitude to those colleagues who agreed to be interviewed, providing me with a kaleidoscope of views and memories with which to paint the mural I attempted to achieve: Bill Brodsky, Charlie Carey, Craig Donohue, Terry Duffy, Brad Ferguson, Marty Gepsman, Phupinder Gill, Rick Kilcollin, John Labuszewski, Jim Krause, Bill Miller, Jimmy Oliff, Jerry Salzman, Don Serpico, Bill Shepard, and the late Fred Arditti. In addition, I must acknowledge the discussions and invaluable material provided to me by the leaders of the Equity Owners Association, Don Karel, Bill Shepard, and Joel Stender.

A book of this nature depends to a large extent on friends and relatives who are willing to read the drafts, offer suggestions, and make corrections.

In this respect, I would put my wife, Betty Melamed, in first place. No matter
what else she was doing, no matter what time of the day or night, she was
always willing to read a passage, offer a comment, or answer a question.
In similar fashion I must single out my daughter Idelle and sons Jordan and
David, all of whom had lived through many of the events and incidents
described and were able critics. Finally, I wish to thank three colleagues,
Arman Falsafi and Beverly Splane, who knew the history and offered a
full range of edits and suggestions, and my administrative assistant, Patricia
Reiffel, who never tired of providing me the entire complement of technical
services required in this undertaking.

L.M.

Author's Note

Human history is replete with new ideas, postulates, and inventions that were so revolutionary or monumental that their advocates were vehemently rebuked and the ideas rejected by the establishment. Milton Friedman defined it as *Tyranny of the Status Quo* (Harcourt Brace, 1983). Historian Barbara W. Tuchman stated in *Practicing History: Selected Essays* (Knopf, 1982), "Men will not believe what does not fit in with their plans or suit their prearrangements!" One of the most celebrated instances, of course, occurred in 1613, when Galileo Galilei published his *Letters on the Solar Spots*, advocating the Copernican model of the universe in which the Earth revolves around the Sun. For that presumption, Galileo was found guilty of heresy by the church in Rome. It took 300 years for the Vatican to recant.

From the buggy whip's displacement by motor vehicles, to New England's whale oil succeeded by Texan crude, to the workshop super-seded by the assembly line, adherents of the status quo have sought to prevent advancement, using whatever means necessary. The futures markets have been no different. The Chicago Mercantile Exchange, now CME Group, Inc. is a well-known poster child for change. From the innovation of live animals as contracts for trade in the 1960s, to financial instruments in place of agricultural markets in the 1970s, cash settlement replacing physical delivery in the 1980s, and electronic trade instead of open outcry in the 1990s, the CME defied the status quo. But it never came easy or without a fight.

PART I

Battling the Tyranny
of the Status Quo

CHAPTER 1

Countdown to Liftoff

"I have detected a sort of squishy rumor that you are supporting Terry Duffy for chairman."

It was vintage Scott Gordon, chairman of the Chicago Mercantile Exchange (CME).[1] We were sitting in my office on the thirty-second floor of the Merc's north tower. He said the words quietly as was his custom, ostensibly in total innocence of their implication. Even the phrase "squishy rumor" was a distinctively Scott Gordon usage of words intended not to be confrontational or offensive—an offhand comment between two friends about a bit of inconsequential gossip on the trading floor in 2002.

It was anything but. We were at a pivotal moment in the extraordinary history of the Chicago Mercantile Exchange. We were at another historic showdown—the corporate equivalent of the gunfight at the O.K. Corral, a confrontation replete with intrigue, conspiracy, and treachery in which the careers of many hung in the balance. We were in a battle that would determine whether past revolutionary labors and innovations would achieve a triumphant destiny for this venerable institution and make millionaires out of thousands of Chicago traders.

I liked Scott Gordon. We had been friends for many years, ever since his mentor and my close friend Leslie Rosenthal, the former chairman of the Chicago Board of Trade (CBOT), asked me if there was a job available for Gordon at my firm, Dellsher Investment Company, Inc. That was back in the 1980s. I made sure there was. It was the beginning of a career path that led Scott to be elected chairman of the CME in 1998. How strange, then, to find ourselves four years later on opposite sides of a struggle for control of the CME. But I am way ahead of the story. That's the trouble with memory. Once you set it in motion, it is propelled like a rocket, never so much as taking a breath or stopping to reflect on the path it has followed. Memory takes far too much for granted. It presumes you know the context of each flashback it conjures and the history that conceived it.

Given the dramatic sea change that the futures industry and the CME in particular have experienced over the last 10 years, let alone the past

three decades, it is already difficult to remember in detail all the twists
and turns of the history that brought the Merc to today's pinnacle, and
even harder to recall some of the life-and-death issues with which we
struggled, the resolution of which now seem so obvious. It is, however,
imperative to record this history not only because of George Santayana's
famous admonition, not only because it might provide a fascinating story,
but because it is representative of the never-ending struggle between status
quo and change.

In 1991—after two decades of leadership—I felt that this immigrant kid
from Bialystok had done enough. Our Exchange was in very strong shape,
success primarily flowing from its first-mover advantage in the introduction
of financial contracts. Further, the soon-to-be-launched electronic Globex
system would in my view provide the technological certainty for its future.
So confident was I of the coming technological age that in November of 1991
I wrote "Tomorrow's Technological Tidal Wave," (see Chapter 11) an essay
that predicted the coalescence of interactive multimedia communications
systems and the dawning of an era demanding 24-hour trading capability.
More to the point, in combination with its strong agricultural base, the CME
represented the most diverse futures institution in the world. Its Eurodollar
contract was the most actively traded futures instrument of any exchange. It
had become the accepted short-term interest rate mechanism for the world
of finance. Membership prices were on the rise. Volumes too were growing
and the open interest, which tabulates the overnight open market positions,
had risen to record proportions. As Jack Sandner, the newly installed CME
chairman upon my retirement in 1991, liked to point out, the large open
interest was proof that the CME had a built-in reservoir for continued growth.
It was a valid observation.[2]

Now I thought it was time to step down and pursue some private-sector
goals. I planned to launch Sakura Dellsher, a futures brokerage firm formed
from a merger between my firm, Dellsher Investment Company, and the
Japanese Mitsui Tayo Kobe Bank. Except that I would remain chairman of
Globex for a while longer, my decision would preclude me for the first time
in 22 years from leading the decisions and actions of the Merc—a move I
thought represented a permanent change in the direction of my life. I was
very wrong.

Few observers would argue that irrespective of what CME titles I
officially held (Chairman, Special Counsel, Chairman of the Executive Committee, or Senior Policy Advisor), from the time I was first elected chairman in 1969 to my retirement in 1991, and again upon my return to the
Board in 1997 as Chairman Emeritus and Senior Policy Advisor—although
I had plenty of help as indicated in the acknowledgments—I was the effective leader of the Chicago Mercantile Exchange. My leadership position

remained in place (with the exception of a brief period under chief executive officer Jim McNulty), until after the Merc's initial public offering in 2002, when the new team of Terry Duffy, as chairman, and Craig Donohue, as CEO, began to take over the reins. To this date, I remain Chairman Emeritus and Chairman of the Board Strategic Steering Committee.[3]

Although this story could begin at any number of junctures, 1996—five years after my "retirement" and about six years before the critical conversation with Scott Gordon took place—is particularly appropriate. Just as the space shuttle is fueled with rocket propellant prior to liftoff, so did the events begun in 1996 provide fuel to the CME for its unparalleled climb to the top.[4] However, to do justice to the pivotal events of that year, one must be conversant with the mortal conflict at the Exchange between the two opposing blocs that dominated CME politics: those who favored "open outcry" and those who supported electronic trading.

The war, and it was exactly that, unofficially began on August 28, 1987, when the CME board approved the plan submitted by its Strategic Planning Committee to create the world's first electronic trading system for futures and options. The plan, of course, needed referendum approval from the CME membership.[5] Its working designation was PMT, which stood for Post (Pre) Market Trade, a nomenclature I purposefully selected to allay any fears that PMT might encroach on the sanctity of open outcry.[6] The system would operate exclusively *before* and *after* regular U.S. business hours. No existing pit-traded instrument would ever need to compete with the electronic screen during the open-outcry session. It was a holy pledge that could not be changed without membership approval.

To say this was a revolutionary idea does not begin to describe the radical nature of the notion. A departure from open outcry was a watershed moment for futures markets, an event comparable in physics to, say, the splitting of the atom, or like announcing the concept of e-mail to a world that had only experienced the Pony Express. As the CME press release explained, "In a bold and far-reaching joint undertaking, the Chicago Mercantile Exchange and Reuters Holdings, PLC, entered into an agreement to create a global electronic automated transaction system for the trading of futures and futures-options." Arguably it put the CME light-years ahead of its competition. I tried to explain this to the membership in my 1987 Annual Report titled "Embracing Reality."

The concept embodied in PMT (Post Market Trade) is clearly an historic milestone in the development of futures trading. It embraces the realities brought about by technological advancements of recent years and takes a giant step toward unification of the world's separate financial center.

PMT combined elements of electronic linkage with those of extended trading and integrates them with the open-outcry system. In effect, it draws the best from the present and marries it to the technology of the future. In all modesty, it put the CME light-years ahead of its competition.[7]

The Merc's announcement served as a decisive contrast to our primary rival, the CBOT, at the time the world's largest exchange. Karsten Mahlman, the chairman of the Chicago Board of Trade, likened the CME's announcement to the development of the H-bomb, stating it could mean the end of futures markets. Indeed, the CBOT's response to the threat of international competition, announced earlier in 1987, had been predictable. Rather than encroach on open outcry, it sought to extend it by creating an open-outcry "Night Trading Session" that would operate from 6 to 11 P.M. Ostensibly, this would discourage the Asian world from creating a competitive exchange in their own time zone and bring Asian futures business to the American shore.[8]

To me, the difference in response to globalization between our two exchanges was fundamental. The CBOT leadership was bending to the political will of its traders and ignoring the wave of technology that was overtaking the world. A night market for a few hours each evening, I stated, "was like trying to hide from a tornado in a cardboard box."

Here is what the *Chicago Tribune* said:

The Chicago Mercantile Exchange announced a revolutionary plan to capture global business through computer trading rather than resorting to night hours.[9]

If the proposal is approved as expected, the century-old futures industry will make a giant leap into high-tech electronics with its first major attempt at automated trading.[10]

This was my statement to the CME membership in the 1988 Annual Report "The Third Milestone":

The CME believes that to blindly assume that open outcry is the perfect system for all time is to be lulled into a false sense of security and forgo any opportunities to strengthen or advance our way of doing business. Such a policy would be both foolish and dangerous and could lead to disaster. While we must always respect our heritage, we must never let ourselves be held back by its limitations. We must recognize the greater truth, that those who ignore or fear to embrace reality will quickly become history. [See Appendix 1A.]

Open outcry, of course, represented a trading regimen by which a group of traders and brokers gathered in a pit (also known as a ring) and competed for transactions by using their voices and hands to shout out the quantity and price at which they were willing to buy or sell a specific product. Until very recently, this methodology universally described and defined the markets of futures. It was a practice as old as the markets themselves, intertwined with their very birth, which, it is said, occurred in Osaka, Japan, in 1730. Feudal lords there established warehouses to store and sell rice paid to them as land tax by their villagers. In order to protect their booty from wild price fluctuations between harvests, they formed the Dojima Rice Market in the house of a wealthy rice merchant named Yodoya—ostensibly the first organized futures exchange. The merchants gathered there and with shouts and gestures negotiated the price of their "rice tickets."

It can of course be argued that open outcry for transactions between buyers and sellers preceded the Dojima premises by a number of centuries. Ancient Phoenicians, Greeks, and Romans openly traded options against the cargoes of incoming and outgoing ships. And in the tenth and twelfth centuries, during seasonal merchant fairs in Brussels, Madrid, and elsewhere, merchants would gather to loudly and openly negotiate for the future delivery of merchandise. It was not until 1826 in England, and two decades later in the United States, that the traditional open-outcry futures market was established. In the United States, Chicago was the natural locale as it represented the great railroad center for products grown in the West to be moved to the population centers in the East. In 1848, the Chicago Board of Trade opened its doors for trading in grain—corn, wheat, soybeans—to become the world's largest futures exchange during most of its history. Its building, erected in 1885, at LaSalle Street and Jackson Boulevard, became the symbol of Chicago's commercial vitality. Fifty years after the CBOT's birth, in 1898, the Chicago Butter & Egg Board was born, the precursor to the Chicago Mercantile Exchange, which was formed in 1919. In the 1960s, the CME achieved fame as the "House that Pork Bellies Built," an exchange primarily trading in meats—cattle, hogs, and pork bellies. This long-standing commercial spirit was recorded by Carl Sandburg in his famous poem about Chicago in 1916:

Hog Butcher for the World,
Tool Maker, Stacker of Wheat,
Player with Railroads and the Nation's Freight Handler,
Stormy, husky, brawling,
City of the Big Shoulders.

In 1971, while chairman of the CME, I conceived of the idea of futures contracts on foreign currencies. Toward this purpose I initiated the founding of the International Monetary Market (IMM), the first exchange created for the express purpose of futures contracts in financial instruments. Beginning with foreign currency contracts in 1972, the IMM served to revolutionize futures markets. In 1976, the IMM merged into the CME and remains its Financial Division to this day. Over the next three decades, Chicago became known as the capital of futures markets, and financial contracts copied by every global center of finance grew to dominate the world's futures trading.

The history of futures trading in other U.S. centers is similar, with futures exchanges founded in Kansas City, Minneapolis, and New York City. Of them, the New York Mercantile Exchange (NYMEX) became the most prominent, trading in energy products and metals. In 2007, the CBOT, and in 2008, the NYMEX, were acquired by the Chicago Mercantile Exchange, to become The CME Group, today the world's largest futures exchange.

Throughout this history, until the beginning of the twenty-first century, all the trading at every U.S. futures exchange was conducted by open outcry. With such deep roots and enduring heritage, for anyone to suggest a different architecture for the execution of futures trade was not only revolutionary, it was crazy. In 1977, as chairman of the CME, I wrote an article for the *Hofstra University Law Review* in which I categorically declared that futures markets could *only* succeed within an open-outcry transaction architecture. My opinion of course was founded on the conventional wisdom of the time, the technological knowledge then available, and my experience in the Chicago trading pits. Eyeball-to-eyeball interaction, until then, provided the only successful means of generating liquidity—the continuous flow of bids and offers. In 1977, personal computers were in their infant cribs, Bill Gates had just recently left Harvard, windows were what you peered through, a mouse was a rodent, and the apple was but a fruit. Computer technology as we know it today was still science fiction. It would be another decade before computers would revolutionize the twentieth century and forever change everything.

Back then, even the mere thought of market automation was heresy. Still, I knew the idea was not new. Beginning in the early 1970s, automation became an intellectual flirtation of the National Association of Securities Dealers, Inc. (NASD). In 1971, the Nasdaq, a subsidiary of the NASD, became the world's first electronic stock market. At first, however, it was merely a computer bulletin board system and did not actually connect buyers to sellers. In 1975, the Securities and Exchange Commission (SEC) proposed the creation of an automated Central Limit Order Book for securities markets, and in 1976, it issued a formal call for automation.[11] In 1976, Professor Junius W. Peake together with Professor Morris Mendelson and R. Williams Jr. responded by proposing to the SEC a plan for an electronically assisted auction market for securities that would include screen-based rather than floor-based trading, auction principles for trade execution, anonymity, price-time priority for all bids and offers, and equal global access by qualified participants—in other words, all of the salient present-day features of electronic systems.[12] It was a revolutionary concept. The idea, however, did not get very far and was attacked by the broker-dealer establishment as a system that would not work and "would destroy the finest capital market mechanism in the world."[13] In 1979, as a result of intensive lobbying efforts by the NYSE and market makers to preserve status quo, the SEC reversed course.[14]

Futures markets were not immune from these pioneering giants. In 1980, Junius Peake actually developed what in my memory was the very first electronic futures market. It was a Bermuda-based, fully automated futures exchange called INTEX. Junius Peake and I shared the same stage at the *Financial Times* conference in London in September of 1982 on the eve of the launch of the London International Financial Futures Exchange (LIFFE). He unapologetically predicted that if INTEX fulfilled an economic need it would be a success, if not "we shall fade from view." Alas, Professor Peake was well ahead of his time and his ambitious pioneering effort failed, but his idea never faded from view. At the time, the so-called "black box" for futures markets was something never to be openly discussed. Automation was viewed as the death knell to our business, and we were bound by an unwritten holy understanding to reject such concepts outright. I recall telling him that while I admired his courage, "he did not have a ghost of a chance." In my opinion, I stated, if someday automation came to futures markets, it could only succeed at an established futures exchange.

Luckily, I was never a captive of what Milton Friedman defined as the "tyranny of the status quo." Indeed, not too many years after my Hofstra essay, I knew that I had been sadly mistaken. Computer technology was moving at unimaginable speed, creating capabilities that in the very near future would make it realistic to consider trade execution within an electronic venue, an architecture that would make trading vastly faster, cheaper, and more efficient. And above all, it would create enormous new transaction flow on which the income of an exchange depended. Once converted, I was now bound and determined to correct my mistake and to follow John Maynard Keynes's admonition: "When the facts change, I change." The facts did indeed change. However, my new conviction represented one of those truisms that intellectual acceptance by itself was insufficient. It required a practical epiphany.

It was January of 1986. The markets were very active. I was standing at my Dellsher company desk station, which faced the Standard & Poor's trading pit on the Merc trading floor, watching the army of clerks—"runners" to be exact—rush to and fro with orders to the pit at a frantic pace. It was a colorful, exciting, and boisterous scene. Normal. And remarkably inefficient. As it happened, I had just put the finishing touches on a science fiction novel, *The Tenth Planet*,[15] my first amateur attempt at fiction writing. The central character was a humanlike computer Putral, who had the incredible wherewithal to serve all the needs of an alien planetary civilization consisting of five planets and a population of 150 billion people. The nexus was striking and obvious: Life had been imitating science fiction since Jules Verne voyaged to the moon—and before that. If I could fantasize an alien computer of such amazing magnitude as Putral, would it be too much to ask of our own civilization to build a computer that could simply transmit orders to and from an electronic screen for execution—in other words, to act as an electronic pit that required no human intervention?

Convinced that technology, whether we liked it or not, would force fundamental changes to our way of life, I refused to be left in the historical trash bin of status quo obstinacy. The idea grew into an obsession—a belief that became my signal mission for the CME. I decided to utilize the Strategic Planning Committee, which I chaired, and which was charged with finding a solution to the competitive challenges of globalization, as the forum to explore everything, including electronic trading. I had carefully appointed to the committee people whom I thought would not be afraid to take on the status quo.[16] In mid-1986, even before the committee's deliberations were completed, I paid a visit to Reuters Holding, PLC to test the water. There I posed the critical question to Andre Villeneuve and John S. Hull, two senior executives of the giant international information company. Would Reuters undertake the mission of creating an automated global electronic transaction system for futures and options with the CME? Their affirmative response paved the way for the committee's decision.

Given today's globalized markets where electronic screens are a ubiquitous fixture on the desks of all traders in every corner of the globe, with market quotations and information flowing in continuous fashion at speeds nearly impossible to fathom, it is counterintuitive to consider a conclusion different from the one reached by the Strategic Planning Committee in 1986. However, it was a vastly different world back then, and the step we were about to take was of incalculable consequence. As I wrote in *Escape to the Futures*,[17] "Just as I had done in 1972 when I entered the unknown waters of currency futures with the IMM, I was now about to ask the futures industry to follow me on yet another odyssey, over oceans, across continents, and through the immeasurable space of high technology."

Barron's printed my views:

> *Marriage of the computer chip to the telephone altered the world from a confederation of autonomous financial markets into one continuous marketplace. No longer is there a distinct division of three major time zones (Europe, North America, and the Far East). No longer are there*

three separate markets operating independently of external pressures by maintaining their own unique market centers, products, trading hours, and clientele.

Today, news is distributed instantaneously across all time zones. When such informational flows demand market action, financial managers no longer wait for local markets to open before responding. Rather, they have the capacity to initiate immediate market positions—a capacity that has come to be known as "globalization." With globalization, each financial center has become a direct competitor of all others, offering everyone new opportunities, challenges and perils.[18]

With hindsight, one can only marvel at our collective courage and pre-science. But what is vision other than imagination extended into the future? As a result, the CME became the first futures exchange in the world with the foresight to embrace an electronic solution to the coming demands of globalization. It was clearly the defining moment in the evolution of the Chicago Mercantile Exchange. More than anything else, it dramatized our leadership in futures markets and was the fundamental ingredient for the CME's current success. For me, it was also personal. Aside from creating the IMM, the world's first futures exchange for trading instruments of finance—and its introduction of currency futures—I consider the development of Globex, the CME's electronic transaction system, preeminent in my achievements on behalf of the Exchange. As I wrote to Milton Friedman at the time, "The idea is so powerful that, in my opinion, it will become the standard transaction system for all futures and options business, and most likely, the model system for securities and all other market sectors, as well." (See Appendix 1B.)

The great man and I developed a close personal relationship over the years, beginning with his embrace of my audacious idea to launch foreign currency futures in 1972. His friendship, a privilege beyond comparison, lasted until the day I was honored to be included to deliver a eulogy at his memorial, on January 29, 2007, at the Rockefeller Chapel of the University of Chicago. (See Chapter 29.)[19]

It is instructive to record how much easier it is to follow than to lead. The CME's electronic announcement was followed, a year or so later, by similar announcements for electronic systems in foreign domiciles, intended either to extend existing trading hours or for the entire transaction process: In 1988 the Tokyo Stock Exchange, the Osaka Securities Exchange, the Copenhagen Stock Exchange, the Danish Options & Futures, the Swiss Options & Financial Futures Exchange (SOFFEX), and the Tokyo Grain Exchange all launched automated electronic systems. The following year, the Irish Futures and Options Exchange, the Tokyo International Financial Futures Exchange

(TIFFE), the London International Financial Futures Exchange (LIFFE), and the Sydney Futures Exchange initiated similar systems. By the end of 1991, 10 more exchanges had followed suit, including the Deutsche Terminbörse, DTB, the London Futures and Options Exchange, the Swedish Options Market (OM), the Finnish Options Market, and Mercado Español de Futuros Financieros as well as the NYMEX.

In congratulating our members on the approval of the PMT referendum, I proudly said to them, "This is our response, to the demands brought about by the technological revolution as well as to the challenges of globalization. We believe it will translate into opportunity and cost-efficiency—whether you are a banker in Tokyo, a risk manager in London, or an investor in the United States. It is a solution in synch with the markets of the future."[20]

It represented but the opening shot in the ensuing life-or-death battle to challenge the status quo.

CHAPTER 2

Globex

The Fundamental Difference

It is true that the Chicago Mercantile Exchange (CME) and the Chicago Board of Trade (CBOT) were known to be archcompetitors. Indeed, historically there were instances when the two exchanges fought fierce competitive battles for business flows to a given market or instrument of trade. But not many. The first of the recorded head-to-head confrontations actually began within the "meats" arena. On November 30, 1964, the CME introduced the revolutionary idea of a "live" cattle contract, offering for the first time futures trade in a product that would be delivered "on the hoof." Although the contract went through some serious revisions before it became a hit, as history is witness, it proved to become one of the mainstay contracts of the Merc's agricultural complex.

In an attempt not to be left out of the meat market, the CBOT launched a steer carcass beef contract six months later. To retaliate, the CME quickly launched a dressed beef contract. Both contracts failed. Then, on April 15, 1966, Warren Lebeck, president of the CBOT, announced plans to compete with the CME by also launching a live cattle contract. It created quite a stir in Chicago, causing some real bad blood between the two exchanges. Merc president Everette B. Harris accused the CBOT of violating an "unwritten law of commodity futures trading which limits the trading of one commodity to a single exchange in the same city." As far as I could tell, old E.B. Harris invented that rule on the spot. The CME even submitted a public petition, demanding that the CBOT cease and desist from mimicking the Merc. The CBOT members refused. Trading in live cattle began at the CBOT on October 4, 1966, and the competitive fray lasted five years. The press had a heyday, building on the natural differences between the two Chicago markets: The CBOT, established in 1848, internationally known as the granddaddy of futures markets (sometimes referred to as the "Irish" exchange), and the CME, a scrappy upstart, 50 years younger, hardly known outside of Chicago (sometimes called the "Jewish" exchange). It was the principal source for the lasting image of rivalry.[1]

Another good example of fierce competitive challenges that I can recall occurred in the mid-1980s, when both the CBOT and the CME sought the rights to the Nasdaq index for futures trade. The CBOT got the license in what turned out to be a costly mistake for Nasdaq. However, it was a serious loss for the CME as well, since we had become the futures "equity" index market for the world. Listing the Nasdaq product at our Chicago rival would alter this reality. To counter the potential loss, we turned to Standard & Poor's, with whom we had a long and highly profitable relationship, for help. I helped convince their officials to design a brand-new over-the-counter index equivalent to the Nasdaq, which the CME would list for trade. We named it SPOC, Standard & Poor's Over-the-Counter index. We even explored the idea of using Leonard Nemoy, the original Mr. Spock from the TV *Star Trek* series, as our bell ringer, but he was too expensive. A heated and rancorous battle between the two Chicago exchanges ensued, costing each in the neighborhood of $4 million in public relations and marketing. I recall personally losing a good deal of money trying to generate trade in the SPOC pit day after day. My presence and trading in the pit of a newly launched contract was always a focal point for the membership, serving to coerce other traders into helping generate initial liquidity. It became one of my trademarks. Alas, neither exchange's contract succeeded in gaining sufficient traction, and both were ultimately delisted. It was a loss for Nasdaq, but I considered our "spoiler" role as a great victory because it preserved the CME as the exclusive exchange for American equity futures. In subsequent years, Nasdaq corrected its mistake by granting the license to the CME Group, where it remains today the second most actively traded index future in the United States.

But things change. During the last two decades or so, with the singular exception of the 1997 battle for the Dow Jones Index, there were fewer and fewer such competitive frays. (See Chapter 4.) Actually, at the launch of our International Monetary Market (IMM) in 1972, there was some serious support from heavy hitters at the CBOT. For instance, the O'Connors, Billie and Eddie, as well as Les Rosenthal, Ralph Peters, Lee Stern, William Mallers, Hank Shatkin, John Gilmore, Eugene Cashman, Pat Arbor, Charlie Carey, Neal Kotke, John Benjamin and a host of other diehard CBOT stalwarts went all out to support our brazen initiative by buying a large number of the originally issued IMM seats at $10,000 each. It turned out to be quite a profitable investment. In similar fashion, I was enamored with the CBOT and its members. I strongly supported the efforts by Fred Uhleman, Joe Sullivan, the O'Connors, and others in their 1973 launch of the Chicago Board Options Exchange (CBOE). For me, the big brother exchange at the head of LaSalle Street in Chicago, with its rich history and huge agricultural markets, was the symbol of strength and substance of Chicago futures. I believe to this day that without CBOT's heritage, Chicago's future markets would not have prospered or maybe even survived. As soon as I could afford it, I bought a membership and became a CBOT member. Ralph Peters, a legendary trader and former CBOT chairman, actually once offered me an opportunity to become his partner; some CBOT members even suggested I run for their board. As I viewed it, our mission was common—to advance the use and value of the futures markets. Although we were competitors, we were much, much stronger together whenever we joined hands in promoting our common interests and defending ourselves against adversaries. In an unprecedented action, in 1976, I dared put Les Rosenthal on the CME board even while he was serving as a director on the CBOT board as well as the board of Trade Clearing Corporation. In my mind, it was the first move toward the possibility of eventual merger. Together, the CBOT and the CME were able to forge many advances on behalf of the industry, such as the critically important creation of the National Futures Association (NFA), a private sector, self-regulatory, customer protection watchdog, whose formulation and federal legislation I led in 1982 with guidance from U.S. Senator Robert Dole. At Rosenthal's recommendation, I even hired the former chief executive officer (CEO) of the CBOT, Robert K. Wilmouth, to become president of the NFA. He made the NFA the effective and respected self-regulatory body that it is today.[2] More and more, the different instruments at our respective exchanges were accepted by the financial world as complementary. More important, the CME and CBOT learned that it was more productive to separately seek different new innovations rather than compete over the same product. We also learned to cooperate, particularly as it related to mutual concerns about international competition as well as regulatory matters emanating from Washington, D.C. Thus, except for some minor product-related skirmishes, the issues between us were reduced to bragging rights: Which was the bigger exchange? The most innovative? And so on. Still, ego and personality clashes between our respective leaders, coupled with memories of past battles, continued to fuel the media and perpetuate an image of jealousy and competition between the two exchanges.

However, there were several fundamental differences between us that were telling, some of which remained more or less constant until the end of the twentieth century. Charlie Carey, the very astute and charismatic chairman under whose leadership the venerable Chicago Board of Trade adroitly escaped the trap being prepared against them by the executives of the Eurex exchange, and who as chairman courageously achieved a merger with the CME, recognized those distinctions. In a conversation with me in February 2008, aboard a jet speeding from Washington after one of our lobbying efforts in Congress, he commented on those differences: first, that the CME gained an enormous first-mover advantage in the launch of the

IMM, which recognized the potential of financial futures contracts at a time when the Bretton Woods system of fixed exchange rates was abandoned. Next, that under my direction there was a continuity of leadership at the CME, while at the CBOT there was a constant change, often in contested fashion.[3] This proved to be a central element in maintaining a continuing theme for directional focus by the Merc. Also, the CME owned and controlled its Clearing House, a critical component in determining the strength and destiny of an exchange, something the CBOT sadly learned in the course of its competitive battles. Its lack of control of the board of Trade Clearing Corporation was the key reason the CBOT moved its markets to the CME for clearing purposes. And finally, most important, was the CME's early embrace of an electronic destiny for futures markets. I agree with Charlie's assessment, particularly as it relates to Globex.

Beginning with the CME's 1987 conceptual embrace of the idea for an electronic trading system, there evolved a wide divergence of opinion between our two exchanges on the future direction for our industry. At the CME, the official stance of our leadership, or so I believed, was to actively pursue an electronic destiny. A good number of our influential members were motivated in this direction. At the CBOT, this was generally not the case. With few exceptions, the concept of electronic trade was at best considered as a distant goal but of little immediate consequence. Clearly, at that time, automation was perceived as contrary to the best interests of the majority of its membership. This difference controlled the relative depth of passion by which each exchange would pursue an electronic solution.

In 1990, the year before I entered my voluntary retirement, completely convinced of an electronic destiny for futures markets, I initiated an all-out attempt to turn Globex into the international standard for electronic trading. The Terme International de France had already come aboard. Negotiations with New York Mercantile Exchange were moving favorably. The London Financial Futures Exchange (LIFFE) was deliberating the idea. But I was willing to suspend all negotiations in favor of the CBOT. Bringing the CBOT aboard Globex not only would totally validate the concept of electronic trade, it would for all time secure the future of the American futures industry; not to mention the fact that it would be a giant step toward eventual merger between us. I convinced Tom Donovan, CBOT president and its most influential voice, and William O'Connor, its chairman, an avid proponent of automation whom I held in the highest regard, to make the attempt. The nature of our deliberations necessitated including Reuters Holdings, which had undertaken to build the system, as a party, making the whole process more difficult by an order of magnitude. Our negotiation teams, which included Jack Sandner and Charles Carey, both destined to become chairman of our respected exchanges, met in earnest on a weekly basis for about a year. It was a Herculean task, one of the most difficult and contentious negotiations I can ever remember, each party having separate demands and reluctant to give up their independence. But it was successful. We achieved what was regarded as a monumental accomplishment—a complex, tripartite agreement for a Globex joint venture (JV).

On October 27, 1990, both memberships overwhelmingly (98 percent at the CME and 90 percent at the CBOT) approved the tripartite agreement. A JV enterprise, The Globex Corporation, was created between the CME and the CBOT for the purpose of maintaining what was to become a jointly owned and operated global electronic trading system. I was elected chairman of the Globex Corporation, and a star-studded cast was appointed as its board of directors: Jack Sandner, John Geldermann, Scott Gordon, Gordon McClendon, Tom Dittmer, Barry Lind, and William Shepard from the CME, and William O'Connor, Dale Lorenzen, David Brennan, Charles Carey Jr., John Conheeney, John Gilmore, Burton Gutterman, and Neal Kotke from the CBOT. In addition, serving as ex-officio board members were William Brodsky, CME president and CEO, Tom Donovan, CBOT president and CEO, and David Vogel, chairman of the Futures Industry Association.

The pact included a set of agreed-to specifications that Reuters undertook to build as well as provisions giving the right to the CBOT and CME to list contracts of their choosing on Globex, at trading hours of their designation, and to share equally in all profits or liabilities.[4] There was also on open-door policy for other exchanges to join the system.[5] Gary Ginter, a futures market expert, was appointed as managing director. It was a happening that if successful would forever change the direction of futures market history. As an expression of gratitude for this huge accomplishment, the CBOT presented me with a world globe. I still fondly display it in my office. A year or so later, on June 25, 1992, the Globex system went live. Although delayed in production, it was the world's first truly international electronic trading system—at the time, all the others were no more than glorified local area networks. Don Serpico and Jim Krause, who headed the Merc's Management Information Systems Department and who made Globex happen, gave me a plaque to record that I had made the first trade on the new system.[6] Nobel laureate Merton Miller, who came to witness the ceremonial event on the CME floor, memorialized the historic occasion by signing a picture to me with these words: *To Leo, If I had only listened to you back in May of 1972, and come to the opening of the IMM, I could have been standing beside you when you began the modern era of finance. At least I didn't miss Globex.*

Again it was a case of man proposes and God disposes. Almost immediately, a critical issue arose that placed the Globex Corporation enterprise in jeopardy. The cause was a proposal made by the CME board and accepted by the CBOT board, that any actions of the board of directors of the Globex JV be made subject to approval by the boards of the two respective exchanges. This provision would create a complete veto power over decisions of the JV board by the boards of either the CME or CBOT. In effect, it made the JV board powerless. The newly appointed star-studded JV board of directors were, to say the least, upset. It is difficult today to describe the full force of my disappointment. Given the veto provision, as chairman of the Globex JV, I would be presiding over a corporate entity that had little power and was likely destined for failure. I would become a champion of a lost cause. It presented me with a dilemma that was nearly impossible to resolve. I correctly surmised that given the history of strife between the CME and CBOT, given the continuing controversy over electronic trade, and saddled with the new veto provision, the fledgling Globex Corporation did not have much of a chance. I decided to do my best to work around the provision for a while and, if unable, to publicly protest by resigning as chairman at the end of my first year's term. It came down to that.

Not much after my departure, bickering between the two exchanges began. There were many causes, some of them substantive, some of them personality clashes. On April 15, 1994, citing irreconcilable differences between the two exchanges, Pat Arbor, the new CBOT chairman, called it quits. Under the headline "CBOT Says Goodbye to Globex," the *Chicago Tribune* reported, "Leaders of the Chicago Board of Trade said Friday that they have voted to end the exchange's affiliation with Globex, the world's only automated after-hours futures trading network."[7] There was a stream of angry accusations between the two exchanges as to who or what caused the rift, but regardless, four years of intensive labor beginning with our tripartite negotiations went out the window. It was a very sad day. I felt that the split represented a grave blow to the advancement of electronic trade and perhaps to Globex itself. Although the CBOT announcement included an avowed intention to rejuvenate its own electronic system, "Project A," I did not put great faith in it. The CBOT's efforts with respect to electronic trading began in March 1989 when it introduced "Aurora," an unsuccessful off-hours electronic replication of pit trading. Aurora evolved into the first "Project A," a local area network begun in 1992 for after-hours trading in low-volume CBOT contracts. This internal CBOT effort, valiantly led by Burt Gutterman, who, like me, believed in electronic trade, never did get much traction.[8] Not much later, LIFFE, which had been considering joining the Globex venture, declined, something I doubt it would have done if the CBOT was still aboard. The *Wall Street Journal* report quoted some analysts as saying that LIFFE's' decision was a death blow for Globex and would have serious implications for Reuters.[9]

In a desperate attempt to save the JV, on April 22, 1994, I wrote an op-ed piece for the *Chicago Tribune* to gain the attention of the members of both exchanges. Although accepted by the *Tribune* for publication, it was withdrawn at my request after I struck a deal with Jack Sandner and William Brodsky to appear instead before the CME board of directors to make a personal appeal. I similarly appeared before the CBOT board. The unpublished *Chicago Tribune* op-ed piece (entitled "Final Appeal") was intended as an appeal to the "Court of Last Resort"—the traders and the Chicago financial community. It embodied the words I later used during my appearances before the board members of both exchanges:

> *There is no comfortable way to phrase it: The recent collapse of the agreement between the two Chicago futures exchanges in Globex is to the detriment not only of the system itself, but to the memberships of both the Chicago Mercantile Exchange (CME) and the Chicago Board of Trade (CBOT), the member firm (FCM) community, as well as Reuters Holdings PLC. What's more, it represents an incredible loss to the U.S. financial services sector in general and the City of Chicago in particular.*

> *To understand the gravity of what has transpired, it is imperative to comprehend what the combined participation of both Chicago exchanges within Globex represents—not just to the members of the exchanges—but to the City of Chicago itself. In its most basic terms, Globex symbolizes the inevitable march of technology, the recognition by futures markets that the era of global 24-hour trading has arrived, and that automation is a necessary adjunct to the infrastructure of futures trade. But Globex means much more. Globex goes a long way toward assuring Chicago's continued dominance as the global capital of futures markets and the center for risk management. This is an achievement that took decades of planning, innovation, and vision by both Chicago exchanges. The consequential result has made Chicago the envy of every other city in the world, copied and emulated by every center of finance. It is folly to endanger this prize.*

> *The intangible benefits to Chicago are immense and impossible to measure; the tangible benefits striking. According to a 1987 study by the Commercial Club of Chicago, more than 33,000 jobs were provided directly by the exchanges, their members and the organizations that provide services to them. Furthermore, more than 110,000 total jobs could be attributed to exchange economic activity, making this industry the city's single largest employer. Nearly $1 billion was spent annually on exchange-related goods and services in the Chicago area and member firms deposited an average of $4 billion daily into Chicago banks. In 1986, exchange spending amounted to nearly $260 million for wages, rent and occupancy, taxes, data processing, telecommunications, and other expenses. And exchange member firms spent an estimated*

$610 million for exchange-related goods and services in the Chicago area. These statistics no doubt have swelled substantially since this study was published.

In making the Globex announcement back in 1987, the CME did Chicago proud by upholding its long tradition of innovation and leadership. There followed a virtual torrent of new electronic systems introduced by most of the world's futures exchanges. However, the crowning achievement of the day was the eventual fusion of the CME and CBOT within Globex. Never mind that Globex did not get off to a fast start, never mind that those who oppose technological inclusion within open outcry took jabs at the difficulties this system encountered, never mind that there were a multitude of complications and negotiations still to overcome. Revolutions do not come easy. At the end of the day, the logic of a single global after-hours electronic trading system containing the markets of both giant Chicago exchanges represented a magnet of irrepressible attraction. This made it all but a virtual certainty that Globex would ultimately succeed, and that most, if not all, of the other major exchanges of the world would eventually come aboard as did the Paris-based MATIF exchange. Globex consequently assured this city a premier seat at the international table of finance well into the next century.

Still another overwhelming bonus was that the CME-CBOT Globex unification created enormous efficiencies and cost savings for our FCM community and ushered in the era of common goals between the two Chicago futures exchanges. United on Globex, the two Chicago exchanges were a much stronger force than their separate parts. United in purpose, the two futures exchanges represented a market colossus that could fend off any would-be foreign competitors. And in today's global competition, this is no small consideration. Where once the preeminence of the U.S. futures and options markets was taken for granted, 1993 will most likely be the last year in which the total transaction volume of U.S. futures markets is greater than that of foreign futures exchanges.

The foregoing is not to say that the concept that Globex embodies has been diminished. Quite the contrary! If there are those who are still skeptical about the road ahead, they are simply deaf to the thundering maelstrom of the technological avalanche around us. Telecommunications has fashioned a global marketplace that demands around-the-clock trading mechanisms. This will not change. Nor is Globex itself now fatally impaired. Globex is right on target. The system's technological competence has been successfully proven. Its substantive potential is intact. But there is no denying that the ultimate success of Globex will not be made easier by virtue of recent events. Indeed, the road ahead is now bound to be more difficult and complex. Most important, the era of common goals has been materially affected. The strength it represented for the members of both exchanges and the value of its potential to the City of Chicago has been jeopardized. The negative fallout may be felt for years to come, all to the advantage of our competitors.

Perhaps it is too late for reconciliation; perhaps these sober assessments will serve to bring the parties back to the table. In any event, it would be remiss not to make this final appeal in a last ditch effort to prevent what is bound to be a grievous mistake for everyone concerned.[10]

It was to no avail. Globex was the innocent victim as the two exchanges went their separate ways, but I wasn't finished yet. In November 1995, in what I would characterize as a final act of "defiance," I wrote an essay entitled "Wake Up Call." It was published in the *Journal of Financial Engineering* and drew national attention. It was directed at the leaders of the Chicago futures exchanges, but was especially meaningful to the members of the CME. Mincing no words, its defining message concluded with this warning:

Futures markets take heed! Complacency is the enemy. Tomorrow's futures traders grew up with Nintendo and Sega. They were given a keyboard for their fifth birthday; their homework was done on a computer; their recreation time was spent in video centers; the worldwide web is their playground; cyberspeak is their language.

When the current transformation process has been completed, when we have crossed the bridge to the new reality, when the new set of rules has been written, futures will still be the primary way to manage risk, but it will be carried out on the information superhighway. Tomorrow's traders will likely execute a complex set of trades from an interactive multidimensional wireless communications system representing the coalescence of key communications technologies: television, telephone, personal computer, and laser storage systems. The only question remaining is whether those trades will still be transacted on our futures exchanges. [See Chapter 12.][11]

That essay, it turned out, did have a significant impact on many members of the Chicago exchanges. However, it was particularly consequential to the members of the CME's Equity Owners' Association.

CHAPTER 3

EOA

The Rocket Propellant Fuel

"I t's Time for a Change" blared the headline. (See Appendix 3A.)
It was the December 1996 newsletter of the Equity Owners' Association, the EOA, formed in January of that year. Richard Ford, Howard Garber, Steve Goodman, Joe Gressel, Don Karel, Sheldon Langer, Kirk Malcolm, George Segal, Aryeh (Leon) Shender, Bill Shepard, Howard Siegel, and Joel Stender—all Merc members, formed the EOA to represent the interests of its equity owners, independent brokers, and traders. Each of a different background and station in life, but all with a common mission on behalf of reform. Their underlying purpose, was to protest the practices of broker groups, promote Globex, which in their opinion had been neglected by the Exchange, bring out into the open issues that were thwarting the Merc's growth, and work toward making the Chicago Mercantile Exchange (CME) a publicly traded entity. (See Appendix 3B.)

At the outset there were just five of them, Don Karel, Bill Shepard, Joel Stender, Leon Shender, and Steve Goodman. They met in secrecy in Bill Shepard's office, where they discussed the Merc's state of affairs and lamented its direction. In particular, they saw the domination of the Exchange by broker groups as the core of the problem, one that in their opinion was destroying membership values and the future of the institution. Their efforts began in December of 1995 by circulating a letter to the membership, signed by twenty-one members, which claimed "Something is Amiss" at the Exchange and demanded a greater voice by independent traders. This was followed by a second letter to the CME chairman and the other directors, citing "members' frustration with the increasing dominance at the Exchange of large broker groups, which have also contributed to the decline of the small, independent trader."[1]

According to Don Karel, the formation of the EOA was cemented after he and Leon Shender came to my office in January of 1996. They said that my essay "Wakeup Call," resonated with many Merc members and requested my return to Exchange leadership. Although I sympathized with their intentions, I pointed out that unless there was sufficient support for change on the CME board itself, it would be futile for any one person to attempt to transform the status quo. They went back to the drawing board, talked with Bill Shepard and others, and proceeded with the EOA. Their immediate objective was to elect a new slate of reform-minded CME directors in the upcoming January 1997 elections. Their platform would be to bring to the Board candidates without a conflict of interest who will be accountable to the membership, who will fully disclose their business development goals, and who will devote themselves to maintain the integrity of membership values. They then made me an offer: If their efforts in the 1997 CME election were successful, would I accept reappointment to a leadership position? It was an offer I could not refuse.

The EOA was born out of sheer frustration. The CME had fallen on hard times—its recent direction ominous. For one thing, the Exchange's transaction volume had been on a continuous downward slide for the last two years.[2] This was not a consequence of lower global futures volume. On the contrary, at the London International Financial Futures Exchange, the Merc's direct competitor with similar products, volumes continued to rise. For the first time in history, it knocked the CME from its historic second-place standing behind the Chicago Board of Trade (CBOT). After two and a half decades of continued growth, this represented a serious blow to our global prestige and was viewed by some as a harbinger of the Merc's downfall. The assessment was reinforced by the fact that all the major European exchanges had surpassed the CME in their electronic trade competence—even though the Merc was the first futures exchange to embrace electronic trade.[3] It also didn't help that toward the end of 1996, William Brodsky, the Merc's president through the past decade, announced his departure in favor of a position as chairman at the Chicago Board Options Exchange.[4] William Brodsky had served the CME with distinction. Jack Sandner and I had recruited him in 1982 from the American Stock Exchange, where he was executive vice president. He represented a perfect fit for us since he was steeped in the securities side of markets, and in April of that year we had launched the Merc's first equity futures product, the Standard & Poor's 500 contract. Three years later, upon the departure of Clayton Yeutter, who was moving on to become U.S. Trade Representative (and later was appointed by President Bush Sr. as secretary of Agriculture), Brodsky was the natural successor to the CME presidency. It was a most fortuitous appointment. Bill was instrumental in solving the so-called triple-witching effects on stock indexes and, after the 1987 stock crash, helped to develop coordinated circuit breakers between the CME and New York Stock Exchange that are still operative. He was also instrumental in the early 1990s bringing to the CME the Nasdaq stock index instrument, which is today one of our major equity products.

But as we know, "All politics is local." As unsettling as was the loss of global prominence, the direct effects at home were worse. Low transaction volume meant less opportunity for traders and lower commissions for brokers. It translated to lower incomes for everyone. Worse yet, the price of membership was highly reflective of business conditions on the floor. Each of the Merc's three divisions, CME, International Monetary Market, and Index and Options Market (IOM), had a separate membership (seat) that could be purchased or sold in open auction.[5] The last sale of a membership was always posted by the Exchange, and every member, consciously or not, would glance at the price every day to see whether its value was higher or lower. The value of a membership was sometimes the only major asset a member possessed. What they saw was not pretty. In the two years between 1994 and 1996, membership values in all three divisions had fallen precipitously. The bellwether of the Merc's strength and potential, the full CME divisional membership had fallen nearly 50 percent—an unprecedented and frightening drop. It caused more than a touch of panic on the CME floor.

As a by-product of difficult times, it caused a good deal of bickering between the CME and the CBOT. So much so that the *Chicago Tribune* carried an editorial in January of 1996, underscoring our "declining trading volume and seat prices" and pointing out that our exchanges "continue to face rising costs and increased competition from foreign exchanges in London, Paris and elsewhere, as well as from customized, off-exchange deals." The *Tribune* lauded a recent CBOT task force that recommended the two rival Chicago exchanges consider a merger. The *Tribune* lamented the fact that this recommendation "produced a loud chorus of derision and doubt" from traders and former officials, and was "pooh-poohed" by the Merc chairman. The editorial pointed out that Patrick Arbor, Board of Trade chairman, was expected to appoint a committee to study this recommendation. The *Tribune* called for "egos and differences" to be put aside and for Leo Melamed to be appointed chairman of the panel. Flattering, but the idea never got off the ground. (See Appendix 3C.)

While nothing inflamed members' fears more than falling membership values, there was much more going on. Beneath the surface at the CME, there was a rupture—a split within the membership so serious and lethal it had the potential to sink the entire enterprise. At the center of the controversy were the interests of traders and independent brokers versus those of broker associations—commonly known as broker groups. On a more fundamental level, the controversy was between open-outcry and electronic trade. Broker groups recognized that advancement of electronic trade ultimately meant the death knell to open outcry.

Seemingly, traders and floor brokers did the same thing.[6] They stood in the pit, shouted out their bids and offers, and executed transactions. But the similarity was surface, the difference was deep. A trader's income depended entirely on the profits and losses achieved as a result of transactions he made for his own account.[7] By definition, his "mind-set" was that of a risk taker. He calculated the potential risk-reward of a given market situation (often in a split-second reaction) and put his own money on the line. In general, floor traders can be divided into three basic categories or variations thereof: (1) position players (traders who maintain a position for a period of time); (2) "scalpers" (very short-term traders who go in and out of their positions throughout the trading session, participating in many transactions and taking a multitude of minimal profits or losses); and (3) spreaders (traders who take positions based on the price-differential between two or more contract months or two or more futures products).[8]

In theory, traders could learn to apply their skill electronically. Not so for floor brokers. A floor broker garnered his income from fees collected for executing customer orders. A clearing firm usually transmitted its customer orders to a given floor broker and paid him an agreed-on fee per contract for every order or part thereof he executed. Although there is risk attendant to this profession as well by virtue of the responsibility for errors, a broker's own money was not otherwise on the line. His income, for practical purposes, was totally dependent on the open-outcry architecture. No floor, no business for brokers. Electronic trade was thus anathema to them. In the pit, both communities needed each other. Brokers generally depended on traders to take the opposite side of their orders; traders similarly depended on the orders coming to the pit through the brokers. Thus, both communities were critically dependent on liquidity—the quantity of bids and offers flowing to the market. In an open-outcry architecture, liquidity was to a very large degree generated by the local floor population (locals).

A broker group by its basic definition was a consortium of floor brokers (a combine of two or more members) that pooled or shared fees resulting from floor brokerage or other floor operations. Broker groups represented a legitimate and innovative response, beginning in the early 1980s, to the growth of futures markets. The ever-bourgeoning flow of business, especially after the introduction of the financials, gave rise to so much new order flow that CME clearing firms needed more and more brokers to execute the deluge of customer orders coming to them. Reputedly the idea was developed by two of my friends, Jimmy Kaulentis and Maury Kravitz. Indeed, with markets in different pits throughout the expanded floor, each demanding execution of orders, sometimes at the same time, it became a physical impossibility for a given broker to handle all the business of a given firm. A broker group offered an excellent solution. Contracting with a firm to provide floor-broker coverage to *every* market, usually at a negotiated fee per trade coupled with the floor broker's assumption of error cost, was a splendid answer to the demands of the time. Although some clearing firms preferred to use their own "in-house" brokers, it was a costly alternative, since the firm would have to buy or lease a membership for each of its own brokers and underwrite the cost of errors. Consequently, the majority of large clearing firms (Futures Commission Merchants) supported the advent of and utilized broker groups. There were many such broker groups, small and large, competing for the business, but the largest of them by far was the International Futures & Options Associates (IFOA), formerly the Associated Brokerage Services. At its height, this group included better than 10 percent of the CME floor broker force.

Thus, the rationale for broker groups was commendable. However, in practice it represented a potential source of serious problems. The most grievous stemmed from a practice known as "dual trading"—the right of a broker to both execute orders for customers as well as to trade for his personal account. Dual trading, of course, was a significant factor in providing the market with additional liquidity. It was also an age-old intrinsic right of membership, common throughout the financial industry in equities, futures, and options.[9] While historically the markets accepted this practice with its inherent conflict of interest, they never envisioned the problems unleashed nor the potential for unethical and even illegal behavior when applied in the frantic action of the open-outcry pit. This potential was exacerbated with the advent of broker groups. Clearly, brokers belonging to the same consortium, when executing orders, had a built-in incentive to favor a fellow broker group member who at the moment may have been acting as a trader for his own account. Such favoritism could then be reciprocated by the trader when he subsequently assumed the role of the broker. This was no violation of Exchange rules but was certainly not a "free market" application.

Another serious potential problem was the negative effect broker groups could have on the competitive open-outcry architecture. For instance, since every member of a broker group could act as the broker on some trades and as a trader on others, a given broker group could theoretically execute every order between its own members, locking out the community of traders and independent brokers. Not only would this affect the income potential of the trader community, it would endanger liquidity and the competitive auction process—critical in assuring the best price to the customer. Some even believed that this was a cause factor in the lower volumes the Merc was experiencing. Still another concern was the fact that dual trading by members of a broker group could potentially provide an illegal means of reimbursing each other—through favorable trades—for the financial losses occasioned by errors made during the auction process. Having said all of that, In my opinion, the vast majority of brokers within broker groups were honest and ethical, operating within the prescribed rules of the Exchange. Of course, it wouldn't take many to sabotage an otherwise honest operation.

On August 5, 1996, Michael Fritz, of *Crain's Chicago Business*, brought the issue to public attention. His article, entitled "Document Untangles Merc

Web," was the result of some provocative investigative reporting. Fritz obtained his information under the Freedom of Information Act from our federal oversight agency, the Commodity Futures Trading Commission. Here is what he reported:

> *Independent traders at the Chicago Mercantile Exchange have long complained that powerful floor brokerage groups have too much clout and control of the action of the futures mart. Merc leaders downplay the criticism, insisting the exchange does a good job of ensuring a level playing field between independent traders and broker-groups. But the Merc's position may resemble the fox guarding the hen-house.*[10]

The facts seemed to bear out his damning contention: The documents Fritz obtained showed that at least three of the five CME board officers were principals or members of broker groups and that nearly half of the board's 24-member elected directors had financial ties to broker groups or worked for clearing firms that collected fees from such groups.[11] He also disclosed that broker-group members "are members of several influential oversight committees that determine everything from who can apply for exchange membership to whether there is sufficient cause to charge a trader with a rule violation." As Fritz noted in a follow-up story, "Despite a 90% rise in Merc trading volume between 1990 and 1994, the number of violations for intragroup trading and trading against broker-group customers fell by 14%."[12]

Michael Fritz's revelations, while serious, were no surprise to Merc members or Exchange officials. The influence of broker groups had been a hotbed of controversy and a major bone of contention at the CME for nearly a decade. Seven years before the EOA was born, back in 1989, the Chicago futures industry was subjected to "Operation Hedgeclipper," an FBI sting operation. As the embarrassing *Chicago Tribune* headline then told the world, "U.S. Probes Futures Exchanges." CME and CBOT members were alleged to have engaged in widespread cheating of customers, market manipulation, fraud, and tax evasion involving millions of dollars.[13] Pretty heady stuff. As the press saw it, at the core of the problem was dual trading and broker groups. Sallie Gaines and Carol Jouzaitis of the *Tribune* ran a comprehensive report on it with the headline "Broker Rings Legal—But Can Lead to Abuse." The article noted that the federal investigation of Chicago's futures exchanges was "putting a spotlight on powerful groups of brokers who often control activity in the trading pits as well as the systems set up to keep trading honest."[14]

I refused to believe the breadth of the accusations. Indeed, when the dust settled a year later, the headlines and media notoriety far, far outweighed the actual findings of wrongdoing. As we always contended, the vast majority of our members were honest and law abiding. But the sting operation had some lasting effects. First, a few members were actually found guilty and went to jail; second, the exchanges substantially strengthened their trading rules and enforcement procedures; and third, there was a concerted effort at the CME to change the rules pertaining to dual trading and broker groups in order to prevent potential abuses in the future. The Blue Ribbon Panel that was organized under my direction to deal with the alleged problems made some major recommendations, which were ultimately adopted by the board. (See Appendix 3D.)[15]

However, as the 1980s evolved into the 1990s, Operation Hedgeclipper became a distant memory. Business growth proved to be an incentive for some to find innovative pit maneuvers and clever methodologies in an attempt to circumvent exchange regulations. According to Michael Fritz, by 1996, members of broker groups were prominent in every facet of the Exchange and their voices often influenced the direction of rules and decisions of the board and committees.[16] The issue was by no means small potatoes. The very successful brokers annually often earned millions of dollars. It is believed that at its height, the cumulative income of these operations at the CME rivaled the most lucrative arenas within the U.S. financial service sector, some said at the rate of $1 billion annually. Little wonder broker groups sometimes held political sway at the Exchange. The tactics and business pressures by a few within these groups were reminiscent of the rough and tumble of the early days in the American labor movement. The "closed shop" approach (made illegal by the Taft-Hartley Act of 1947), which excluded someone from a job unless he was a union member, found its counterpart at the Chicago Mercantile Exchange. In an incident reported by the *Chicago Tribune*, Leslie Rosenthal, the former CBOT chairman and cofounder of Rosenthal Collins, a prominent CME and CBOT clearing firm, could not get four of his own brokers into the Eurodollar pit to execute firm business. According to Rosenthal, his brokers were "frozen out" by the broker groups and physically intimidated. This was not an isolated incident.[17]

Given the conditions revealed by Fritz, one cannot underestimate the courage of the members of the Equity Owners Association. First, because in taking on this issue, they took on the tyranny of the status quo and opened themselves up to abuse from the broker-group constituency. Second, because they had to confront the potential fact, as was rumored, that CME chairman Jack Sandner was associated with a broker group. While this was no violation of Exchange rules, it was certainly problematical. The rumors were indeed correct. In December of 1996, Sandner publicly admitted selling his long-held 10 percent equity interest in the IFOA broker group, the CME's largest broker association—clearly, a lucrative source of income.[18] In addition, his firm, RB&H, earned fees by being the clearing firm for a vast number of broker-group members. In effect, the EOA was taking on the chairman of the CME.

Further, since some members of broker groups were also influential members of the board, the EOA organizers feared they could become subject to trumped-up allegations over trading-rule violations. EOA members' trading income could also suffer. In the competitive frenzy of pit trading, brokers held sway selecting with whom they traded, thereby controlling traders' potential income. "Certain order-fillers attempt to punish locals by actually making an effort not to trade with them," stated Yra Harris, an independent trader who won election to the board in 1997 with support from the EOA.[19] Indeed, if a trader was ignored or boycotted by a broker, there was little he could do. And there was even the potential of bodily harm. In the aftermath of the "FBI sting operation," when some of us were championing rules to limit the number of trades a broker could make with members of his own broker group, I received several anonymous death threats. The Exchange provided me with an off-duty Chicago policeman to act as a bodyguard and protect the entrance to my office. Finally, and most important, the direction of the CME was at play. In the opinion of the EOA, the dominance of broker groups in Exchange affairs was to the detriment of Globex. It was the reason, in the EOA's view, that international exchanges had leapfrogged the CME in electronic transaction technology. They demanded that we regain the momentum toward advancement of electronic trade. Unfortunately, this issue sometimes put me and Jack Sandner on opposing sides. To underscore its unqualified support for Globex, the *EOA Newsletter* carried an interview with me conducted in June of 1996 about the destiny of electronic trade. (See Appendix 3E.)

In taking the bold action it did, the EOA changed the course of CME history. In my book, its members are all heroes. They took on those broker groups that would tolerate improper trading practices and ignited the simmering war between proponents of open outcry and those in favor of automation. In doing so they paved the way for the advent of electronic trade as the ultimate direction of futures markets. Instantly, the EOA, its members, the issues it brought into the open, and the accusatory tones of its message became the only topic of conversation on the Merc floors. Given the business downturn at the CME, lower income levels, a precipitous drop in membership values, and coupled with the media's attention to broker groups, the EOA's timing could not have been more provocative or more effective. Although carefully worded not to overly inflame their adversaries and provoke retribution, this was the EOA's initial mission statement on February 26, 1996:

The Equity Owners' Association was formed to be a catalyst for creativity and vision as much as to challenge perceived inequities and inferior business practices. Our goal is to improve business prospects for our equity members. . . . Today, we have an opportunity to constructively influence our own destiny. The EOA has identified numerous crucial areas of concern. . . . CME leadership must respond positively to our initiative because our strength comes from the entire membership and cannot be denied. [See Appendix 3F.]

It didn't take long for the organized broker community to counterattack. By September 1996, the National Alliance of Futures and Option Brokers (Broker Alliance) was formed. It issued its first newsletter offering this declaration:

The National Alliance of Futures and Option Brokers is committed to the principle that brokers are in a position of public trust and, therefore, have a special obligation to uphold and protect the highest standards of professional conduct on their exchanges. Our mission is to assist our members and exchanges in maintaining those standards through professional education, peer review, participation in exchange governance, and the preservation of the open-outcry system of trading. We believe that the maintenance of fair and efficient markets is best achieved through the process of self-regulation and we dedicate our efforts to protecting and enhancing that process. [See Appendix 3G.]

Clearly, the Broker Alliance tried to wrap itself in the flag, so to speak, and put brokers on the front line of the public trust—"to uphold and protect the highest standards of professional conduct." Formation of the Broker Alliance, it claimed, was not a counterattack to the EOA but rather a response to those "few who prefer to ignore the facts, disseminate misinformation and are seriously attempting to disturb the unity of the Exchange." Noble causes, to be sure. However, its unabashed mission on behalf of "preservation of the open-outcry system" was much more telling. Surely that mission had little to do with protection of high standards and professional conduct. Even more revealing was the opening sentence of its editorial, which derided an *unnamed industry leader* who claimed that "open-outcry is an anachronism." I wonder who the Broker Alliance had in mind. The closing sentence of the editorial minces no words: "We must use our voice whenever, wherever, and however open outcry is challenged. We must use our voices not at one another, but for one another. And now is a good time to start." (See Appendix 3G.)

CHAPTER 4

E-Mini

Springboard for the Merc's Success

The Equity Owners' Association (EOA) delivered and I made good on my promise. On Thursday January 23, 1997, the *Chicago Tribune* business page headline announced "Melamed Returns to Power at the Merc."[1] Six of the 12 Chicago Mercantile Exchange directors up for election were ousted from office, representing a rejection of incumbents unprecedented in the CME's 100-year history.[2] Not only were all the newly elected directors strongly supported by the EOA, three of them—Leon Shender, Bill Shepard, and Joel Stender—were top officials of the EOA itself. As the *Tribune* article reported, I was given a permanent appointment by the board as advisor to the board and its Executive Committee. However, as George Gunset, the *Tribune* writer saw it, this title "belies his influence."[3] Given the huge victory, Gunset was correct. He later called it "Leo's Second Coming."[4] *Crain's Chicago Business* writer Michael Fritz, who first exposed the broker-group issues at the Merc, declared the outcome as a "potent repudiation" of CME leadership and of its powerful floor broker associations. His report underlined the fact that Terry Duffy, an independent floor broker, led the ticket, taking that distinction away from CME chairman Jack Sandner. The election, Fritz stated, "signals a stirring shift in power to independent traders and their supporters, such as Merc Chairman Emeritus, Leo Melamed."[5] It was an important indicator of things to come. We now had the votes to make a difference.

At the first meeting of the new board, on February 5, 1997, with Jack Sandner set to finish the final year of his chairmanship term, I accepted the permanent appointment as "Senior Policy Advisor," and read into the record a prepared statement. (See Appendix 4A.) Although promising to become a unifying force, I recognized that in defeating 50 percent of the board incumbents, the election represented a clear-cut mandate for change and that I would do my very best to provide "new thoughts and a new

33

direction." It was an emotional moment for me. The election process and victory were invigorating, making me realize how much I missed being at the table. I knew my role would be unusual, but not so different from the one I played during much of my official career at the Merc. It wasn't the title that I sought—I always thought titles were overrated—it was the position to use my talents and help direct the destiny of the institution I loved so much. It was where I began my career, where I learned every nook and cranny of our marketplace, and where I had left my mark. Sakura Dellsher, the brokerage firm I was running, was very successful, but its demands on my time and talent were not sufficiently stimulating or satisfying. And yes, I was a trader, something that would never change. It was second nature, inbred, and in my veins. For me, trading with one's own money on the line (I never managed customer funds) represented the ultimate challenge of one's intellect, personality, and stamina. It was where you could test your acumen and agility against the best of the best. While I was often wrong as a trader, I had the will and courage to come back. This I could not give up, nor would it affect my ability to carry out the responsibilities of leadership. The Merc boardroom beckoned, where I wanted to be. There was yet so much to do. So many ideas seeking a chance to be nurtured. I was happy to be back.

What I did not want was to be distracted by past squabbles and acrimony. I said that directly to Jack Sandner. To his credit, he offered his hand in cooperation, and I gladly accepted it. Jack and I had met for dinner after the election and spent several hours burying the hatchet. During that session we touched on all the hot-button issues and differences between us, perceived or real, and left the meeting with an understanding that we would put the past behind us and work together. It didn't result in making us the best of friends, but it enabled us to work hand in hand over the ensuing years. Jack Sandner told the *Tribune*: "Leo and I forged new ground for the Merc and made a great team for many years. I welcome him back and look forward to his return in an advisory capacity to the Board." In turn, I said that I was humbled "by the strong outpouring of sentiments expressed by a multitude of Merc member that I return in an advisory capacity to the Board. I promise to do my utmost to serve the best interest of this institution and all its members."[6]

I had, of course, campaigned for the entire EOA slate, but in particular I concentrated my efforts on behalf of Bill Shepard whose chances for election were considered slim to none. Shepard was a fiercely outspoken critic of broker groups, a strong advocate of Globex, and openly opposed Jack Sandner's leadership. The entrenched forces at the CME were hellbent on keeping him from being elected. For me, Bill Shepard represented exactly the type of director the CME needed, someone smart and unafraid to take on the status quo. Although this virtue included a stubborn streak that sometimes created differences between us, I formed a friendship with him from the day he joined the International Money Market (IMM) back in December of 1971. Our alliance cemented in 1987 when he initiated an effort to limit dual trading in the Standard & Poor's (S&P) pit. I took up the cause and achieved board passage of the "Top Step Rule." The rule limited the top step of the S&P pit—a highly advantageous position in the pit—to floor brokers and, while there, prohibited them from trading for their own accounts. The rule, still in force today, was later adopted in other pits and helped curb the potential of front running and other abuses.

I had a strong indication that the election was going our way when, separately, five old-line members—Joel Greenberg, Louie Madda, Mike Sturch, Bruce Johnson and Yra Harris, astute observers of floor politics whom I trusted, each from a distinctly different floor constituency—came to tell me that the EOA was on the right track. Against the odds and by the slimmest of margins, Bill Shepard was elected to the board. It proved to be most fortuitous. Bill Shepard, together with a small band of trusted associates, Fred Arditti, Rick Kilcollin, and my closest personal friend, Barry Lind—a former board member and the founder and chairman of Lind-Waldock, the first futures discount enterprise—joined me in forming an internal CME team committed to the advancement of electronic trade. Over the next several years, under our mutual guidance, and in close liaison with Jim Krause, who was the project manager for Globex (and subsequently became management information system [MIS] chief), we advanced the technical capabilities, created the operational rules, achieved the necessary funding, and guided the formative evolution of the Globex platform.

Upon returning to the board, I quickly initiated two major actions. The first was to establish a Broker Association Task Force for a comprehensive review and recommendations of the issues attendant broker groups. Irwin Rosen, a trader and former lawyer, was appointed as chairman and Bill Salatich, a broker, as vice-chair. Both were newly elected members of the board whom I had strongly supported and trustworthy independents. In due time the recommendations of this task force became the policies adopted by the board, greatly alleviating some of the past grievances. The second action I undertook was to officially remove the constraints on the development of Globex. I called it my "Technological Emancipation Policy." Until this point, technological advancements of Globex, such as there were, were limited to those applications developed and brought forward by the Exchange itself. In practice, this meant no new technological applications unless sanctioned by the chairman and approved by the board of directors. In the opinion of our internal information technology (IT) experts, Krause and Serpico, this constraint was the primary reason for the lack of Globex advancement. I made clear to the board and stated for the record that "the Exchange must no longer impede the progress of new technology, but rather, the MIS department must assist and encourage this process." I was consciously moving to usher in a revitalized technological era at the Merc. The new policy removed any impediments to the development of new applications on the trading floor and encouraged the CME membership to use its ingenuity to do so. I made certain that Bill Shepard, a technological cognoscente, became chairman of the Globex Oversight Committee, which had direct responsibility for Globex development.

Separately, on the advice of Jim Krause and Don Serpico, I encouraged them to complete the ongoing negotiations which would replace the present Reuters technology for Globex with what was viewed as superior technology developed by the Nouveau Système de Cotation (NSC) and owned by the Paris Stock Exchange, Société des Bourses Françaises Bourse (SBF). With Reuters' approval, the complex agreement with SBF was hammered out in 1998 under the guidance of Craig Donohue and Jerry Salzman. Referred to for a time as "Globex2," the new system became operational in September of 1998 and gave the CME control and eventual ownership of the Globex platform. Fate has many partners. My return—the *Chicago Tribune* called it "Leo's Second Coming"[7]—also coincided with the alignment at the Merc of two other individuals, both economists and both with a long history in CME affairs. On February 5, 1997, T. Eric Kilcollin assumed the duties of CME president, replacing the departing William Brodsky. Not only were Rick and I good friends, he had come to the CME under my leadership in 1981 from the Federal Reserve and later became our chief economist. Kilcollin, a proponent of automation, was among the first to provide me with strong encouragement in the conceptual birth of Post (Pre) Market Trade (PMT).[8] Although Rick's tenure as president was quite short, his predisposition toward technology was a welcome backdrop for my mission. About a month later, one of my closest friends and associates, Fred Arditti, returned to the Merc after an extended leave. His return—which coincided with my own—was not by happenstance. Fred was a brilliant financial engineer, with a Ph.D. in economics from the Massachusetts Institute of Technology. In 1980, when Fred was chairman of the Economics Department at the University of Florida, I recruited him with the help of Beverly Splane, our chief operating officer, to become CME's chief economist.[9] His primary assignment was to find an acceptable mechanism by which to cash settle the soon-to-be-launched Eurodollar contract. The Eurodollar futures contract was to be the first cash-settled futures instrument, replacing the need for physical delivery at the time of contract maturity. To be successful, it was imperative that we devise a mechanism for establishing a settlement price at the close of the contract's life that would universally represent the price for 90-day interest rates for Eurodollars at that moment in time.

Within a year, Fred was instrumental in devising the IMM Eurodollar Index upon which the launch of our most successful contract was based.

Fred's methodology was hugely successful and was later adopted by the London Bank Inter Offered Rate (LIBOR), the global standard for short-term spot interest rates. In 1982, Fred Arditti left the CME to serve as president of GNP, a futures firm, and later went to Drexel Burnham. Thereafter he returned to teaching, becoming an economics professor at DePaul University in Chicago. During the 1990s, Arditti was commissioned by Harvard University to write one of the world's definitive books on derivatives.[10] Over the years, Fred and I formed an inseparable bond as personal friends, meeting frequently and enjoying each other's company. Upon my urging, in 1997 he accepted the offer from the new CME president, Rick Kilcollin, to become CME's senior executive vice president. Fred's second CME tenure was unfortunately cut short because of internal CME political maneuvers and then due to illness, but his presence until March of 2000 was for me and the CME of singular significance. Sadly, Fred Arditti passed away on October 30, 2004, after a protracted battle with pancreatic cancer. Prior to his death, at my initiative and with board approval, the CME's Center for Innovation established the CME Fred Arditti Innovation Award.[11]

About midyear, a unique and unexpected opportunity for Globex materialized that dramatically changed the direction of the CME. To understand what happened, it is necessary to know some of the history of stock index futures. The S&P 500 was listed for trade at the Merc back in 1982. Fifteen years later we had attracted over 90 percent of the business flow of that futures business—no small reason for the Merc's leap to preeminence. The critical element behind this success was a fatal error made by the Chicago Board of Trade back in the early 1980s. The CBOT believed, pursuant to conventional thinking, that the Dow Jones Industrial Index was "public domain." Therefore, it could replicate the Dow Index for futures trade *without license* from the Dow Jones owners. The CBOT was in error. Fortunately, I held a contrary opinion. I believed that the S&P 500 index, which I had targeted for our futures trade, was the private property of Standard & Poor's. Although Jerry Salzman, our general counsel, disagreed with me, I insisted that we negotiate for a license from S&P Corporation before we launched their index. Thus, together with Jack Sandner we successfully negotiated with Brent Harries, the president of Standard & Poor's, for an exclusive license—still in force today, some 28 years later. The CBOT ended up in a protracted court proceeding, which they ultimately lost. Consequently, the CBOT was shut out of U.S. stock index futures and the CME was without equal in this arena for the next nearly two decades.

In 1997, the Dow Jones organization finally reconsidered its nonlicensing stance. What was left to decide was which futures exchange to license and at what fee. The battle for the Dow Jones license between the CME and CBOT proved to be the last great competitive clash between the two Chicago exchanges. The outcome was considered critical because the equity world, as well as our respective memberships, believed—wrongly as it turned out—that a Dow Jones futures contract would dominate stock-index futures trading. Both exchanges went all-out to win the deal. Not long after my return to the board, I joined the team with Jack Sandner, Fred Arditti, and Rick Kilcollin to convince Dow Jones the CME was the best venue for its index. We were, after all, the established "stock-index" futures exchange, and logic dictated that the Dow Index contract would more likely succeed where stock-index business was already flourishing. It was an accepted market truth that a new futures contract had a better chance of succeeding when listed alongside other related futures instruments. Pat Arbor, chairman of the CBOT, however, contended that at the Merc, the new Dow Jones instrument would be second fiddle while at the CBOT, the world's largest Exchange, the Dow Index contract would get top-dog standing and 100 percent of the exchange's marketing attention. Arbor had a potent argument which rang true. When coupled with the CBOT's offer of a huge licensing premium, it was believed to be an unbeatable proposal.

However, long before the decision by Dow Jones was made, I quietly began discussions with some of my insiders, Arditti, Lind, Shepard, and Kilcollin, about an alternative idea in the event we lost the bidding contest. The concept was quite simple. Many of us had become convinced that in spite of our huge success with S&P 500 futures, our contract was underutilized. At about $250,000 per unit of trade, it was structured primarily for the institutional world, far too large for the average retail trader.[12] An S&P 500 index instrument at about one-fifth the size—call it a mini contract—would present the trading public with an ideal index trading vehicle. Indeed, the retail crowd, larger than the institutional community by an order of magnitude, might very well create a much more liquid futures product. Such a contract, we thought, would certainly give the potential CBOT Dow contract, which was directed at retail trade, a run for its money.

Privately, however, I wanted to go much, much further. My underlying motivation was to make the new S&P mini contract the first futures instrument ever to be electronically traded around-the-clock—in other words, during the open-outcry trading session as well as after business hours. My principal co-conspirator was Barry Lind, someone who over the years served as my primary advisor and soul mate. Not only was he thoroughly steeped in the flows of futures markets, he joined my unshakable belief in the future of electronic trade. More to the point, his firm's customers were predominantly retail traders. Lind's steadfast opinion that his customers not only would support but would prefer an electronic venue was sufficient foundation for me to champion an exclusive Globex listing for the mini S&P contract. Lind's support not only gave me the courage but the practical rationale. If successful, it would once and for all settle the critical question of whether an electronic venue could generate sufficient liquidity to be a viable alternative to open outcry. It would represent the defining moment in the battle with the status quo.

In the first week of June 1997, we received the bad news. The Dow Jones Index was officially awarded to the CBOT. We tried to soften the blow with the announcement of the mini S&P concept, but the news hit the CME like a ton of bricks. Our members regarded Dow's decision as a death knell to the future of the Merc, and our membership prices headed south. While disappointed, I was far from despondent. I was in London at a conference at the time, and I recall immediately calling Barry Lind for assurance that his firm would provide all-out support to the electronic venue. He was unequivocal. Hastily returning to Chicago, I huddled with Jim Krause on whose shoulders the technological development of Globex would lie. Could he make Globex ready for an early September launch of the E-Mini? That would be even before the CBOT could launch its Dow contract. It was a tall order. Krause did not disappoint me—then or since. I wrote an upbeat letter to the membership and left with Jerry Salzman and Rick Kilcollin to negotiate an exclusive license with Standard & Poor's for the new mini contract. (See Appendix 4B.) It was achieved in record time. At the July 1997 board meeting, I was able to report a licensing agreement with S&P through 2014 for the new mini product along with an accord to jointly market the instrument. A new special Mini S&P Ad Hoc Committee was formed, of which I assumed chairmanship, with powers of a mini board. The S&P mini contract officially became the "E-Mini," to signify its exclusive electronic venue.

As soon as our floor community realized that the new mini contact would exclusively be traded electronically—and during the open-outcry session—the revolt began. Wasn't this the ultimate threat to open outcry? The nose of the camel under the tent? The first live missile directed at pit trading? In my heart of hearts, I realized that it may very well have been the case. But if so, did it not represent the direction the world was taking? Was this not in line with my "Tomorrow's Technological Tidal Wave"?" (See Chapter 11.) Wasn't this the exact reason I was returned to the CME board? Was it not my mission to convince the CME floor community that telecommunications had fashioned a global marketplace that demanded around-the-clock trading mechanisms? That by ignoring this truth they would simply be inviting the same fate that has historically befallen all who would deny the advances of technology? Deaf to the thundering maelstrom of the technological avalanche around us? And that if we as leaders failed to take the indicated action to preserve our future, would we not be guilty of misfeasance or worse?

Several years later, in reminiscing about those heroic days, Fred Arditti said something that I will never forget: "There are three important things in leadership," Fred told me, "creativity, timing, and risk taking. Your timing was brilliant," he said. "You used the crisis moment to change direction for the Merc. If you would have done that a few years earlier, you couldn't get it through. You told me," he reminded, "we have to take some risks here. These are things that you have to do to change the direction of the people you're working for. If they don't understand what's best for them, a leader shows them which way to go."

Small additional problem: The 1987 PMT referendum that gave birth to Globex prohibited the listing of an existing pit-traded contract on the screen during open-outcry hours. Since the S&P 500 contract was traded in the pit, the listing of another S&P 500 instrument on Globex, say the E-Mini—with some similar specifications—during regular trading hours might be considered in violation of the referendum. If so, it required membership consent, something that would be dead on arrival. Both Jerry Salzman, our general counsel who had helped draft the wording of the original referendum, agreed on a contrary opinion. In our view, the E-Mini represented a new instrument, one with sufficiently distinguishing specifications to differentiate it from the full-size S&P 500 index contract. Therefore, it did not violate the referendum. Mini versions of existing products had not been considered at the time of the PMT referendum. While Jerry's legal opinion was important, the controversy the issue generated was legendary.

I became an obsessed evangelist with but one holy mission: to get the contract off the ground. I put all my credibility on the line. First, I argued, the E-Mini was a brand-new instrument and did not violate the referendum; second, because of its small size, it would not directly threaten the existing open-outcry S&P product; third, it represented the smartest defense against the Dow futures contract; finally, if the electronic venue was the future of futures, then it was imperative that the CME be the first to capture this destiny. Toward this goal I organized a floor marketing campaign together with members of the new E-Mini board. We held meetings with members individually as well as in groups, on the floor and offsite, arguing, cajoling, and imploring. I called in all the chits accumulated over the years. I went to speak at all relevant committees. In particular, I spent time with the Equity Indices Committee, a key forum whose approval was absolutely critical. Fortunately it was chaired by Jack Bouroudjian, a very smart equity market expert who was a strong supporter of electronic trade. After a three-hour confrontation we gained their approval with a 22-to-2 vote. However, after all the efforts, when we held the mandatory open members' meeting to discuss the subject, the issue was still touch and go. Some members even threatened a court battle. At the end of the day, the majority acquiesced, becoming convinced that the E-Mini was the best weapon in the battle for retail equity-index business and that it would bring a wave of new business to the Merc.

There was one additional element that was vital, both in placating our members as well as insuring success of the contract. It was an adroit adjunct to the E-Mini proposed to me by Bill Shepard. Since the primary reason for the failure of new futures instruments was their lack of liquidity, Bill came up with an innovative idea to help ensure liquidity right from the start. It also provided floor traders a special role in the electronic development of the E-Mini. He suggested that we place Globex terminals within an especially built arbitrage unit on the trading floor with proximity and visibility to the S&P 500 pit—which Bill called the "price-discovery pit." A group of selected electronic floor traders could then act as arbitragers, signaling orders to the big contract of the outcry pit—which was very liquid—while laying them off onto the mini contract on the Globex terminal that they commanded. Presto, instant E-Mini liquidity courtesy of the so-called price-discovery pit. In addition, this approach would help build open interest in the E-Mini because traders could be encouraged to keep their arbitraged positions intact until maturity when the big and little contracts would converge and offset each other. In short, Bill's adjunct was a superb innovation. It was pure brilliance. It served as an insurance policy for E-Mini success. In embracing his idea, I hesitated only long enough to record my strong conviction that ultimately electronic trade would become the real "price-discovery pit."

But the battle wasn't over. Next, there developed a floor movement ostensibly aimed at preventing "cannibalization" of the successful pit-traded contract by its electronic upstart cousin. If too much of the S&P trade was directed to the electronic screen, the argument went, it would jeopardize the liquidity of the successful pit contract. To prevent such cannibalization, it was proposed that we place an upper limit on the quantity of any order that could be directed to the electronic venue. Today such a thought would be laughable if not inane. But in 1997, when electronic trade was still viewed in some quarters as the end of civilization, the idea was considered rational. For me and our inner group, it was just one more obstacle in the long journey to electronic trade. Any limitation of order size to Globex would act as an impediment to its success—the lower this threshold, the higher the obstruction. Knowing we had a difficult fight on our hands, Bill Shepard and I sought solid support from our E-Mini board. The mini board voted to proceed with the E-Mini contract with an upper limit of 50 contracts for electronic trade—at the time, a sizable retail quantity.

However, the opposing forces would have none of it. There was a petition signed by 130 members threatening a referendum and court proceeding unless the maximum E-Mini order was limited to 10 contracts, a ridiculously low number. When this issue was brought to the CME board meeting in late July 1997, it became as heated and boisterous a meeting as I can ever remember. There was a move for a maximum of only five contracts. The controversial battle lasted until sometime around midnight, with an intense and continuous debate and numerous motions. The final outcome was a compromised maximum of 30 E-Mini contracts for members and 15 for nonmembers. Bill Shepard and I considered it a victory.

The IMM's E-Mini S&P 500 was launched on September 9, 1997, the first American futures instrument for electronic trade around-the-clock, in other words, concurrent with pit trading. Richard A. Grasso, New York Stock Exchange chairman, did the honors of ringing the ceremonial opening bell, with Harold McGraw III, president of The McGraw-Hill Companies (the owner of Standard & Poor's), as the special guest of honor. To say it was an instant success cannot begin to describe the triumph it represented. It recorded 8,000 transactions, the highest number of opening-day trades in the history of futures trades.[13] A month later, Dow Jones News reported: "After five weeks of trading, the E-Mini S&P 500 futures contract has broken the 10,000 mark in open interest at the Chicago Mercantile Exchange . . . the fastest growing of any CME traded equity futures contract, in terms of open interest."[14] The CBOT's Dow contract, while successful, never came close to the volume recorded by the E-Mini contract.

About a month after the E-Mini launch, on October 30, 1997, I faced the CME membership at its annual meeting—my first appearance before all the members since my return. It was at the Renaissance Hotel in Chicago and the ballroom was packed. Called "A Return to the Table," I carefully wrote out my remarks. I thought it was imperative to touch all the major issues we were facing and highlight some of the actions we had already taken. In particular, this was my opportunity to explain why I returned to leadership and to assure the members that any perceived or real differences between Jack Sandner and myself were behind us. I told the members, "We are working together in harmony with a unification of purpose." It was also my opportunity to acknowledge Jack at the close of his six-year chairmanship term and publicly express our thanks for his years of service. I also used the opportunity to make a strong appeal for the members to put aside past differences and join hands in order to persevere and succeed. And it was a chance to acknowledge a number of people who made a special contribution during the course of the year. I offered singular praise to the E-Mini effort—with special recognition of Bill Shepard and Barry Lind for its successful launch. Throughout my remarks ran a "Technological Emancipation" theme as well as a recognition of the enormous asset Globex represented. Upon conclusion of my remarks, I recall a personal gratification for the overwhelming applause my words seemed to generate. (See Appendix 4C.)

The impact of the E-Mini far, far outweighed its record volume. It constituted a watershed in the history of markets, single-handedly making Globex a household name in financial circles and forever changing the course of futures. With the benefit of hindsight and without fear of contradiction, I can categorically state that the E-Mini was the springboard for the CME's ultimate success, putting our Exchange on the world's modern financial map. It forever proved that an electronic platform could generate sufficient liquidity to support a futures instrument and act as alternative to open outcry. It was the launching pad for our eventual initial public offering. It served as the compass for all markets, bringing the imperative of "electronics" to the top of everyone's agenda—be it in futures, options, or securities. Not only were there a rash of new E-mini instruments everywhere, virtually no new contract at the CME was ever again launched other than on Globex. In a relatively short time span, the E-Mini S&P 500 stock index contract, whose volumes continued to soar, became the U.S. equity market's directional leader—the price discovery "pit" for equities. Arbitrage between the big and the little index contracts still goes on, but the large S&P 500 pit is a ghost of its former self and its traders look to its younger sibling for direction. In 2007, the E-Mini traded a record of over 415 million contracts, and as of this writing, in December 2008, it represents some 30 percent of the CME's overall volume.

Exhilarated by the E-Mini success I could not possibly guess in 1997 that the struggle with the forces of the status quo had only just begun.

CHAPTER 5

Strategic Commotion
Planning the Journey

In January of 1998, Jack Sandner's six-year tenure as Chicago Mercantile Exchange (CME) chairman was coming to a close and the Exchange's political juices were beginning to flow.[1] The Melamed-Shepard alliance was activated again as we huddled to find a candidate whom we could both support. We agreed that the next chairman should symbolize the coming of a new era at the Merc, one who would put an end to recent strife on the floor and help heal the wounds within the membership. To do that, we wanted someone who had an unblemished reputation, embraced technological advancement, and was free from broker group influence.

There were three front runners, all were board members: Two were Silvermans (not related), Jeffrey and David, the other was Scott Gordon. All of them were experienced and had the necessary qualifications. But there were clear differences. Jeffrey Silverman was very intelligent and a highly successful cattle trader. He was a strong proponent of technology, and very independent. But he was not well-known outside the meat complex. David Silverman, while not in Jeffrey's league, was also a trader, but not exclusively so. He was also very intelligent and a proponent of technological advancement. In fact, David had been the leader in developing the Merc's Globex Foreign Exchange Corporation (GFX) unit, a successful foreign exchange liquidity-providing mechanism for currency futures. It represented the type of innovation that I heartily embraced—the creation of a CME-sponsored unit, GFX, to do foreign exchange arbitrage between futures and cash. However, reputedly David was favored by Jack Sandner, which made his candidacy problematical—as everywhere in politics, perception was as good as reality. Scott Gordon, on the other hand, was neither a trader nor a broker, he was an officer of a member firm. When he worked for my firm, Sakura Dellsher, he was its marketing director. Throughout the ensuing years, we maintained a loose friendship, sometimes jogging together at the East Bank Club, and often discussing the Merc and its future. Now he was chief executive officer of the Mitsubishi clearing firm, a small futures enterprise operating exclusively for the proprietary futures business of the Mitsubishi Bank. He had been a member of the CME board for many years and risen to the office of secretary. Mild mannered and well known, he was easy to get along with and thoroughly expert on the workings of the Exchange. He was, however, viewed as vacillating and without strong convictions and did not own his membership, a fact generally viewed negatively by the membership. Still, he was the most noncontroversial of the three candidates.

Based on our reading of the 30 members of the board, none of the three candidates yet had commitments for the necessary 16 votes—the majority it took to win. All three candidates had some hard-core supporters. Our count had David with eight or nine, and both Scott and Jeffrey with five or six each. When Shepard and I tested the water with a few of the noncommitted board members—our first meeting was at Hackney's on Willow Road—it became apparent that they would follow our lead. Thereafter, the boardroom of my firm, Sakura Dellsher, on the thirty-second floor of the north tower of the Merc building became our campaign headquarters. Our goal was to create a block of votes sufficient to swing the election. Although the voting was in secret and anyone could change his mind without detection, as a very strong rule this did not happen—as traders who traded with each other daily in transactions that amounted to millions of dollars with but the wave of a hand or nod of the head, we all lived by our word. The pre-election politics went back and forth, the outcome fluid until the very last hour when our group swung from Jeffrey Silverman to support Scott Gordon. I was dispatched to advise Scott of our decision. I met him in hurried fashion just before the board meeting in the elevator vestibule of the north tower. To this day, I think he believed he had sufficient votes without our support. Scott was wrong. As I recall, it actually took three ballots before Scott Gordon received the necessary 16 votes to become CME chairman. By contrast, Terry Duffy was unanimously elected on the first ballot to the office of vice chairman.

The issue of controversy was whether to find a continuing role for Jack Sandner, given that he had just completed three consecutive terms as chairman. There was a strong division of opinion. Directors from the EOA contingent were very much opposed, but I took the other side of the argument. I pointed out that upon my return, I had publicly promised to work with Jack as a unified team. Indeed, he had become most cooperative in my leadership and we had rekindled a friendship. I therefore thought that providing Jack with a continuing senior role would promote the spirit of unity and help us lead the Exchange toward a technological future. It was an instinctive gesture on my part. My opinion prevailed. A new post was created, "Special Advisor to the Board," a counterpart to my title of "Senior

Policy Advisor to the Board." Although Jack's post was not made permanent as was mine, it did include a stipend equal to the one I was receiving. On the surface at least, peace and harmony prevailed.

To his credit, Scott Gordon came to office recognizing that world markets were changing. Not long after he assumed his position as CME chairman, he created a Strategic Planning Committee (SPC) with full authority and scope to chart a new course for the CME. He made the SPC very large. It included three vice chairmen, Yra Harris, Thomas Kloet, and Bill Shepard, with Jack Sandner and me as advisors. It also included the principal officers of the Exchange, President Rick Kilcollin, Executive Vice-President Fred Arditti, Chief Operations Officer Jerry Beyer, and General Counsel Jerry Salzman.[2]

"Initially I declined," remembers Jim Oliff after being asked by Scott to take the committee's chairmanship. "I told Scott that this is the natural position for Leo Melamed, that's how we've gotten to where we are." Oliff, a Brandeis Liberal Arts graduate who received a law degree from Northwestern law school, became an International Monetary Market (IMM) currency broker and trader in 1976. He began his trading career at the Mid-America exchange, where many of our members got their feet wet in the small-size versions of the Chicago Board of Trade (CBOT) grain contracts, and was among the army of newcomers to the IMM who helped build our revolutionary exchange. I strongly supported Jim Oliff for election to the board in 1982. Jim's father, Hershel Oliff, a dear friend and a CME member since 1964, had a marvelous sense of humor, which his son inherited and made him fun to be around. "Leo will be on the committee as Advisor," Scott assured him, explaining that he wanted an elected director to be the chair. Jimmy and I talked about it and he reluctantly agreed, worried that I was insulted. I wasn't. But I too thought Scott's decision had a political twist to it, an attempt to be nonpolitical and not anger Jack Sandner. As it turned out, Oliff did an outstanding job as chairman while providing me the full latitude to act as the internal and de facto chair of the undertaking. Our tacit and practical understanding was that I would lead the direction of the SPC, and he would carry the plan forward to the board and membership. I wanted no more. We thus became partners in the difficult mission. The arrangement worked exceptionally well.

The Strategic Planning Committee had its work cut out for it. The three years following its creation were to become pivotal years for the CME and the CBOT, indeed for the futures industry. On the surface, things were going well. The Merc's E-Mini contract continued to be hugely successful, bringing new business flows to the CME. All our other markets were booming. The CBOT similarly was also doing well, and together our Chicago markets were drawing world attention to our space, its potential, and profitability. But success has its downside. Severe problems were brewing. For the first time in 1998, one could hear some serious rumblings from the international community as well as from members of the American banking industry and over-the-counter (OTC) entities about a competitive run for market share of our futures markets. Behind the scenes, stock exchanges, investment banks, financial intermediaries, and information providers were planning a head-long race to set up new electronic derivatives/futures trading systems. The potential competitors were noted global financial players, some of whom were our markets' biggest customers, contributing well in excess of 50 percent of futures business. We were viewed as easy pickings. After all was said and done, we were still primarily ensconced within an open-outcry architecture. And it didn't look as if we would ever change. Our big-volume arenas—at the CME, Eurodollars, at the CBOT the 10-year note and 30-year bond contracts—were seen as huge trophies worth the effort. From their point of view, the efficiencies of electronics, the speed of execution, the lower execution fees were overwhelming attractions, making our markets easy prey. As the E-Mini demonstrated, world competitors could fairly easily replicate any of our nonlicensed products onto an automated platform. So the question was still which venue would prevail—electronics or open out-cry? The answer would determine whether Chicago—where futures markets were developed and where financial futures were invented—would remain the epicenter of their trade, or whether the capital of this gigantic enterprise, an economic engine for the locale that housed it, would be wrested from its birthplace, perhaps to the OTC universe or to the European continent. It was a serious question and created an obvious sense of nervousness among the leaders of U.S. futures exchanges.

Ironically, in 1998, the answer to this issue was at the heart of a competitive struggle playing out in Europe. It happened in the form of a do-or-die battle for trading control of the 10-year German government bond known as the Bund, the major instrument for European long interest rates. Since its launch as a futures product 10 years earlier by the London International Financial Futures Exchange (LIFFE), the Bund had become one of the world's most successful futures contracts. This proved to be a bit of an embarrassment to the German financial community since the product (the German Bund) was obviously their turf, yet they had no futures exchange to house it. Two or so years later, the Deutsche Terminbörse (DTB), a German version of the LIFFE exchange, was born. It soon launched the identical Bund futures contract. However, because of its tardy entry to the universe of futures markets, it was given but a small chance of success. Nevertheless, there was one significant difference—the DTB was the first European futures exchange to be launched on a totally electronic platform without an open-outcry component.

LIFFE, a British carbon copy of the IMM initiated at the instigation of John Barkshire, a London money broker, was born in 1982 to trade financial products. It was an instant winner, enjoying overwhelming success, with a growth rate on the order of 45 percent per annum. In, 1992 LIFFE merged with the London Traded Options Market (LTOM) and in 1996 with the London Commodity Exchange (LCE). By the end of 1996, LIFFE was by far the biggest futures exchange in Europe, followed by the Marché à Terme International de France (MATIF) in Paris and the DTB in Frankfurt. But just like its Chicago counterparts, LIFFE was committed to open outcry. I recall chairing a Futures Industry Association–sponsored debate in Chicago in November of 1996 on the potential of electronic trade. I was the odd man out. "Surely, Leo, you recognize that liquidity can never be produced on the screen," I was told by LIFFE's officials. (The S&P E Mini was yet to be born.) The chairman and CEO from LIFFE had joined the chairman and CEO from the CBOT to vehemently disparage the idea of electronics as a substitute for open outcry. LIFFE's management felt secure ignoring its German rival because even three years after its launch, the Frankfurt exchange could capture only about 25 percent of the Bund futures trade. In July of 1997, LIFFE officials published a strategy report reaffirming their unshakable commitment to open outcry, "the fairest and most efficient way of executing business in high volume."

But in early 1998, the DTB and the Swiss Options and Financial Futures Exchange (SOFFEX) merged to form the European Exchange (Eurex). Its new general manager, Werner Seifert, instituted an aggressive plan of action, and things began to heat up. Seifert pushed a price war on fees and began installing electronic trading screens in Chicago. It took an amazingly short span of time for this plan to become effective and to begin decimating the Bund futures business that LIFFE had generated. In short order, Chicago market makers, operating electronically under very favorable financial arrangements with DTB, were able to generate up to 20 percent of the DTB's Bund-trading volume.[3] By June of 1998, DTB's Bund contract achieved critical mass and surpassed LIFFE in futures volume. The battle was all but over.

While one can attribute other causes for this unexpected and dramatic result, the central and controlling reason was that electronic trade was immensely more efficient and cost effective. The principal commercial customers of the Bund instrument, global banks, made it clear they much preferred DTB's screen-based technology over LIFFE's open outcry. The outcome of this competitive battle became the first striking exception to the accepted principle that the exchange launching the product first will overcome all subsequent competitive challenges for the same product. Indeed, that rule was so hard and fast, I had coined the saying "The Firsteth with the Mosteth, Winneth." But now there was clear evidence that in a contest between an electronic platform and open outcry for the same product, the old principle could be undone. It was a sobering awakening, especially for the Brits. To their credit, having waited too long to save the Bund instrument, they acted quickly and forcefully. On June 9, 1998, members of LIFFE voted to approve the introduction of electronics as well as a new management structure for its exchange. Not much later, LIFFE announced a $100 million program to devise and launch by the end of the year LiffeConnect, an electronic system for its futures markets.

Did anyone hear the alarm that was sounded?

CHAPTER 6

Global Competition

The Ultimate Enforcer

The Deutsche Terminbörse–London International Financial Futures Exchange (DTB-LIFFE) confrontation, a direct result of the technological revolution, set in motion a number of unintended, but in some cases predictable, consequences. The predictable was that it energized all our competitors, both domestic and foreign: "Let's go after those bums in Chicago." After months of speculation, rumors, and hype, Howard Lutnick, a creative and resourceful market player, president and chief executive officer of Cantor Fitzgerald, the giant inter-dealer in the U.S. Treasury cash market, was the first to officially throw down the gauntlet. On April 6, 1999, he announced the creation of the Cantor Financial Futures Exchange (CX), which was to offer Future Commission Merchants (FCMs), locals, and other market participants a low-cost, anonymous alternative for trading U.S. Treasury futures contracts. CX proposed to use its e-speed electronic platform, the same electronic platform used by dealers in the cash market, to form a global bond and derivatives trading system and become the first to link European and U.S. fixed-income markets into a single trading platform. The announcement which sent shock waves through our Chicago markets initiated a deluge of new "me-too" would-be electronic competitors. By July, the *Financial Times* reported that Cantor Fitzgerald had made good on its promise with the launch of "the first global electronic trading platform for international bonds."[1]

Going after Chicago's markets thus became the newest fad in global finance. Almost immediately, the creation of BrokerTec Global was announced. It represented a mega-attack on our markets by none other than our principal customers, the world's largest banks. The new enterprise, composed of Citigroup, Credit Suisse First Boston, Deutsche Bank, Goldman Sachs, Lehman Brothers, Merrill Lynch, and Morgan Stanley Dean Witter, would set up a new interdealer structure to transform the annual multitrillion-dollar trade in U.S. Treasuries, Euro-denominated debt, and their own derivatives into a global electronic bond trading system. Only J.P. Morgan was missing from the megabanker consortium because it had decided earlier to create its own rival electronic bond broking system called Euro MTS, based on the Italian government bond trading system. MTS actually became the first to launch an electronic platform for Euro-denominated government bonds. Not much later, Intercapital Plc., which had become the world's largest money broker by merging with Garban Plc., held talks with BrokerTec to join its venture. Intercapital Plc. subsequently announced a new venture with Bloomberg, the global information vendor, for an order matching service for cash and derivative securities. At about the same time, the American National Association of Securities Dealers (NASD) was vying to tie up with top investment firms to set up an electronic futures trading system. Even Reuters got into the act by considering an electronic bond trading through its own Instinet platform.

The Chicago Board of Trade, considered highly vulnerable for its lack of an electronic system and its passionate commitment to open outcry, was the initial target, its flagship U.S. Treasury bond and note futures contracts seen as a most lucrative prize. Stunned, the CBOT at first reacted by seeking an alliance with BrokerTec itself. It thought that such a compact would allow the CBOT to share the system for trading bond futures next to the underlying cash market. That idea was aborted quickly when BrokerTec began talking with LIFFE for the use of its new electronic system, LiffeConnect. Such an arrangement would transfer the cash and futures markets onto one common trading platform with the potential of clearing the trades through a common clearing house, the London Clearing House (LCH). Arguably this combination would offer market participants savings of billions of dollars in margin and settlement costs. It was a frightening competitive prospect.

Although the CBOT's treasury complex was the initial target, it wasn't difficult to conclude that the Eurodollar contract of the Chicago Mercantile Exchange, with its unparalleled volume and liquidity, was the ultimate grand prize. Whoever owned Eurodollar futures owned the interest rate market and arguably the future of futures. Indeed, the Electronic Broking Services (EBS), a potentially serious competitor that provided electronic foreign exchange dealing services, was considering creating an electronic forward-rate-agreement (FRA) market, a cash market substitute for the Eurodollar product. There seemed to be no end to potential competitors. While the CME possessed an electronic platform, our competitors were aware that CME rules did not allow *existing* floor-based contracts to be electronically traded during regular trading hours. The E-Mini was a singular exception to the rule because it was defined as a new instrument. Aside from this issue, Globex was technologically incapable of handling the humongous volume generated by Eurodollars.

And there was still another problem. American futures exchanges, anchored as they were in a not-for-profit membership structure, did not have the agility or capital to compete against the formidable global competitors mounting the attack. This brought into focus the idea of demutualization, a process of converting a not-for-profit membership organization into a for-profit corporate structure. Richard Sandor, an esteemed market observer who was instrumental in developing financial contracts at the CBOT and who launched Chicago's and the European Climate Exchanges, summed it up succinctly: "Mutual forms of ownership are not a twenty-first century way of doing business. Speed and flexibility are business assets, and mutuals have neither."[2] The New York Stock Exchange and the Nasdaq Stock Exchange were talking about demutualization. So were the CBOT and CBOE. So was almost everyone. The NASD, parent of the Nasdaq stock market, reportedly said its board had approved plans that could involve selling shares in its exchange to participant brokers and eventually to the public.[3] In some places it had already happened: The Stockholm Stock Exchange became the first stock exchange to convert, and the Australian Stock Exchange was a close second. Steven Strahler of *Crain's Chicago Business* summed it up:

> *The industry's buzzword is demutualization. Institutions from the NYSE on down are studying it, converting from member-driven organizations into less democratic but potentially more competitive and technologically advanced corporations that could go public and list their own stock. The established exchanges are being forced to react to rival upstarts that are busting open what for decades has been a cozy, members-only club. Unfortunately, it may already be too late for many existing exchanges.[4]*

To say that the American futures markets' organizational structure was cumbersome does not begin to explain its unwieldy legal, regulatory, and political makeup. As I told Reuters News, "The problem we face in our industry is that as a membership organization, we have to live within the structure of politics that requires decisions to go through a very tortuous process."[5] That said a mouthful. At the CME there were 39 members of the board of directors who met twice a month; there were over 200 committees; and there were over 3,000 members aligned in three divisions with everyone having a personal say-so and in some matters even a veto right. Additionally, since this was before congressional adoption of the Futures Modernization Act (FMA) of 2000, there were also cumbersome procedural regulatory requirements by the Commodity Futures Trading Commission (CFTC). Needless to say, in the globalized world of present-day competition, which often required rapid response and instant action, such a ponderous structure was doomed to failure. Increasingly, many of us reached the understanding that the CME had to shed its ancient not-for-profit design in favor of a modern for-profit structure. Implicit in this conclusion was the judgment that such a redesign would lead the CME down the path of becoming a public company, the best means of attaining the kind of capital necessary to build a first-class electronic system with which to defend our turf in the coming century.

Toward that purpose, the CME board did what most corporate organizations do: It authorized Scott Gordon, our chairman, to retain a consultant. McKinsey & Company was our choice. Andrew Eichfeld and John Ott, McKinsey's project managers, became a permanent addition to the Strategic Planning Committee (SPC). Jimmy Oliff set the SPC on an aggressive schedule with meetings on a once-a-week basis. The McKinsey managers attended most of these meetings and in addition held conferences with committee members. Years later, Craig Donohue, who was assigned as the coordinator between the Strategic Planning Committee and the board, offered his opinion that the McKinsey experience was mostly a dud. In the sense that they provided no acceptable solution, no magic bullet, he was quite correct. Indeed, McKinsey's main idea for the CME was to use its Globex system to become the electronic turnstile and gatekeeper for the world and charge everyone for using our system. A grand thought, but seriously unrealistic. Still, in another sense, McKinsey's role was important to the process. For one thing as Jimmy Oliff stated, "They helped organize our thoughts." Indeed, their conclusion followed the standard consulting road map: Draw on the expertise existing within the client, add information and experience from your own resources, organize the findings, put fancy words to the conclusion, and wrap it with your credibility ribbon. Or in Oliff's words, "Mostly, they gave us back what we fed them." In truth, however, I liked the McKinsey people and found them very experienced. It was important to see that expert outsiders agreed with our private conclusions. While I have no doubt that McKinsey's own experience and rationale led them to their recommendations, Oliff and I did a good job in making certain that they spent some quality time with some of us. I know that I held a number of private in-depth conferences with both Andrew Eichfeld and John Ott. It certainly did not hurt our cause.

Essentially, they recommended to our committee that the CME pursue expansion of our electronic system, urging us to include all elements of trading used on the trading floor, and to continue to be "the Firsteth with the Mosteth." In other words, speed and aggressiveness in electronics were of the essence. An ancillary recommendation was that the CME consider using our electronic system as an enticement for a joint venture with the CBOT in order to have all of the interest rate products listed electronically on a single platform. Not a new idea. McKinsey also supported the need for demutualization and recommended that it allow current members to have trading rights on both the trading floor and the electronic platform.

None of this represented new ground to Arditti, Kilcollin, Oliff, Shepard and myself, who were leading the same charge. But in the end, when it came to recommendation to our board, we could point to confirmation from a respected outside expert.

In mid-August 1998, the McKinsey managers made their initial report to the CME board. It represented a view from 30,000 feet. Their report covered the whole gamut of possible reactions by the CME to the rapidly changing futures world. At one extreme was the do-nothing option, which would result in the CME becoming nothing more than a minor player in the world market. By following this option, we would be destined to live out our remaining years as a small open-outcry exchange, trading our exclusively licensed Standard & Poor's (S&P) products (until we perhaps lost this license) plus a few agricultural commodities. A possible middle ground McKinsey described would be to continue along a line that we had already been considering—to form an alliance with one of the new electronic networks being created elsewhere. The most aggressive option was to go all out to win the central role in the electronic future. This would require us to make a complete commitment to the electronic platform and to invest in joint ownership of technology, what they called the "Shaper strategy."

Oliff and I agreed that the first two alternatives were losing propositions. By then, DTB's electronic venue had captured over 90 percent of Bund futures volume; EBS with its 2,100 screens globally compared to the CME's 600 in North America had proceeded with its competitive plans for an electronic FRA market; and other European exchanges were similarly developing short-term interest rate functionality. Most important, both Jimmy and I harbored the belief that in the not too distant future, LIFFE would undertake a full-blown assault on the CME. In fact, in an attempt to divert LIFFE from this course, the CME for a time attempted an alliance with them. It was unsuccessful. We thus agreed—a direction from which I never wavered—that it was imperative to pursue an aggressive expansion of our electronic capability and migrate our franchise product to the screen before someone stole our golden goose. We also both agreed, as did the majority of the SPC, that while we explored partnerships with other exchanges and market participants, we proceeded with a policy toward demutualization.

Jimmy Oliff and I convinced Scott Gordon to prepare the board for what we had in mind by presenting an interim report to the board. Built around the McKinsey recommendations, the SPC developed a slate of six preliminary actions. which we reported out. Of these six, four were imperative: full commitment to protect our products by improving the technical viability of our electronic system and providing open and equal access to our customers; an aggressive plan to migrate liquidity from open outcry to Globex; negotiating multiple partnerships with other exchanges and market participants; and changing CME's ownership structure to a for-profit entity. Each recommendation was hotly discussed. To no one's surprise, the issue of migration to the screen drew the most fire. The open-outcry old guard was still alive and kicking with enough votes to derail this recommendation. The final language of the recommendation was modified to read that migration to the screen would be instituted selectively, *for those products that the board decides to list electronically.* In other words, the real battle over electronic migration of Eurodollars was yet to be fought. Still, it was progress. The general commitment toward electronics as well as demutualization was clear. We even agreed to retain an investment banker, and the SPC 'eventually hired Salomon Smith Barney in an advisory capacity.

Three months later, in November of 1998, the Strategic Planning Committee made its final report to the board. Jimmy Oliff took the lead. As I recall, it took us more than an hour to read into the record the gist of our long deliberative process and to present our recommendations in detail. We had condensed our recommendations into four salient points. The first two were relatively noncontroversial: it was to have the SPC begin working on the necessary steps to lead us to demutualization by becoming a for-profit corporation (talk about your unintended consequences of the technological revolution), and for the board to agree that we strengthen our competitive position by reaching out to possible partners to develop strategic alliances. The final two recommendations were explosive, contentious, and demanded immediate action. They represented the SPC's decision to bite the bullet. We asked for a two-pronged effort toward advancing Globex as a world platform. First, to invest the large sums needed (about $65 million over the 14 months through January 2000—serious money at the time) to build up the capacity of Globex so it could handle the entire breadth of 40 contract months of the Eurodollar. Jim Krause had advised me that the first phase of Eurodollar capability would be ready no later than June 30, 1999, and the entire range of Eurodollar futures and options contracts would be able to trade side-by-side by January of 2000 (an ambitious but doable schedule and hopefully in time). Second, we proposed that the CME hold a membership referendum to approve side-by-side (concurrent) trading of the Eurodollar contract with Globex. The board knew this was coming and prepared to do battle.

When the arguing was over and the smoke cleared, the board of directors of the CME voted approval of all recommendations of the Strategic Planning Committee with only four dissenting votes. It was a historic achievement. Without doubt what turned a number of votes was the convincing argument made by both Jimmy and myself that an assault on our Eurodollar franchise contract was imminent. We argued that it would be the height of misfeasance if we remained unprepared. This view was emphatically supported by the members of the SPC as well as Scott Gordon. It was also very helpful that in August, several months earlier, the CBOT membership had approved by a five-to-one margin side-by-side trading for its Treasuries futures contracts. Of course, Treasury futures at the CBOT did not hold untouchable status as did their agricultural complex of corn, soybeans, and wheat, nor as Eurodollars did at the CME. Still, CBOT chairman Pat Arbor hailed it as preemptive action: "We must be competitive and visionary to remain the industry leader. To preserve these markets, particularly open out-cry, we are making a preemptive strike on any entity which might emerge as our competitor." [6] I recall calling Pat to offer my congratulations.

There was one ancillary recommendation by the SPC of critical im-port: to proceed with development and deployment of a new handheld technology, the so-called Galax-C. It would enable local traders to con-duct interactive Globex trading from anywhere on the floor. Jim Krause to this day believes that Galax-C represented the biggest boost for advancing Globex. Because the currency complex had already approved side-by-side trading, the handheld instrument could be deployed to that quadrant by March of 1999. [7] However, for the big-enchilada, Eurodollars, it would have to wait for referendum approval.

The board agreed to advise the membership of the SPC proposal in its entirety at special members' meetings scheduled for the end of November 1998. It was also to be the main topic of discussion at the forthcoming Annual Members' meeting in December. At that meeting, I was heartened by the fact that the proposition seemed to receive a favorable reaction. Again, I believe the fear of a competitive assault on our markets was a most convincing factor as was the favorable vote by CBOT for their Treasuries markets. Referendum on the proposition was scheduled for January 14, 1999. As expected, it was the only topic of discussion by the floor community during the two months leading up to the vote. A group of us, including Jimmy Oliff, Bill Shepard, Scott Gordon, Jack Sandner, and myself, spent countless hours on the floor with groups of members or one-by-one. We lobbied as if it were a holy mission. I insisted that our sole common hymn be that this was an "imperative defensive action against competitive threats." The referendum passed overwhelmingly with 92.8 percent of the weighted votes cast in favor of the proposal. The gigantic Eurodollar contract along with all other futures had gone side by side with Globex.

One of my closest friends, Dr. Henry Jarecki, an original board member of the IMM and an astute observer of the market scene, jubilantly called to say he never believed he would see this day. The event was historic, but sadly, pyrrhic. Like the guy said, we called for a celebration but nobody came. With few exceptions, the Eurodollar community—traders, indepen-dent brokers, members of broker groups—continued to trade in the pit as if nothing happened; similarly, the traders in the agricultural sector. Aside from the S&P E-Mini and foreign exchange trading, Globex generated vir-tually no additional business. Since liquidity begets liquidity, the dealers and hedgers could not budge from the open outcry arena so long as the locals' business flows on which they depended remained rooted in the pit. In 1999, the Eurodollar complex of futures and options represented nearly 59 percent of the Merc's total financial volume and a whopping 76 percent of its total open interest. Without Eurodollars, the evolution to electronic trade was stalled. In Jim Krause's words, "The side-by-side approval was important from a political standpoint, but from a technology standpoint it was a dud. We just spent a lot of money for nothing."

I disagreed. We were battling a century-old tradition. The tyranny of the status quo was not so easily reversed. I was certain that between the launch of the E-Mini and the current side-by-side referendum, the foundation for the electrification of the Merc had been laid. "Jim," I said, "Patience. It took two centuries to make the Renaissance."

CHAPTER 7

Demutualization

Stepping on the Moon

On Monday, April 12, 1999, Zhu Rongji, premier of the People's Republic of China, came to the floor of the Chicago Mercantile Exchange (CME). It was a consequential happening in the world of finance. Not that a head-of-state visit to the Merc was so unusual. The CME, no differently than the Chicago Board of Trade (CBOT), had more than its share of such high-level personalities over the years. Not counting the innumerable visits by U.S. Senators and Congressmen, the CME hosted a multitude of national and international dignitaries and officials of every brand. While the Merc's compelling image was built primarily on its innovative ideas, it gained enormous value from such visitations. The visibility and PR was impossible to estimate. Beginning in 1975 with the visit by Hubert Humphrey, Vice President of the United States, there was a steady stream of U.S. Presidents, Vice Presidents, as well as heads of state of foreign nations.[1]

The commencement of this tour de force at the Merc coincided in 1975 with the establishment of the CME's Political Action Committee—an idea suggested to me by William Bagley, the initial chairman of the Commodity Futures Trading Corporation (CFTC). The Merc's PAC, like the majority of similar political action committees in the United States, acted under the authority of the Federal Election Campaign Act of 1971 and as clarified through subsequent court decisions.[2] Over the years, as a result of the joint leadership efforts by Jack Sandner and myself, along with the early fund-raising prowess of Harry Lowrance, the Merc's PAC became one of the most respected in the nation, giving the CME a solid voice in our nation's capital. Equally important in these efforts, in the 1980s, it led the way to a joint floor visitation program maintained by both the CME and CBOT, which provided us with a unique opportunity to bring to the floor elected officials and explain firsthand how the markets worked and their contribution to the economy. The program provided visiting guests with a priceless educational lesson about how the world markets work, a lesson that could never be duplicated simply through textbooks. To paraphrase a saying often attributed to Confucius, one personal visit to the Exchange was worth a thousand pictures. At the same time, it raised the profile of the Chicago Exchanges and served to invigorate our members' political interest. The photo opportunity with a well-known political official was a priceless memento and an incentive for their voluntary contributions to our PAC.[3]

During the 1970s, 1980s, 1990s, and extending into recent times, the success of this undertaking was in great measure due to the efforts of some very talented and dedicated CME executive personnel in Washington, D.C., principally Dayle Henington, Lita Schilling Frazier, and recently Bo Chambilis. Early on, Dayle Henington prevailed on then House Agriculture chairman, Kika de La Garza, to allow the Merc to use his spacious House hearing room for an annual reception for members of the U.S. Congress, a custom that has continued to this very day.[4] The total measure of credibility and goodwill engendered by the CME's PAC, visitation, and Washington educational programs over the past three decades with members of both bodies of Congress and within both political parties represents an incomparable asset, nearly impossible to assess. Still going strong, our current combined CME/CBOT PAC (and now with the addition of NYMEX) has in recent years been significantly enhanced by the additional leadership of Terry Duffy (CME Group chairman), Charlie Carey (CME Group vice chairman), Craig Donohue (CME Group chief executive), C.C. Odom (CME Group director), and the organizational talents of CME PAC directors David Wescott and Ronald Pankau.

The mission of raising the stature and image of the CME was an ever-present underlying force and took many forms. It was meaningfully advanced by the public directors we sought to serve on our board. This mind-set for me began with the very creation of the International Monetary Market in 1972, where I sought appointment to the board of such internationally prominent personalities as Robert Abboud, executive vice chairman of the First National Bank of Chicago; Dr. Henry Jarecki, chairman of Mocatta Metals; Beryl Sprinkel, senior economist for the Harris Trust Bank of Chicago; and William J. McDonough, executive vice president of the First National Bank of Chicago. It was a custom followed by every Merc chairman and similarly conducted by the CBOT. Sometimes, as in the case of Nobel Prize winner in economics Merton Miller, the appointee would, at different times, serve on both our boards. Often the people were dignitaries whom I personally became acquainted with and befriended. At all times, we sought people who were not simply well-known but those whose credentials and expertise would serve the needs and best interests of the CME.

Over the years, these appointments included such notables as Gerald Corrigan, former president of the Federal Reserve Bank of New

York; Tom Eagleton, former U.S. Senator from Missouri; Rudy Boschwich, former U.S. Senator from Wisconsin; Paul Simon, former U.S. Senator from Illinois; and Myron Scholes, Nobel laureate in economics. In more recent times, our appointments have included Dan Glickman, former U.S. Secretary of Agriculture, and Dennis Hastert, former Speaker of the U.S. House of Representatives. Often our selections were lucky (some might be generous and say prescient), as in the case of Beryl Sprinkel, who eventually became chairman of the Council of Economic Advisors under President Reagan, and William J. McDonough, who followed Gerald Corrigan as president of the Federal Reserve Bank of New York. Similarly, in 1999 I met with my friend of many years, Rahm Emanuel, after completion of his official term as senior advisor to President Clinton for Policy and Strategy to discuss the possibility of a board seat on the Merc. He accepted my invitation and on May 5, 1999, was duly appointed to the CME board, where he served for several years. As we all know, Rahm Emanuel, in November 2008, was appointed by President Obama as his chief of staff.

But Rongji's visit of 1999 was of special import because China's phenomenal development was finally getting widespread attention. His visit wasn't an accident or good luck. Just as every long journey begins with a single step, so are relationships built over long periods of time—especially within the Asian world. This was not the first time one of the highest officials of the Chinese Republic would personally honor the Merc in this fashion. Fourteen years earlier, on July 26, 1985, communism officially shook hands with capitalism when President Li Xiannian became the first high-ranking Chinese official to pay us a visit. It was an unheard-of gesture back then. In fact, the U.S. Treasury, whose responsibility it is to guard foreign heads of state, called me to ask if it was true. Yes, I had personally invited the president of China to come to the Merc floor during the visit by our board officers to the Chinese Republic a year earlier at the behest of the Chinese Central Bank. That visit laid the foundation for the Merc's long-standing and ongoing friendship with the People's Republic of China. It is a foundation of friendship and trust established over two decades that will pay the CME untold dividends as the Chinese economy meets the promise of its enormous business potential in the decades ahead.

While Rongji's visit momentarily caught the attention of the Merc's trader community, it was not the most important topic on their minds. Nor was the historic referendum that theoretically put Globex on a par with open outcry. Nor was Fred Arditti's brand-new idea of Weather Futures—a new dimension for futures with which to manage weather-related financial risks in specific major population centers, such as Atlanta, Chicago, Cincinnati, Dallas, New York, Philadelphia, Portland, and Tucson, with other centers to follow. What was occupying the attention of many brokers and traders on the floor at the moment, at least those in the Eurodollar pit, was "pit space-dispute guidelines." In other words, by what rules should a given broker or trader be entitled to the location of his one or two square feet of space in the Eurodollar pit over another broker or trader? As nothing else, the importance of this issue revealed the true mind-set of the Eurodollar pit community: *Eurodollar futures would never move to the screen.*

Pit location was everything. As the saying went: "Where you stand is where you eat." Millions of dollars were at stake. In a well-publicized 1996 incident, a Eurodollar broker reputedly sold the rights to his one-square-foot top-step pit location to a fellow broker for $1 million.[5] The issue remained so pronounced and controversial that in 1998, Scott Gordon appointed a special committee to make location determinations. The discussion at the board centered around who was to serve on the committee and the guidelines the committee should follow. After hours of debate, by a razor-thin margin of 13 to 12, ten guidelines were adopted with equity ownership, volume of business, and tenure to carry the most weight. It was viewed as a loss to the broker groups. In hindsight, all of this may seem rather trivial—but it was deadly serious at the time.

That mind-set was totally ignored by those of us who were seeing the electronic handwriting on the wall. Fred Arditti and I privately agreed to concentrate in two directions: first, to find the correct path to demutual-ization, and second, to internationalize Globex. An earlier Globex initiative had been known as the "Globex Alliance." It proposed that CME partner with other futures exchanges to make Globex the standard for the industry. This grandiose idea, which I heartily supported at the outset, had its ups and downs over the years. Rejuvenated by McKinsey & Co, it was embraced by both Scott Gordon and Jim Oliff as the surest way to achieve Globex validation. While I was no longer certain we could pull it off, I joined the efforts. Scott Gordon asked me, Jack Sandner, and Fred Arditti to act as emissaries and begin the negotiation process with the CBOT, Singapore International Monetary Exchange (SIMEX), Marché à Terme International de France (MATIF), and even London International Financial Futures Ex-change (LIFFE). In short, we held discussions with virtually everyone in the global futures space. As Scott Gordon pointed out at the annual 1999 Futures Industry Association convention in Boca Raton, we had agreements with Singapore's SIMEX, the French MATIF, and potentially others. "At the end of the day," Scott said, "numerous alliances, covering numerous aspects of the business will be forged . . . to share a common trading platform."[6]

I agreed with the McKinsey people that the CBOT represented our best opportunity and the most telling flow of business for Globex. Having spent years opposing the advancement of electronic trade, the CBOT was now under the gun and in dire need of an electronic order-matching engine to protect its financial markets. It was in not-so-secret discussions with Eurex for an electronic system arrangement. Such a deal would have serious international competitive implications for the CME, and it therefore made sense for us to go all out in an effort to discourage those discussions and convince CBOT to choose Globex instead. Scott Gordon asked me to lead a special negotiation team for this purpose. We met with the CBOT leadership, including Bernie Dan, eventually the CBOT chief executive officer (CEO), a very capable manager, and made them what for all intents and purposes was a very attractive offer (some believed it was too generous): no charge for our Globex developmental cost, CBOT expense limited to what it would cost it to interface with our electronic platform, prospective development costs to be shared jointly, and each exchange to maintain control of its own products. The proposal would not preclude either party from pursuing other joint ventures. It was but one of a number of initiatives I led in an attempt to bring the CBOT and CME together on Globex, a move that I believed would ultimately lead to merger. It took several weeks for the CBOT to turn down the offer and tell us that it had decided on a deal with Frankfurt.

Ostensibly, the CBOT decision was based on the fact that the Eurex technology was superior to that of Globex. Perhaps, but Jim Krause assured us that this was not the case. He agreed with our conclusion that the CBOT's underlying motivation was to deny the CME this "Globex" victory. Ironically, internal politics caused the CBOT's membership in the first instance to turn down the Eurex proposal. Nevertheless, given CBOT's choice in favor of Eurex, the Merc had nowhere else to go internationally but to deal with LIFFE. Scott Gordon led the effort and we went full speed ahead. By August, an agreement seemed at hand. LIFFE and the CME would provide cross-exchange access and interconnection of trading platforms; cross-margining of our Eurodollars and LIFFE's Euribor (a European short-term futures interest-rate instrument similar to Eurodollars) contracts as well as other initiatives; and would create an innovative joint venture between the CME and LIFFE that would be structured as a fully electronic for-profit entity to capitalize on new markets. With a good deal of media fanfare, a memorandum of understanding was signed on August 5, 1999. "With today's agreement," said CME chairman Scott Gordon, "the world's premier exchanges for short-term interest rates provide a linkage that will give our customers innovative global trading opportunities, along with greater market efficiency and cost savings."[7] Hugh Freedberg, LIFFE's CEO, concurred: "This agreement will meet the needs of our customers through the innovative use of technology and the provisions of a wider choice of products."[8] None of it came to pass.

In the meantime, given the unfavorable reaction from their members, CBOT's chairman David Brennan and Tom Dononvan, its president, returned to Germany and the negotiating table with Eurex. What evolved was a new deal, "Alliance/CBOT/Eurex" (A/C/E), a common trading platform for the two futures exchanges. "The time is ripe to make the alliance

with Eurex. This partnership has my full support," stated Brennan.[9] The
European press couldn't resist taking a shot at the CBOT:

> *In a week when the Chicago Board of Trade, the world's largest floor-*
> *based derivatives exchange, finally embraced the electronic wizardry*
> *behind Eurex, seven of the world's eight largest fixed income houses*
> *announced plans to set up a new screen broking system for the cash*
> *bond markets, and immediately signaled an intention to open up talks*
> *with LIFFE. The developments underscore the speed with which the fixed*
> *income markets are changing. The CBOT, steeped in bureaucracy and*
> *conservative to the point of indolence, will have a fully operational elec-*
> *tronic capacity in a matter of months.[10]*

However, before the new alliance took effect the following year, internal politics at the CBOT, never far below the surface, erupted again,
This time in a rupture between chairman David Brennan and CBOT's long-
standing president, Tom Donovan. Contrary to the outcome of altercations
with Donovan in past political squabbles, on this occasion the chairman prevailed, ending the tenure of the strongest CBOT voice for the past 18 years.
Reputedly receiving a $10 million payment, Tom Donovan left the CBOT
in April 2000.[11] He thus was not present when on August 25, 2000, Project
A, the internal CBOT electronic system launched under his command, was
switched off for the last time. It was duly replaced with A/C/E under the new
alliance agreement with Eurex at a moment of high expectations. Andreas
Preuss, Eurex director, proclaimed: "The alliance is not limited to simply the
implementation of a joint technology, but much more than that. We intend
to exploit the synergies of a single team, and single platform."[12]

Promising sentiments! However, life is full of surprises. As reported by
Melissa Goldfine of Reuters, "From the inception, the relationship between
the two exchanges has had its tense moments." Calling it a "clash of cultures," she reported that at the press briefing ahead of the A/C/E launch, former Eurex CEO Joerg Franke said he saw the partnership's ultimate goal as
a Eurex-CBOT merger, a sentiment which the two exchanges later denied.[13]
Within a year, trouble within the alliance began brewing. Political infighting,
changes in leadership at the CBOT, and inadequate technological A/C/E capabilities caused wide-ranging disputes between the partners. Eventually,
the CBOT refused to pay for the latest software upgrades, a cost of about $15
million, acknowledging that the expected benefits from improved software
would not justify the costs. Eurex took it as a breach of formal agreements and threatened to invoke "dispute resolution" procedures against
the CBOT.[14]

The dispute ended when again a new agreement was reached by short-
ening the termination date from 2008 to 2003, allowing the two exchanges

to form new partnerships prior to expiration of the alliance, and a settlement of the cost issues. "We wanted to resolve a situation which had been a little bit too complex, a little bit too exclusive and a little bit too restrictive for both parties to develop their business," said the new Eurex chief executive, Rudolph Ferscha.[15] Actually, it was the beginning of the end of the relationship. By January of 2003, there were rumors that the CBOT was looking to end its A/C/E deal with Eurex in favor of a technology license from LiffeConnect of Euronext Liffe.[16] The rumors were correct. At a special news conference on January 10, 2003, Nickolas Neubauer, the new chairman of the CBOT, announced that Eurex's A/C/E platform would be replaced with its London counterpart, LiffeConnect. The reason for CBOT's sudden turnabout became clear when Rudolf Ferscha of Eurex issued a blockbuster announcement that the German-Swiss Exchange was planning to become a direct U.S. competitor to the CBOT. The announcement acknowledged that Eurex had had advanced talks with the CFTC about its plans to launch a full-fledged U.S. exchange that would trade a full range of derivatives on U.S. interest rates, indexes, and equities in early 2004.[17]

But there I go again letting memory run way ahead of the story. While the foregoing international maneuvers and machinations kept everyone busy during the last year of the twentieth century, some of us at the Merc never lost sight of what was our highest immediate priority: demutualization. Although it was a goal fraught with danger, an untested adventure not unlike exploring an alien planet, for some of us it was axiomatic—it was the only way to prepare the Merc for the twenty-first century. Steve Strahler of *Crain's Chicago Business* captured the essence of this difficult mission:

> *When Chicago's futures exchanges talk about transforming their splintered, membership-owned organizations into nimble, for-profit corporations, an infamous Vietnam analogy comes to mind: they may have to destroy the village in order to save it. . . . Indeed the light at the end of the tunnel on LaSalle Street could be as elusive for the city's exchanges as it was for the United States in Vietnam. . . . Simply put, Chicago's futures and options exchanges are contemplating the most radical restructuring in their storied history . . . converting from member-driven organizations into less democratic but potentially more competitive and technologically advanced corporations that could go public . . . one that promises to alter them radically if not kill them outright*

> *Changing their stripes not only will require a new mind-set by member-owners, who must wrestle with how much power to cede, but it also hints at self-destructive tendencies by introducing for-profit concepts, such as revenue-raising strategies, that are antithetical to the cooperative nature of an exchange. Ultimately, lumbering decision-making*

processes could doom many exchange conversions from the start. The spoils likely will go to the industry's first movers—those that jump into the public markets, raise capital for acquisitions and foreclose options for competitors.[18]

Strahler explained it well. *It will require a new mind-set by member-owners to willingly cede their power.* In practical terms, I was convinced that a successful demutualization plan would require two parts: a legal structure and a political deal. Both parts would have to be to the liking of the brokers and local traders. Finding that holy grail became the mandate for the Strategic Planning Committee.

Right from the outset of this mission my greatest fear was that during the deliberations there would be leaks to the floor, which inevitably would become garbled like in the game of "Telephone." I had of course directed a similar undertaking years earlier, when in 1987 we unveiled the idea of Post (Pre) Market Trade (PMT)—the after-hours electronic transaction system that became Globex—a concept so antithetical to floor traders that the chances of approval were considered small to none. Similarly, I knew that if demutualization had any chance at all, it would be *only* if the idea were presented at one time, after its full formation, after every conceivable error had been addressed, when every query, no matter how wild, had a prepared and credible response, and only when its unveiling was made under precisely prepared and orchestrated conditions. Even a breath or hint of what was being formulated could become a flash point of gossip and distortion so that by the time the plan was fully divulged, the built-up fears, misrepresentations, and misconceptions could not be overcome. Now again, my demand, "under penalty of death," was that not a word, not a sound of what was being discussed by the SPC ever leave the room. Any leak was tantamount to a subversive act. Jimmy Oliff christened our process a "Code of Silence." It worked. Not one member of the press, try as they did, could learn anything of what we were considering. This report in *Securities Week* pretty well summed up the general view held by the world.

> *Work on proposals to go about demutualizing the CME has been proceeding methodically for close to a year and has suggested to many observers the difficulty of coming up with an acceptable plan that could be sold to members. One big potential obstacle to the effort has been finding a way to offer a direct payment, or the guarantee of a payment to member who essentially would be giving up the rights they now have under the exchange's structure as a member organization.*

> *While CME members would probably be given shares in a new corporation that would place most of the power and authority in the hands of*

the board, most observers have suggested that their approval will only be forthcoming if they perceive that they are certain to receive compensation for the value of their seats while retaining trading rights that could be bought and sold. Finding the money to pay members for their seats, either all at once or through a payout over time, has been the most vexing problem facing all U.S. exchanges considering plans to demutualization and become for-profit institutions.

In the Merc's case, based on current seat values, about $700 million would be required for a complete buyout of the seats owned by members. In general, though, industry observers have had a difficult time imagining anyone willing to buy any exchange when computerized trading operations can be launched for less.[19]

Since no American exchange had ever undertaken this revolutionary step, no road map or blueprint existed. It was to be an original work of art. There were two house artists who must be given a lion's share of the credit: Jerry Salzman and Craig Donohue. I had known Salzman from the time I took over the CME chairmanship in 1969. He was then fresh out of Harvard Law School and became our outside legal counsel. He had served us in this capacity during every major turn in the many twists of our history. Over the years, Jerry gained a well-deserved national reputation as the foremost legal mind in matters of futures markets. But he became much more to us than legal counsel. Hugely talented, Jerry Salzman became someone whose advice and counsel I have trusted and relied on throughout the years. While sometimes we found reasons to disagree, sometimes strongly, I never really questioned that our divergent points of views, when they happened, were based on honest differences of opinion on what was in the best interest of the CME.

Craig Donohue was a relatively fresh face for me. An attorney by profession, who had come to the CME a decade earlier, rising through its ranks to become in 1998 CME senior vice president and general counsel. When Fred Arditti took over, becoming responsible for the work product of the SPC, he called my attention to two star employees at the Merc, Craig Donohue and Phupinder Gill, both of whom in his opinion were "extremely talented, valuable and devoted." He appointed Craig Donohue vice president of strategic planning, which brought Craig into my sphere of influence. It provided me with my first opportunity to work with Donohue and get to know him. As usual, Fred Arditti's instincts were letter perfect and, as history is witness, proved to be a most fortuitous occurrence for both Craig Donohue and the CME. From this point forward, Craig Donohue became involved in virtually every facet of CME's business and the upper echelon of decision making. He became both general counsel and head of strategic planning and business development, responsibilities that made him indispensable for the demutualization process and beyond.

In an entirely separate dimension of Merc affairs, until Fred Arditti called my attention to Phupinder Gill, whom everyone referred to as Gill, I hardly knew him. A Singaporean by citizenship and Indian by birth, Gill came to the Merc from the CBOE in 1988 because, in his words, "I discovered the Merc was a much better place to work." Fortunately, the CME was then running educational courses for members, and Gill signed up for every class he could. With an unparalleled inquisitive and insatiable mind, Gill quickly learned every aspect of the Exchange. His first assignment was at the Clearing House, working for John Davidson, a senior CME clearing-house executive, and Kate Meyers, who was its director. His first important responsibility was to run the risk management and financial management department, a highly critical aspect of Exchange clearing. His performance was considered nothing short of brilliant. When John Davidson left, Gill was appointed second in command, and when Kate Meyers departed in 1998, Gill was the unanimous choice to take the top slot. Fred Arditti's return to the Merc provided Gill with the first opportunity to get to know him. He became an instant Arditti fan. Gill, Fred, and I quickly formed a special mutual admiration society that was to become of critical import in the years that followed. Highly intelligent, with a penchant for diplomacy, Phupinder Gill went on to become for me the single most important Exchange management official, as he personally knew and understood every segment of the complex underpinnings of the Exchange, their relationship to each other, and the management of their personnel. Upon Fred's death from pancreatic cancer on October 30, 2005, Gill and I remained as brothers.

But as everyone will agree, the Picasso of the legal structure of demutualization was Brad Ferguson, the Merc's special tax attorney from Sidley & Austin. Brad, an old CME hand, had his first taste of Exchange matters in 1981. As a member of the firm of Hopkins and Sutter, he collaborated with Fred Hickman and CME's tax counsel Ira Marcus to resolve the sticky issues emanating from the era when so-called "tax spreads" were a legal means of transferring income forward. Now Ferguson was called on to use his magic paintbrush and create the legal blueprint for converting the existing CME from an Illinois not-for-profit membership corporation into a Delaware for-profit stockholder corporation in an equitable fashion without incurring tax liability to the members. In seeking this objective, Ferguson invented the perfect model, which thereafter every American exchange utilized. As with many bright solutions to complex problems, the answer was in keeping it simple. All he had to do, he decided, was to transfer the existing makeup before demutualization to the new model. His brainchild was based on the realization that every member owned certain "buckets" of rights. There were rights specific to a futures exchange: the right to enter the floor, the right to trade, the right to execute orders for customers, lower trading rates and margins, the right to lease out the membership, and so on. In addition, members also owned such traditional equity rights as the right to vote and to share in residual exchange assets in the event of liquidation. This brought him to the "A and B" configuration, where A and B shares between them would collectively incorporate all the existing buckets of rights. All we had to do was structure an entity that stapled these membership rights onto Class A and Class B shares of common stock within the "New CME." As finally designed, both Class A and Class B shares would have the traditional features of common stock. However, the primary purpose of Class A shares would be to confer most of the equity value in the corporation in the event of a public offering, while the primary purpose of the Class B shares would be to confer the trading privileges associated with membership in the existing CME along with some equity value. It was a work of art.

In September of 1999, Brad Ferguson unveiled to the board the legal structure for demutualization with the blessing of the SPC. There was instant acceptance by the board. That took care of part one, the legal structure, the easy part. But there was still the proverbial elephant in the room: the political deal. How could we resolve the membership fear that the board could mandate the closure of the floor or any portion of it? What would we have to give the members to relinquish control over the right that most mattered to them—the third rail of our world—open-outcry trading? The right that ignored the referendum on side-by-side listing. *What would it take to make the trade?*

In spite of my unalterable belief that electronic trading was the destiny for futures markets, I had a great deal of respect and sympathy for the floor community. For much of my adult life I had been one of them—earning a living as a trader in the pits, depending on the open-outcry architecture. It was our mother's milk, what we knew, how we lived and survived. For that reason, I would not join any draconian measures to get to the promised land—or in other words, force the result by, for instance, making the floor antiquated, impractical, or too expensive. In my opinion, one could not, and should not, *forcibly* direct or interfere with the natural evolutionary forces that I believed would ultimately choose electronic trade. In plain English, if electronics were to happen, it must be by a decision of the floor itself based on natural evolution or change in circumstances. But I was equally determined that the evolutionary contest be fair. Until now the scales were tipped in favor of open outcry. How to get the vote while balancing these conflicting equities was the $64 billion question.

From the start, I had a sense of how this could be done, but the trick was to get the committee to agree as a consequence of their own logical conclusion—a process of examination and elimination. My partner in this effort again was Bill Shepard. He, no differently than I, was weaned on the floor, had great respect for the floor traders, and understood the mentality of this diverse constituency. With Jimmy Oliff's oversight, Bill and I carefully navigated through the Strategic Planning Committee's thought processes—avoiding a myriad of shoals and whirlpools that could sink the enterprise. We would analyze a given approach and, if it led to a dead end, discard it and begin again. What made this difficult task even tougher was that to maintain our code of silence, we could never actually test any deal with anyone on the floor. It was like walking a tightrope from 10 stories up without a safety net. Slowly we reached a unanimous conclusion—a plan that we believed would be embraced by the majority of members. It was where I knew we had to end up.

It took about a year, but in retrospect, it was a thing of beauty: to allay all naysayers and skeptics right from the get-go, we began with a sacred "Commitment to Maintain the Floor." No tricks, no gimmicks, no subterfuge. The floor was sacrosanct. We would do nothing untoward to the floor. However, we also had to be fair to electronic trade. Both venues would coexist, competing with each other, until one or the other took over. The foundation for this approach was already in place by virtue of the side-by-side referendum previously approved. The mantra we adopted was honest and flexible—an offer we thought the floor would buy: The market—*read, our customers*—would decide which architecture suited them best. Liquidity would be the key determinant. As long as an open-outcry market remained liquid, we guaranteed to maintain trading floor space and support facilities, provide clearing facilities, disseminate prices, and, importantly, continue to support the contract at 1999 financial levels. Nothing in this deal, however, would prevent a given floor community from choosing to abandon an open-outcry forum for a given contract at their discretion. Nor could the Exchange use any gimmick, such as fees, to direct the business one way or another. We agreed that the clearing fees charged for floor-based business would never be greater than those charged for electronic trade. The beauty of this proposition was that adherents of the respective venues were equally convinced that theirs would be the one to win. The open-outcry constituents needed only to look at the ineffectiveness of the side-by-side referendum to sustain their beliefs. Those of us who understood the strength of technology knew otherwise. Dave Carpenter of the AP Newswires quoted me correctly: "Be it open outcry or be it electronic, both systems will be viable for this exchange. We would turn to the marketplace for the final word."[20]

And we knew how to make a fair liquidity determination. We used a formula principally devised by Jerry Salzman previously applied and acceptable to the floor. In simple terms: A market would be deemed to be liquid: (a) When a comparable exchange-traded product exists, and our open-outcry market has maintained at least 30 percent of the average daily volume of such comparable product, or at least 30 percent of the open interest of such comparable product measured on a quarterly basis; or (b) When no comparable exchange-traded product exists, and our open-outcry market has maintained at least 40 percent of the average quarterly volume in that market as maintained by the CME in 1999, or at least 40 percent of the average open interest in that market as maintained by the CME in 1999. Not only was this liquidity test deemed fair by the floor, it was viewed as a high enough threshold to allay the fears of the "floor-forever" crowd. Changes to liquidity rules, or other "Core Rights" of B shareholders, such as product allocation rules, trading floor access and privilege rights, or other inherent floor membership rights, could not be made without a referendum by the B shareholders. It was an explicit and ironclad guarantee. Five years later, in 2004, we brought forward a referendum requesting a change, but that's getting ahead of our story.

The Strategic Planning Committee's demutualization plan also included a dramatic proposal to change the composition of the CME board. A modern corporate entity, I insisted, could not operate efficiently with 30-plus members of the board. I also knew this to be a most difficult and sensitive issue that, unless it was included as part of the demutualization package, might never be accomplished. We agreed on a plan to achieve this result. After demutualization, there would be a year of transition following the December 1999 election during which nothing would be changed. After this first year, the size of the board would begin to be reduced, in two stages, from 39 to 19 directors. (Later this was amended to 20 directors to include an automatic seat for the CEO.) The final composition would include six board members elected by Class B shareholders, six by joint Class A and Class B shareholders, and as many as seven would be elected by joint A and B shareholders from a board-nominated slate. Finally, pursuant to the guidance of Simon Hewitt and Gideon Asher of Salomon Smith Barney, the SPC agreed to authorize 100 million Class A shares and to initially issue and register 25,855,200 of such shares. Each CME member would receive 16,200 A shares, IMM members 10,800 A shares, and Index and Options Market (IOM) members 5,400 A shares.

Oliff and I presented the Demutualization Plan at a special board meeting late in October 1999. It was approved in its entirety. The Code of Silence would remain in force until it was unveiled at the annual members' meeting, on Tuesday, November 2, 1999. Curiously, Scott Gordon virtually turned the entire show over to Jimmy Oliff. It was well that he did. While I spoke passionately on behalf of the recommendations, it was Jim Oliff's finest hour. To a packed house, in meticulous fashion, he explained the complex proposal, its rationale and essential nature. Oliff was exceptional, self-assured, and thoroughly convincing. There was tremendous applause when he was finished. It boded very well for the plan. Craig Donohue then explained to the members the ins and outs of the process and time line of demutual-ization. Basically, nothing could happen until the Securities and Exchange Commission gave formal approval. After that happened, for the first time in American history, a demutualization plan would have been presented to an American exchange membership for ratification. In the course of time, the date of that membership vote was determined to be June 6, 2000. The day after the members' meeting, Dave Carpenter of Associated Press Newswires reported: "The plan met with loud applause Tuesday night when it was unveiled to the exchanges approximately 3,000 members." He quoted me as stating that "the plan turns over the final word on whether electronic or open outcry is more desirable to the marketplace."[21]

There was just one additional *small* matter: sale of the deal to the membership. Although there prevailed a strong sentiment in its favor, many months had passed since the member's' meeting. The task was left to the leaders of the Strategic Planning Committee, the CME board of directors, and the key members of management, Rick Kilcollin, Craig Donohue, and Fred Arditti. We viewed it as a once-in-a-lifetime proposition. There had been lots of talk by others, but no other exchange in the United States had the courage to bite the bullet. In addressing the floor community, that message was one of my strongest personal points: "The members of the CME and IMM were always trailblazers. Here was a magnificent opportunity to do it again and seize the moment." During that time period, as I recall, I may have personally met with every member of the floor community. And successful we were. As Reuters News reported on June 6, 2000, "The vote was 98.3 percent in favor, the highest margin of approval in the history of the CME." The achievement was heralded by every financial publication throughout the world. Peter A. McKay of the *Wall Street Journal* stated it well. The CME members, he said "had approved to turn their nonprofit market into a streamlined business, making it the first US derivatives-exchange so constituted."[22]

For all intents and purposes, the new CEO of the CME, one we had not yet chosen, would be handed a brand-new exchange, the first of its kind in the United States, ready, willing, and able to compete in the twenty-first century. It was a giant step for financial markets, by some measurement, the equivalent of stepping on the moon.

CHAPTER **8**

Dot-Coming
The False Paradise

In all fairness to Jim McNulty, our new chief executive officer (CEO), it must be noted that he assumed the Chicago Mercantile Exchange (CME) chief executive post on February 7, 2000, the exact moment when the tech bubble was at the peak of its madness. The dot-com mania was a virus that infected nearly everyone in the financial sector. It was the culmination of a frenzy that had witnessed the Nasdaq Composite Index rise above 5,000, having moved 86 percent higher in the final year of the twentieth century. During this so-called Goldilocks era, more than 180 U.S. and foreign stock funds doubled in value in 1999 alone, propelled by uninhibited investments primarily in technology and telecommunications. More than $400 billion streamed into technology growth funds. It was the climax of a perverted epoch of the late 1990s that infected a majority of the investment community and saw suspension of nearly all rational thought. "Irrational Exuberance" was the phrase coined by Alan Greenspan which forever defined that era. An era when the "story" of how a company hoped to make money was far more consequential to its stock value than bottom-line results; when every harebrained idea could be the foundation of a fortune; and when every concept had the potential for a new Internet market. Shares of these companies routinely doubled and tripled on their first day of public trading. Their eventual demise is the stuff serial killer movies are made of. Having peaked in March of 2000, the Composite Index fell 59 percent by the end of the year, on its way to a dismal 1,100 bottom. There are market experts who cynically doubt whether the Nasdaq Composite Index will ever get back to the record high. Parenthetically, I might add, the free-fall ending of the dot-com era of 2000 seems to have been but a preview of coming attractions, given the market meltdown that occurred eight years later.[1] Had the CME tied its future to this mirage, its destiny might very well have ended as did the dot-com aberration.

Like so many others, it seemed to me, Jim fell victim to this hysteria, coming to the Merc with a plan, one that was completely embraced by Scott Gordon: The CME would become a prime benefactor of the dot-com revolution. It was to be a new futures dawn, a new dimension. On the surface, it sure sounded enticing. In reality, it was an idea based on illusion. Among many new things, CME would become the clearinghouse for products or services launched by the dot-coms—be they in the realm of energy, chemicals, food, grease, fish, or fowl. A brand-new CME department, e-business, would be created to house, promote, and develop this enterprise; and a brand-new managing director, Satish Nandapurkar, would be brought aboard to lead the undertaking. The e-business department would signify a new direction for the Merc, a course no other futures exchange had yet considered. To put it another way, the CME's age-old model of trading and clearing products that were benchmark instruments with which to manage business risk would be given a major face-lift and transformed into a trading, trade-processing, and/or clearing venue for the fathomless opportunities created by the dot-com revolution.

Satish, a very smart and charming guy, was commissioned to find business models that were in tune with the current e-commerce rage and could be wedded to our futures market, utilizing one or more of our systems of transactions, processing, or clearing. The potential targets for futures application could spring from any one of the myriad of cyber-space commerce ideas that were permeating the Internet, the so-called B2B, business-to-business models (describing transactions of goods or services between businesses), or B2C, business-to-consumers models (describing transactions between businesses and individual consumers, such as online catalogs), or C2C, consumer-to-consumer models (describing transactions between consumers through some third party, such as eBay), and so on.

Having spent my whole life at the vanguard of an industry that thrives on innovation, having led the revolutionary idea of financial futures and spearheaded the radical move toward cash settlement as well as electronic trade, I was no shrinking violet when it came to change. Count me among the last to be beholden to the status quo. However, the essential component in advancing change is that it be built on a bedrock of reality. Without that essential constituent, change is but a fancy word, an imaginary concept, a wishful notion. The dot-com era was no more than an illusion. In reality, no more than a handful of the multitude of would-be dot-coms ever had a ghost of a chance of lasting success. As the market ultimately determined, the vast majority were no more than make-believe. To structure a revolutionary futures enterprise on a mirage was in my opinion a recipe for disaster.

More than that, aside from the fact that the dot-com revolution ended in smoke, and putting aside for a moment the concerns whether the proposed enterprises could ever work within the structures of a futures market model, or whether they represented a valid value proposition for the marketplace, or whether they were founded on enduring business demands, and ignoring the question whether such undertakings could ever make a sufficient profit to warrant the risk they represented, some of us read the underlying motivation as an attempt to wrap our markets with a dot-com ribbon as we prepared the CME for an eventual initial public offering (IPO) liftoff. The goal: to pump up our multiple from a valuation of 8 to 10 to something on the order of 25 to 30—the multiple enjoyed by enterprises associated with e-commerce.[2]

The CEO selection process had been long and arduous, lasting almost a full year. There were actually two search committees, the full committee and the special "inner committee," both operating under the guidance of a professional "headhunter." Some of us of course believed that a search was unnecessary. In our opinion, the CEO job should be given to Fred Arditti. However, in private conversations that I and others had with Fred, he absolutely rejected the idea. "I will not accept under any circumstances," he told me. When pressed for a reason, at first he was noncommittal, but eventually confided that he could not work with some of the CME folks and did not believe that Scott Gordon's exploratory offer to him was genuine. I could do nothing to change Fred's mind. The full committee, appointed by Scott Gordon, comprised exclusively of CME board members, included himself, Terry Duffy, Jim Oliff, Marty Gepsman, Tom Kloet, Jack Sandner, Verne Sedlacek, David Pryde, and myself. But the full committee did not get to see or interview every candidate.[3] First a candidate was reviewed and interviewed by the special-inner committee, and only those candidates deemed acceptable moved on to the full committee. The inner committee was composed of what Scott Gordon considered his "loyalists," Tom Kloet, Verne Sedlacek, and Jimmy Oliff. Those of us on the full committee actually never knew who the other candidates were. Nevertheless, we all saw so many candidates that the process became confusing, counterproductive, and burdensome. Many of the candidates had fine credentials and were accomplished individuals in their own fields; however, precious few, if any, actually understood the workings of a futures exchange.

By the time Jim McNulty was directed to the full committee, some of us were very tired of the process. Jack Sandner and I sort of bonded again during this period, agreeing the sooner this was over, the better. We actually saw eye to eye on the potential of each candidate and were relieved when we heard from the inner folks that a "perfect" candidate had been found. Jim McNulty had many talents. One of them, in the words of Jimmy Oliff, was that "he was a dynamic speaker." I agreed with that assessment. More important, McNulty told the Selection Committee what they wanted to hear. He stressed both that we were entering a new market era and also that it was an era in which the CME could excel. He was clearly a beguiling and superb salesman. While Jack and I had similar reservations upon interviewing Jim McNulty, since, like the other candidates, he had little if any futures exchange expertise, we agreed that on the surface he certainly had the other qualifications we were seeking. I must, however, admit that in going along with McNulty, I ignored the advice from my good friend and professional associate Robert K. Wilmouth, the former president of the National Futures Association, who privately told me that "McNulty's appointment was not a good idea."

In January of 2000, Scott Gordon reported that the Search Committee had finalized the financial arrangements with the chosen candidate for Exchange president. Actually, the financial negotiations were exclusively conducted by a special subset of the board, Scott Gordon, Tom Kloet, and Jerry Salzman.[4] Still, there was no question about the qualifying credentials of James J. McNulty. He had made his mark as a general partner of the Chicago-based O'Connor and Associates, a pioneer in applying sophisticated risk management technology and quantitative techniques to securities, futures, and options markets. He went on to become a managing director for the international investment banking firm Warburg Dillon Read and was cohead of the Corporate Analysis and Structuring Team within the firm's Corporate Finance Division. Scott Gordon proudly reported to the membership in an open letter on January 18, 2000, "Our new president and CEO has a thorough understanding of derivatives, technology, and the global financial services landscape, has managed organizations through change and will provide us with the creative vision and strong leadership needed to propel us forward at Internet speed." (See Appendix 8A.) He would begin as the Merc's chief on February 7, 2000. (See Appendix 8B.)

Jim McNulty wasted no time. Privately and publicly he told CME members that the Year 2000 Strategic Plan would focus on as many as five initiatives: The first two were mere extensions of the CME's existing priorities, which were to position the CME's staff and operating systems to function well post-demutualization and to improve our technological self-sufficiency. The most important thrust of McNulty's priorities was to develop CME-2 Business opportunities. The final two initiatives, as I recall, focused on increasing our customer base with both retail and institutional traders. Soon after, McNulty presented a new senior management organizational chart noting that the team was designed to capitalize on the demutualization plans so as to position the CME as the premier and global marketplace in the twenty-first century. The new management team included some old hands: Craig Donohue as managing director, business development and corporate/legal affairs, and Phupinder Gill as managing director and president of the CME Clearing House Division. Two new members of the management team were also introduced, Satish Nandapurkar, who, as previously mentioned, was to serve as managing director, e-business, and Lewis Ting, as managing director of organizational development. Mr. Ting would spearhead the efforts to emphasize employee and organizational development opportunities at the CME, while Mr. Nandapurkar would assume overall responsibility for developing new e-business and business-to-business opportunities. Later, Scott Johnston would join the management team as the Merc's chief information officer, putting Jim Krause on the sidelines.

It seemed to me that the central mission of Satish Nandapurkar, who was totally enthralled by the dot-com revolution and its unending opportunities for the CME, was to make good on his boss's promise to establish three substantial B2B alliances, or "NewCos," within the first 18 months of his appointment. Consequently, over the span of the next year and a half, Satish labored and lectured at length about the merits of moving into the B2B market space and the huge revenue streams available from a CME B2B initiative. Underscoring the enormous size of the B2B marketplace and its utilization of cost-efficient Internet technologies, Satish talked incessantly about relevant industry trends and the value of transactions conducted online between companies. He identified the essential ingredients of what he referred to as a "complete market ecosystem," explaining the CME's prospective role in creating, promoting, and managing markets for commerce. He stated that the CME had a strong potential for a leadership position in clearing service to B2B exchanges, but it had to organize and move quickly to capitalize on that position. He also introduced us to the structure of two models for moving forward: "B2B Lite" and "B2B Heavy." In B2B Heavy, the CME would structure a NewCo clearinghouse for a B2B exchange, while in B2B Lite, the CME would codevelop and market futures contracts with a B2B exchange.

For those of us who had never considered utilizing the CME as a counterpart to the B2B Internet revolution, the idea was a bit mind-boggling if not bizarre. To say we were skeptical is a huge understatement. Call it a culture clash. Still, Satish was an excellent presenter, spoke with great authority, and was clearly furthering our new CEO's ideas. He explained that to accelerate and jump-start the B2B initiative, the CME must utilize cooperative development partnerships with "marquee" exchanges in each "vertical." For some of us, the concept made our heads spin; for others, it sounded like so much hokum.

The best way to fully comprehend what McNulty and Nandapurkar envisioned for the Merc is to examine the so-called "CheMatch Project." Totally embraced by Scott Gordon, it was the first of an array of enterprises that in their opinion would spring from the dot-com revolution and be utilized by the Merc in its futures markets applications. In their view, this deal and others like it would position the CME as part of the new wave of Internet business (coincidentally I must add, perhaps raising our multiple on Wall Street). The project envisioned forming a B2B alliance between the CME and CheMatch.com, Inc., an Internet-based marketplace and information resource for buying and selling bulk commodity chemicals, plastics, and fuel products. Toward that purpose, the CME entered into an exclusive B2B agreement with CheMatch to jointly develop and market a cobranded complex of certain chemical futures and options products that would trade on Globex and clear through the CME Clearing House. Approved by the Board, the projected launch date was set for June 2001. The following partial report in Houston Business Wire Report provides a more in-depth description of the idea:

> *The Chicago Mercantile Exchange (CME) and CheMatch.com, Inc., today announced that they have signed an exclusive agreement to jointly develop and market a co-branded complex of certain chemical futures and options products that will trade on the CME's GLOBEX(R)2 electronic trading system. The agreement, which formalizes the CME's entry into the business-to-business ("B2B") arena, represents the first joint development project between a futures exchange and a B2B marketplace to create risk management products targeted to a specific industry.*

> *The agreement also marks the first time futures products will trade on a futures exchange with an electronic link to an online B2B marketplace. Linked via the Internet, CheMatch.com's secure, neutral trading platform and the GLOBEX2 system will provide seamless transitions between the two sites and offer chemical companies, traders and financial institutions the ability to trade both physical and derivative products.*

> *Chicago Mercantile Exchange officials said the CME's new B2B initiative will offer a variety of services to certain online marketplaces that have been established within a broad cross-section of industries. The agreement with CheMatch.com is the CME's first as part of its new effort.*

> *CME Chairman Scott Gordon said: "We are pleased to launch our B2B initiative through this agreement with CheMatch.com. We are being very selective—joining forces with those premier B2B marketplaces such as CheMatch.com that we believe will enjoy accelerated growth with the help of our services."*

> *Carl McCutcheon, Chairman and Chief Executive Officer of CheMatch. com, said: "This agreement is an important development for the chemical and derivatives industries. A liquid futures market will be a great tool to help our clients hedge risks, remove pricing volatility and make better capital expenditure decisions. We're excited to be working with the CME to usher in this new order of electronic trading and to set the stage for trading cash markets and derivative products side by side in one global platform."*

Said CME President and Chief Executive Officer Jim McNulty: "Our entry into the B2B arena will leverage the CME's many years of experience and expertise in applying a comprehensive package of critical processes and technology to markets. CheMatch.com is an excellent choice for us because of its focus and domain expertise in the commodity chemicals industry."

Through its B2B initiative, the CME will offer a variety of "horizontal infrastructure" services customized to the needs of "vertical" B2B marketplace clients, including market structuring, such as product design, self-regulation, rules enforcement and arbitration; clearing services, such as transaction processing, payment and settlement, credit administration, risk management, fulfillment management and guarantees; risk management products, such as futures and options; and traders experienced at providing liquidity to markets. "The CME is known for its neutrality, transparency, credit risk management and financial integrity, which will benefit B2B marketplaces," Gordon said.

During a senior management restructuring announced in March, the CME tapped Satish Nandapurkar to serve as its new Managing Director, e-Business, and oversee the new B2B effort. Since that time, Nandapurkar and other CME officials have met with numerous B2B marketplaces such as CheMatch.com to explore possible areas of cooperation, and the CME has chosen CheMatch.com as its exclusive electronic trading platform for certain chemical futures and options products.[5]

It was certainly a first of its kind for the CME and, as far as I know, for futures markets anywhere. Unfortunately, there were few adequate answers to a host of questions, such as verification of the specifications of the products, their quality or lack thereof, who would be their guarantor, the method of delivery, liabilities stemming from injurious usage and environmental issues in the event of a spill or other mishap during product delivery, and on and on. To say the least, for some of us, the concept was downright frightening. Nevertheless, the CheMatch futures enterprise was launched, complete with a floor bell-ringing ceremony. Thankfully, it never got off the ground. Indeed, to this day such B2B enterprises have not found a successful niche at the CME nor to my knowledge anywhere in the futures arena.

In my opinion, as well as in the opinion of many on the board and a number of senior executives, the thrust toward Internet-based B2B commerce in futures trade was a dead end or much worse. Unfortunately, while Jim McNulty, our new CEO, possessed many talents, he had insufficient appreciation of the fundamental nature of a futures exchange. The new senior management team Jim put in place, Satish Nandapurkar and Lewis Ting, while perhaps knowledgeable in their own fields, in my opinion knew even less about exchanges. Indeed, Lewis Ting, as chief of personnel, in very quick order gained the displeasure of a host of veteran CME staffers. As time went by it became the collective opinion of many of us that—with Scott Gordon's full approval—they were taking the Merc down a path that was fraught with danger. If the CheMatch deal was a metaphor for what was coming, we wanted none of it. The "Gordon Growth Model," which McNulty spoke a good deal about, or the laminated wallet-sized CME Mission Statement and Values cards that he distributed to the staff as well as Merc directors to help us remember our priorities, didn't give us great comfort. Without experienced futures hands taking part in the critical decisions and guiding the CME's future direction, many of us felt like we were watching a movie whose ending was unlikely to be pretty.

Still, I must believe Jim McNulty wanted to make the CME successful and profitable. One of his best achievements came very early. On August 30, 2000, within six months of his appointment, McNulty moved for unlimited, direct electronic access to products traded on CME's Globex system for all market participants. The move included removal of limitations on customer access to the "book," allowing customers to view bids and offers in Globex products, and eliminating restrictions on the number of Globex workstations that members and customers could have. Previously, Globex was accessible only to members, clearing members, or those with Electronic Trading Hours permits. For me, this action represented a critical milestone in the evolution of the Merc's electronic stystem. It opened Globex to the entire world. Although McNulty had no role in the development of Globex itself, he deserves full credit for taking this ultimate step. McNulty also reorganized the CME staff along professional corporate lines. To his credit is the fact that he directed Craig Donohue to redefine our complex fee structure to better reflect current business flows and had the good sense to embrace Craig's proposals. Craig had the necessary depth of knowledge so that together with CME staffers Arman Falsafi and John Curran, they were able to correctly map the pricing and fee levels as well as cost reductions. The objective, of course, was to increase overall profitability rather than the profitability of each product and service.

I also credit the McNulty administration for the opportunity to bring aboard as a public director Nobel laureate Myron S. Scholes. Early in his tenure, McNulty asked if I would reach out to my friend Myron and see if he would be interested in such an appointment. In 1997, Myron Scholes, along with Robert C. Merton, was awarded the Nobel Memorial Prize in Economic Sciences. Together with Fischer Black, they developed the Black-Scholes options model, the cornerstone of modern options markets.[6] Scholes, of course, had been among the star-studded team of Long Term Capital Management, a hedge fund that failed in 1998. However, its demise did nothing to diminish Myron's credentials, and I was only too happy to oblige. Indeed,

I knew that Myron's appointment would complete a promise I made to my close personal friend, the 1990 Nobel laureate in economics Merton Miller, who until his passing on June 3, 2000, was a prized member of the CME board and, previous to that, of the Chicago Board of Trade board. Near the end of his days, I visited Merton Miller and he asked me whether his place on the CME board would remain a "Nobel" seat. I promised him it would. On August 30, 2000, Myron Scholes joined the CME board and brought to it a distinction that few American corporate boards can match.[7] Parenthetically, I also take pride in suggesting for the CME board Terry Savage, the author, television commentator, and nationally known expert on investing and personal finance who cut her eyeteeth as a trader on the International Monetary Market.

One of Myron Scholes's lasting achievements was in assisting the creation of the CME Competitive Market Advisory Council (CMAC), a select "think tank."[8] In 2003, both Terry Duffy and Craig Donohue enthusiastically endorsed my idea of creating such a council composed of the highest strata of financial experts who could provide the CME board with advice in the form of policy, analyses, position papers, and other strategic recommendations. Without Myron Scholes, who accepted the role of its first chairman, it is doubtful that we could have attracted to CMAC dignitaries such as Nobel laureates Gary S. Becker and Robert C. Merton; former dean of the University of Chicago Graduate School of Business Professor John F. Gould, who is the current CMAC chairman; international economist David D. Hale; Yale University Professor Robert J. Shiller; and recently, the former president of the Chicago Federal Reserve Michael H. Moskow. Today CMAC represents an unparalleled resource of independent thought and opinions that is rare in the corporate world. One of its hallmarks is the annual Fred Arditti Innovation Award—representing the CME's equivalent to the "Nobel Prize"—to "an individual or group of individuals whose innovative ideas, products or services have created significant change to markets, commerce or trade."[9]

Jim McNulty's most important contribution, of course, was bringing investment banking experience to the CME, which eventually served to take us public. Without his presence, this process would have been slower and more difficult. For most of us, it was a brand-new experience. Jim was "in" with the investment banker crowd and used his relationships right from the beginning of his CME tenure. Under his direction, the CME began interviewing potential investment bankers for the express purpose of an IPO. As Gill once commented, "We had so many investment bankers around you couldn't turn around without bumping into one of them." Eventually, Morgan Stanley was chosen and did a fine job in providing the CME board with the education and information necessary to make some informed decisions. They ultimately took us public. Thus, I have no reservations in crediting Jim McNulty with leading the CME through the IPO process.

Of course, to bring Jim's IPO efforts to fruition it required—as described in the following chapters—a new CME regime to wrest control from the Gordon/McNulty management and take over in 2002. Further, it should be noted that the essential groundwork for the IPO had been completed long before Jim's arrival. As Jerry Salzman said to me at the time, "McNulty had no heavy lifting as it related to demutualization." Fully a year before McNulty became CEO, the plan for demutualization had been hammered out by the Strategic Planning Committee, passed by the board, and successfully negotiated with the floor community. Without this successful achievement, no IPO would have been possible.

Indeed, well-meaning contributions aside, little by little under the Gordon/McNulty tenure, the experienced members of the board and our senior executives were shunted to the side. Terry Duffy, Barry Lind, Bill Shepard, Jack Sandner, and myself, as well as the ranking members of CME management, such as Jerry Salzman, Craig Donohue, Phupinder Gill, and Jim Krause, were excluded from the deliberation process. Others like Jerry Beyer and Fred Arditti preferred to resign, leaving within a few months of McNulty's arrival. Jerry Beyer was the first casualty. He and I had a close relationship, developed over many years as he often assisted me in navigating the dangerous shoals of Merc politics. As chief administrative officer, Jerry had one of the most difficult positions at the Merc. He had to juggle the many conflicting political and regulatory currents resulting from demands by the chairman, the board members, and the floor traders, that were always in motion underneath the surface of the Exchange while keeping the institution within some semblance of order. I often marveled at his adroit ability to keep things straight. Jerry was *all* CME, someone I trusted, whose leaving was unfortunate.

A few months later, Fred Arditti left. According to Phupinder Gill, he had the following interchange with Fred Arditti directly after their first get-acquainted meeting with Jim McNulty at an offsite location at the Civic Opera House. Fred Arditti, who hardly ever said anything negative about anyone, tried to convince Gill that Jim would turn out okay and made a $500 bet with Gill that within six months, Gill would like Jim. In turn, Gill bet Fred that within six months Fred would not be there. Fred duly paid up on both bets. His departure for me was a personal body blow and for the Merc an immeasurable loss. Similarly, David S. Goone, a very talented product marketing senior vice president and rising star, saw the handwriting on the wall and left.[10] As Marty Gepsman, one of our old-line board members, cynically remarked to me: "Jim McNulty has his own agenda. He made it very clear he wanted his own people." But in the opinion of many of us, it was much more than that. He wanted the lot of us to be gone. According to Bill Miller, one of our public directors who served on the Audit Committee, and as straight-up a guy as you could find, the McNulty people viewed us, the old guard, (Tim Brennan, Terry Duffy, Marty Gepsman, Yra Harris,

Bruce Johnson, Gary Katler, Pat Lynch, John Newhouse, Jim Oliff, William Salatich, Jack Sandner, William Shepard, Howard Siegel, and myself) as representing the past and having inherent conflicts. At one point the Audit Committee was asked by management to retain an outside consultant for recommendations regarding the composition of the board. It seemed to Bill Miller that such an exercise should come from the full board rather than the CEO unless, in Bill's words, "it was postured to a specific conclusion" against existing board members. In March of 2002, Bill called me in Arizona to alert me of this eventuality in order that I could make it known to the entire board.

A telling example of lack of recognition of the history and culture at the Merc was evidenced in a conversation that I once had with Satish Nandapurkar in my office sometime near the end of 2001. Satish had come up with a chart to show me the plan he and Jim had devised showing the CME's potential massive revenue stream. The plan had a specific purpose, to attract investors to the forthcoming IPO planned for some time in early 2002. (The IPO, at the insistence of some of us, was delayed and later delayed again.) His chart showed how in the following year, on a given date, the CME's revenue stream would suddenly rocket skyward. Puzzled, I asked, "How is this going to happen?" Satish explained that on that day, the Eurodollar futures complex would go exclusively electronic. It was the business model on which they planned to take the Merc public. In theory, he was correct. Transition of the Eurodollar contract to Globex after closure of its pit would result in a dramatic increase to CME's revenue. But of course that was not my question. I explained that the CME could not blithely order a closure of the Eurodollar pit. By virtue of the demutualization referendum, there was a precise liquidity formula that determined when and under what conditions a given pit trade could be shut down. Indeed, it was that formula which gave the floor sufficient comfort to achieve passage of the referendum. The CME, I stated, would have to explain this fact to potential investors. Our conversation ended abruptly.

The underlying thrust of McNulty's design for the Merc was a Five-Year Strategic Plan that was still to materialize. In his words, it was based "on the current shift in the ecosystem." In his opinion, this would lead to the beginning of collaborative commerce among financial institutions. Over the next five years, Jim explained, there would a consolidation of derivatives, securities, and B2B marketplaces and clearinghouses, something that was later referred to by him as the "Perfect Storm."[11] Consequently, the future success of the CME, he predicted, depended on its ability to position itself as a consolidator and preferred partner in the new marketplace and its ability to be a world-class applied technology firm. In simple language, in his view the vertical model of the CME—initiating instruments for hedging business risks, providing an execution forum, processing and clearing of the resulting transactions within a secure financial structure—had seen its best days. The future CME would primarily be a "trade-processing" and an "applied-technology" enterprise.

We had an indication of what Jim was talking about when he unveiled a grandiose plan for a joint venture with Morgan Stanley in a project labeled "Jumbo." It would create a giant entity that combined the CME's clearing capabilities with Morgan Stanley's extensive market breadth to capture the full potential of the B2B business. The plan included the most disquieting concept of a sale or transfer to the proposed joint venture of the CME's most precious jewel, its Clearing House. The plan made me shudder. Many of us felt that the CME Clearing House was the single "untouchable" component of the CME integrated structure—its worth nearly impossible to fully evaluate. In our opinion, a sale or transfer of this asset would cause irreparable harm to our enterprise and serve to severely diminish our ability to innovate. During the three or so decades during which I led the CME, even during the brief industry exploration of a so-called "common clearing" arrangement, I consistently repulsed all proposals to detach, dislodge, or displace the Clearing House or diminish its functionality. As history is witness, the CME Clearing House was fundamental to our exceptional success in the years that followed. The recent (2008–2009) global meltdown, as nothing before, proved the incalculable and indispensable value of the CME Clearing House—its central counterparty clearing apparatus (CCP), and its bedrock mechanism of financial safeguards. Those very systems and safeguards kept the CME secure during the past and particularly the current financial crisis, differentiating us from what occurred in other parts of the financial world. Indeed, the CME Clearing House represents the model for the future of markets as well as OTC derivatives.

Bottom line, after two years of the Gordon/McNulty regime, many of us on the board had become disillusioned and apprehensive of their leadership. For some, like Terry Duffy, it didn't take that long. From the outset, Terry was not enamored with Jim McNulty and told him so. But even those of us who tried to give Jim the benefit of the doubt saw few accomplishments, listened to a lot of fancy talk, and heard of plans that were very scary. The concept of depending on the Internet for new futures business was dumbfounding. The idea of primarily becoming a technology company seemed wrong. The thought of endangering the status of our Clearing House was downright frightening. This feeling resulted in a good deal of behind-the-scenes discussions and the stirring of some internal strong political machinations. The thrust of those discussions gave rise to the idea of a change in CME leadership. Jim McNulty was under contract until 2004, but Scott Gordon was up for reelection in April of 2002. Our path was obvious. A plan evolved to contain McNulty, without facing contractual issues, by focusing instead on a new chairman of the CME.

CHAPTER 9

Cabal
Boardroom Intrigue

It was Saturday, April 27, 2002. As planned, Terry Duffy, Craig Donohue, and I gathered at my home to plan the new Chicago Mercantile Exchange (CME) era. We were sitting in the kitchen, my wife, Betty, supplying a continuous round of snacks and coffee. It was a triumphant moment. During the past six months, all our waking moments, every thought, every action was devoted to but one mission: an ambitious and dangerous corporate coup. Now it was done. The previous Wednesday, April 24, 2002, Terry Duffy had officially replaced Scott Gordon as CME chairman with a vote of 15 to 5. It was a huge victory representing a sea change at the Merc. (See Appendix 9A.) The wide margin was a testament to the fact that our rationale for change found resonance with many on the board. The planning, skullduggery, and secretive engineering had been in the works for months. We were taking the CME back from people who in our minds were leading the Exchange in the wrong direction. Our goal was to put the Merc back on its tried and true path—to reestablish control of the Exchange under the watchful eye of experienced CME board members and futures professionals.

In my opinion, the central reason for the eventual decision to replace Scott Gordon as chairman was that he allowed the Exchange to give up its system of checks and balances. Before demutualization, when we were still a membership organization, all decisions were subject to an unending process of scrutiny, deliberation, and voting. In fact, so much so that it was difficult for the Exchange to operate or move forward. In describing this Exchange decision-making structure, I used to cynically explain that you had to go before the Washroom-Facility Committee before you could change the color of the washroom walls. This structure made it nearly impossible to compete in the fast-moving business world of the late twentieth century, let alone the next century. It was one of the principal reasons to demutualize. However, be careful of what you wish for.

It didn't happen overnight, but in a matter of a short couple of years, so revolutionary was the CME transformation that it was mind-boggling. We were now operating with a 20-member board of directors, half of what it was, that met but once a month, there were fewer than a dozen committees, down from 200, and with few exceptions there was no necessity for a membership vote. That is progress with a capital P. Unfortunately, under Scott Gordon, the lessening of vetting and accountability standards were quickly taking the Exchange to the other extreme. In the two years following Jim McNulty's appointment in February of 2000, Scott had nearly entirely handed the reins over to the new chief executive officer. As I saw it, their philosophy was to have the board in a purely oversight-of-management role, without any strategic planning input. It was beginning to become, at best, an exclusive senior management operation or, at worst, a two-man enterprise. However, a board must be integral to the major decisions in order to be in the position to accept ultimate responsibility for the direction of the enterprise. Besides, an exchange is far more complex than a standard manufacturing or service-providing enterprise, having too many moving parts to be governed without a complement of checks and balances at the top.

Further, as the *Financial Times* noted on the eve of our election, "Perhaps the single most important thing a board can do is to have a chairman who is independent of management."[1] The opposite was becoming true at the CME. Bill Shepard once confronted Scott Gordon on this point directly, complaining to him that *"Jim McNulty doesn't understand he works for you."* Coincidentally, about the same time, Gretchen Morgensen, financial editor of the *New York Times*, urged shareholders to remember that "corporate executives are your hired hands."[2] And Jerry Salzman once said to me that McNulty and Gordon were joined at the hip, and complained that "a lot of stuff was blacked out for me." Although McNulty and Gordon were perhaps a bit more respectful of me, I had the identical opinion. Similarly, Jack Sandner told me he felt like a "nonentity." Terry Duffy once confronted Scott directly and told him, *"You're not nearly independent enough as chairman. You've become Jim McNulty."*

To add insult to injury, it became personal. On March 20, 2002, a surprise letter from Scott Gordon to the Audit and Compensation Committee became public. (See Appendix 9B.) In effect, it suggested that the CME do away with the standing of its two senior advisors, Leo Melamed and Jack Sandner. "I would ask the Compensation Committee," Scott Gordon wrote, "to consider the advisability of compensating Board Advisors in a manner different from other Board members." (See Appendix 9B.) Gordon knew very well that the letter was an insult, not only as a matter of form but with respect to the unparalleled contribution Jack and I had made and continued to make to the Exchange, as well as the prestige we engendered for the institution. Neither of us were likely to continue to devote the inordinate amount of time we did without receiving the long-established relatively small stipend. That was, I believed, precisely what Jim McNulty and Scott Gordon wanted to achieve. Without the two of us on the board, they would have far less critique and interference with their proposals or direction for the Exchange. Less critique and less light. Our presence on the board, represented an authoritative voice that provided the board with both the weight of nearly unequaled expertise as well as an invaluable historical perspective. In formulating policy for the institution, most members of the board deeply appreciated the counterweight of knowledge and experience we represented—the loss of which could only be detrimental to the best interests of the CME, but considerably beneficial to the plans and intentions of the Gordon/McNulty partnership. Aside from that, in my case, Gordon's attempted action was most likely also a violation of a CME board agreement. My appointment in 1997 as Senor Policy Advisor was a *permanent* board resolution that included the monetary stipend. Not stopping there, to further their goal of control and entrenchment, Jim McNulty made another move with an overt attempt to make Scott Gordon's tenure permanent by making him "executive chairman"—with a significant raise in salary. The combination of those two initiatives caused a rebellious outcry from a large number of senior board members and served to energize our eventual cabal.

It caused Terry Duffy to come to my office and say that it was "the last straw!" We had talked about it often before. He was now prepared to run against Scott Gordon for chairman if I would lead the effort. We met at the Drake Hotel for dinner sorting out all the issues, planning the future, and agreeing to take on the challenge. We have remained close personal friends since that moment. As vice chairman, Terry Duffy was the perfect choice with the necessary talents and credentials. He had long experience on the board as well as on important committees. He was very knowledgeable about floor operations and knew the futures business. He was very smart and presented a good image. His popularity within the membership was broadly based and, most important to me, he was trustworthy—a straight-up guy whose word was solid. In 1980, Terry Duffy came to the Merc after meeting Vince Schreiber at the University of Wisconsin. Schreiber, an original member of the International Monetary Market, was one of my good friends and strong supporters who first introduced me to him. Terry began as a runner, but a year later, with borrowed money from his parents, became a member of the CME. Eventually he rose through the ranks, started a successful brokerage business, and was elected to the board in 1995. It was a typical Merc story and a good one. More than one Merc member became chairman on the basis of those credentials. Of course, not every Merc member found his true love on the floor and married her, as in the case of Terry and his beautiful wife, Jennifer. Most telling to me was the fact that Terry Duffy was an independent floor broker and one of the first pit brokers to boldly adopt the new CME electronic technology for his brokerage business in the hog pit—clear proof of his willingness to face down the status quo. It set a meaningful example for others. There was still an additional factor that was appealing to me—his sense of politics. It was in the genes. In 1921, his grandfather, John J. Duffy, became Alderman of Chicago's Nineteenth Ward and remained in that office for the next 25 years. He was elected Cook County board president in 1959, a big deal in Chicago.

I never doubted that Scott Gordon, while misguided, had the best of intentions. In my opinion, had he not so completely embraced the McNulty/Nandapurkar dot-com mantra for the CME without listening to some of our concerns, and without any significant internal vetting or scrutiny by some of the old CME hands, history would have judged his tenure as CME chairman as one of great distinction. After all, during his watch the historic CME referendum to demutualize was authored and approved—the first American exchange to do so. As Scott said to Peter McKay of the *Wall Street Journal* the day following the referendum, "The resounding endorsement of demutualization by the members of the Chicago Mercantile Exchange brings the CME to the most significant turning point in the more than 100 years of history and culminates two years of deliberative strategic analysis, planning and execution."[2] Scott was ever so correct. He could have used this accomplishment as a stepping-stone to build the Merc's future together with the people whose ideas and efforts brought the CME to this remarkable juncture. For whatever reason, Scott chose a different path.

During the length and breadth of the conspiratorial plan that the three of us engineered, we were aware the odds were very much against us. Jim McNulty was a smart guy and a willing combatant. With Scott Gordon's support, he had taken control of the relevant corporate machinery during his two-year tenure. We had precious few left in the upper management to rely on with the departure of many of our trusted senior officials, including Fred Arditti, Senior Executive Vice President, Gerald Beyer, Executive Vice President and Chief Operating Officer, David Goone, Senior Vice President for Product Marketing, and Dick McDonald, Chief Economist. The new management team that McNulty put in place was considered merciless, willing to remove anyone who was perceived as interfering with their control or direction. Everyone's job at the Merc was subject to review.

Our task was made much more difficult by the fact we did not want to rock the boat publicly. We were acutely aware that we were in the process of preparing for an initial public offering. Any unfavorable publicity could hurt our stock value. We hoped our decision to simply seek a new chairman would be a mitigating factor to limit the perceived damage. While chairmanship change was a significant event, it was not an unusual happening at futures exchanges—a matter of internal politics. Once we had accomplished that feat, we could decide about McNulty. But in the course of events, the pre-election media coverage generated a good deal of attention, some of it very negative for us. There developed the distorted view, we thought intentionally planted by the opposition, that the team led by Leo Melamed and Jack Sandner seemingly formed in support of Terry Duffy but actually represented an attempt to move the Exchange back into its open-outcry past. It goes to show how easily people can be misled. Given that my life during the past decade and a half was devoted to a battle on behalf of Globex and electronic trade, with arrows in my back to prove it, for anyone to believe that I would participate in a move back to open outcry was sheer lunacy. And yet more than one member of the media bought into this view.

Indeed, by the time of the election, the direction of the Chicago Mercantile Exchange in favor of electronics was not in controversy, at least not at the board level. Nor was it even an issue between the two factions battling for election votes. Nor was Globex the basis of the conversation between myself and Scott Gordon that fateful April day in 2002 when we met in my office and I admitted that the "squishy rumor" he heard about Terry Duffy might be true. Rather, at issue was the most critical element in the evolutionary metamorphosis: How do you get to the promised land without turning into pillars of salt? In other words, how does an open-outcry exchange get transformed into an electronic enterprise without losing its essential asset, its continuous liquidity? How does demutualization affect the direction of a futures exchange? What value do you place on experience and internal expertise as you prepare for the future? But that is not how the press read it. Days before the election the headline from Dow Jones Commodities Service read "CME's Chairmen Vote about Keeping Old Ties in the New World." The story explained: "On the top level, it seems to be a battle between the old order and new order over how quickly the exchange replaces its traditional pits with an all-electronic trading system." To his credit, Terry Duffy did his level best to keep the focus on the real issue of the election. He told the Dow Jones reporter, *"We need a chairman who is independent."*[3] On the other hand, David Greising, of the *Chicago Tribune*, preferred to be philosophical:

> *In their day, Melamed and his feisty protege (Sandner) helped make the Merc one of the world's most influential and innovative exchanges. Too bad old times aren't what the Merc needs right now. The exchange is preparing to offer stock to public investors. It fights to adapt to electronic trading. It is a leader in Chicago's effort to control the new market for futures contracts on individual stocks. And in all these areas, the Merc is faring well. Under Chairman Scott Gordon and new Chief Executive*

*Jim McNulty, the Merc has avoided the pratfalls that the Chicago Board
of Trade has endured. It has a chance to convert electronic trading from
a threat to an ally for growth. . . . And yet, with all this on the line, what
is the talk as the Chicago Mercantile Exchange heads into a vital annual
meeting Wednesday? They're talking about Jack and Leo. The wonder if
the two fading legends really will make their move, first to oust Gordon
and later McNulty.*[4]

Thus, this was a political chess game with the highest of stakes—the
futures market's version of "Barbarians at the Gate." If we lost, we would
not only lose our standing and reputation, we would lose our only chance
to save the CME from what we believed to be a terrible destiny. The three
of us, Terry, Craig, and I, became a team, relying on each other's skills
and operating as a synchronized unit. It required all our talent, credibility,
and intellectual capital. It required a comprehensively designed blueprint,
meticulous execution, complete coordination, and an ability to be in constant contact. We met several times every day, most of the time in secrecy
in my office. We kept each other totally informed. What made matters most
difficult was that everything we planned had to be done under the wrap
of secrecy. Our goal was to gain a majority of the 20 votes on the board.
Some of those votes we knew were impossible to wrest away from Gordon,
who was a likable person with deep roots at the Exchange and perceived
favorably by the media. Outwardly, he had done a credible job as chairman. His alignment with Jim McNulty, who had a very good image with the
press, also served him well. On the other hand, Terry Duffy was a virtual
unknown quantity to the media or the public directors on the board, whose
votes were critical. Being vice chairman of the Exchange did not generate
a great deal of public recognition. Nevertheless, I was convinced that Terry
was a quick study and had all the attributes of leadership. Flashing forward,
there can be no doubt that this proved totally on the mark. Sure, Terry had
the guidance and assistance of some savvy and experienced people around
him, but clearly he possessed the necessary talents. Seldom have we ever
witnessed as quick and as successful an on-the-job training as occurred with
Terry Duffy.

Besides, our effort was not based on any one individual's capability but
on the totality of our mission on behalf of the Exchange. We were representing a time-proven record based on innovation and success. We were
speaking with credibility, experience and expertise. Our views had already
found resonance with many of the board. I inherited the responsibility to
orchestrate the lobbying effort to reassure those board members, especially
the public appointees, of the validity of our cause, the direction we planned
for the Exchange, and our choice for the next chairman. I began the process
with my good friend Myron Scholes. Over the years, we had developed a

strong respect for one another. Myron and I had often met for dinner during his trips to Chicago and always our conversation was directed to the CME, its plans and future. As a Nobel Prize recipient, Myron was highly regarded on the board, and his views would be extremely helpful in the undertaking at hand. If I won him over, we judged, it would go a long way to sway others around the table. If not, the odds against us would become larger. In truth, even before the campaign began, Myron had confided in me that in his opinion the CME was moving in the wrong direction under the Gordon-McNulty leadership. Since our views were in sync, the dinner meeting we had at the Ritz Carlton was much easier than I had anticipated. Although Myron did not know Terry Duffy, he was willing to rely on my recommendation. His agreement provided me with a strong foundation to move forward. Carefully choosing the board members whom we believed we could persuade, over the next several weeks, I held one-on-one as well as group meetings with every one of the 15 board members who ultimately voted with us. In similar fashion, Terry Duffy, using his natural political skills, held similar one-on-one meetings with each of the board members whom he had known over the years. Terry and I met daily to compare our results. Our combined victorious efforts served to cement our lasting friendship. Mercifully, because Craig Donohue was not an elected official, we spared him from this exercise. But his guidance and the continuous flow of information he provided about the maneuvers by our opposition was crucial.

In the case of Jack Sandner, it was different. Jack met with Terry, who told him to talk to me. Jack had a sense of what was going on and wanted to help execute the plan. It was no surprise. From the beginning of the McNulty/Gordon era, Jack had become, in his words, "invisible." He was given no role in the new administration and was not an active participant in any of the inner deliberations. He had been removed from most committees. It was clear that he had become an outcast. Jack and I had been at peace for a number of years; in fact, as the memory of past difficulties faded, a friendship of sorts was rekindled based on our store of common experiences and a desire to serve the CME. Since I never had any doubt about Jack's intellect and capabilities, our common opposition to the present regime had an additional bonding effect. Jack was also politically very astute and could be most helpful in the battle we were facing. Terry Duffy left the decision with me, although Jack's vote was important to him. I first touched base with Bill Shepard. Bill had been an early detractor of Jim McNulty and had lost confidence in Scott Gordon. He told Scott so directly, questioning his independence from McNulty. So Bill was squarely with our plan. However, early on, Bill expressed concern that Terry Duffy might be a secret open-outcry adherent, just as some of the media speculated. He wanted nothing to deter us from moving forward with technology. I convinced Bill otherwise, that Terry had always maintained his independence in relation to the broker group issues. It was the independent vote that got him elected to the board in 1995 and to lead the ticket in 1997. My assessment could not have been more correct. Convincing Bill about Jack was more difficult because of their history. But in the end, he too left the decision with me. After further reflection, Terry and I met with Jack in my office and I asked him what he wanted if we were successful. Jack responded, "I want my dignity back." It was an honest answer with which I could commiserate. I welcomed Jack aboard. It was a decision I made instinctively, one I never regretted. Having been cast aside by the McNulty/Gordon administration, it provided Jack an opportunity to again use his talents and wealth of experience on behalf of the Merc. As I anticipated, from this point forward Jack Sandner became a charter member of the new leadership team that was formed along with Terry, Craig, and myself. We again became comrades in arms. I dare say that the CME was the beneficiary.

It was also important to bring into our fold some of the remaining notable members of the management team. Having been generally disen-franchised by the Gordon-McNulty regime, they would be willing allies. While there were rumors of what was going on, they had no firsthand knowledge of our plans. I carefully contacted a number of them, includ-ing Jim Krause and David Gomach, our CFO, explaining that if there was a change in the chairmanship, it would not affect their standing. It was also imperative to meet with Jerry Salzman and Phupinder Gill. Both were among the wiser and more experienced hands at the Merc. Over the years, Jerry Salzman had assumed the role of an integral member of the inner brain trust. But he had been shunted to the side by the McNulty regime, and I vowed to change that. Once, when Scott and Jim tried, or pretended, to seek my counsel and approval on matters that they were considering, they invited me into their exclusive "Wednesday Morning" briefings led by McNulty. I agreed on the condition that Jerry Salzman also be included. Outside of the fact that I knew his contributions would be meaningful, my private reason was to gain independent confirmation of my belief that some of the ideas being discussed by the McNulty's team were off the wall. When Jerry confirmed my worst fears, it went a long way in convincing me to lead the effort to correct conditions before it was too late.

In the case of Gill, it was equally important. As I have previously noted, Phupinder Gill had become the de facto chief of staff of the Exchange, personally knowing nearly everyone on the staff and understanding the ins and outs of every segment of the Merc's mechanisms, particularly the clearinghouse operation, where he began his employment. He was trusted by the Merc staff. It was critically important that he be made aware that he would be included in the hierarchy of the administration, should we be successful. To that end, I took Gill out to dinner at Gene and Georgetti's one evening and, under the wrap of secrecy, outlined the idea of a new chairman and a new regime. Gill, an outspoken individual, wasted little time in offering his opinion that if we did not succeed, the destiny of the Merc was in clear danger. Although I did not ask Gill to do anything to advance our cause, I left our meeting satisfied he fully supported our undertaking.

Our Saturday kitchen cabinet meeting lasted all day. We agreed on four key actions: First and foremost, we wanted to correct the procedure that in our view represented the greatest peril to the CME. The McNulty modus operandi was to bring to the board for approval proposals that were inadequately vetted. Often they were actions based on ideas that the board was seeing for the first time, sometimes, in our opinion, half baked, without adequate deliberation. Such a procedure presented a clear and present danger. To correct this flaw and reinstate some critical checks and balances that had been shattered, we proposed to create a Board Steering Committee, which I would chair, that would act as a filtering mechanism for examination and discussion of major actions before advancing them to the board for approval. The committee would be appointed with seasoned market veterans from the board and management.

Board Steering became operative immediately upon Terry Duffy's election, during Jim McNulty's tenure.[5] Every committee chairman has his own style. As I visualized it, the purpose and function of Board Steering would be to elicit debate and discussion between all participants, allowing ideas to be freely discussed and examined. I was particularly concerned that members of staff and management be encouraged to voice their opinion without intimidation by its chairman or members of the board. It worked famously well. For one thing, it provided senior management an opportunity to present ideas, proposals, and reports for discussion in a format that was more informal and much less structured than such presentations necessarily become during board or Executive Committee meetings, where a vote of approval was being requested and required. It became a testing ground, allowing new ideas to be fleshed out, amended, and examined against questions and comments from influential board members. For another, the committee served as a learning experience for board members, giving them a firsthand look at management's direction for the exchange. It also provided the board an opportunity to present their own ideas and innovations in a forum that invited discussion.

An outstanding example for the value of an independent filter such as Board Steering occurred the following year in a most explosive fashion. Howard Siegel, a CME director and one of the committee's new members, came to me with some disturbing hearsay he had come across. It seems that some customers had privately advised him that the CME had conducted a Globex "Customer Satisfaction Survey" with some devastating results. It caused me to do some checking. I learned that indeed a survey had been authorized by Arman Falsafi, CME Managing Director, Global Electronic Trading and Data, and conducted by Loran Marketing Group, an independent consultant, to measure and track user satisfaction with various aspects of our electronic trading systems including speed, reliability, cost, and customer service. The results showed the Globex platform rated last, far behind that of Eurex and LiffeConnect, our principal international competitors. Trouble was, while Falsafi immediately submitted the report to her superiors at management, it never went any further nor was it presented to the board. Jerry Salzman told me he was dumbfounded over the apparent lack of action by higher-ups on this critical issue. Needless to explain, members of the board labored under the impression that Globex—the Merc's poster child for our "advanced technological state"—was the number-one system in the world. The truth would be a shocking revelation. I huddled with Craig Donohue and Terry Duffy, and advised them that I would request Falsafi to present the report to Board Steering at its next meeting in February 2003. Thereafter, Terry asked her to present it to the board. The consequential result was that under Arman Falsafi's and Jim Krause's direction, fixing Globex became the top priority of the Exchange. It took about two years and a large dose of money, but it was done.

Over the ensuing years, with the administrative assistance of Pat McGill, Associate Director of Administration and Planning, the Board Steering Committee (now Board Strategic Steering), was the forum to which major policy actions of the CME were presented in the first instance for discussion and eventual recommendation to the board (for example, such defining matters as the defense strategy against the attack on Eurodollars by Euronext Liffe, described in detail in Chapter 10). Similarly, the strategy relating to the so-called "Common Clearing Link" between the Chicago Board of Trade and CME, which brought all CBOT futures products for clearing to the CME Clearing House, and which was the gateway to the eventual merger with the CBOT. No differently, the strategy relating to bringing the New York Mercantile Exchange (NYMEX) markets onto the Globex platform was the purview of Board Steering and hotly discussed by its members for over a year. At issue was whether the CME should instead pursue an alternative strategy by listing for trade its own energy contracts in direct competition with NYMEX. Ultimately, the Board Steering Committee's recommendation for a Globex–NYMEX connection was adopted and accepted by the CME board. As history is witness, it was the critical step leading the CME Group to complete a successful acquisition of NYMEX.

In both latter instances, however, the actual merger negotiations were ultimately delegated by the board to a special negotiations committee led by Terry Duffy and composed of Craig Donohue, Phupinder Gill, Jack Sandner, Bill Shepard, and myself. In the case of the CBOT, the close personal friendship between CME chairman Terry Duffy and CBOT chairman Charlie Carey, played an invaluable role in making it happen.[6] In the case of the NYMEX acquisition, the extraordinary efforts of our CEO, Craig Donohue, overcame the reluctance by some NYMEX members to approve the proposal. In both instances the negotiation subcommittee did an outstanding job in maneuvering through the long and complex process. The CBOT negotiations became complicated by an order of magnitude after Jeffrey Sprecher, the very capable chairman and CEO of the Intercontinental Exchange (ICE), entered into the bidding contest. In the final analysis, however, as is the case in many such efforts, it was the undeniable logic of establishing Chicago as the capital of futures markets that made the elusive CBOT deal come about. I should also note that the CME–CBOT merger represented an immense personal triumph for me. From the start of my CME tenure in the 1970s it had been a goal I coveted. (See Appendix 3C.) Then, in 2006, the day immediately after the New York Stock Exchange (NYSE) announced its plans to merge with Euronext Liffe, I realized that the moment was ripe. It didn't take much to convince Terry Duffy, Craig Donohue, and the others that the only meaningful response to the NYSE action (establishing a transatlantic securities behemoth with a strong futures component), was by creating what I called a "futures supertanker." The only way to achieve this was *not* to seek an international link, but to bring about a merger with the CBOT.

The second of our key decisions adopted during our Saturday meeting was to create a Governance Committee, which Jack Sandner would chair, for the purpose of establishing a governance structure of the Exchange that conformed with modern practices. This action proved valuable since the new committee under Jack was very effective in impeding some of the mischievous internal restructuring planned by the McNulty management. Third, we would create an "Electronic Transition" Committee" to help our members migrate to the electronic venue. Jim Oliff was the perfect choice as chairman for this committee. It represented a strong signal to the floor community that the direction toward electrification of the Exchange was not about to change and gave them an educational forum to learn how to transfer their trading skills to the screen. It also served as an extension of CME's long-standing tradition to promote educational programs and facilities relating to markets. Under Jimmy's leadership, the Electronic Transition Committee established a CME center that served both as a place for service providers to exhibit and demonstrate their wares and as an academic laboratory for our members to be exposed to the newest technological applications and to hone their skills. Separately, we also all agreed to promote Phupinder Gill to his well-deserved eventual office of CME president. (Gill unsuccessfully tried to get me to take this honor.) Finally, Craig Donohue, who was then managing director for business development and corporate/legal affairs, suggested we create the "Office of the CEO" and elevate him to that office. In this fashion we would not only ensure that Craig was included in major decisions by the CEO but would position him as the potential successor to Jim McNulty.

On January 1, 2004, Craig Donohue actually became chief executive officer of the CME, replacing Jim McNulty. As I had learned firsthand throughout the years of working with Craig, confirmed by the unparalleled experience of our successful corporate coup, Craig Donohue possessed a combination of legal, strategic planning, technological, and business-development skills that were perfect for the Exchange we were planning. His intellect, experience, and temperament were ideal for the eventual CEO slot we had in mind from the beginning. He received his Juris Doctor degree from my alma mater, John Marshall Law School, in 1987, a Master of Law in Financial Services Regulation from Kent College of Law in 1989, and completed his studies with a Master of Management from the Kellogg Graduate School of Management in 1995. He had a brief legal stay at the law firm of McBride, Baker & Coles before becoming a staff attorney for the CME in 1989. At the Merc, Craig's experience included every facet of Exchange operations, people skills, and international competition. When combined with his instinctive ability to assess business opportunities, it offered us a chief executive officer candidate who was right out of Central Casting. As history is witness, our expectations were rewarded. In my opinion, based on four decades of futures markets development, Craig Donohue became the very best CEO that any futures exchange could hope for. I seriously doubt that the CME could have achieved everything it did during his time in office without Craig at the helm. Our personal relationship quickly evolved into an intellectual bond and close friendship that has lasted to this very day.

A new day had dawned. In our collective minds, we had saved the institution. And we did it without any personal monetary gain, which in today's financial landscape must seem impossible. Both Terry Duffy and I turned down the offer to receive any stock options or the like which was awarded to senior level CME management. Although few deserved an award more than the two of us, we both privately agreed that at the time it didn't seem proper. We reasoned if the CME were successful, we would eventually be rewarded. With the advantage of historical hindsight, our achievements—the electrification of CME markets, our rebuff of international competitors, our merger with the CBOT and NYMEX, our number-one status in the world of futures, and our flawless performance during the current financial crisis—more than validate our bold action. We accomplished what I daresay few believed we could. Indeed, most informed observers, including Jerry Salzman and Phupinder Gill, gave long odds against us being successful. Even Craig Donohue admitted to me that until it actually happened, he was never quite certain it would. Some of us were certain. In fact, Bill Shepard told me that in order to spare Scott the embarrassment of losing, he had asked a mutual friend to tell Scott to withdraw his nomination. Scott refused. Most remarkable was the fact that we carried out the plan to the exact letter of the blueprint the three of us devised at the outset, and under a layer of secrecy. Remarkable also was the fact that going into the fateful board meeting in April of 2002, I have a suspicion that neither Scott Gordon nor Jim McNulty were truly prepared for its outcome.

But there is no rest for the wicked. We had precious little time to savor our incredible victory. Even as we planned to institute a new regime, fast-moving events from abroad were about to challenge the CME as had nothing before. Our new administration, our new chairman, our new CEO, our chairman emeritus, and our former chairman were about to be subjected to an acid test on which once again the fate of our beloved CME would rest.

CHAPTER 10

Baptism by Fire

Sweet Victory

On Friday, December 6, 2002, the Chicago Mercantile Exchange Holdings Inc. (CME) became the first major U.S. financial exchange to go public, completing its initial public offering (IPO) at $35 a share and receiving net proceeds of $117.8 million. It was clearly historic. One has to tip his hat to Jim McNulty, who orchestrated the IPO, and to Morgan Stanley and UBS its lead managers, as well as Citigroup, J.P. Morgan Chase, and William Blair & Co., who comanaged. But in all humility, it was Leo Melamed and Jack Sandner who should get the lion's share of the credit in successfully selling the Merc to the investment community during the "road show" that preceded the IPO.

People often use the term "capital formation," but until one has experienced a road show led by a prominent investment banker in conjunction with an imminent IPO, the words have little context. To put it as concisely as possible, capital formation, or at least one form of it, occurs when a group of selected corporate officers (the sellers), accompanied by a designated official from the investment banker—in our case, Morgan Stanley—board a chartered private jet and for the next three weeks or so are rushed around within a harrowing schedule to and fro some 30 cities across the United States and Europe to meet with potential investors (the buyers) for scheduled one-hour or so presentations and questioning during which the sellers put their best case forward to the buyers. The more sales, the more capital formation. The memory of those weeks is now but a blur of harassed activity, but to name a few of the places on the schedule, in no particular order, they included New York, Chicago, Houston, Denver, Minneapolis, Madison, Menomonee, Milwaukee, Kansas City, Boston, San Francisco, San Diego, Los Angeles, London, Milan, Frankfurt, Zurich, Rotterdam, and Amsterdam....Some of these locations required several different visits.

We had to fight our way onto that airplane. Originally, Jim McNulty convinced the people from Morgan Stanley that the team to make the sales pitch and persuade potential U.S. and global investors to buy CME shares should be led by himself as chief executive officer (with fewer than 24 months of CME history), and should include only the chairman (originally scheduled to be Scott Gordon, but in fact was Terry Duffy) and the chief financial officer, David Gomach. It took all of my persuasive skills to force Jack and myself (with a combined total of more than 50 years of CME history) onto the sales team. Ironically, only six months earlier, on May 16, 2002, the CME held a grand celebration in honor of the anniversary of the International Monetary Market (IMM). It was the creation of the IMM three decades earlier that set in motion the incomparable rise of the CME, bringing it to the juncture of a public offering and a listing on the New York Stock Exchange (NYSE), an event in which I played so singular a role. Presiding at the anniversary celebration and keynote speaker was William J. McDonough, president of the Federal Reserve Bank of New York and one of the original members of the IMM board; contributing also was Nobel laureate Milton Friedman with a specially prepared video in which he jokingly called me "the biggest crap-shooter of them all" for taking on the New York banks and daring to launch currency futures contracts in 1972;[1] and a special message from Federal Reserve chairman Alan Greenspan which ended with the following statement: "What is clear is that participants in financial markets across the country and around the globe have good reasons to join the International Monetary Market in celebrating their 30 years of accomplishment."[2]

And yet our CEO did not judge that this history demanded my participation in order to tell prospective investors firsthand something about how we got to where we were and where we might be heading. Similarly, that Jack Sandner, who served as CME chairman for so many terms throughout the years, had knowledge about our Exchange that was of special value in this sales effort. But it didn't take more than one presentation to prove that Jack Sandner and I were indisputably and exceptionally well qualified for this task. One must remember, few investors at that time knew what or who the CME was. As the first of the American exchanges, let alone futures exchanges, to do an IPO, public exchanges were pretty much of a mystery to the investing community. One cannot tell how the sales process would have proceeded without the two of us. But this much is clear: Leo Melamed and Jack Sandner knew more about the CME, its successful history, its unique innovations, its operational capability, how it works, what it does, and its future potential than anyone on the planet, and we were better equipped from the point of experience and ability to present the CME's case and respond to questions than anyone on that team. Nothing succeeds like success. Our stock exploded on the scene, doubling in value during its first year of trading on the NYSE (now listed exclusively on Nasdaq), then skyrocketing to a $700 high by its fifth birthday from its IPO price of $35. The recent global financial crisis, which has taken a heavy toll on the shares of all enterprises in the financial sector, including the CME, takes nothing away from our enormously successful IPO.

But even before we could settle into our new surroundings among the listed NYSE and Nasdaq elite, we were confronted with a do-or-die battle. The never-ending rumors about an eventual all-out attack by our European rivals, Eurex and Euronext Liffe, were about to turn into reality. The *Chicago Tribune* gave our traders the official news early in January of 2004, a sort of perverted New Year's greeting: "A European-based exchange is planning to grab business away from the Chicago Mercantile Exchange—beginning March 18."[3] War on the Merc had officially been declared by Euronext Liffe. However, this news—so well anticipated—did not produce the media buzz that was created by Eurex's announcment. On February 4, 2004, Eurex received Commodity Futures Trading Corporation (CFTC) approval to open for business on these shores. As announced a year earlier by Rudolf Ferscha, CEO of Eurex, the new enterprise, Eurex US, was established to compete on our turf for futures business. While this was a very serious challenge to all U.S. futures exchanges, for the Chicago Board of Trade (CBOT) it was of much more immediate and deadly concern since the Swiss–German futures bourse had the Chicago Board of Trade in its crosshairs. Ironically, 60 days earlier, the CBOT had still been a partner of Eurex, utilizing its A/C/E electronic system.

Eurex's plan was as treacherous as it was clever. The CBOT was caught in a nightmarish vice. On the front end, its electronic business could be faced with identical competitive Eurex contracts listed for trade on an electronic platform owned by Eurex where the CBOT's own business already flowed. At the back end, Eurex planned to gain ownership control of the Chicago Board of Trade Clearing Corporation (BOTCC), the clearing facility where CBOT cleared its transactions. It was a juicy story, winning the headlines and, some would say, the hearts and minds of the American press. This love affair with the media began well before their American launch. For years, Eurex had cultivated an expansive image, for one thing, by annually staging a most impressive party at the annual Futures Industry Association (FIA) conference in Boca Raton, which provided all conventioneers, the media included, with main-line entertainment. The press couldn't be blamed—after all, the CBOT was a stodgy, old-line enterprise, clinging to the past, and a bit arrogant. Eurex, on the other hand, the world's top futures exchange, radiated sophistication, owned a first-class electronic trading system, and reputedly had a $40 million war chest—which could be used to pay brokers for order flow.

Exuding confidence, even before its first trade, Eurex US leased 20,000 square feet of office space in Chicago's Sears Tower. Its opening celebration came amid a blitz of publicity that targeted CBOT users, and included staged parties, press conferences, free coffee to traders on La Salle Street (where the CBOT resided). At night, Eurex also lit up the top of the Sears Tower in Eurex's colors of green and blue[4] and taunted its intended target by beaming a searchlight on the outer walls of the historic Board of Trade building; during the day, "Hooters-looking" damsels passed out free Eurex T-shirts to CBOT traders. To his credit, CBOT president Bernie Dan heroically succeeded in thwarting the efforts of a determined and attractive young lady to get him to accept one.

Kopin Tan, Barron's top-notch financial columnist, set the table in September of 2003 with an article entitled "European Invasion: New electronic exchange takes on Chicago."[5] The article left the impression that the CEO of Eurex US, Rudolf Ferscha, was an ever-so-sophisticated giant killer who at last would rescue the deprived American futures markets—wedded as they were to an archaic past—and slay the Neanderthal dragons in Chicago, bringing America a modern, efficient, technological future:

> *Rudolph Ferscha lives in Frankfurt, Germany, but the Eurex chief executive has become so at home in Chicago on his frequent visits that he jogs at dawn along the Lake Michigan shore. His next big run will attract a larger audience, and will take him from Lake Shore Drive right onto turf long staked out by Chicago's venerable futures exchanges. Eurex last week said it will launch on Feb.1 a fully electronic derivatives market, called Eurex US. Based in Chicago, it will go head-to-head with the Chicago Board of Trade and the Chicago Mercantile Exchange. The new exchange will start trading futures on U.S. Treasury bonds and European interest-rate products, before adding a family of dollar and Euro-denominated futures and options.*
>
> *The announcement was long anticipated but still created a buzz. Even skeptics who talked down the Eurex plan heard the bigger message: that next year could bring accelerated change for Chicago's futures markets, which despite recent electronic embellishments are still devoted to manual trading through "open outcry" auctions on exchange floors.[6]*

I traveled to New York to meet with Kopin in an attempt to change his views about the Chicago's futures establishment. Still, I give Eurex top grades for courtesy. Indeed, as the code of civilized adversarial relationships probably requires, before hostilities begin the leaders of the attacking faction often make a final gesture of goodwill to the intended victim to explain, in the parlance of the underworld, *"There's nothing personal involved. It's strictly business."* Rudi Ferscha, a highly likable European, would have it no other way. On September 20, 2003, he came to Chicago with a high-level

Frankfurt delegation, led by Hartmut Schwesinger, the mayor of Frankfurt, to meet with the leadership of the CME, Terry Duffy, Craig Donohue, Jack Sandner, and myself. It was a very *gemutlich* gathering. The mayor explained in a most congenial manner that although Eurex would surely win over the futures business from the two Chicago markets, we should all remain good friends. Months later, Colleen Lazar, CME Director of Public Affairs who had carefully arranged the get-together, said she would forever remember the look on the mayor's face after my response to his statement. When I asked her to remind me what I said, she laughed and told me that I assured the Frankfurt mayor we would remain good friends because "Hell will freeze over before Eurex will win!"[7]

"It will happen on February 8," stated Joseph Weber of *BusinessWeek*, "when Eurex ramps up its Chicago-based computers to handle an anticipated tens of millions of dollars worth of business. Expected to provide cheap and fast trading—without many of the costly middlemen now filling the pits at the Chicago Board of Trade and the Chicago Mercantile Exchange—Eurex aims to steal away plenty of contract trading from its less-automated rivals."[8] It sounded as if we had already lost. I recall asking Charlie Carey, the CBOT chairman, what he thought. He responded something to the effect that "Well, they got our attention."

And did they ever! Five months after Eurex launched its effort to steal the CBOT's business in U.S. Treasury futures, the 156-year-old Chicago Exchange—whose financial contracts by then were predominantly trading on the LiffeConnect electronic platform—was posting record volumes. The incredible mistake the Eurex executives made is failing to recognize that the critical moment had passed. This was not a PR contest, nor was it a payment for order-flow challenge. It was first and foremost a battle between open outcry versus the efficiency of electronics.

The plan fashioned by Eurex US was based on three critical assumptions: (1) because a portion of the CBOT's financial customers were already trading on its A/C/E electronic platform, the customers would, more likely than not, remain there to trade the same contracts when listed by Eurex; (2) since electronics was far more efficient than open outcry and CBOT members were antithetical to electronic trading, they would not provide the necessary liquidity to support an electronic venue; (3) that the CBOT fee structure could never compete with Eurex's low-fee standards. Wrong on all counts.

Use by CBOT of the A/C/E platform ended on December 31, 2003. This was followed by a 30-day grace period during which Eurex could not compete. The question was how fast the CBOT could transition to LiffeConnect. A year earlier, in a letter to members, then chairman Nickolas Neubauer stated, "We believe we can sufficiently establish our liquidity during this transition and so meet and beat any competitive threats." He was right. The electronic switch to LiffeConnect went quicker and smoother than Eurex calculated. Partly this was due to the fact that the Eurex electronic system was based on old technology and not as efficient as the newer LiffeConnect system. President Bernie Dan correctly predicted at the time that "the integration of the platform with our floor will be much more efficient."[9] Charlie Carey, who took over as CBOT chairman in March of 2003, left no stone unturned, coercing his board to adopt a highly competitive fee structure—which they did in the nick of time—and energizing the CBOT floor to give their all-out support. Indeed, given the competitive threat, CBOT floor traders became totally supportive and CBOT's Treasury business flowed to LiffeConnect like fish to water. By the time Eurex got its American license, some 80 percent of CBOT's U.S. bond and T-note futures contracts was successfully trading on the London platform.

The most cunning component of Eurex's plan was to gain control of BOTCC, an independent clearing facility where for the past 77 years all of the CBOT's futures business was cleared.[10] If this plan succeeded, Eurex US would have a stranglehold on CBOT's business. CBOT's customers could effectively become Eurex US customers without the need to change any clearing procedures. It was a valid assumption. However, it turned out to be Eurex's biggest miscalculation. Eurex totally underestimated the determination of the CBOT board and the leadership skills of its chairman, Charlie Carey. As a successful trader of many years, Charlie was as bold as he was agile. According to Charlie, on the close of business, February 8, 2004, the very first day of the Eurex US launch, Joe Murphy, president of RFCO, a former major clearing firm that had strongly supported the competitive attack by Eurex US, told him that Eurex had lost because the CBOT chairman's defensive actions were letter perfect. To his credit, Joseph Weber of *BusinessWeek* did his best to correct the record:

> To the Europeans at the world's largest futures exchange, Eurex, Charles P. Carey may have looked like a hayseed. The jovial, burly chairman of the Chicago Board of Trade is much happier trading corn futures in the raucous pits than hosting meetings in the exchange's elegant boardroom. Eurex officials, who pan the open-outcry pits as a throwback to the pre-computer age, won't say what they thought. But Carey figures "they viewed me as a corn trader who didn't know what I was doing." If so, the Swiss and Germans who run Eurex are the ones who look like rubes now.[11]

The CBOT of course tried to buy control of BOTCC, but when it couldn't, Charlie Carey did what Rudolf Ferscha never expected could be done. Of course, to do it, Charlie needed the open arms of the Chicago Mercantile Exchange. As Russ Wasendorf, chief executive officer of Peregrine

Financial Group, put it, "Wars make strange bedfellows. What happened here is that the Chicago exchanges got the sense that they were facing serious foreign competition and they were forced to get together."[12]

As history is witness, the CME was more than willing to come to the CBOT's rescue and at the same time achieve an incredible business coup for itself. Of course, there was a real risk. If the CME Clearing House was not able to carry out in time the gargantuan task of transferring CBOT trades from BOTCC, the plan in its entirety would fail miserably. Still, in our view, the reward far outweighed the risk. Again the association and friendship achieved over so many years between many of us with members of the CBOT leadership proved invaluable, providing a strong factor of trust; this was especially true with respect to the friendship between Terry Duffy and Charlie Carey; but give major credit to CME's CEO, Craig Donohue, and CME's president, Phupinder Gill, for their leadership in the sensitive negotiations. Indeed, Donohue and Gill drove the complicated fee structure negotiations until the exact common denominator was found that would make both exchanges happy and at the same time gain the applause of the FCM community who would benefit from the cost savings the new clearing arrangement would engender. By April of 2003, the agreement (which I named, "the CME/CBOT Common Clearing Link") was hammered out. The CME would provide transaction processing, guarantee, and other business services. The Clearing Link was set to begin operations on January 2, 2004—a full month before Eurex US would gain regulatory approval as an American company.[13] Miraculously it did. CME chairman Terry Duffy hailed the agreement as "good for our customers, our clearing firms, our exchanges and certainly Chicago."[14] He was ever so right. Based on combined first-quarter 2003 figures, if this agreement had been in place in January of 2003, the CME Clearing House would have cleared an average of a whopping 4 million contracts a day.[15] As I said to the *Financial Times*, "This agreement is truly historic. The link represents the culmination of many years of efforts to bring the CME and CBOT closer together."[16] Rhetoric to the side, the ultimate credit must go to Phupinder Gill and the Clearing House officials for their tireless efforts, working day and night to accomplish the Herculean transition from BOTCC clearing to the CME. As Clearing House president Kim Taylor explained it, "Billions of dollars worth of positions had to be moved on time without any interruption of trading." In my mind, the achievement ranks up there with the Seven Wonders of the World.

However, as previously noted, the honor of being the first European exchange to take on the CME and its flagship Eurodollar futures and options contracts went to Euronext Liffe, the London-based futures and options exchange. As *Securities Week* pointed out in its February 2, 2004 edition, "Last week, while everyone was looking the other way—toward Eurex and its soon to be launched U.S.-based futures exchange—along came LIFFE, owned by Eurex's rival Euronext, with the news that it will launch electronic Eurodollar futures to compete with the Chicago Mercantile Exchange's most popular contract."[17] LIFFE's chief executive, Hugh Freedberg, confirmed this fact and told the truth: "This is something that we've always envisaged since we started the development and introduction of LiffeConnect."[18] In other words, as many of us in Chicago suspected, the negotiations over the years between the CME and LIFFE to establish a permanent alliance between our two markets papered over the real truth. But that is a fact, not a complaint. In the world of international competition, one can never ignore opportunity whenever or however it appears. The *Wall Street Journal* gave context to the threat and put its finger on the problem:

> *Eurodollar futures are the CME's most popular product. But while the exchange's equity-index futures and currency-futures products have seen explosive growth on its Globex electronic-trading platform, Eurodollar futures haven't. Last year, a total of 309.6 million Eurodollar contracts traded, with electronic trading accounting for only 4% of total volume.*[19]

We had already seen this movie and knew its ending. Back in 1997, LIFFE was the precise victim of such an electronic attack by the Deutsche Terminbörse, (later to become Eurex). LIFFE's franchise contract, the 10-year German government bond known as the Bund, was wrested away by the Frankfurt-based exchange primarily because it provided an electronic venue for the same futures instrument. LIFFE ignored the electronic threat and continued to trade the Bund in the pit until it was too late. It was nearly the death knell of the London market. Lesson mastered, now it was Euronext Liffe's turn to apply what it learned to the CME. The similarities were frightening: The Bund instrument was to LIFFE's overall volume what the Eurodollar contract was to ours, both products similarly represented leading futures instruments for interest rates, the Bund for European long-term rates, the Eurodollar for global short-term rates, and just as at LIFFE, our contract traded nearly exclusively in the open-outcry venue. Our vulnerability was obvious. The Brits saw the opportunity and seized on it.

To put it in plain English, the IMM Eurodollar contract *was* the CME. At the close of 2003, the Eurodollar contract—futures and options— represented 50 percent of the total CME volume, 84 percent of its total open interest, and 75 percent of its net income. Euronext Liffe had a fine reputation, an excellent electronic platform, virtually the same global banking membership as we did, and was damn serious about its intent. Aside from the inherent and obvious efficiencies of electronics over open outcry, as far as fee structure went, no matter how low we reduced exchange transaction fees, it was impossible to compete unless the brokers gave up their fee as well. That could never happen. It was our worst nightmare. And it wasn't a surprise. Indeed, we had tried to prepare for it. Recall that on January

14, 1999, after a long harangue and much grief, the side-by-side referendum was overwhelmingly passed by the CME membership—a referendum branded as an imperative to thwart competitive threats. It was enacted to begin the process of migration of our floor-based products to the electronic venue. As the *Wall Street Journal* pointed out, it worked exceptionally well for equity index and currency futures. But as far as Eurodollars went—*nada*. The Eurodollar floor broker and trader community ignored the referendum, its intent and purpose. For the best of reasons, of course: their income. And without the liquidity provided by this community—the commercial users of the contract, in other words—the hedgers had no choice but to stay where they were.

Some within the American community saw it as a good thing: John Damgard, president of the FIA, welcomed the Liffe announcement as part of the emergence of head-to-head competition among exchanges. "We are now seeing exactly what Congress intended with the passage of the Commodity Futures Modernization Act of 2000," Damgard stated.[20] Competition, yes, but those of us at the CME had a different take: We would move heaven and earth to protect our franchise contract. Craig Donohue, exuding confidence, told the *Securities Industry News* that he believed the old adage, "winner takes all," will once again prove true in derivatives markets. "Yes, winner takes all, and yes, the CME will be the winner," he stated.[21] Indeed, the consequential effect of the Euronext Liffe attack on the Chicago Mercantile Exchange cannot be better described than in the famous statement attributed to Isoroku Yamamoto—Japan's greatest naval strategist in World War II and commander in chief of the Japanese fleet. When presented with the news on December 7, 1941, that Pearl Harbor had successfully been attacked, he prophetically said: *I fear all we have done is to awaken a sleeping giant and fill him with a terrible resolve.*

The Board Steering Committee went into crisis mode. I invited to the deliberations several members of the Eurodollar pit, including John Newhouse, a former board member and an extremely active Eurodollar broker from the inception of the contract. Merc management began presenting various defensive strategies, such as extension of the existing Eurodollar market-maker program, expanding regular trading hours, increasing the number of participants and expanding participation by proprietary trading firms, offering a more favorable exchange fee structure, waiving exchange fees for the Galax-C handhelds to encourage floor traders to use this electronic connection to Globex, enhancing the technical ability of floor traders to access Globex, and so forth. All of those actions were excellent ideas and worthwhile; however, it was recognized by most of us that the only certain defense to an attack by Liffe was to increase the liquidity of Eurodollar trading on the electronic venue. The only way to do that was to *mandate* migration from the pit to Globex. But how? I recalled my conversation with Satish Nandapurkar when he suggested we could force Eurodollar trade onto

Globex on a given date. As I pointed out then, that could come about only through a referendum; it was written in stone. To have a chance, the proposition must make sense to a majority of the floor.

The modus operandi instituted for Board Steering, encouraging open debate so that ideas could be explored, built on, or rejected without embarrassment, served its purpose. Our discussions suddenly took a new path. Bill Shepard, vice chairman of Board Steering, made the telling argument that our focus should be on the so-called "whites"—that is, the first two quarterly Eurodollar contracts.[22] If we could effect a sufficient volume increase on Globex of the two "near-by" trading months, our vulnerability diminished considerably because Liffe had little liquidity in the so-called "back months." It made sense. Then John Newhouse built on that idea: If the near-bys could achieve at least a 25 percent electronic trading threshold (of total Eurodollar volume), it would serve to create enough liquidity on Globex to discourage commercial disaffection. From the moment John made the suggestion, I knew we had found our "holy grail." Terry Duffy and Craig Donohue were instantly aboard. After a good deal of further discussion, a recommendation to the board was hammered out, one we thought had a chance for passage by the membership: If the required percentage of trading volume on Globex for the two near-by contracts was not met by a certain date, the board would have the right to shut down floor trading for those two contracts. It was left up to the traders to keep the contracts alive in the pit. The board approved the concept, later refined by the Executive Committee, and a referendum, now called a "Special Meeting," was set for March 16, 2004.

Now came the hard part. Member meetings were scheduled for February, 11, 12, and 13, 2004. In my heart of hearts, I knew this moment represented the final battle in the war between status quo and change—a war that had begun 17 years earlier, in 1987. The floor was worried and riled. All sorts of rumors were flying. Everyone was focused on the meetings. The leadership of the board would have to face the extremely hostile Eurodollar trading community, together with its powerful broker groups, all in all, nearly 3,000 strong—the most successful and hard-bitten open-outcry constituency in existence anywhere. And we had to win enough of them over to pass the proposition. It would be a no-holds-barred confrontation. I had been there many times before. But this would be Terry Duffy's first test as chairman, a baptism by fire. Fate had given him a chance to prove his fortitude and leadership skills—an opportunity to test his mettle.

As expected, there were 1,000 angry faces in the room—2,000 angry eyes. The fear, frustration, and distrust was palpable. The emotionally charged atmosphere had many characteristics of a lynch mob. Both sides took turns to speak. Terry was first, meeting the challenge with courage and determination. He never wavered and never lost his cool. Craig Donohue made a fantastic presentation, I followed with my version of a Knute Rockne "The Merc members always respond in a crisis" address, and others from the board followed. But the hostility did not dissipate. There were angry statements made, there were arguments and suggestions, there were answers given, explanations offered, refuted, rebutted, again and again. We had to do this three times. The outcome would determine the destiny of our exchange.

There was only a month between the meetings and the vote. All of us spent every waking moment pleading our case. We were fighting for the life of the Exchange. Perhaps the imminent threat from Euronext Liffe would make the difference. We had the facts and the logic. There are times when that is enough. This was one of those times. The proposition passed overwhelmingly. And it worked. The required 25 percent of trading volume was reached long before the deadline. The real surprise was how quickly the vast majority of Eurodollar futures business transferred to the screen once critical mass was achieved. It was like the floodgates had opened. Clearly, the inescapable logic of electronic trade over open outcry was irresistible . . . *Hell did not freeze over.* Fortunately, Globex itself was ready, willing, and able to do the job.

Looking back, there were plenty of scary moments. Things could have gone either way. But in the end, our crowd came through. And, yes, there are many heroes to this history. But it was Globex that gave us the magic. It represented the stuff that dreams are made of. Its development was symbolic of the global technological revolution that transformed every aspect of civilization over the past three decades. It made the CME Group what it is today. This time the tyranny of the status quo was vanquished.

Suddenly a wave of remorse overcame me. I had a flashback to that day when as a young law student I first encountered the Merc's trading floor at 110 N. Franklin and remembered my feelings. I recorded them in my memoirs at the time:

> *I was Alice stepping through the Looking Glass into a world of not just one Mad Hatter, but hundreds. The shouting among the traders, the movement of their bodies and hands, captivated me like nothing before. Dumbfounded, I watched the clerks darting across the floor at road runner pace with buy and sell orders in their hands for brokers in the trading pits. If it wasn't the Looking Glass then it must have been the Twilight Zone, a dimension of sight, sound and mind. Maybe it was both. Whatever it was, there was a life-force on that floor that was magical and exciting, and though I didn't understand what was going on, I wanted to be a part of it. I had no doubts or illusions that this wasn't a law office. It was whatever it was, and it paid $25 a week. I was thrilled beyond words.*[23]

Globex Time Line

- On October 6, 1987, Globex was conceived with approval of the CME membership.
- On June 25, 1992, Globex was officially launched.
- On September 9, 1997, the CME E-Mini Standard & Poor's 500 was listed on Globex, becoming the first U.S. futures instrument to begin 24-hour electronic trading.
- On August 18, 1998, the CBOT membership approved concurrent open-outcry and electronic trading in its U.S. Treasury futures contracts.
- On January 14, 1999, the CME membership approved concurrent open-outcry and electronic trading in all futures and options contracts.
- On May 18, 1999, the CBOT membership voted to accept an electronic alliance with Eurex.
- On November 2, 1999, CME members embraced a board proposal for demutualization—adopted on June 6, 2000.
- In January 2002, LIFFE was acquired by Euronext, joining the exchanges of Amsterdam, Brussels, Paris, and Lisbon, to become the continental European exchange known as Euronext Liffe.
- On December 6, 2002, the Chicago Mercantile Exchange became the first U.S. financial exchange to go public.
- In January 2003, the CBOT transferred its financial futures from A/C/E to the LiffeConnect system.
- On February 4, 2004, Eurex received CFTC approval to open Eurex US.
- On March 18, 2004, Euronext Liffe began trading the CME's Eurodollar futures contract.
- On March 16, 2004, CME members approved the board proposal to begin the transfer of Eurodollar futures to Globex.
- In January 2004, the CBOT moved its futures and options clearing operations from BOTCC to the CME Clearing House.
- In April 2006, the New York Mercantile Exchange (NYMEX) approved listing its energy contracts on Globex.

- On April 4, 2007, Euronext Liffe merged with the NYSE to become the NYSE Euronext Group.
- On July 12, 2007, the CBOT merged into the CME to become the CME Group.
- On August 22, 2008, the NYMEX merged into the CME Group.

PART II

Messenger from the Futures

CHAPTER 11

Tomorrow's Technological Tidal Wave

Futures markets, as their name implies, should provide a glimpse into the future. In truth, they often don't. The future is habitually too clouded and burdened with too many imponderables to be seen clearly.

For instance, here we are at the start of the twenty-first century in the midst of a global rebirth, one that should offer an unequivocal picture of a bright tomorrow. Communism slain, the tyrannical order of the Soviet Union dismantled, East European nations freed, market economic order embraced by all, apartheid in retreat, emerging nations in the Pacific Rim, the European Economic Union about to commence. Good stuff.

And, yet, something gnaws at making an unguarded optimistic prediction for the world. Perhaps it is because we know of the contradictory and uncertain nature of mankind. Perhaps it is because we know the steep price tag of all that lies before us. Perhaps it is because we are concerned that the global credit spree of the 1980s will demand payment in the 1990s.

So instead, allow us to stay clear of the unknown. Allow us to talk about the inevitable. Allow us to predict that whatever ensues, the role of futures and options will be significant. Allow us to predict that whatever ensues, our markets are about to be engulfed by a technological tidal wave.

* * *

Robin Maxwell settles back and buckled the safety belt around her as the British Airways 787 taxies out to the runway at Kennedy. She pulls from her briefcase an IBM IAM-Port, her interactive multimedia portable system, and turns it on. After the screen in front of her comes to life, she executes a few

Presented at the Seventh Annual London International Finance Symposium conducted jointly by the Chicago Board of Trade and the Chicago Mercantile Exchange, London, November 7, 1991.

115

directions using the system's electronic mouse and is instantly connected to the Equity Information Center at her Goldman Sachs office in New York. A few more clicks on the mouse gives her the information she requested as well as an online data feed to various markets around the world. Robin studies the information, then calls up a trader friend in Chicago, who appears on her online video screen for a brief discussion of her market theory.

As the airplane levels off at 35,000 feet, Robin checks the time in London, calls up for a Globex connection on the screen, and initiates orders to buy December S&P 500 contracts on the CME, sell March FTSE contracts at the LIFFE and CAC-40 contracts on MATIF, a complex DAX/Nikkei options spread on the Deutsche Terminbörse and Osaka exchanges, and to buy February U.S. Bond puts at the CBOT.

When she is finished with the transaction, Robin watches the market for a while, sends a fax to her London office, takes a sip of the coffee the stewardess provided, and asks her IAM-Port to review the current crop of plays showing in London so that she can make reservations for that evening.

Science fiction? Don't bet against it. Interactive multimedia—a multidimensional vehicle of communication representing the coalescence of key communications technologies: television, telephone, personal computers, and laser storage systems—is coming. When these technologies merge, life as we know it will never be the same.

While Robin Maxwell's interactive multimedia system is not yet available, what *is* available is quite amazing. Robin can easily install a calling card that provides her with 24-hour real-time market information in stocks, futures, options, and mutual funds.

Or she can install a real-time spreadsheet system which will display, analyze, and monitor continuously current financial data with electronic online data feeds.

Or she can install a portfolio information management system designed to document and control transactions and positions in actively managed portfolios or funds.

Or she can install a software product providing a host of analytical calculations, regression analysis, and exponential smoothing from single or multiple databases.

Or she can install a software providing daily investment performance calculations by account, currency, group, sector, and industry.

I could go on and on, but you get the point. These are not esoterica of a future tomorrow. I am describing a bit of present day avant garde technology. A few years ago, these systems were but on programmers' drawing boards. A dozen years ago, they were someone's overactive imagination. And 20 years ago? Well, let me tell you.

In 1972, the markets of futures and options were among the very first to discern the meaning as well as the potential of the coming new financial age, an age that above all was to be directed by a new technological standard. The new technology, while still then in its infancy, was to instigate an information revolution that would dramatically change the scope, nature, and structure of financial markets forever.

As Walter Wriston then predicted, by virtue of the information revolution we would be witnessing a galloping new system of international finance, one that differed radically from its precursors in that it "was not built by politicians, economists, central bankers or finance ministers . . . it was built by technology . . . by men and women who interconnected the planet with telecommunications and computers."

The results were spectacular. As a consequence today we live in one interrelated, interdependent world economy. Distinct divisions based on time zones have vanished. Geographical borders that once could limit the flow of capital are history. Internal national mechanisms that once could insulate one's population from external price influences are impotent. Financial markets are now virtually unencumbered, continuous, and worldwide in scope.

Because the markets of futures and options understood the consequences of the new technology, embraced and adapted to its demands, our markets blazed the trail for much of what has since followed in world capital markets. We established that there was a need for a new genre of risk management tools responsive to institutional money management and modern telecommunications; we introduced the idea of risk management as a regime; we fostered the concept of financial engineering as a commercial necessity; we became the catalyst for the invention of a multitude of new products, both on and off exchanges; we caused the acceptance and integration of futures and options into the infrastructure of the financial establishment; and, we engendered the development of futures markets worldwide.

But that was the first phase. And while exciting and highly successful, it was only the beginning. The evolution of our markets is a continuous living thing and cannot stop. Nor, I daresay, will the breathtaking speed of technological innovation. I speak not of the good or bad of it, I speak only of its inevitability. Indeed, as the guy said, "You ain't seen nothing yet." What is coming down the technological trail in the very near future will again completely transform our marketplace and make trading unrecognizable from what it is today. What is coming is a computerized trading competence undreamed of but a mere decade ago.

Some of it is structural. Computer-aided systems engineering, the so-called CASE, represents a new wave in programming. CASE moves systems development away from its traditional art form and more into the realm of science. It applies engineering discipline and computer support to systems building. It allows software development to focus on solving business problems. Its applicability is boundless. The Paris Bourse, for example, used

CASE to overhaul and streamline its clearing system in order establish a competitive edge in Europe. Similarly, PaineWebber, by enlisting CASE, will become one of the first wire houses to attempt to retool itself for the 1990s with a state-of-the-art distributed computer system that will provide round-the-clock online availability for trading, marketing, and customer data.

Some of it is being developed by the exchanges. For instance, on the Chicago Mercantile Exchange and the Chicago Board of Trade, systems are being jointly developed to accept trading instructions from market participants worldwide and deliver them electronically directly into the trading pits. Orders will be routed through the CME's TOPS or the CBOT's EOS system for electronic switching to the proper pit broker who will utilize a computerized broker's workstation to organize and instantly report trade status back to the customer. Independent traders in the pits will utilize the latest innovations in handheld technology with which to do their proprietary trading and to instantly report their trades for clearing. These so-called AUDIT terminals will use advances in pen-based handheld computers including handprint recognition.

But most of it is in software. Intelligent agents will "reside" in computers to create a world we can hardly envision. As Craig Torres of the *Wall Street Journal* recently reported, during the past five years, major American market participants have spent millions of dollars to advance their computing potency. Indeed, one estimate says U.S. securities firms will spend some $7.5 billion on technology in 1991. Firms the likes of Morgan Stanley, First Boston, O'Conner & Associates, Salomon Brothers, Kidder Peabody, and Goldman Sachs and others are using automated development tools to build brand-new software programs. They are venturing to achieve a new generation of "analytics"—sophisticated mathematical computer models that can act as giant think tanks in order to identify hundreds of never-before-imagined trading strategies in securities, futures, and options.

While the trend is still in its infancy, its direction is unmistakable. Until now computers were used mostly as spreadsheets, or as fast calculators, or to analyze risk, or to run accounting or other programs. In the coming age, computers will no longer act within the framework of their traditional competence, they will have gained artificial intelligence. The next generation of analytics, now in development at sophisticated research laboratories, seeks to apply brand-new financial theories and allow the trader to apply them to markets on an ongoing basis. The evolving new mathematical formulas will imitate how traders think and look at markets—but several thousand times faster than humans can. In fact, a new supercomputer has just been unveiled that runs at a speed of one "teraflop," a trillion floating point operations per second.

As a consequence, computers are on the verge of generating a wave of pristine trading strategies that will offer heretofore unheard-of opportunities.

Computers are searching for price correlations and connections between markets that human traders never thought possible or never thought about at all. Computers will invent virgin tactics within a complex set of transactions inconceivable for the human mind to have perceived. Computers will create synthetic options and futures far beyond human imagination. Computers will find ways to blend these new analytical transactions with traditional strategies to produce even more complex possibilities. And while the bulk of the new wave of technological transactions will be utilized off exchanges—within the cash markets—the markets of futures and options are bound to be substantial beneficiaries as well.

For example, computers recently created a synthetic option on the Nikkei Index. It was produced out of a combination of Nikkei stock index futures and exchange-traded stock index options. The synthetic Nikkei option cost less than the real thing and allowed traders who recently used it to make $500,000 on a single trade.

In another instance, a managing director of a major securities firm recently created a two-year option that gives an investor the right to buy the S&P 500 stock index at its lowest point of 1991 in Swiss francs. Without analytics, such products could not even be imagined.

IBM's mathematical sciences department, very much involved in the development of analytic market math, is working on a mathematical model that will allow investors to assemble hundreds of portfolios in seconds and have various shadings of investment risk and reward.

Anticipating a constant 24-hour market, IBM has also been working on a mathematical model for the past two years that will scan the trading pattern of stocks or bonds around the world and around the clock. Says the department's director, "Time shouldn't be measured by how the clock ticks, but by the level of trading activity." By creating a model that uses trading activity as a measure of time, IBM hopes to create a new vantage point for spotting price trends.

As one would expect, competition in this emerging field will be fierce, every new analytic a most closely guarded secret. Remember, the only proprietary component for the inventor is the mathematical formula he devised which offers unique profit opportunities in markets that are extremely efficient and extremely competitive. Consequently, while many of the major firms are working feverishly to develop analytic competence, much of it is hush-hush and most of it behind secured doors.

But the secret is out, anyway. New computer-generated mathematical analytics are coming whether we like it or not. Says Myron Scholes of the coming new age in trading, "People who don't have analytics are going to be relatively obsolete." What he didn't mention is that not only will analytics achieve a myriad of new trading opportunities, they will also result in a myriad of new regulatory concerns, issues, and problems. How will these new transactions be regulated? Will they be regulated? Can they be regulated? And, in any event, what dangers do they pose for the financial structure of the world? Those are legitimate and important issues yet to be recognized by the federal regulatory bodies of the world as well as, I might add, the traditional exchanges. Sad to say, very few understand the full scope and nature of the technological tidal wave coming, let alone comprehend what its ramifications will be or how to cope with them.

Finally, it is important to note that as IBM suggested, the new technological trading competence will be structured to capitalize on the coming global 24-hour market. Yes, the revolutionary Globex concept fostered by futures markets has now become establishment even for the securities markets and even before our own international system is functional. Thus, you not only see the NYSE moving in the desired direction with after-hours trading sessions, you see the launching of NASDAQ International, a trading system for U.S. stocks on an electronic screen; you see the Japanese over-the-counter market launching a similar system; you see the Italian securities market leaving the traditional open-outcry stock trading for computerized screens; and, of course, you see similar systems such as at LIFFE, MATIF, Sidney Futures Exchange, TIFFE, SOFFEX, and DTB springing up all over the world.

The coming new technological age, when combined with more globalization, instant informational flows, 24-hour trading, immediate access to markets of choice, and intensified competition, offers immense opportunities for the markets of futures and options. In a world where financial risk is constant, where financial volatility is commonplace, where innovation is rewarded, where demand for unique risk management strategies will increase, where financial engineering is prized, where opportunities will rapidly appear and disappear on a constantly changing financial horizon, and where professional management will continue to demand efficient instruments of trade, in such a world, the role of futures and options is fundamental.

CHAPTER 12

Wakeup Call

We are at an unprecedented moment in the evolution of finance and markets. We find ourselves at the vortex of three primary crosscurrents that have converged to create some turbulent waters and whose resolve is still uncertain. The rush of these currents has been extremely rapid and has advanced upon the world at nearly the same time. Their remarkable history is quite recent and still very fresh in our memory.

First came globalization. Walter Wriston, the former chairman of Citicorp, sensed it early. In 1985 he told us we were witnessing a "galloping new system of international finance," one that was not built by politicians, economists, central bankers or finance ministers, but by men and women who interconnected the planet with telecommunications and computers. As a result, Wriston stated, the world had replaced the gold standard with the information standard.

Indeed it had. Our separate financial existence was transformed into one interrelated, interdependent world economy. Geographical borders that once could limit the flow of capital are history. Internal national mechanisms that once could insulate a population from external price influences are increasingly impotent. Financial markets have become virtually unencumbered, continuous, and worldwide. A company located anywhere in the world can use resources located anywhere in the world, to produce a product anywhere in the world, to be sold anywhere in the world.

Second: political. As Nobel laureate Milton Friedman predicted, the free economic precepts of Adam Smith combined with the principles of political freedom espoused by Thomas Jefferson have resulted in an unmitigated triumph of market-driven economic order over central planning, of capitalism over communism, of democracy over dictatorship. The world experienced the incredible might of these two ideals as together they seemingly overnight forced the unification of Germany, the liberalization of Eastern Europe, the

---

Presented at the Annual Meeting of the International Association of Financial Engineers, November 9, 1995, New York.

fall of communism, the collapse of the Soviet Union, and the dissolution of apartheid.

This political/economic transformation has propelled virtually every nation in the world to move to a market-driven economic order. It is a unique historical happenstance. For the past 20 years when we spoke of a global economy, we were only talking about 25 percent of mankind—mostly North America, Western Europe, and Japan. As recently as 1988, almost 70 percent of mankind was living under Marxist or socialist economic systems. Suddenly, there are 3 billion more participants in the capitalist system. Suddenly, every country on the planet is a competitor in the global marketplace.

Third: microdynamism. This is a word I made up to explain that the world has moved from the big to the little. In physics we traveled from General Relativity to quantum mechanics. We went from contemplating atoms to inspecting their nuclei and discovering quarks and leptons. Particle physics was upon us. Similarly, in biology scientists migrated from examining individual cells to peering within their structure and ushering in the era of gene engineering. Molecular biology was born.

This microdynamism and downsizing can be seen in every aspect of our lives. Today's personal computer, small enough to be stored in a briefcase, can do much, much more than the UNIVAC, the world's first computer, which required an entire room to be housed. We wear much lighter material that is warmer and stronger than the bulky clothing of previous eras. Fiber optic cables are replacing mountains of copper wire. Transistors transformed the radio and a myriad of other electrical appliances into handheld devices. Microprocessors miniaturized the entire technological world and keep getting smaller and smaller. And on and on.

In markets, the evolution was strikingly similar. When advancements in computer technology were applied to established investment strategies, the result was remarkable. Just as it did in the sciences, market applications went from macro to micro. Intricate calculations and state-of-the-art analytical systems ensued, offering financial engineers the ability to divide financial risk into its separate components. Derivatives—the financial equivalents to particle physics and molecular biology—were born. Investment methodologies were transformed from all-encompassing traditional strategies to finely tuned modern portfolio theories. Long-term hedging evolved into continuous online risk management.

The foregoing three primary crosscurrents, coupled with a swarm of secondary flows, have converged to create our present financial market environment. It is unique to history. It is still undefined and not understood. It is volatile and dangerous. At times the whirlpool is smooth and easy to anticipate. Suddenly it is vicious and unpredictable. Markets go up with unrelenting force, only to turn without warning and collapse without end. Participants find inventive ways to cash in, only to be caught in unsuspecting savage traps. Rogue traders unearth ingenious techniques to deceive or cheat as traditional controls are found antiquated or woefully inadequate. Market regulators, along with business managers, seem helpless and off guard.

What shall the world do? Condemn the events that produced the turbulence? Curse the reality of the present? Outlaw the markets? Restrict price movement? Ban futures? All of the above?

We can neither expunge the history that brought us to this fate nor prevent its ultimate resolve. We are in the midst of a great transformation. We are negotiating an unknown expanse between a world we knew and the one we know not. We are on a gigantic bridge between past political arrangements, past economic orders, past technical capabilities, past market applications, past internal controls, and a new reality.

We are yet insufficiently conversant with the new order, its dimension, its demands, its potential, to write the rules. If we act in haste to severely harness the currents, rigorously restrict its flow, or sternly direct its course, we take the risk of creating conditions far, far more dangerous than what is naturally in store for us. If we so fear the computer that we adopt a Luddite philosophy, if we so recoil from Procter & Gamble, Orange County, Metallgesellschaft, Barings Bank, Daiwa Bank, or similar debacles yet unknown that we enact Draconian rules to prevent their occurrence, if corporate boards shrink from the use of futures because of fears of consequential losses to their corporate bottom line, civil actions by shareholders, or sanctions by regulators, then at best corporate profits are headed south, and at worst Western civilization has hit its top.

At this juncture in the transformation, while we dare not ignore the dangers it has engendered, we must not cower in its presence. Just as we found it impossible to curtail the developments in gene engineering, so we will discover that financial engineering also cannot be stopped. Instead, we must be prudent and vigilant. We must set standards, benchmarks, and especially internal controls. We must heed the lessons we have learned and adopt the prescriptions that are warranted. We must enforce the recommendations of such forums as the Group of Thirty, the Windsor Declaration, and the FIA Global Task Force on Financial Integrity. We must observe and learn and intensify our education process. Risk management implicitly must include risk enlightenment.

And, above all, we must be realistic. There are but two certainties. Neither is surprising. First, that the metamorphoses I described are unending—by definition evolution is a continuing process, whether in physics, biology, or markets. Second, that the unmistakable common denominator of recent crosscurrents has been technology. Indeed, throughout the ages, technology has consistently been the foremost force in dictating fundamental and revolutionary change in the political and economic landscape of our planet. In the past decade, the technology of telecommunications forced a stark, uncompromising examination of political and economic systems, bringing down state-controlled economics and racial inequalities, while the technology of computers enabled physicists, biologists, and financial engineers to peer into the smallest detail of our structure and manipulate its makeup.

Clearly, the introduction of fire brought about a profound change in the life of our species, as did the invention of the wheel, electricity, the printing press, and the industrial revolution. But events speeded up. The technological revolution of recent years was of a larger magnitude and came upon the world in a shorter time span than ever before experienced. At an unprecedented pace that continues to accelerate, technology has produced, and continues to produce, fundamental changes that reverberate through every facet of our civilization, but nowhere more than in financial markets, where the transformations have been spectacular, global, and absolute.

There are still within our markets those who would ignore these realities. These souls are simply following historian Barbara Tuchman's prediction that "Men will not believe what does not fit in with their plans or suit their prearrangements." Pity! For no longer is there a valid debate on the subject. Anyone who is still skeptical about the direction we are headed is simply deaf to the thundering maelstrom of the technological avalanche around us. Anyone who had not seen the handwriting on the wall is blind to the reality of our times.

One can no more deny the fact that technology has and will continue to engulf every aspect of financial markets than one can restrict the use of derivatives in the management of risk. The markets of the future will be automated. The traders of the future will trade by way of the screen. Those who dare ignore this reality face extinction. Round-the-clock electronic information in stocks, futures, options, and mutual funds is now commonplace. Real-time spreadsheet capabilities which display, analyze, and monitor current financial data with electronic online data feeds are old hat. Portfolio information management systems designed to document and control transactions, provide real-time positions, P&L, and credit limit updates are routine. Electronic alerts, predetermined target prices, complex option spreads, currency conversions, and volatility cones are now standard trading applications. Software products providing a host of complex analytical calculations, multidimensional charts of theoretical pre-expiration curves, historical comparisons, projections, regressions, and exponential smoothing from single or multiple databases are abundant. Risk analysis modules providing a snapshot of the portfolio under varying market circumstances are standard. Support programs for exotics such as average rate, chooser, corridor, digital, double digital, dual, lookback, quanto, and trigger/barrier options are available. There are even computer trading systems that anticipate and incorporate the human thought process of traders, so-called artificial intelligence. And there are much, much more. For the information standard has become the information superhighway. There are 37 million users of the Internet on the North American continent alone.

In the 1970s and 1980s, futures markets led the way. We recognized that to survive competitive pressures, we had to embrace new technologies and integrate them with open outcry. To compete globally, we recognized that telecommunications was fashioning a global marketplace that would necessitate electronic trading mechanisms. Proudly, in 1987 the Chicago Mercantile Exchange membership overwhelmingly approved Globex. It was the first embrace of an electronic screen-based system for futures anywhere in the world. And almost on cue, the Globex pronouncement resulted in a virtual torrent of electronic systems devised either to extend existing trading hours or to conduct the entire transaction process.

The following year, the Chicago Board of Trade, the Tokyo Stock Exchange, the Osaka Securities Exchange, the Copenhagen Stock Exchange, the Danish Options & Futures Exchange, the Swiss Options & Financial Futures Exchange (SOFFEX), and the Tokyo Grain Exchange all launched automated electronic systems. The next year, the Irish Futures and Options Exchange, the Tokyo International Financial Futures Exchange (TIFFE), the London International Financial Futures Exchange (LIFFE), and the Sydney Futures Exchange (SFE) initiated similar systems. By the end of 1991, ten more exchanges followed suit, including the Deutsche Terminbörse (DTB), the London Futures and Options Exchange, the Swedish Options Market, the Finnish Options Market, and the Mercado Español de Futuros Financieros (MEFF). Indeed, except for Brazil's BM&F and the MATIF in Paris, all new futures exchanges built since 1986 are fully automated.

Alas, in recent years, the process toward technology in futures markets seems to have come to a screeching halt. Suddenly, our market establishment reverted to establishment ways. The evidence to support this conclusion is overwhelming. While Globex volume statistics are growing, they are still pitifully small and the system itself has become enveloped in politics. It still accounts for only 1 percent of the Merc's annual volume. That is about the same percentage as the ACCESS system of the NYMEX. The LIFFE APT system does a little better with about 3 percent of its annual volume, and the MATIF has done much better. Its Globex volume has grown from 5.5 percent in 1993 to 8.7 percent in 1995, proving that technologically the system is sound. Similarly, Sidney's SYCOM system has grown from a 5.1 percent of its volume in 1993, to a 1995 total of 8.9 percent. In contrast, the evening session of the CBOT is losing volume, from 1.6 percent in 1993 to a projected 1.1 percent in 1995.

The low level of screen-based transaction volume on after-hours exchange systems gives testimony to a lack of understanding by many futures exchanges that—like it or not—a screen-based transaction process is in their members' future. While it is comforting to know that the mass of futures liquidity is still on the floor today, it represents a false security blanket. Foreign exchange, a market institutionalized by futures exchanges, offers a stark and sobering comparison between electronic-driven volume and open outcry. The average daily FX turnover measured in U.S. dollars was approximately 200 billion in 1986 compared to 1 trillion in 1995, a 500 percent increase. In the last several years, the world experienced the wildest swings in FX prices ever recorded, accompanied by huge increases in transaction volume. According to figures recently released by the Bank for International Settlements (BIS), the turnover figures for major forex centers in cash markets between 1992 and 1995 (on a net basis, with data adjusted for double counting) shows a whopping increase of 60 percent in London, 46 percent in New York, 34 percent in Tokyo, 43 percent in Singapore, 30 percent in Switzerland, 49 percent in Hong Kong, and 40 percent in Germany. However, CME foreign exchange contracts did not benefit from this growth. It registered a mere 9.5 percent increase in volume in 1993 and another 6-plus percent increase in 1994. While admittedly some of this OTC volume can be attributed to exotics not traded on the exchange, one must accept the fact that OTC screen-based technology is an extremely attractive medium for FX market transactions.

Indeed, it is estimated that overall electronic order matching in foreign exchange has grown from virtually nothing in 1992 to over one-half of FX transactions in 1995. Reuters Holdings revenue from electronic transaction products in both equities and FX experienced an increase of 165 percent from 1990 to 1994. Its Instinet Corporation—whose affiliates are members of 15 exchanges and trade equities in 30 countries—did 20 percent of the Nasdaq's daily volume in 1994. Its 1995 volume shows transactions of 1 billion shares per month. Meanwhile, Reuters Dealing 2000–2 averaged as much as 20,000 FX trades per day in 1995, double its volume over the last four months. And Reuters is no longer alone. Electronic Broking Services (EBS), the consortium made up of some of the world's largest banks and FX dealing institutions—ABN-AMRO, Bank of America, Barclays, Chemical, Citibank, Citicorp, Commerzbank, Credit Suisse, Lehman Brothers, Midland, J.P. Morgan, NatWest, Swiss Bankcorp, and Union Bank of Switzerland—has also come of age. EBS reported that daily volume has risen from 2,000 a year ago to 10,000 recently. Third in line is Minex, a two-year-old Asian consortium backed by Dow Jones/Telerate, Tokyo Forex, and KDD among others, which already accounts for 20 percent of all FX brokering in Tokyo and is doing well in Hong Kong and Singapore.

The global trading day begins in Tokyo and Sydney and is virtually unbroken 24 hours a day, as it moves around through Singapore and Hong Kong to Europe and finally the United States before starting again in Japan.

How can the open-outcry hours of any single exchange hope to capture a significant portion of such business without a continuous screen-based system? Not to mention the fact that the fraud perpetrated on Barings and Daiwa Banks would have been near impossible in any automated trading system or within an electronic data management environment.

While I do not advocate turning off the lights on existing trading floors—that would be unforgivably stupid—it is equally suicidal not to seriously prepare for a technological tomorrow. Whatever progress there has been in recent years was at a snail's pace. In almost every critical area of advanced technological competence, exchanges with trading floors have fallen behind. For instance, LIFFE is the only exchange with real-time clearing capabilities. Futures exchanges are far behind securities exchanges in automatic order routing. No futures exchanges have advanced capabilities for floor communications with brokers and have limited capabilities for handheld price reporting. Only the CBOE has developed a system for handheld terminals. No futures exchanges are developing automatic small-order execution systems. Use of electronic books in the transaction process can be found only at securities exchanges.

And everything within the technological revolution of the last two decades—which produced the present information standard and transformed the world into what we know today—is about to become old if not obsolete. For technology is poised once again to take a quantum leap. The computers that Walter Wriston wrote about and that wired the world in the mid-1980s are about to go wireless in the mid-1990s. Satellites will soon allow wireless communication from anywhere on the planet. When this wireless transformation goes into high gear—over the latter half of this decade—we will literally transfer information over thin air.

Today's cyberwizards have combined the sorcery of electrical and electromagnetic waves, and propelled them at the incredible speed of 300 million meters per second, about three-quarters of the way to the moon with every second. In doing so, they have produced an invisible wave of energy that can carry a computer command, the human voice, or virtually any program including market information, quotations, analysis, and orders from anywhere to anywhere. The new technology will create a world in which applications impossible with wires will result in not just a series of new technological marvels but a spectacular lifestyle emancipation.

By unplugging us from existing infrastructures, networks of information, and communication hookups, we will suddenly have many more choices about where we live, work, or how we trade. This new freedom of wireless communications can be best illustrated with how the simple pager is already transforming our lives. So-called alphanumeric pagers with small LCD screens can show not only a phone number but a complete message. By the end of this year, a so-called bidirectional pager will enable us not only to receive e-mail but to acknowledge these messages by choosing one of the 100 set responses. Think of the possibilities for trading, if the response is buy or sell and is linked into an automated trading system.

Millions of people in African countries are sidestepping their backward infrastructures with cellular phones. Many millions more in China are already using pagers to communicate in places where no wired telephone network exists. Nor will we be limited to the telephone boundaries of today's cellular capabilities. New phone networks, operating by way of satellites, will begin providing round-the-globe service later in this decade. Without the limitation of land-based antennas, everyone on the planet, and especially market traders, will be able to trade from places never before thought possible. Are today's exchanges preparing for this world?

Futures markets take heed! Complacency is the enemy. Tomorrow's futures traders grew up with Nintendo and Sega. They were given a keyboard for their fifth birthdays; their homework was done on a computer; their recreation time was spent in video centers; the World Wide Web was their playground; Cyberspeak is their language.

When the current transformation process has been completed, when we have crossed the bridge to the new reality, when the new set of rules has been written, futures will still be a primary way to manage financial risk, but it will be carried out on the information superhighway. Tomorrow's traders will likely execute a complex set of trades from an interactive multidimensional wireless communication system representing the coalescence of key communications technologies: television, telephone, personal computer, and laser storage systems. The only question remaining is whether those trades will still be transacted on our futures exchanges.

CHAPTER 13

Reminiscences of a Refugee

We are all but a product of our parents, our education, and our experiences.

I was only nine when we arrived in the United States, but what an unusual history I had already endured. I was party to a miraculous escape—the only family to escape from Bialystok, Poland, intact at the outbreak of World War II. I was the product of fear, danger, strategy, and luck. I had witnessed my parents playing hide and seek with the Gestapo and the KGB. I had spent two weeks on the Trans-Siberian railroad and traversed three-quarters of the way around the globe. I had been taught in six languages: Yiddish, Polish, Lithuanian, Russian, Japanese, and English. I had been baptized into my parents' movement whose ideal was human dignity and equality for all. And I had learned firsthand the harsh realities of political dictatorship. While I had a great deal of trouble with playing baseball in my new homeland or adjusting to new friends and a new social order, I had forged an inner resolve that would see me through.

In a very real sense, I was saved from the ovens of Treblinka by the eighteenth-century philosopher Moses Mendelssohn, the little hunchback from the Dessau ghetto in Germany and grandfather of composer Felix Mendelssohn. Mendelssohn together with dramatist Gotthold Lessing had become the pioneers of Jewish emancipation and advocated that Judaism must leave the ghetto.

It was this movement, a century later, that snared my father, Isaac Moishe Melamdovich, and mother, Feygl Barakin, into its current and carried them into the era of new enlightenment. In doing so, the movement wrestled them away from the all-consuming religious moorings of the shtetl and replaced it with an ethnic identity based on biblical morality, the printed word, the Yiddish language, and the ideals of one of the prevalent political movements of the day.

Friends of the Chicago Public Library, Freedom to Read Award, Union League Club, Chicago, November 1, 1996.

My parents were ardent Bundistn, a Jewish faction of the Socialist movement that fought for the working man, was adamantly opposed to communism, and was eternally committed to preserving Yiddish as the language of the Jewish masses. Indeed, my parents were both Yiddish school teachers in the parochial schools of Bialystok. Their new bible included the writings of the giants of Jewish literature: *Sholem Aleichem* (*Peace be with you*—Salomon Rabinovitch—from the original *Sholom Nochem Veviks*) on whose writings *Fiddler on the Roof* is based; *Mendele Mocher Sforim* (*Mendel the Bookseller*—Shalom Jacob Abramowits); and Itzchok L. Peretz, the philosopher-writer who taught the Jewish masses that morality was the highest of all the commandments.

My parents were among the intellectuals of Poland, leaders in a movement that demanded equal rights for Jews along with all nationalities. They were building a new utopian world, one based on freedom of thought and equality for all. The movement had catapulted my father to its forefront and resulted in his election to Bialystok's City Council; for a Jew, an honor without parallel. My mother was one of the pioneers of the modern women's movement, outspoken in social affairs and an equal breadwinner in our household. Indeed, one of her favorite songs was Beethoven's Ninth Choral symphony with Friedrich von Schiller's words, "Alle Menchen Seinen Breeder," "All humans are brothers."

Alas, on September 1, 1939, the Nazis marched into Poland, shattered Schiller's ideal and all normalcy. Although at the time we didn't know it, our destiny was to be doomed along with 6 million other Jews of Eastern Europe.

Miraculously fate intervened. Moses Mendelssohn's movement had provided my father with an escape route. Bialystok councilmen, my father included, were advised to leave the city lest they be taken as hostages by the Nazis. My father had to make the painfully difficult decision to escape and leave his wife and only child behind. Fortunately he did. It was the first of many life-or-death decisions made by Isaac Melamdovich over the course of the next two years. They were decisions in a chain of events that led the Melamdoviches out of the clutches of both the Nazis and the Bolsheviks, across the steppes of Siberia, through Japan courtesy of Ambassador Sugihara, and eventually to the freedom of these shores.

But no transition of this magnitude is without pain. Although Chicago was a far cry from what was experienced by the generations of immigrants who were thrust into the tenements of New York's Lower East Side, there were many similarities and common ordeals. This was especially true for the children who, like myself, were unmercifully immersed in a foreign environment and left to cope with the unvarnished and often cruel demands of their fellow compatriots. Indeed, I was a struggling, unhappy, greenhorn kid until I entered Roosevelt High School on the North Side of Chicago.

Suddenly, it was as if I were reincarnated. No one knew of my refugee history, no one cared. At last I was accepted as an equal.

Life in Chicago's inner city for teens during the late 1940s was right out of J.D. Salinger's *Catcher in the Rye*. We hung around the neighborhood drugstore, we had social and athletic clubs; we had best friends and worst enemies; we played baseball and basketball; we dated, loved, and tried to make it with girls; we drove old beat-up cars; we jitterbugged and crooned with Frankie Lane, Peggy Lee, Perry Como, and Frank Sinatra; we listened to the radio soaps and thrived on the adventures of Tom Mix, Captain Midnight, and Jack Armstrong.

Then came the 1950s and, while none of us knew it at the time (no one does while it is happening), those were undoubtedly the best years of our lives. Just as *Diner* and other movies of note attempt to depict the years following the end of World War II, life was relatively simple, well organized, and pleasant. You followed the rules—whether it was the rules of your family, your social sphere, or the neighborhood. Although as young adults we sometimes experimented with the forbidden and often skirted the niceties of the social structure, we knew where the lines were drawn and, for the most part, did not transgress them. Although there was great social strife around us, it didn't frighten us; although there were street gangs, the inner city streets were still safe; although there were reefers, there was really no drug problem. Most of all, government was still "good" and federal officials still respected.

And when we entered college, there was a world of literature to be consumed: Lawrence Durrell, Ernest Hemingway, Aldous Huxley, James Joyce, D.H. Lawrence, Thomas Mann, Henry Miller, Erich Maria Remarque, and so many others that one's lifetime seemed far too short. These literary greats became our personal friends, offering us a never-ending parallel, albeit informal course of education. It is this beholdency to literature that makes tonight's Chicago Public Library's Freedom to Read Award so exceptionally meaningful to me. Books were always a profound part of my life, I suppose a consequence of my parents' deep-seated respect for education and literature—after all, they were teachers first and foremost.

And, as I noted in *Escape to the Futures*, my zeal for education had a very practical application in advancing the cause of futures markets. Futures were an arcane and mysterious neck of the woods that most of the world considered a sub-rosa activity, best left to the zany and the gamblers. We were shunned, not only by the public at large, not only by our respected cousins on Wall Street, whose activities were really not so dissimilar, but even by the financial media:

"It's ludicrous to think that foreign exchange can be entrusted to a bunch of pork belly crapshooters," so proclaimed a prominent New York banker back in 1972 on the eve of the Merc's launch of the International Monetary Market.

"The New Currency Market: Strictly for Crapshooters," echoed *Business-Week*.

And the respected *Economist* in 1976 compared the International Monetary Market (IMM) to Linda Lovelace, the girl with the deep throat. How dare we, it asked, trade the sacred Treasury bill on the same floor with pork bellies.

Derogatory comments, defamatory innuendos, inflammatory jokes, false accusations, misleading opinions, half-truths, out-and-out lies—such has been the burden and fate of futures markets. And why not? From time immemorial, predicting the future has been a hazardous occupation. "Behead the messenger of bad tidings!"

As a result, I knew that our only hope was in education of the public and made it a permanent fixture at the Merc: workshops, seminars, global symposia, the publication of books, brochures, trading analysis, the establishment of programs and courses at colleges and universities, grants for fellowships and studies, lecturers, educational programs, and even permanent university chairs for the study of futures.

But I've gotten ahead of the story. Back in the 1950s there was also politics. In our college crowd, political interaction, whether by personal involvement or simply by way of heated discussion, was a holy and daily ritual. I was more fortunate than most. What better way to learn civics than to experience the Joe McCarthy era from the vantage point of John Marshall Law School. Gunner Joe represented a very real danger to the basic tenets of individual freedom, and this was critical to law students who, by definition, were ardent protagonists of the American ideal and for whom the Bill of Rights was a holy sacrament.

Indeed, for college students of the 1950s era, the civil rights movement that unfolded wasn't a mere intellectual exercise—something to be studied, to write essays about, and to answer questions about—it was a living monument, an everyday event, a happening in real time. There was a revolution in the making before our very eyes and the world was never to be the same. We were online witnesses and participants—marchers in the marches, singers of the songs—*We Shall Overcome!* Montgomery, Alabama, Martin Luther King Jr., Governor Orval Faubus, sit-ins and boycotts, Justice William Brennan, the National Guard in Little Rock: Those weren't historical references, they were our everyday newspaper headlines.

Earl Warren was appointed as Chief Justice of the Supreme Court by President Eisenhower just as I entered law school. What better way to study the magnitude of *Brown v. Board of Education*—that segregation was a violation of the equal protection clause of the 14th Amendment to the

U.S. Constitution—than from within Professor Braunfeld's classroom where constitutional law was alive and the only subject that mattered.

But constitutional law meant much, much more for me than the 14th Amendment: It put into focus for this law student the rights of the individual as measured against the rights of the state. Constitutional law became an intellectual learning experience that opened for me an entire new thought process and a roadway to my understanding of capitalism. Whereas my father's socialism focused on the betterment of society as a whole, capitalism focused on the betterment of the individual to the benefit of society as a whole. This proved to be a cataclysmic revelation and caused a revolutionary reversal in my inherited beliefs. Ultimately it brought this young patriot to the realization that the socialistic concepts of his parents were in conflict with precepts of the free market and contrary to the very essence of the American success story—and were wrong!

One day I privately confronted my father on this issue. He and I quite often engaged in serious discussions of a political or social nature. Sometimes these discussions became quite heated, and on occasion ended in shouting matches that to my children, who watched from a respectful distance, no doubt seemed like arguments of a life-threatening nature. Actually, I considered my father the smartest man I ever met, our discussions notwithstanding. His instinctive feel for an idea or situation was nothing short of uncanny.

In most matters, my father, who was highly opinionated, would take the so called traditional European and *intellectual* side, and I, what was to him the modern American and *superficial* point of view. For instance, one of his favorite topics was the American preoccupation with sports, which to his way of thinking, except that which was practiced in school, was a complete waste of time; anyone sitting around listening or watching a sports event was allowing his brain to atrophy. In similar fashion, but to a much harsher degree, he detested card-playing of any sort, which for him was the unquestionable work of the devil and a direct path to a life of depravation and sin. My love of tournament bridge was a source of unending grief to my father and a topic of constant discussion.

But on this occasion my father was unusually subdued and thoughtful. Yes, he admitted, in America some of the old notions under socialism had less validity, but, he explained, it was a hard-fought-for transformation: The workers of America had won most of the demands which he and his fellow European socialists had stood for and never achieved. It took, he said, the American union movement and socialist ideals to overturn the sweatshop mentality of the early 1900s. Now, my father agreed, an individual had the ability to pursue his or her own dreams, which could result in a betterment of society as a whole.

Not too many years later, the economic lessons and theory learned in constitutional law at John Marshall Law School could suddenly be put into practice. The floor of the Chicago Mercantile Exchange became the laboratory. But by then, this student of law had fervently embraced Milton Friedman's conviction that the story of the United States was a story of two separate but interdependent miracles: an economic miracle and a political miracle. Each miracle based on a separate set of revolutionary ideas, both of which by a curious coincidence were formulated in 1776.

One set of ideas was embodied in Adam Smith's *The Wealth of Nations*. It established that an economic system could succeed only in an environment that allowed the freedom of individuals to pursue their own objectives for purely personal gain. The second set of ideas, drafted by Thomas Jefferson, was embodied in the Declaration of Independence. It proclaimed a set of self-evident truths: *that all men are created equal, that they are endowed by their Creator with certain unalienable Rights; that among these are Life, Liberty, and the pursuit of Happiness*. The success of our nation, as Milton Friedman asserted and Merton Miller will certainly attest, is a consequence of the combination of these two basic ideals. Economic freedom coupled with political freedom. One without the other cannot work.

As chairman of the Chicago Mercantile Exchange, this graduate of John Marshall Law School was provided an opportunity to implement these ideals in an exchange that was but a backwater marketplace with a questionable future, dealing in butter, eggs, and onions. The process involved some diverse and special ingredients:

First, as I already mentioned, it required a modern rule book, for without law and order, no economic house can exist. Next it required a bit of imagination coupled with a healthy dose of innovation. Then it needed a great deal of good luck. As futures traders, all we ever asked for was maybe a little war, some pestilence, a couple of floods, an occasional famine. On this occasion the Almighty was very generous. We were benefactors of a world in chaos. I daresay, if ever one needed proof that "necessity is the mother of invention," one need only review the economic disorders leading up to and following the creation of the International Monetary Market.

For a setting, there was, of course the breakdown of Bretton Woods, the system of fixed exchange rates. Then on August 15, 1971, President Nixon closed the gold window, releasing a seismic economic shock with financial reverberations to be felt even a decade later. This precipitated unprecedented economic disarray, which included the oil embargo of 1973. What followed was an era of financial turmoil rarely equaled in modern history: The U.S. dollar plunged; U.S. unemployment reached in excess of 10 percent; oil prices skyrocketed to $39 a barrel; the Dow Industrial Average fell to 570; gold reached $800 an ounce; U.S. inflation climbed to 20 percent; and interest rates went even higher.

For us it was a virtual paradise. These events ensured that the IMM's formula for successful innovation based on necessity of the times would be a sure-fire success. Indeed, in May of 1986, precisely 14 years after its inception, Merton H. Miller bestowed upon the IMM a supreme and unparalleled honor by nominating financial futures as "the most significant financial innovation of the last twenty years."

The process also required people who could be molded into an army, an army of traders—for no one person alone could do what had to be done. They came from all walks of life, and as I stated in *Escape*, they had two common denominators: tenacity and a dream! I described them in this little poem which I read at the IMM's 10th anniversary:

> Who were we?
> We were a bunch of guys who were hungry.
> We were traders to whom it did not matter—
> whether it was eggs or gold, bellies or
> the British pound, turkeys or T-bills.
> We were babes in the woods, innocents—
> in a world we did not understand,
> too dumb to be scared.
> We were audacious, brazen, raucous pioneers-
> too unworldly to know we could not win.
> That the odds against us were too high;
> That the banks would never trust us;
> That the government would never let us;
> That Chicago was the wrong place.

The final ingredient was a tribute to my parents' equality ideal. The markets we built epitomized Schiller's *Alle Menchen Seinen Breeder*. No, it is not utopia yet, but I know of no other private sector establishment that is more free of human prejudice and less concerned with race, gender, or religion than are the free market structures of American finance.

Indeed, tonight's master of ceremonies, Terry Savage, is a first-class example of the Merc's nondiscrimination ideology—and living proof of the equality between genders. In 1967, one of my first actions was to expunge the discriminatory rule at the Merc which prohibited floor participation by females. Terry was one of the early women to come to our pits, hold her ground with the male traders, and learned economics from the bottom up. As I stated in the book, Terry was smart enough to parlay her acquired trading skills into a career as a superb national business newscaster. Similarly, my personal friend and former bridge partner Carol (Mickey) Norton, who was the first lady trader at the IMM—indeed, the first in futures markets.

She too never gave an inch in the male-dominated world of futures, and became one of the outstanding traders of the era.

Yes, in our markets, the trophy goes not to the Catholic or the Jew, not to the white or the black, not to the man or the woman, it goes to those who understand the economic principles of supply and demand. No, it is not utopia yet, but in Chicago's financial markets it is not what you are—your personal pedigree, your family origin, your physical infirmities, your gender—but your ability to determine what the customer wants and where the market is headed. Little else matters.

As an eight-year old sitting on that Trans-Siberian train and staring out the window for days on end, I could no more imagine the course my life would take—that I would escape to the futures—than I can today discern what the world will be like, say, 50 years from now. We are all captives of events and circumstances over which we have so little control. In my case, fortune was most generous. It offered me the opportunity to partake in the American miracle. And if this refugee has in any small way contributed to the precepts of Thomas Jefferson and principles of Adam Smith, he is humbled, but it is not to his credit. He is after all but a product of his parents, his education, and his experiences.

CHAPTER 14

The Need for Futures Markets in an Emerging World Economy

"The Mediterranean is the ocean of the past, the Atlantic the ocean of the present and the Pacific the ocean of the future," so said John Hay, the American Secretary of State at the turn of the century. While it can certainly be argued that the future took its good time in getting here, make no mistake, the future of the Pacific Rim has arrived.

Today, the countries of the Pacific Rim represent a combination of developed and developing nations that jointly embody an economic force equal to any region of the world. "Today," states John Naisbitt, in his *Megatrends 2000*, "the Pacific Rim is undergoing the fastest period of economic expansion in history, growing at five times the growth rate during the industrial revolution."

The geographic area involved is as large as it is diverse. By its all-inclusive definition, it accounts for two-fifths of the world's surface and nearly half of the world's population. By any standard, the nations that encompass the Pacific Rim are dissimilar in many fundamental respects, with differences ranging from culture to political systems to economic orders. Their differences also run the gamut from those, in the words of the *Economist*, that are "as rich and stable as Japan and as poor and turbulent as China, as big and open as America and as small and closed as North Korea."

Japan is, of course, the financial colossus of region encompassing a vast and complex business infrastructure which includes some of the world's largest securities firms and banks. Australia and New Zealand provide the anchor on the South. Australia, almost as large as the continental U.S., is more British than Asian but its location makes it imperative for the continent

---

Presented at the Future of Fund Management in India 1998, Second Annual Conference, Mumbai, India, April 16–17, The Taj Mahal Hotel.

137

to think Asian. The newly industrialized countries, or NICs as they are sometimes called, include Singapore, Hong Kong, South Korea, and Taiwan. Hong Kong, of course, will revert back to China in 1997 and become an uncommon segment of this vast and underdeveloped giant. Then there are the members of the Association of South East Asian Nations, which include Indonesia, Malaysia, the Philippines, and Thailand.

Although there are many ties other than geographical between these nations, for the purposes of this publication there is a sufficient common denominator based on a similar economic evolution which brought some of these states to employ or consider employing the markets of futures and options. While their current experience with these markets is of recent vintage, as most learned observers are aware, futures markets are nothing new to the region. Indeed, it was in Japan during the Edo period (1600–1867) that centralized futures markets were born. The place was Osaka, where feudal lords established warehouses to store and sell rice that was paid to them as land tax by their villagers. In 1730, to protect themselves from wide price fluctuations between harvests, these merchants established the Dojima Rice Market, the first organized futures exchange.

Over the span of the next 200 years, there were from time to time some small agriculturally based futures markets in Japan. However, it was not until the birth of the Sidney Futures Exchange (SFE) in 1960 that futures again made their presence felt in the Pacific Rim. The SFE was also the first Asian futures exchange to launch a financial contract in 1979. Then came the critical catalyst in the modern development of futures and options markets in the Pacific basin; it was the revolutionary link in 1984 between Singapore's SIMEX and the Chicago Mercantile Exchange (CME). This innovation served to spur the race for financial futures dominance in the region. A year later, Japan re-entered the futures markets arena in a meaningful fashion when the Tokyo Stock Exchange (TSE) launched its successful Japanese Government Bond contract. This important event was quickly followed by the inception of futures trading at the Osaka Securities Exchange (OSE) and the birth of the Tokyo International Financial Futures Exchange (TIFFE). There was no stopping the process now. The community of nations of the Pacific Rim had fully embraced the financial futures revolution.

Nor could it be otherwise. The vibrancy and native talent of Pacific-based populations, the wealth achieved as a consequence of decades of successful manufacturing and export, the resulting potential of their financial centers, all combined to make the region a vast store of financial strength and a force equal to any in the world. This expanding base of capital markets could not continue very long or compete on a global scale without the development of futures markets. The advent of globalization, greater interdependence, modern telecommunications capabilities, instant informational flows, immediate recognition of financial risks and opportunities, and intensified competition made the management of risk an essential prerequisite of success for every financial community. To address this new financial imperative, it was mandatory for the nations of the Pacific Rim to turn to the unique mechanisms provided by futures and options markets.

It was axiomatic. The financial futures revolution, launched in Chicago in 1972, blazed the trail for much of what has since followed in world capital centers. The CME was the first major exchange to recognize the significance of the demise of the Bretton Woods Agreement, the post–World War II pact that instituted a fixed exchange rate regime for the major world nations. To capture the potential of the free market epoch that was about to ensue, the CME created the International Monetary Market (IMM), the first futures exchange for the specific purpose of trading in financial instruments. The era of financial futures was thus born. While the new wave of futures began with currency contracts, it was quickly followed by futures contracts on U.S. government securities—Treasury bills at the Merc, and Ginnie Mae certificates and Treasury bonds at the Chicago Board of Trade (CBOT). Later, when in the early 1980s the concept of cash settlement in lieu of physical delivery was instituted, the stage was set for the CME's introduction of Eurodollar futures. This led the way for stock index futures and initiated the era of index markets.

The financial futures revolution was destined to profoundly alter the history of markets. It established that there was a need for a new genre of risk management tools suitable for sophisticated strategies and responsive to professional and institutional money management. As a consequence, it proved the necessity of futures and options within the infrastructure of finance and alongside other traditional structures of capital markets. Most significantly, from their inception, the markets of futures and options understood and embraced the common denominator of recent world upheavals: the spectacular advances in technology. Clearly, no other single factor was more instrumental in influencing political and economic change than was the technological revolution of recent years.

On the political front, modern telecommunications fostered instant mass and personal informational flows in total disregard of national boundaries. It offered everyone a stark, uncompromising comparison of political and economic life, making it nearly impossible for governments to hide the truth from its people. On the economic front, modern telecommunications made instantaneous price information available to everyone around the globe and fostered massive capital flows in unencumbered fashion. It dramatically changed the nature of global capital markets forever. The markets of futures and options recognized this march of technology, understood its inexorable impact on commerce and trade, and willingly adapted to its demands. It is no accident that our markets thus represent one of the greatest growth arenas of the last two decades.

As logic would dictate, events in Eastern Europe and the Soviet Union during the last several years have dramatically confirmed the significance of the financial history of the last two decades. The bankruptcy of command economic order, the downfall of communist rule, and the collapse of the Soviet empire serve as undeniable testimony to the value of capitalism and market driven economics. The markets of futures and options are integral to that victory. Indeed, what markets better epitomize price determination by virtue of the free forces of supply and demand than do the markets of futures and options?

During the past decade, beginning with the 1982 establishment of the London International Financial Futures Exchange (LIFFE), new financial futures exchanges have opened in virtually every major world financial center, including the Marché à Terme International de France (MATIF) in Paris, the Swiss Options and Financial Futures Exchange (SOFFEX) in Zurich, the Deutsche Terminbörse (DTB) in Frankfurt, not to mention the exchanges in the Pacific Rim itself. The dramatic success of this history prompted Nobel laureate Merton Miller, University of Chicago professor of finance, to nominate financial futures as "the most significant financial innovation of the last twenty years."

Indeed, if financial futures and options were not yet in place, they would have to be invented:

- They are indispensable in a world that demands the ability to swiftly institute complex strategies or to cost-effectively adjust portfolio exposure between securities and cash.
- They are ideally suited for a world where tailored risk management strategies are on the increase and where opportunities rapidly appear and disappear on a constantly changing financial horizon.
- They are a vital option in a world in which it is often imperative to utilize a creditworthy mechanism that preserves credit lines.
- They are without equal in providing a vast array of products combined with an envious measure of liquidity and an incomparably narrow bid/ask spread.
- Finally and most significantly, they are well positioned for a world where professional money management is the wave of the future.

Thus, what was imperative for the financial structures of other global regions became equally imperative for the Pacific basin. Nor should we forget that the process is incomplete. Some of the Pacific Rim communities are just beginning to emerge from their formative development stage. More to the point, the vast financial potential of mainland China is yet to be unleashed. Is there any doubt that the same forces which brought about the downfall of command order economics in the Soviet Union will achieve a similar result in China? Is there any doubt that its highly competent people will someday in the coming decade join the market rebirths occasioned by the other Asian populations? I daresay no. And, when it happens, it will exponentially affect the strength and vitality of the Pacific Rim.

Although there are some heavy macroeconomic clouds overhead, the long-term direction in the evolution of global markets is unmistakable. In a world where the distinctions between the major time zones has vanished, in a world where geographical borders that once could limit the flow of capital are but history, in a world where traditional internal protections that could insulate one's citizenry from external price and value influences are no longer valid, in such a world market-driven economic order is quintessential and futures and options a critical component. For the expanding region such as the Pacific Rim, with its vast and diverse cultures and infrastructure, and with its still-untapped and developing potential, there can be no other course.

*   *   *

This leads us directly to the recent problems and controversies in Southeast Asia. Last August, an Indonesian newspaper close to the government ran an advertisement with a picture of a currency trader wearing a terrorist mask made of American $100 bills. "Defend the Rupiah," the ad urged. "Defend Indonesia." Indeed, recent financial troubles in Southeast Asia have resulted in some of its leaders accusing currency speculation as the main culprit of their problems. Nothing new about that. Currency speculators have been a convenient scapegoat throughout the centuries whenever government policies fail and a country's currency begins to devalue.

The main villain in the current attack has been George Soros, the billionaire financier who is clearly the most colorful and notorious of the speculator lot. Soros was called a "moron" and a "rogue" by Malaysian prime minister Mahathir Mohamad at the recent IMF World Bank Conference in Hong Kong. He declared that "currency trading is unnecessary, unproductive, and immoral . . . and should be made illegal." He accused the "great powers" of pressing Asian countries to open their markets and then manipulating their currencies to knock them off as competitors.

Serious accusations. Unfortunately, they rang a bit hollow. They came from a man who loudly applauded his government's string of economic successes of recent years—built on foreign capital—and who pronounced grandiose plans to build airports, dams, and a Southeast Asian Silicon Valley. The same leader who gladly used foreign investments to build the world's tallest building, Southeast Asia's largest airport, and harbored visions of a glittering new capital.

Suddenly he sings a different tune. Now he proclaims his theory of Western desires to suppress Asian competitors. The reason for his change in opinion is obvious. After a decade of advances in this region's journey toward open and efficient markets, serious problems have erupted. Indeed, Southeast Asia was and still is in a financial crisis. It began in Thailand, one of the most successful of the "tiger" economies which attracted billions of dollars in foreign investment, more than it could wisely invest. Thailand's currency, the ringgit, has plunged 30 percent against the dollar, its banking system began to creak, and the Thai stock market crashed. Foreign investors fled, and the crisis quickly spread to Indonesia and Malaysia. It is instructive to examine why this happened, what mistakes were made, and how to avoid them.

While there have been financial crises before—Latin America in the early 1980s and Mexico in 1995—the feel of what has happened in Southeast Asia is in some ways quite different. From afar, it is easy to think of Asia as a seamless whole. But, in fact, it is made up of distinct regional economies that these days find themselves competing against one another. The explosive boom in exports to the developed world from low-wage China, for instance, is a large part the underlying cause of Southeast Asia's slump. A few years ago, the VCRs, televisions, and toys that lined the shelves of American stores most likely had a *Made in Thailand* or *Made in Malaysia* label. Today they say *Made in China*.

Asia's southeastern emerging markets unfortunately came to regard the private foreign investors as a virtually unlimited source of funds. Only seven years ago, private investment in developing nations around the world was a mere $30 billion, compared with official development aid of nearly $65 billion. Now the proportions are starkly different. Official aid has declined to $45 billion last year, and private investment ballooned to roughly $245 billion. When the money was flowing in, Asian leaders had no complaints. They were being rewarded, they said, for hard work, rising productivity, and emergence of an educated middle class that saved at rates that put Americans to shame. Now that the money has begun to flow the other way, leaving many countries with huge debts denominated in dollars that must be paid back with devalued local currencies, their attitudes have begun to change. Quickly the argument has become a debate over "Asian values" versus "Western values." Never mind the facts. Never mind that the market always reacts to perceived realities. Never mind that the credit rating of Malaysian paper was lowered by Standard & Poor's from stable to negative because of Malaysian reluctance to curb rapid credit growth when inflation was building in the economy.

It is always easier to blame currency problems on speculators than to admit to excessive government spending or lax monetary policy. And the perfect whipping boy in all this is the United States, the champion of financial liberalization. Thus it was left for U.S. Treasury Secretary Robert Rubin to lead the defense on behalf of free markets during the Hong Kong conference. He remained the standard-bearer of Western view that markets impose discipline on nations, economies, and, most of all, politicians. His 26 years in investment banking at Goldman Sachs & Company steeped him in the belief that markets go to extremes but that, in the long run, they reward countries that keep their houses in order and punish those that do not. He countered Mr. Mahathir by saying that currency speculation is "part of the total activity in secondary markets" which "increases liquidity and lowers costs."

The real problem in Southeast Asia is not George Soros. It's the lack of sound economic policies, sober banking practices, and open markets. Put simply, Southeast Asian nations were living beyond their means. It began with several years of excessive money and credit growth. The problem was accentuated when huge amounts of foreign capital in the form of loans and direct investments poured into the region. All this encouraged the local population to spend freely and splurge on imported goods. The predictable result was that the countries' trade deficits ballooned and their currencies came under severe pressure. The gravest deficiency was inadequate government supervision, particularly in the Thai banking sector. This was a formula for serious trouble. "We became too rich too quickly," said Thai Finance Minister Thanong Bidaya, in a display of abject honesty.

Of course, we don't need to feel sorry for George Soros. He was fully capable of defending himself and did. The outspoken financier was eminently correct when he said that the Malaysian prime minister's suggestion to ban currency trading is so inappropriate that it does not deserve serious consideration. "He is using me," declared Soros, "as a scapegoat to cover up his own failure." A failure that was exacerbated when Prime Minister Mahathir ordered restrictions on short sales and moved to prop up stock prices for Malaysians, but not for foreign investors. That led investors to flee, and Mr. Mahathir was soon forced to make a sharp reverse turn. But the damage to his country's financial credibility was done and will last for a long time. As Soros told the government officials who gathered in Hong Kong, "Interfering with the convertibility of capital at a moment like this is a recipe for disaster."

CHAPTER 15

Panel on the Stock Market Crash of 1987

Thank you very much, Tony. I am delighted to be part of this important conference and to be included in this prestigious panel.

I do not have any prepared remarks. Instead, I am going to go back and forth between my memories of the past, thoughts about the present, and hopefully provide a bit of a peek into the future as it relates to financial markets.

I can embrace most of what Nick Brady and Jerry Corrigan said this morning. The three of us have had numerous occasions over these years since 1987 to reflect on those times. During that period, we saw each other often, sometimes more than we wished, but often enough to recognize the similarity of the lessons we learned, and to respect each other's opinion on most of the matters involved.

Let me also state that as a representative of futures markets, I probably saw Bob Glauber more than anybody during those times. On more than one occasion, during the time Nick Brady was leading the so-called "Brady Task Force," I was thankful that Bob Glauber was there because often he was one of the very few who understood that "futures" represented a market, and not simply something about "tomorrow." In fact, I'm not at all certain how many futures exchanges Nick Brady had visited previous to his visit to the Merc directly after the crash. That visit stands out in my memory.

It was about a week after the crash and we who were about to receive Nick Brady were very concerned. To put it mildly, often members of the New York market community came with a built-in negative bias about futures. So we were apprehensive and wanted to make a good impression. We were

With Nicholas Brady (Former U.S. Secretary of the Treasury), and Gerald Corrigan (Former President of the Federal Reserve Bank of New York). Brookings-Wharton Papers on Financial Services First Annual Conference, Washington, DC, October 29, 1997.

lucky in that visit. Not only did it go very well, Mr. Brady unexpectedly gave us an opportunity to shine.

As the Merc officials and the Brady Task Force officials sat around the Merc's boardroom table, it became obvious that Nick Brady was very concerned that the market may have more to fall and that things could get worse.

"When is the next shoe going to fall?" he asked.

I had thought about that question often and had come to a conclusion. "I think both shoes are off!" I replied.

He was surprised at the certainty of my answer. "How can you tell?" he asked.

"I do not know," I said. "It's my trader's instinct. I think all the air is out of the system."

Fortunately, in the days and weeks that followed, that turned out to be right. I was lucky, but I think it impressed Mr. Brady.

The second thing that must have impressed the head of the Brady Task Force during that visit was when he asked how long it would take us at the Merc to give him a complete transcript of all the transactions of October 19 and 20. Nick had been a professional in the securities markets and was used to the fact that a complete transaction record of the trades on any given day at the New York Stock Exchange would take a very, very long time to produce. Indeed, it actually took years before the NYSE produced the full record. Still, Brady knew that in order to complete the Brady Report, he would need to know all of the facts, the figures, and the statistics of what happened during those critical days—not just in New York, but in our markets in Chicago as well.

Imagine Nick Brady's surprise when in response to his question, our president, Bill Brodsky, who winked at me with a smile, responded, "How about before you leave?"

Actually, that answer epitomized one of the main differences between futures markets and securities markets. While that difference has been significantly corrected since then, at that time futures markets, in contrast to their New York counterparts, represented a market that was almost always current—not only in flashing the immediate S&P futures price, but in its ability to instantly provide the facts, figures, and statistics about the transactions. We knew almost everything the following morning. Not only the exact prices and times of the transactions, but who did what to whom, and how. And, as a result, we knew with certainty the following morning that futures were not the culprit as the media portrayed us and as much of the world believed in the aftermath.

That is what the world thought. So much so that Congressman Ed Markey, of Massachusetts, I believe, made a public statement to the effect that: "We have found the culprit and it is index arbitrage." He could not have been more incorrect. We could confirm with exactitude the next morning what some of us knew intuitively even on October 19, 1987—that there was very little index arbitrage going on. How could there be? The New York Stock Exchange had never really opened. Oh, the lights were on and the air conditioning was working, but there was hardly any trading. You cannot have index arbitrage unless you have a cash market. And there was none. For hours, many of the NYSE specialists did not or could not open a multitude of major stocks. And index arbitrage cannot be done without two markets: One must buy in one market and sell in the other. By definition, you cannot arbitrage against only one market.

Thus, I and many of our officials knew that in reality there was hardly any index arbitrage going on. I was watching the index arbitragers. They were holding their hands in their pockets. What could they do? As the statistics later confirmed, there was no more than 10 percent index arbitrage on October 19. Ninety percent of the sales that occurred were direct sales by investors.

Our market opened on time and there was a price. Problem was, no one liked what the price was saying. But there was a price, and the price correctly reflected what the buyers and sellers were willing to do. It was horrible. It was the most frightening moment in my life, but at least there was a price. We answered the telephone. Our traders were in the pit. Hardly anyone left.

Clearly, there was one big lesson of the 1987 crash. As the Brady Report said, "We are one market." Yes we are, totally connected, not just New York and Chicago, but worldwide.

Witness what happened this very week during the minor Asian contagion which spread across the world from the East to the West, from Hong Kong to New York, to Chicago. The world again reacted to it just as we expect all humans to do—just as happens when someone shouts "Fire!" in a crowded theater.

In recent months and weeks, while prominent stock market analysts at Goldman Sachs and other places kept saying that it cannot happen, I was conscious of something wrong with that statement. Because emotion takes over whenever greed and fear are in contention. Emotion has not been outlawed, nor has panic or greed or fear. As long as there are human beings, there will be expected reactions based on greed and fear and market crashes.

I do not know one specific cause of the crash of 1987. As Mr. Corrigan indicated, there was no specific cause. There were a combination of causes. But the cause certainly was not the futures market.

The one major difference between 1987 and 1997 is that today we immediately knew that no one would be blaming futures. And no one did. One marked difference between then and now is that the exchanges and market participants are much, much more technologically advanced. We can all better handle the influx of large volumes. The NYSE, in particular, has greatly advanced since 1987. But perhaps the greatest difference between then and now is that today the world has a much better understanding of OTC derivatives and futures markets, their differences, their importance, and their interaction with each other and the cash market. The knowledge that has permeated the financial communities about futures, options, OTC derivatives, and the cash markets is light-years different than what anyone knew ten years ago. Credit academia, credit the information revolution, and credit the media.

Mr. Brady still has his fear of derivatives and leverage. I do not blame him. I do too. In fact, we both agree on that more than he probably realizes. I too recognize that there is a certain unknown degree about leverage that is out there, what it can do and how it will react and impact the markets during an emergency. But, as he correctly stated, "The genie is out of the bottle." There is nothing any of us—including Jerry Corrigan—can do about that, even if we wanted to. Financial OTC derivatives and exchange-traded futures are with us for the foreseeable future, and we must learn what we can about them and to live with them.

This has been an extraordinary century—and here we are at its end. It was a century during which mankind traveled from the big to the little. For instance, in physics, in 1905, Albert Einstein taught us about relativity, the universe—the very big. And from there we went to discover the atoms, electrons, and protons. Enter quantum mechanics. Later we dug deeper and unearthed quarks and leptons—the very, very little. In biology, the same happened. We began the century learning about the human body. We learned about cells and thought they were the ultimate element within the human body. Then we discovered genes. Enter gene engineering. We learned to look inside the genes and discovered we could break them open. We learned how to manipulate genes and create living things—even sheep.

So you see, it was a century in which we went from the big to the little. The central reason, of course, was the advancement in technology and the invention of the computer. And what happened in physics and biology also happened in markets. In 1972, when we launched a market in currency futures, we launched a big financial instrument. Currency markets, Eurodollars, stock index instruments—the big financial tickets. Today's quants use their computers to create 14 separate little derivatives which are the equivalent to the Deutsche mark. Forget the currency market, forget the Deutsche mark, forget the Eurodollar; these guys can create what ever you want through the computer. The derivatives they create in markets are the financial equivalent to the creation of sheep in biology. Yes, again from the big to the little. So, the genie is out of the bottle. You are not going to change that.

Right now, as we sit in this room, there are thousands of financial engineers creating new financial derivatives, products we never heard of with names we cannot even pronounce. And yes, a lot of that creates leverage. And I too worry about that. Indeed, if Jerry Corrigan tells you that we should be vigilant, he knows what he is saying. And I agree. But we are not going to stop it. The computer gets better and faster with every passing day. The financial engineers get better and faster with every passing day. The process is unending. Our only hope is that the information age we live in will keep us informed and that we can keep pace with it.

I do not pretend to know what the future will bring. I do know that the world now understands that the futures markets are an integral part of finance. That was a clear result of the 1987 crash. Risk management is today a prerequisite to survival, and instruments such as futures and options are the mechanisms of choice. And will be in the world of tomorrow. That will not change.

Alan Greenspan will tell you that this ought not change. In the years following the crash, the Fed chairman testified that futures markets were the messengers that in 1987 were first to advise the world that suddenly prices were a lot lower and values had changed dramatically. The messengers, he said, did not cause the change in price value. Nobody on our futures floor caused the change in price value. We rapidly reported the change and reacted to it. In similar fashion, during the recent correction—which should not be labeled "crash"—futures markets were again the messenger. They quickly reported the truth of what occurred. Of course it is incorrect to compare the recent upheavals with the 1987 crash. Mr. Brady is correct when he states that while the absolute numbers may sound the same, a 7.2 percent drop in one day, as we just had, is a far cry from the 1987 drop of 22.6 percent.

Reflecting back again to 1987, I agree with Mr. Corrigan when he stated that the day of danger was the day following the crash. I offer the following as evidence of what I mean.

In the futures markets, as you know, all the pays and collects must be completed before the market can open. Futures are $T + 1$. Unlike the securities markets, we don't have the luxury of three days to settle up; or five days like back in 1987. In futures markets, the money owed as a result of the previous day's market movement must be paid for in cash by the following morning. It is a no-debt system. If the change in value is not paid for, we cannot open.

The value change between the longs and shorts on the day of the crash, October 19, 1987, was $2.5 billion. That was—and still is—a very large number. And when you are talking about it in cash, it is even a larger number. We had never encountered or imagined such numbers in our previous pays and collects. As I said to our clearinghouse chief, John Davidson, "That is more money than the GDP of some countries." And the longs had to pay the shorts that amount by 7:20 A.M. on October 20. Would they do it? was the question. It was the question asked of me by Alan Greenspan when I spoke to him very late in the night of October 19. "Will you open tomorrow?" he asked.

That was the scariest moment because the truthful answer I gave was, "I do not know."

What the Fed chairman was really asking was: "Will the longs pay the shorts? Will you get the money?" Because if we did not, then we would not open the next day. And then the scare scenario Mr. Corrigan described earlier would begin to unfold. It is the fear of not being paid that throws the system into gridlock. If someone fails to pay, it sends a shiver through the financial system. Who failed? becomes the question of the moment. If anyone believed that a firm failed, it would have a domino effect. "I am not going to pay that [guy] until this [guy] does not pay me." So the critical question was whether the Merc would open. It was the most dangerous time of the crash.

I did not sleep that night. I was in the clearinghouse of the Merc the entire night together with the other officials of the Merc. It evolved that there was one major player who had to pay $1 billion. And we were told the money was slow in coming in. No one had a doubt that this player had the money, but if he did not pay in time for our opening, we could not open. Then the rumors would start and fear would take over. It is what happened in 1932.

In the middle of the night, we had to call the chairman of that financial giant and alert him to the problem.

"Who are you?" he asked being awakened in the middle of night.

"We are the Chicago Mercantile Exchange," we said, "and you owe us a billion dollars."

Can you imagine waking up to a telephone call at 2:00 A.M. and someone telling you that you owe $1 billion and where is it?

A few hours later, at 7:00 A.M., twenty minutes before the opening, I was on the phone with the Continental Bank, which was the Merc's settlement bank. Wilma Smeltzer was the officer of the bank charged with handling the Merc's account. She knew that there had to be $2.5 billion paid before that account was cleared.

I asked, "Wilma, how are we doing?"

She replied, "Leo, we have $2.4 billion. There is still $100 million missing, and it does not look like it is going to make it."

I shouted, "You mean you are going to let a stinking 100 million stand in the way? Just advance the money!"

"Leo," she said, "I cannot do that."

I said, "Wilma, we know the customer. They are good for the 100 million."

She said, "I know that too, Leo, but I do not have that kind of authority."

Well, fate intervened. Tom Theobold, chairman of the Continental, arrived at that very moment.

"Hold it, Leo, there is Theo. I'll ask him."

A moment later, Wilma said, "Leo, Tom said it was okay to advance the money."

We opened at 7:20 A.M. The money actually did come in 30 minutes later.

And that is the fear Jerry Corrigan was talking about. The pays and collects that he was worried about and that we were worried about. It certainly represented the most dangerous moment of the crash. In the recent market movement, by comparison, it was no sweat at all. There was no doubt at the Merc that the $3.6 billion change of value at our markets was ever in jeopardy of being paid. Similarly, the coordination between us and the securities markets was now totally different. In 1987, we were in total disconnect, today we were completely in sync. We learned how to coordinate from the 1987 crash.

As a free market devotee, I do not like the idea of circuit breakers any more than any free market economists. In fact, in 1987, I had a two-hour telephone conversation with Milton Friedman trying to convince him that it was okay to try circuit breakers. Well, I never convinced him of that. Still, I did embrace the concept. The key is that everyone knows long in advance what they are and how they will work. And as far as I am concerned, they pretty much worked. I do agree that circuit breakers now require some serious adjustment to reflect current percentages and current market realities. But, all in all, I think the circuit breakers worked. This time, there was total coordination between the markets of New York and Chicago.

So, as I indicated, we learned a great deal from the 1987 crash and are much better for it. But I am not here to say that it cannot happen again—no, I am not. We had better stay vigilant because no one has outlawed the fundamental reasons that cause crashes: fear and greed. Thank you.

CHAPTER 16

Preface to the Japanese Translation of *Escape to the Futures*

My special affinity for the Japanese people can of course be attributed to the most obvious reason: Japan and its people saved my life as well as the lives of my parents. And while that singular reason is more than compelling for these memoirs to be translated into Japanese, there are several other and equally important reasons for the friendship between myself and the Land of the Origin of the Sun.

In 1940, I was only eight years old when the Trans-Siberian train brought us to Vladivostok, our gateway to freedom—far too young to appreciate the extraordinary deed of the Japanese official who had made our flight to safety possible. It wasn't until many years later that my father recounted to me the story of Sugihara, the Japanese Consul General to Lithuania who defied orders from his own foreign ministry in order to save the lives of some 6,000 doomed refugees.

In the beginning, even my father didn't know the full truth of Chiune Sugihara's courage. The details of this Schindler-esque story weren't immediately available to the world at large. But what my father did know was that this uncommonly humane Japanese official recognized the plight of Jews trapped in this Lithuanian corner of the world who were about to be consumed by the insane hatred-flames of the Nazis. Sugihara did the one thing in his power to do: He granted the refugees a lifeline—a transit visa through Japan.

Years later we all discovered the full magnitude of Sugihara's deed. Not only did this great and honorable man save the lives of thousands, he acted against the orders of his government who three times had rejected his pleas for authority to do the right thing. In *Visas for Life*, the life story of Chiune Sugihara written by his wife, Yukiko, she recounts how her husband

Published by Edward Brothers, Inc., 1993.

brought together the members of his family—including her younger sister, Setsuko, and their three sons, Hiroki, Chiaki, and Haruki—to advise them of his decision: "I may have to disobey my government," he said, "but if I don't, I will be disobeying God." In following the dictates of his conscience, Chiune Sugihara became one of this world's sacred righteous. As the old Jewish proverb states: *He who saves one life saves a whole people.*

I did not return to Japan until several decades later, in May 1985. I was now leader of the Chicago Mercantile Exchange and invited to speak in Tokyo at a financial seminar together with my friend and mentor Nobel laureate Milton Friedman. The seminar, sponsored by Arthur Andersen, offered the Japanese business community a chance to hear Professor Friedman, one of the brilliant economic minds of our century, lecture about free markets, and afforded me an opportunity to speak about futures markets.

Indeed, futures markets are another and equally important reason for translating this book into Japanese. It is no secret that I have devoted almost my entire adult life to the understanding and furtherance of futures markets, particularly financial futures. And while futures markets have been in existence from time immemorial, their official beginning on an centralized exchange did not occur until the Dojima Rice Market was organized in Osaka in 1730. Thus Japan has a special and unique tie to my life's work in the promotion of organized futures exchanges throughout the world.

Of course, the futures markets I was advancing were very different than the rice tickets traded at the Dojima Market centuries ago. I was championing futures contracts on foreign exchange, interest rates, and stock indexes—financial futures. This was a new concept in futures markets, introduced in 1972 at the International Monetary Market of the Chicago Mercantile Exchange. Today, financial futures have become an indispensable tool of risk management throughout the world with financial futures exchanges developed in nearly every center of finance. Indeed, the phenomenal success of these instruments during the past two decades has few equals in the business world and symbolizes the power of an idea whose time had come.

The first financial futures contract to be offered in Japan was on the long-term government bond contract, the JGB, listed at the Tokyo Stock Exchange (TSE) in October 1985. This was followed in June 1987 by the launch of the Stock Futures 50 contract—a basket of Japan's 50 leading stocks—on the Osaka Securities Exchange (OSE). In 1988, the Japanese Ministry of Finance passed the Revised Securities and Exchange Law and the Financial Trading Law, lifting the ban on Japanese investors from trading futures and options in any product that was not backed by a physical commodity. Following the lifting of this ban came the introduction of stock price index futures in 1988, the introduction of stock price index options, and an OTC government bond futures options market in 1989. I was greatly privileged to be the guest of honor at the opening of the Nikkei 225 Stock Price Average futures contract at the OSE on September 2, 1988. And with the introduction of the Financial Futures Trading Law, which opened up new opportunities for risk management and investment on an international scale, in June 1989, the Tokyo International Financial Futures Exchange (TIFFE) was organized and began trading its first product, the three-month Euroyen interest rate futures contract.

It was during this time period that I rediscovered the beauty of the Japanese people and the reason for my fascination with them as a youngster years before. Memories of our short but happy stay in Kobe came flooding back. I was again reminded of the sensitivity and beauty of Japanese culture, its many forms of the fine arts and folk arts: flower arrangement, woodblock printing, calligraphy, dance, theatrical plays, puppet theater, and Kabuki. I was again awed by Japanese reverence for ancient customs and rituals; its deference for elders; its consideration for foreigners. I was again taken by Japanese sense of color, their orderliness, cleanliness, and awareness of natural beauty. Indeed, childhood feelings and experiences that had remained frozen in my memory were suddenly released to be revisited in my adulthood. It was a unique and joyous occasion.

My friendship with the Japanese people continues today. Not only have I made many lasting personal friends during my frequent visits to this country, not only have I delivered business lectures and held seminars, not only have I offered my expertise to government officials in matters concerning futures markets, I have had the honor of establishing a partnership arrangement with one of Japan's premier banking institutions, the Sakura Bank.

This country saved my life. It afforded me the opportunity to extend to the world the Japanese-inspired idea of an organized futures market. In publishing my memoirs in Japanese, in a sense I have come full circle. I am forever grateful.

CHAPTER 17

Pain, Progress, and Promise
Reflections on the Twentieth Century

We stand near the finish line of the second millennium Anno Domini. It is a momentous milestone. Yet, except for the fear of mass computer malfunctions—the so-called millennium bug—this landmark seems of little consequence. Clearly, 10 centuries of human history is far too long a period to reflect upon. A thousand years ago, the Sung dynasty was about to dawn in China, the Capetian dynasty was ruling France, and the Persian scholar Avicenna was preparing to write his treatises on the law, medicine, and metaphysics—writings that would influence much of the philosophy of the Middle Ages. While those occurrences may be an integral part in the quilt of human history, they are of little moment for us today.

But we also stand near the finish line of the twentieth century. And the comparisons and lessons to be drawn from the world as it stood but 100 years ago are quite another matter. Indeed, as you receive your law school diploma—you who will fashion and lead the next century—it is not only relevant but highly instructive to take a glance back, scan the highlights of the twentieth century, examine the pivotal junctures that shaped its destiny, and in so doing perhaps glean something about the road ahead.

Perhaps my father summed it up best. Prior to his death in 1990, he told me that even though the horrors of the twentieth century included a new low in the history of mankind—two world wars and the Holocaust, an indelible blot that can never be expunged—he nevertheless felt it was a most remarkable century. In spite of the atrocities, he watched the world go from the horse and buggy (the main form of transportation at his birth in 1904), to Apollo Eleven, which in 1963 took Neil Armstrong to the moon.

John Marshall Law School Commencement Address, McCormick Place, Chicago, Illinois, Sunday, June 7, 1998.

Indeed, it is hard to fathom that at the dawn of my father's century, Britannia was still the empire on which the sun never set; the railroads were in their Golden Age, automobiles were considered nothing but a fad, codeine was touted as an excellent cough syrup, the phonograph was the most popular form of home entertainment, life expectancy for the American male was 48, and the death of Queen Victoria assured that the Victorian age was in its final act. Oscar Wilde, Friedrich Nietzsche, Giuseppe Verdi died, but Louis Armstrong, Humphrey Bogart, Spencer Tracy, and Thomas Wolfe were born. And in Europe, Sigmund Freud published his *Interpretation of Dreams*, unlocking the mysteries of our subconscious, and Albert Einstein, the foremost thinker of the century, published his famous three papers, which included his special theory of relativity that forever changed the destiny of mankind.

From the beginning of the century, there was extensive testimony of its message of hate and violence. In France, the Dreyfus Affair (1894) had reared the ugly head of prejudice; in the U.S., the Supreme Court delayed genuine civil rights by embracing the separate but equal doctrine in *Plessy v. Ferguson* (1896); the Spanish-American War (1898) had begun with its cry to "Remember the Maine"; President William McKinley was assassinated (1901); and not much later but a continent away, the barbarous two-day Jewish pogrom in Kishinev occurred (1903); the Russo-Japanese War (1904) broke out; followed by the bloody rebellion in St. Petersburg (1905) which rang the bell on what was to become the Russian Revolution a decade later (1917).

There was evidence also of cultural enlightenment. Emmeline Pankhurst lit the torch on behalf of women's right to vote (1903); the modern version of the Greek Olympic Games were reborn after being missing for 3,000 years (1896); and the Boer War finally ended. Then in an unconnected burst of innovations whose social value some might question, Picasso entered his "Blue Period"(1901); Boston defeated Pittsburgh in the first World Series games (1903) ever played; the theory for IQ tests was introduced (1903); the concept of the Boy Scouts was fashioned (1907); and the *Count of Monte Cristo*, the world's first motion picture, was produced in Hollywood (1908).

In addition to Einstein, there were other strong signals that science and technology would force its way onto center stage. Russia had begun construction of its colossal Trans-Siberian railroad (1891); Guglielmo Marconi took out his first patent for the radio (1896); J.J. Thompson detected the electron (1897), proving the ancient Greek theory that atoms were at the foundation of matter; Max Planck proposed the quantum theory of light (1900); Gregor Mendel's discovery of how inherited traits are passed was finally accepted (1900); Walter Reed conquered yellow fever (1902); and Wilbur and Orville Wright changed human transportation forever at Kitty Hawk (1903).

That was the stage setting, so to speak, for the production known as the twentieth century. Looking back, we can see that the playwright provided plenty of clues for what was to come. Accordingly, it is highly instructive to look around us today for a sneak preview of what we can expect tomorrow. However, one of the most profound events that would direct much of our present century occurred long before it began, back in 1848—smack dab in the middle of the nineteenth century. In that year, Karl Marx and his associate, Friedrich Engels, published the *Communist Manifesto*. Its goal was novel and even noble: "To create a new society where there would be a fair and equitable distribution of wealth, ending the vast disparities between the rich and the poor." The concept of Marxism, more commonly known in practice as communism, would dominate the political thought of Europe and later Asia for most of the twentieth century.

Today, some 150 years after the concept was conceived, we know it to have been an unmitigated failure. The truth was officially flashed to the world in 1990 at what seemed like another traditional May Day celebration in Moscow Red Square. As usual, all the government top brass were present, as usual there were banners and marches and songs, as usual there was all the expected pomp and circumstance. But something was drastically different. It was the banner! "Communists: have no illusions—you are bankrupt," it blatantly proclaimed—right there, in the middle of Moscow Red Square, on May Day 1990!

Indeed, those of us, citizens of planet Earth, fortunate enough to be present in the final decade of the twentieth century, have been privileged to witness events equal to any celebrated milestone in the history of mankind. In what seemed like a made-for-TV video, we were ringside spectators at a global rebellion. In less than an eye-blink in terms of world history, the Berlin Wall fell, Germany was unified, apartheid ended, Eastern Europe was liberated, the Cold War ceased, and a doctrine that impaired the freedom of three generations, wrecked the economics of scores of nations, and misdirected the destiny of the entire planet for seven decades was decisively repudiated.

What a magnificent triumph of democracy and freedom. What a glorious victory for capitalism and free markets. What a majestic tribute to Thomas Jefferson, Adam Smith, Abraham Lincoln, Friedrich Hayek, and Milton Friedman. What a divine time to be alive. Surely these represented the defining moments of the twentieth century. But let us be clear: What transpired was not the result of a single influence but rather of a multitude of forces. Nor did the wildfire of freedom we witnessed occur by virtue of a random spark. The underground flame took years to overpower the forces of tyranny. It was fueled by some universal truths: that fundamental human rights cannot forever be denied; that totalitarianism is evil; and that an economic system based on central planning is vastly inferior to a market-driven economic order.

Still, if there is a single lesson to be gained from these events, it will not be found in the political or economic arena but rather in the sciences. For it is axiomatic: Human events are but links of an unending chain forged to the greatest extent by the inexorable march of science and technology. Ironically, the lynchpin of all that occurred was devised precisely 100 years after the *Communist Manifesto*, on December 23, 1947—smack dab in the middle of twentieth century. For on that day, two Bell Laboratory scientists demonstrated a device made of strips of gold foil, a chip of semiconducting material, and a bent paper clip that could take an electric current, amplify it, and switch it on and off. They had invented the first transistor. It was the birth of a technology that would serve to dominate the balance of this century and much of the twenty-first century as well. The Digital Age was upon us.

Transistors and their offspring, the microchip, transformed everything: the computer, the space program, the television, the calculator, the automobile, the telephone, and, to be sure, telecommunications. We had migrated, said Walter Wriston of Citicorp, to the "information standard." Modern telecommunications capabilities fostered instant mass informational flows in total disregard of internal prohibitions or national boundaries. This proved to be the common denominator for the dramatic upheavals we witnessed. Modern telecommunications gave everyone the ability to make a stark, uncompromising comparison of political and economic systems. Everyone had the ability to judge their government, compare their economies, scrutinize their moral codes, examine their individual freedoms, and weigh them against that of their neighbors. The truth could no longer be hidden from the people. Thus, as it has throughout the history of mankind, science and technology again dictated fundamental reform in our social structure and reshaped both the political and economic landscape of our planet.

In a very real sense, the technology of the twentieth century moved mankind from the vast to the infinitesimal. It is a trend that will surely continue. In physics, this century began with the theory of General Relativity; this dealt with the big, with the universe. From there we journeyed to comprehension of the little, of quantum physics. Indeed, physicists have now decoded nature's age-old secrets, bestowing upon the world perhaps the single greatest achievement of the human mind—the atomic theory. Similarly, in biology we also moved from macro to the micro—from individual cells to gene engineering. This led us to the discovery of DNA (deoxyribonucleic acid) and provided geneticists the ability to manipulate cells, where the ultimate secrets of nature reside. We entered an era where we can probe the fundamental components of life and, among many things, remedy mankind's most distressing afflictions.

And even in the world I represent—the financial markets—the evolutionary process was strikingly similar. When financial engineers applied advancements in computer technology to established investment strategies, market applications went from the big to the little just as in the sciences. Charles Sanford, the former chairman of Bankers Trust, dubbed it "particle finance." The idea was to take every form of finance and investment—from alimony to zero coupon bonds—and break them up into tiny bundles of risk for trade. Derivatives, the financial counterparts to particle physics and molecular biology, were born. One might even say that the Scottish-cloned sheep "Dolly" is the biological equivalent to its financial cousin, the interest rate swap.

Clearly, Planet Earth itself went through the miniaturization process. We call it globalization. As a consequence, today, for the first time in human history, nearly every country on the planet has a market-oriented economic system and is attempting to be a competitor in the global marketplace. For the past 20 years when we spoke of a global economy, we were talking about only 25 percent of mankind—mostly North America, Western Europe, and Japan. As recently as 1988, almost 70 percent of mankind was living under Marxist or socialist economic systems. Suddenly, there are 3 billion more participants in the capitalist system.

This has spelled unequaled opportunity for Americans and made our nation the unrivaled leader of the world. Among the many effects, it produced the current strong U.S. economic climate and our dominant position in financial services. But leadership has brought us burdens and responsibilities as well. Bosnia and the Middle East are but two examples. China and India are two more. And globalization also means competition. Contrary to what our Washington officials are publicly saying, the financial union in Europe, should it be formed (between Germany, France, Italy, Spain, Portugal, Austria, Belgium, the Netherlands, Luxembourg, Finland, and Ireland), will produce an economic giant equivalent to the U.S. in population, output, and trade. By introducing the euro (with Britain, Sweden, and Denmark poised to join in 2001), Europe may alter the financial map of the next century.

There are also other ramifications of globalization. The rise in financial assets led by the American stock market may have created a global financial bubble. If so, when it bursts, the effects from the fallout may be staggering. Of equal concern is the fragile nature of emerging economies throughout the world, economies that were not devised for the stresses of the open marketplace. The rapid flow of capital to nations that are still mired in nepotism, corruption, or an old-boys' network—to systems without free market structures, without cash market capabilities, without transaction transparency—sets the stage for more economic turmoil such as recently transpired in Southeast Asia.

And globalization has its dark side as well. It has unleashed a tide of nationalistic fervor that is as dangerous as it is infectious. The experience in the former Yugoslavia taught us that ethnic cleansing did not die with the Nazis; nor is what happened in Rwanda anything but an appalling example of genocide. Moreover, the rise of fundamentalism represents a serious menace to the next century. We can coexist in a global environment only if there is flexibility and compromise. With fundamentalism there is none. Furthermore, the gap between the "haves" and the "have-nots" continues to widen both within nations and internationally. Ultimately, this could produce an explosive condition. When you add to this mix the fact that the modern technology has made democratic societies highly vulnerable to cyberspace terrorism, and that weapons of mass destruction are present and available to rogue nations, or to those with traditional enmities, or to villainous opportunists, you must conclude that our world is as dangerous a place as it ever was.

Still, in stark contrast to the signals at the turn of the last century, the evidence today is overwhelming that the next century will be dominated by the information standard. As Dr. Carver Mead of the California Institute of Technology stated: "The entire Industrial Revolution enhanced productivity by a factor of about a hundred, but the microelectronic revolution has already enhanced productivity in information-based technology by a factor of more than a million"—and you've seen nothing yet! Today, millions of transistors are etched on wafers of silicon. On these microchips, all the world's information can be stored in digital form and transmitted to every corner of the globe via the Internet. Thus, the Digital Revolution will impact the next century just as the Industrial Revolution directed much of the nineteenth and twentieth century. Or to put it as Harry Seegers, chief executive of GE Information Services, said, "Information technology will be to the twenty-first century what electricity has been to the twentieth century."

Indeed, the Digital Revolution will change the way we live, work, and play. Everyone will be wired, carrying small pocket devices that can be used to communicate, or as a computer, or a fax, or to download money. Tiny chips might even be implanted in our bodies that could act as a universal credit card, passport, or driver's license. Telephones as we knew them will be history. Wireless e-mail in the twenty-first century will be the dominant personal telecommunications instrument. Surely national and economic borders, which have already been blurred, may dissolve completely, as communication satellites enable consumers to do transactions in cyberspace.

And perhaps it won't be long before there is one world currency—digital money. Yes, instead of storing value on paper, the twenty-first century will surely allow us to put money into electronic digits. It will be more portable and certainly smarter than its paper counterpart. It can be stored in your laptop, on a credit card, or on a chip implant in your hand. And because digital cash will be highly compliant, you will be able to control it much more precisely than paper money. Not only will the next generation of law students receive their allowance on e-mail through the Internet, it will come programmed as how they can spent it—so much for food, so much for books, so much for beer.

Finally, in the Age of Cyberspace we can envision an enormous shift of power from producer to user. Technology is a force for democracy and individual empowerment. The consumer will become king because the Internet changes the old rules. Consumers who don't like what they see will just click, delete, and move on to the next screen. Those corporations that are currently merging and are betting that bigger is better may be looking in the rearview mirror and could be completely wrong. With the cost of entry lower and easy access to the global marketplace via the Internet, competition will come from smaller entities with a flexibility to offer innovative services. In the past, success had a lot to do with real estate; in the future, where you are located may not matter.

So there you have it: the pain, the progress, and the promise of the twentieth century. It would be grand to tell you that we have learned from our mistakes, that we will not repeat them, that only enlightened times await us, but I am afraid that would be a bit Pollyannaish. Still, there has been great progress and the future looks brighter than it ever was, even if somewhat formidable. Indeed, if what lies ahead sounds a little scary to you, then you are realistic and have learned well. And if as lawyers you see vast challenges and great opportunities, then John Marshall has done a good job. Congratulations and good luck.

CHAPTER 18

There Are No Jews in Bialystok

We arrived at Warsaw. It was the first leg of a long-awaited family trip that would take me back to Bialystok, the city of my birth.

In my heart, I always knew I would make the trip. While my parents, Icchok and Faygl Melamdovich, were alive, I had often offered to sponsor a trip that would take them back to where they grew up, where they were educated and became teachers, where they were married. They had been at the forefront of Yiddish culture in Bialystok, in the movement out of the shtetl so that Jews could become equal citizens in the world society.

But they repeatedly declined. "There is nothing there left for me," my father would say. Perhaps he was right. I wouldn't know unless I found out for myself.

I was a child in 1939, when the German army attacked Poland and began to turn Europe into an inferno of death. World War II had sprung its frightening trap that would ensnare millions of Europeans and deliver them into the hands of the Nazis. The story of our escape, as my parents, with me at their side, miraculously outwitted the Gestapo and KGB, is not material to these reflections. Our two-year odyssey spanned three continents, six languages, the Trans-Siberian railroad, and Japan (a life-saving transit visa was issued by Chiune Sugihara, Japanese Consul General to Lithuania), and happily concluded in the United States in 1941.

In this circuitous fashion, acutely aware that I was among the few fortunate souls who escaped the horrors unfolding in Europe, I found myself on the inner city streets of Chicago's Northwest side. We settled in a neighborhood that was an ethnic melting pot of Italians, Poles, and Jews, and where "Hey, you dirty kike" was not an uncommon greeting. Still, despite my precarious start in life, irrespective of the special strife I faced, as do most foreign children unfamiliar with the culture of their new homeland, one could say that my achievements exemplified the splendor of America.

Reflections and Memories, August 2000.

For it was here, in this land of the free and home of the brave, that this refugee from Bialystok, without American roots, without wealth, without proper credentials, without clout or influence, was given the opportunity to enter the world of futures markets and climb to the top of its complex structure. Within that arena, at a moment that was ripe for change, I was invited to use my imagination and skills, to innovate and invent. I was lucky. The world in the early 1970s had entered the first stages of globalization. There was a need for new instruments of finance. My colleagues and I responded to the need and our ideas gave rise to the era of financial futures. In this fashion, in a small way I was able to contribute to the growth of Chicago and American markets. A contribution which in the eyes of some—the editor of the *Chicago Tribune*, for instance—would merit my inclusion in a list of the "Ten most important Chicagoans in business of the twentieth century."[1]

While this background may be instructive and provide some standing for my point of view, it is also not material to these contemplations. Two facts are, however, germane to this story. First, emotionally, my parents never left the Old World; consequently, I inherited a portion of their mindset. Second, as a child, I had never been to Warsaw—not physically, that is. Spiritually . . . well, that was another matter. In literature, theater, politics, culture, prose, song, and poetry, Varshe—as the capital of Poland is called in Yiddish—was alive for me, as if I were born there. Varshe was a constant and consequential topic of conversation at our home whenever my parents met with their group of Yiddish intellectuals as I was growing to adulthood. Varshe, I learned quickly, hosted the modern Jewish thought that emanated during Poland's exciting years: the early 1900s through the beginning of World War II. During that era, Jews flexed their cultural muscles, forcing the greater Polish society to contain its embedded anti-Semitism and at least begin to accept them in the social structure.

Jewish roots in Warsaw are deep. They were there as early as 1414. But Warsaw's status as the main center of Jewish population growth in Poland was not visible until the second half of the nineteenth century. In the 1860s, in an effort to win support from Jews against the Poles, the Russian czar lifted from Warsaw and its surrounding provinces many of the existing anti-Semitic taxes as well as the residential and employment restrictions against Jews which were ubiquitous throughout Poland. As a consequence, Jews fled the small towns of Poland and migrated to Varshe to participate in the economic opportunities that the liberated laws allowed. This process unleashed powerful evolutionary forces. By the end of the nineteenth century, Varshe had been transformed into the Jewish economic, political, and cultural capital of Poland.

Many other cities, within Poland and elsewhere in Europe, made significant contributions to the total body of Jewish culture. Near the top of any list would be the legendary city of Wilno (Vilna in Yiddish), known as the "Jerusalem of Lithuania." In the latter half of the eighteenth century, under the influence of the fabled *Vilner Gaon*, Rabbi Elijah ben Shlomo Zalman, Vilna blossomed as the center for rabbinical studies and for the Haskala, the Jewish Enlightenment movement. A century later, in 1897, the Algemeyner Yidisher Arbeter Bund ("the Bund"), a Jewish faction of the Socialist movement, was conceived in Vilna.[2] My parents were ardent Bundistn, and I most certainly would have been inducted into the movement had the world not been turned upside down by Adolf Hitler. Over the years, Vilna, which produced some of the greatest Yiddish writers and poets, evolved as a flourishing source of Hebrew and Yiddish literature. Chaim Grade, Shmerke Katsherginski, Moyshe Kulbak, and my personal favorite, Avrom Sutzkever, were among them. The acclaimed Vilner Teachers Seminary, where my mother earned her teaching degree, was situated there. And, of primary significance, Vilna was the birthplace of the Yiddish Scientific Institute (YIVO), the preeminent center for the study of the Yiddish language, literature, and folklore. Founded in 1925 under the direction of Yiddish linguist Max Weinreich, it was miraculously transplanted to New York in 1940. For Yiddishistn, such as my parents, the YIVO was the equivalent of the bible on matters of Yiddish language.

Still, no other city could equal Varshe as a center of Jewish cultural life at the beginning of the 1900s. Varshe represented the largest concentration of Jews in Europe, and the second largest in the world, after New York. (At the start of World War II in 1939, Varshe's population included 380,000 Jews, or almost 30 percent of the total population.) Varshe became the unquestionable capital of modern Jewish thought and the epicenter of an emancipation movement—a metamorphosis that was sweeping over Jewish masses and uncoupling world Jewry from its ancestral religious moorings. Yet this transformation did not diminish traditional religious participation—in the 1920s, there were over 400 synagogues within Varshe.

In the first three decades of the twentieth century, Varshe evolved into a vibrant and dynamic center of secular Jewish life. The city became the headquarters for a large number of diverse political parties, including a strong Orthodox religious faction. Jewish cooperatives, credit unions, orphanages, hospitals, newspapers, publishing houses, theater companies, orchestras, choirs, sports clubs, and cultural societies were formed there, and became the center of a European network that reached every touchstone of Jewish existence.[3]

Most important, Varshe was also the official seat from which Icchok Leybush Peretz presided over the Jewish cultural renaissance of that era. Without taking anything away from the other two classic giants, Mendele Moscher Sforim and Sholem Aleichem, I.L. Peretz has to be regarded as the most influential Yiddish writer of all time. From 1890, when he settled in

Varshe, until his death at the beginning of World War I, Peretz shaped Yiddish literature into an instrument of national cohesion. His writings served as a pulpit from which he educated, admonished, and, in the words of historian Ruth R. Wisse, "[led] Jews away from religion toward a secular Jewish existence without falling into the swamp of assimilation."[4] Under his influence, the city became the center of a rapidly growing modern culture that was based in the Yiddish language and acted as a magnet for Yiddish novelists, poets, journalists, and thespians. From his Varshe home, Peretz transformed the teachings of the Ten Commandments into a modern paradigm of moral consciousness. He taught uneducated Jews how to liberate themselves from the controls of orthodoxy. He inspired young Yiddish writers to join in his mission of creating a national literature, and he championed the Yiddish language, declaring it central to Jewish life. He educated Jewish workers to understand their own self-worth, and he freed Jewish women from subjugation to male domination. Peretz gave the Jews hope that a new and better world was coming: *Hof Un Gleib, Nisht Veit Is Noch Der Freebling* (Hope and Faith, Spring is Not Far Away).

My parents' generation embraced Peretz's ideals as gospel and used them to build the Bund into what Motl Zelmanowitcz described as "a vision of democratic and liberal socialism—not as a dogma, but as a way of life—as a garland of values which incorporate social justice, internationalism, and brotherhood of nations."[5]

That was the Varshe I knew without ever stepping inside its borders; or sitting within its restaurants and cafés and listening to heated discussions by Varshever Jews of current events, politics, or the latest literary works; or attending one of its plays in which the fabled Ida Kaminska reigned supreme and taught the Yiddish masses the cultural value of theater. That was the city I visualized even though I never participated in the plans of its residents for the new world that was soon to come, and even though I was far too young to join them in singing "Di Shvue," the Bundist anthem that, in the lyrics written by the renowned Shimon Anski, swore boundless loyalty to the Bund.

The images of *that* Varshe remained alive for me until—until the moment our British Airways plane touched down at Okecie, Warsaw's international airport. They were instantly shattered. My father was right on. The Jewish Varshe that was frozen in my memory, placed there by his reminiscences, had vanished from the face of the earth. Intellectually, I had always known this fact, but I was unprepared for the psychological impact of facing the reality. To be fair, I suppose my reaction was a purely "Jewish" reflex. Were I, say, an Indian or a Brit or a Pole, or anyone except a Jew coming to today's Warsaw, I would not have had to endure the devastating emotional letdown that I experienced. What I found was a nondescript city bereft of vigor, rebuilt cheaply by communists after World War II, with hardly a trace remaining of its historic and distinctive past. And, for all intents and purposes, it was devoid of Jews. For me, without Jews, Varshe might as well have been the capital of Azerbaijan.

From this point forward, I was sleepwalking, as if in a dream. I was conscious of people—my wife, Betty; my daughter, Idelle, and her husband, Howard; my four grandchildren—and of the places and things on our tour—old buildings, statues, and sights tourists should see. But, for me, a strange surreal silence, the silence of those who were missing, enveloped everything and everyone. Author Jozef Hen, in defining Warsaw's old Jewish Cemetery, which contains the gravesites of some esteemed historical personages in our culture and was somehow left virtually untouched by the Germans, explains: *The cemetery is a peculiar monument, unique evidence of what has happened. No, not because of the graves of those resting here. On the contrary, because of the graves that are not here. The Absent give evidence to the crime committed.*

In a similar vein, the greatest impact to my consciousness was caused by what was absent from Warsaw. The Yiddish language was gone. It was missing from the names of shops and restaurants, from the chatter of voices on the streets, from the haggling between buyers and merchants in the marketplace, from the babble of discussions in the coffee houses, from the playful cries of children on the streets and in the courtyards.

The Polish government, with help from the Ronald S. Lauder Foundation and others, has done its best to mark the sacred and notable sites. The Polish tour guides are very professional as they carefully escort their clients through the history of the city. We too had done our part in preparing ourselves and telling Joshua, Aaron, Jared, and Mara, our grandkids, who ranged in age from 16 to 7 years, the story of the Holocaust. The older two boys had visited the U.S. Holocaust Memorial Museum in Washington, DC, and were provided with written material that they judiciously studied. But how is it possible to do justice to demonic acts that, in President Dwight D. Eisenhower's words, *beggar[ed] description?*[6]

The missing voices that I sought have been replaced by plaques; the haunting sense of vibrant Jewish life has been marked by monuments. These were all around me. I found it difficult to repress a sudden desire to run away, as if somehow, by leaving, I could preserve the images of the Varshe that had been infused in me. My fingers trembled as I touched the plaque for Icchok Kacenelson, the great Yiddish poet. As a child, I had recited his words. His voice was silenced in Auschwitz. My heart pounded as we stopped at the plaque for Janusz Korczak, the Polish physician (born Henryk Goldszmit), who chose to perish in the Treblinka death camp, together with the Jewish children from his orphanage, rather than continue to live when they were being taken to their death. I couldn't find the words to explain to my grandchildren the majesty of his martyrdom. There is a plaque honoring

Icchok Nyssenbaum, the rabbi leader of the Mizrachi and a member of the Warsaw underground. He perished in Treblinka. The members of the Bund who died in the Ghetto Uprising also have a plaque. Another, in the form of a manhole cover, memorializes the sewers through which Jewish inhabitants clandestinely entered and escaped from the ghetto; still another is dedicated to Shmul Zygelbojm, a member of the Warsaw Ghetto's first Jewish council. He escaped but later committed suicide in London—his way of protesting the world's indifference to the Holocaust. His final words were addressed to the exiled president of Poland: *"I cannot remain silent, nor can I remain alive, while the last remnants of the Jewish people perish in Poland."* The plaques and monuments house the ghosts of those who lived and perished here. Their silence speaks volumes.

On the mandatory tour through the "Memorial Route of Jewish Martyrdom and Struggle," I steeled myself and tried to overcome the icy chill that encased my being. The tour route begins at the Monument to the Heroes of the Ghetto, runs down Zamenhof Street, past Shmul Zygelbojm Square, and arrives at the memorial to Mila 18, which gives special honor to Mordechai Anielewicz. His name has been etched in my memory since childhood. His plaque is silent, like so many of the others. He was the 23-year-old commander of the Jewish Fighting Organization, known in Poland as the Zydowska Organizacja Bojowa (ZOB) who, on April 19, 1943, the eve of Passover, stood fast with his brave contingent of 750 Warsaw Ghetto fighters and faced the onslaught of the powerful German army.[7] The story has assumed hallowed proportions and is recited at all uprising commemorations. On the exact day when Jews throughout the free world would sit down for their traditional Seder feast, SS Gruppenfuherer Jurgen Stroop, commander of the Warsaw occupation forces, led a trained German army into the ghetto to deliver its final liquidation. By then, only 50,000 Jews were left in the Varshever Ghetto. No longer did anyone have illusions about their destiny. Anielewicz's Resistance Fighters—poorly armed with handguns, a few rifles and grenades, iron rods, and Molotov cocktails, some made from lightbulbs filled with sulfuric acid—stood ready to greet the foe.

They were prepared to die fighting. Against impossible odds, without military training, they inflicted considerable casualties on the Germans and were victorious in forcing the invaders to leave the ghetto and regroup. Although the outcome was a foregone conclusion, it took 28 days of intense fighting and the full might of the German Wehrmacht—tanks, artillery, and fighter planes—to firebomb the ghetto and quell its defenders. Not until May 16 could Stroop report: "The Jewish Quarter of Warsaw no longer exists."

In 1951, Jurgen Stroop was sentenced to death and executed in Poland.

Mordechai Anielewicz couldn't have foreseen the full significance of the Warsaw Ghetto Uprising. In a defiant act reminiscent of the heroic deed of his brethren, centuries earlier, at Masada, he and some of his brave compatriots committed suicide in their Mila Street bunker rather than allow themselves to be captured alive. But he sensed that the ramifications of the ghetto battle would go far beyond military reports and casualty statistics. In his last letter, written two weeks before his death on May 8, 1943, Anielewicz wrote: "I feel that great things are happening and that this action which we have dared to take is of enormous value."[8] Indeed, news about the uprising inspired Jewish underground resistance elsewhere. There were revolts in more than 60 ghettos and in about 100 regions, including those well-documented in Kovno, Vilna, Minsk, Bialystok, Lachva, Novogruok, Lublin, and Krakow.[9] And, ignoring the certainty of severe retribution, and irrespective of fences, guard towers, machine guns, searchlights, and vicious dogs, uprisings occurred in death and concentration camps, including those in Treblinka, Sobibor, and Auschwitz/Birkenau.[10] Of a different dimension and of incalculable magnitude is the fact that the Warsaw Ghetto Uprising will forever remain an exalted flashpoint of pride for Jewish people everywhere.

Elie Wiesel, a Nobel laureate author and a Holocaust survivor, in his introduction to *On Both Sides of the Wall*—the memoirs of Vladka Meed, whose real name was Feigele Peltel-Miedzyrzecki and who acted as a courier during the Warsaw Ghetto Uprising—asks a puzzling question: Where did Mordechai Anielewicz "draw the strength, the knowledge, to go out in battle against the most awesome army in Europe?" One might think, Wiesel muses, that, as a consequence of German atrocities, the Jews would turn into animals. After all, as he suggests, "there are limits to human endurance. One must break at last." And yet, "the hangman was mistaken." Throughout the ghetto years, Wiesel writes, the Jews refused to break: "The ghetto, half-a-million souls, for the most part did not become a jungle. Quite the contrary; people tried to help each other." Therefore, as Wiesel points out, "One must marvel even more at the fighters and couriers. Instead of falling into despair, they found reasons and strength to help others."[11]

The silent Anielewicz plaque tried valiantly to tell my grandchildren all of that.

The Memorial Route then took us to its conclusion. We followed the tour guide down Stawki Street: past numbers 5 and 6, which once housed the SS Unit Command; past numbers 6 and 8, the former school and Jewish transit hospital; and to the intersection of life and death—the entrance of the Umschlagplatz. At this place, Varshever Jews were loaded into cattle cars and delivered to the gas chambers of Treblinka or other extermination centers. To distinguish the ignominy represented by this site from the evil of the others, four plaques, inscribed in Polish, Yiddish, Hebrew, and English, silently explain: *Along this path of suffering and death over 300,000 Jews were driven in 1942–1943 from the Warsaw Ghetto to the gas chambers of Nazi extermination camps.*[12] It doesn't—it can't—describe the starvation, disease, terror, and torture that were daily fare for those who managed to survive long enough to be brought here. Next to the Wall Monument are the remaining traces of the brickwork comprising the gate of the Umschlagplatz. Above the gate is this inscription from the Book of Job, XVI, 18: *O Earth, Cover Not My Blood, and Let My Cry for Justice Find No Rest*. Job's words don't register; instead, I hear the ringing words of children singing: *"Hof Un Gleib, Nisht Veit Is Noch Der Freehling"*—Hope and Faith, Spring is Not Far Away.

Visiting the Warsaw Jewish Cemetery proved to be a momentary respite from the oppressive strain of the ghetto experience. The contrasting psychological effect between the death we encountered along the Memorial Route and its counterpart within the Warsaw Jewish Cemetery was as remarkable as it was immediate. There is silence here too, but this silence represents normalcy. As Jozef Hen notes, *"Silence hangs above the place, but it is not a deathlike silence, not torpor."* It is the silence of historic acknowledgment—of reverence toward past deeds and accomplishments. Whatever events defined the life and death of someone who found a final resting place in this venerable cemetery, they have no compelling comparison to the circumstances surrounding those who perished in Varshe during the Holocaust. The fact that this Jewish cemetery, the largest in Europe, exists at all is one of the wonders of the world. During the Nazi occupation, the cemetery was part of the ghetto. How and why the Nazis forgot to—or chose not to—destroy it will forever remain an enigma of wondrous proportions.

Established in 1806 and surrounded by a brick wall, the Warsaw Jewish cemetery contains some 250,000 tombstones. The celebrated names inscribed there—names spoken with reverence in my parents' household—offer a rare walk through Jewish history. They include: Shimon Askenazy, a historian and diplomat; Adam Czerniakow, president of the Warsaw Jewish Community, who became head of the Warsaw Judenrat and took his life rather than obey the S.S. order to deliver 10,000 Jews to the Umschlagplatz; Bronislaw Grosser, a Bund activist for whom the Yiddish school at which my parents taught in Bialystok was named; Esther Rachel Kaminska, the "mother of Yiddish Theater"; Ber Meisels, a legendary rabbi of Warsaw; I.L. Peretz, the father of modern Yiddish literature, whose funeral on April 3, 1915, was attended by more than 100,000 people from all over the world (Peretz's monument, created in 1925 by sculptor Abraham Ostrzega, is shared with writer Jacob Dinezon and with Shimon Anski, the author of *The Dybbuk*, which premiered in 1920 at the Warsaw Elizeum Theater); Feliks Perl, a political activist and head of the Polish Socialist party; and Ludwik Zamenhof, who created the international language Esperanto.

Visiting the gravesite of Esther Kaminska, who was compared during her life to the likes of Eleonora Dusae and Sarah Bernhardt, was of special moment for me. Her daughter was the fabled actress Ida Kaminska whose performances on the Varshe stage as well as throughout the world materially advanced I.L. Peretz's goal in establishing Yiddish as the centerpiece of modern Jewish life. Although my parents often saw her perform, I was never privileged to meet her. However, I did get to know her niece, Dina Halperin, who carried forward their family tradition and became a renowned international star of the Yiddish stage. Dina Halperin was a close personal friend of our family. She would often call on my father to discuss the deeper meaning of a given playwright's writing or in her quest for an unfamiliar Yiddish word. More to the point, I had the good fortune of performing in Chicago Yiddish theater productions under the direction of Dina Halperin.

My career in Yiddish theater was strictly as an amateur. Still, I did get recognition from a large segment of the Jewish population, both in Chicago and New York, as a Yiddish actor. My parents were responsible for launching my acting career. Upon arrival to Chicago, they arranged my appearances at many of the Jewish cultural events with which they became associated, where, to the delight of the audience, I would recite poetry in an infallible Yiddish. Under my parent's' tutelage, I spent countless hours preparing poems and learning to properly emote the poet's words and meaning. These public undertakings brought me a measure of fame. It also led me to participate as an actor on the legitimate Jewish stage in Chicago as well as to partake in soap operas on Jewish radio programs. Subsequently, when the Chicago Yiddish Theater Organization was organized under the direction of Dina Halperin, I became a proud member of its permanent troupe.

These distant connections to the life of Esther Kaminska flashed though my mind as I stood in reverence in front of her grave.

If the visit to Warsaw left me unexpectedly shaken, the one to Bialystok did little to grant relief. The two-hour trip northeast from Warsaw was across flat and monotonous farmland that seemed frozen in a time warp. It offered no clue to the cataclysmic events that, half a century before, had occurred here and had altered the course of history forever. The country-side is peaceful now; the farmers plow and till their land, and their family members dutifully sell mushrooms to motorists passing along the highway. Life is now—as it always was before 1939—as it should be. But nearby is Treblinka; to the southwest is Gross-Rosen; to the southeast is Majdanek; and farther south, behind Warsaw, is Auschwitz. The black storks that for generations have made their homes here still return to their former nests. If they could speak, I wondered, would they remember to inform their off-spring that in this region of the world, where once lived 3 million Jews who spoke in Yiddish, their winged ancestors witnessed the darkest days in human history?

Elie Wiesel remembered. He wrote: *The beginning, the end: all the world's roads, all the outcries of mankind, lead to this accursed place. Here is the kingdom of night, where God's face is hidden and a flaming sky becomes a graveyard for a vanished people.*[13]

Although it is the city where I was born, I found myself less connected to Bialystok than to Warsaw. Upon reflection, this is understandable. My memories of Bialystok are those of a seven-year-old. They remained frozen in that time-space construct. My subsequent strong connections to Jewish life—those that molded my identity—were formed by actions and events that occurred thereafter, either with a historical Varshe reference, or as a consequence of an educational format directed mainly by my parents, or based on world events that took place as I grew up. The images I retained of Bialystok were only momentary memory snatches: my immediate family, the house I lived in, the street I played on, some familiar city sights, and a few critical flashes after the onset of the war and during our escape from the Nazis. Some of these snapshots I was able to get close to during our visit, but most of them were gone forever.

When I was a child, the Bialystok *stotzeiger,* or town clock, seemed of landmark proportions. My recollection was not far from the truth. Renovated now as a museum piece, its structure still stands proudly in the middle of the city and offers a warm welcome. Constructed circa 1900, the clock's four faces look down on the citizens of Bialystok and provide a reassuring image of a small but ambitious Polish town. Bialystok, the largest city in northeastern Poland, now has a population of 280,000 and acts as the seat of a land region that encompasses over 10,000 square kilometers. Deriving its name from the Biala River (*biala* is the word for "white" in Slavic languages), which runs through the city, it was founded in 1320 by Prince Gedimin of Lithuania. The first Jews came there in 1558, but, for some 200 years, until the rule of Count Jan Branicki, whose heirs governed the Bialystok province from the seventeenth to the nineteenth centuries, Jews were denied full citizenship. In 1939, just before the Germans invaded Poland, there were 110,000 Jews living in Bialystok, representing over 60 percent of the city's population. It meant that Bialystok had the highest percentage of Jews among the world's cities with more than 100,000 inhabitants. Bialystok also had the greatest number of synagogues per capita, with 33 rabbis in attendance.[14]

Upon our arrival, the mayor of Bialystok, Richard Tur, sadly advised us through an interpreter (an appointment had been arranged, courtesy of the Polish Consulate in Chicago) that we had come too late. The last Bialystoker Jew had died three weeks before. "Just think," my wife whispered, "had you come back to Bialystok a little sooner, there would have been two of you." The tragic reality that had haunted me throughout our time in Varshe had followed me here. The great Jewish center of Bialystok was *Judenrein,* just as Hitler had intended. Alas, the black swastika painted on the adjacent wall of the archival building reminded us that you don't need the presence of Jews to have anti-Semitism.

I had clear memories of our home and the neighborhood where I grew up. Our house, a simple wooden bungalow, sometimes referred to as a *chaate* in Yiddish, was inherited by my mother from her father, who died before I was born. It stood in the heart of the Jewish section and had a dining room, a kitchen, and one bedroom. The kitchen was dominated by a black potbellied stove that sat in the middle like a headless dark Buddha. The dining room boasted a white-brick wall oven that allowed my *babba* (my maternal grandmother) to prepare *cholnt* over the weekend. Cholnt was East European manna: a thick stew made of pieces of beef, potatoes, onions, carrots, beans, and a host of spices mixed together in a thick pot and cooked overnight. The house also had an attic where babba slept and a cellar where she stored the bottles of pickles and preserves that she prepared during summer months. We also enjoyed indoor plumbing, a luxury seldom found in Jewish homes. My father, who, along with my mother, was a teacher by profession—and who, in my childish mind could do almost anything—had built the washroom, complete with a pull-chain for the overhead water box. That room lifted our family well above the station of our neighbors.

To my surprise, although most were abandoned, we found a number of such chaates still standing in what once was the Jewish quarter. I was now faced with the moment of truth I had often contemplated—my reaction to an encounter with a close and personal object of my childhood. Sighting the Bialystok *stotzeiger* was exciting but had brought on no deep emotional response. However, seeing the row of old dilapidated wooden houses, any one of which could have doubled for the house I was born in, suddenly brought forward unexpected waves of nostalgia that were as frightening as they were welcome. I experienced an immediate rush of disparate childhood memories—the youthful faces of my parents; my mother's white satin blouse that she sometimes wore to work; my babba's black woolen shawl, and how she placed it over her shoulders on the Sabbath; the outline of our kitchen cabinet; the voices of my friends—some of whom I didn't know that I remembered—shouting out my name in Yiddish and calling me to come outside to play—all these came at me at once, causing gooseflesh along my spine and—for the first time in many, many years—bringing tears to my eyes. A similar effect, perhaps in combination with the wooden relics from the past, came from seeing the cobblestones beneath my feet precisely as I had remembered them on Fastowska Street where we lived. If I had any remaining doubts that I was again standing in the neighborhood of my childhood, they were completely dispelled by a nearby structure that was amazingly similar to the little Beth Midrash synagogue that had been at the foot of our block. The plaque on its wall confirmed that it was indeed the former Piaskower Synagogue. Built in 1890, it had survived the decades almost intact. Its renovated structure now serves as offices for a construction firm and for the Zamenhof Esperanto Society. The entire episode was for me an emotional watershed.

In our search for the area where the Great Synagogue of Bialystok once stood, we were directed to the wall of a small building, where a plaque memorialized the victims who died when this illustrious house of worship was burned. Designed in 1908 by a renowned architect, Shlome Jakow Rabinowicz, the Great Synagogue's dome exhibited a Byzantine-Muslim influence and was famous throughout Europe. In this synagogue, open only on Saturdays and holidays, women prayed together with men, although in separate halls. Between World Wars I and II, national holidays were celebrated there and the services were attended by such authorities as the mayor and the governor of the region.[15] I was suddenly confronted by a flashback of tragic proportions. The Nazis recaptured Bialystok on June 27, 1941. Six days later, to celebrate their victory, German soldiers, at gunpoint, forced 800 Jews, mostly women and children from the neighborhood, into the Great Synagogue. They locked the doors and then set the structure on fire. Both of my grandmothers and my only aunt, Bobble, were among those who burned to death. How was it determined, I wondered, that I should escape their fate?

There is another visible commemoration of the Great Synagogue of Bialystok. On the fiftieth anniversary of the end of World War II, a monument was erected in its honor in a small square near its original location. The monument corrects some of the errors contained in the original plaque and exhibits the only remaining part of the structure: the iron beams that once supported its magnificent dome. In another flashback, my father's determined face appeared as he lectured me about the importance of holding true to one's principles. That incident happened just after the outbreak of the war. The mayor of Bialystok asked the synagogue's rabbi, Dr. Gedali Rozenman, for permission to hold a City Council meeting there because the City Hall had been destroyed by bombs. The rabbi agreed but requested that all City Council members wear a yarmulke. The mayor readily agreed; council members would surely respect the nature of such a request. Well, not everyone. My father, one of the few Jewish representatives to the Bialystok City Council, was an ardent Bundist. Although steeped in the Talmud, my father and the legions of his fellow Bundistn had found religion too restrictive in their battle for equality and social justice for Jews. Their god was the Jewish worker. My father refused the rabbi's request because the wearing of a yarmulke might compromise his oath to the Bund. It was a matter of principle.

We visited the memorial to the leaders and fighters of the Bialystok Ghetto Uprising. It was led by Mordechai Tenenbaum, one of the organizers of the Warsaw Ghetto Fighters. Upon his arrival in Bialystok in November 1942, Tenenbaum, convinced that the Germans meant to murder them all, advanced this credo: "Let us fall as heroes, and though we die, yet we shall live." As a youngster, I first heard those words in conversations around our kitchen table. The motto unified the various underground factions, who then formed the Bialystok Organization of Jewish Self-Defense. The new organization issued the following manifesto: *Don't be lambs for slaughter! Fight for your life to the last breath. . . . Remember the example and tradition of numerous generations of Jewish fighters, martyrs, thinkers and builders, pioneers, and creators. Come out to the streets and fight.*

On Sunday night, August 15, 1943, the call was answered. It is a story I know well. The ghetto fighters attacked three rings of German soldiers and police surrounding the ghetto. Two days later, Bialystok was a city under siege. The Bialystoker Self-Defense Organization, with more than 200 armed Jewish fighters, were holding the ghetto hostage. The fighting lasted six days; the Germans used tanks, artillery, and airplanes to quell the uprising. Unofficial data and eyewitness accounts put the Nazi losses at 100 soldiers killed or wounded. The name of one of the heroes of the uprising was strangely similar to my father's, Icchok Malmed. After throwing acid in the faces of some particularly savage Nazi soldiers, Malmed gave himself up when the Germans threatened to retaliate by shooting 1,000 Jews. He was executed by hanging. A plaque in his memory was placed on Malmeda Street, named for him.[16]

The memorial to the Bialystok Ghetto Uprising stands on the site of the old Jewish cemetery on Zabia Street. A telling story is connected with this site. After the war, when about 1,100 Jews returned to Bialystok, the damage to the old Zabia Street cemetery at the hands of the Nazis was repaired. Then the remains of some 3,500 ghetto victims were buried, a wall was built around the cemetery, and several obelisks were erected. Two decades later, in 1971, an anti-Semitic wave, allegedly incited by communist authorities, caused the Bialystok ghetto cemetery to be destroyed once again. Its monuments and obelisks were blown up. This incident provoked former Israeli Prime Minister Icchok Shamir, who, as a youth had attended the Bialystok Hebrew *Gymnasium* (high school). to remark: "The young Polacks destroyed everything the Nazis did not—even the Jewish cemeteries."

Little wonder that there are no Jews remaining in Bialystok. And without Jews, Bialystok has lost its meaning, its raison d'être—or so it seems to me. And something else is missing. Bialystok was the Polish center for textile production and finished goods. It was also a bustling city filled with Jews from every walk of life. Some of them became quite distinguished.

Icchok Shamir, who served as Prime Minister of Israel in 1983–1984 and again in 1986 to 1992, was a Bialystoker; so was Dr. Ludwik L. Zamenhof, an ophthalmologist by profession, who, in 1887, became world famous as the inventor of the international language Esperanto. Dr. Albert B. Sabin was also a Bialystoker. As a microbiologist in the U.S., Sabin improved on the Salk polio vaccine and developed an oral equivalent. A renowned Parisian, international lawyer Samual Pisar, who spent his adolescence in Auschwitz, was a Bialystoker. His autobiography, *Of Blood and Hope*, published in 1979, has been translated into 20 languages. And it should not be forgotten that, beginning in the 1880s, Bialystok thrived as a center of the Jewish labor movement, a revolutionary arena that produced many prominent personalities and writers.

However, more than the weavers of Bialystok or its citizens who distinguished themselves in medicine or in politics, it was the bakers of Bialystok who exported the fame of the city to the world. Over the years, Bialystok would leave its gastronomical mark, especially on the United States, where bakeries, delicatessens, and food stores would sell the "bialy," a breakfast roll—the creation of Bialystok bakers.

Mimi Sheraton, the respected food aficionado, recently wrote a book, *The Bialy Eaters*, devoted to this subject. She talks of the success of the bialy—a distant cousin of the bagel but without the hole in its center—and describes her search for the original "Bialystoker Kuchen," a baked roll about nine inches in diameter (larger than a bialy). It had a perimeter of raised dough, and its flat, crisp, disklike center was impressed with *mohn* (poppy seeds) and shreds of roasted onions. Bialystoker Jews who loved the kuchen (that included nearly everyone) were known as "Bialystoker Kuchen *fressers*" (immense eaters). Sheraton tells how she traveled far and wide to record personal memories of those who had firsthand experience with this fabled delight. She also reports that Nina Selin, of Washington, DC, describes her family as descendants of three generations of bialy bakers. Ms. Selin claims that her maternal great-great-grandfather, Moshe Nosovich, born in Bialystok in 1835, was the inventor of the Bialystoker Kuchen.[17] Perhaps. But what every Bialystoker, including myself, can testify is that the Bialystoker Kuchen was the original McCoy and was far tastier than its current counterpart. Alas, there no longer are any Bialystoker Kuchens nor, for that matter, any Jewish Bialystoker bakers. Sadly, my father's "There is nothing there left for me" echoes through my mind.

A strange and infectious silence overcame our group upon departure. There was much to think about, and many emotions had to be sorted out. My daughter, recognizing that, after all the anticipation, I might be experiencing a letdown, quietly said, "Well, at least, it was closure." That it was! But I wasn't so certain that closure was what I had been looking for. Much later, when we returned to our hotel in Warsaw, news of an astounding nature hit us. The coincidence was strange and ironic. Here we were, at the very heart of the Holocaust—the place where Hitler's *final solution* for the Jewish people had begun. Six decades later, a Jew, U.S. Senator Joseph Lieberman, had been chosen as the Democratic Party's candidate for the office of Vice President of the United States.

CHAPTER 19

Chicago Futures in the Twenty-First Century

The world of futures that I encountered when I came to the Chicago Mercantile Exchange as a runner in the 1950s is long gone. Our technology was then chalk, blackboards, and the teletype. Board markers scribbled transaction prices and volumes on the blackboard, and Sammy—best described as the Merc's first CIO—sitting in a booth above the crowd, recorded the trade on the teletype. His work product was a tape that wound itself into the wastebasket. About a decade later, beginning in the late sixties and extending into the seventies, we graduated to computer-driven wallboards and a punch-card-driven clearing system. These became increasingly more sophisticated as the new technologies of the eighties and nineties infiltrated the business world. Still, the brick and mortar remained, as did the flashing quote boards and the shouting and pushing of traders, runners, and phone clerks. The world hasn't seen a new exchange like that since 1986. Modern exchanges are incorporeal. Soon the only reminder of the past will be the flashing quotes, but these may mostly be on computer screens.

In few places has the impact of the computer and modern information technology, which affected every nook and cranny of life on this planet, been more pronounced than in the financial markets. Alas, U.S. financial exchanges, especially U.S. futures markets, have been slow to grasp the full implication of these transformations—their neglect eclipsed only by the inertia of U.S. regulators. The consequence of this compounded inaction, indifference, or ignorance may very well serve to validate last Sunday's *Chicago Tribune* lead editorial which spoke of the imminent demise of Chicago as the capital of futures markets. The *Tribune* lamented the fact that "Anyone looking at the future of futures at the dawn of the twenty-first

The Future of Finance, University of Chicago Graduate School of Business, Gleacher Center, Chicago, April 28, 2000.

century must look east—across the Atlantic Ocean—to Eurex," who surpassed the CBOT to become the world's largest futures exchange. (See
Appendix 19A.) But the editorial, as Mark Twain might have said, is a bit
premature—maybe even dead wrong. Besides, it hardly touches the surface
of the complex issues involved.

It is now within the grasp of most financial institutions to acquire and
operate trade execution systems that duplicate the trading function of exchanges. As a result, every dealer is poised to create an exchange or join and
expand the operation of an existing exchange. There is a major story almost
every day announcing a new alliance to operate an exchange or a quasi
exchange. There is no technological barrier to cross-border operations, and
foreign exchanges want their share of the U.S. transaction business.

The only barrier to chaotic competition and a shakeout, are regulatory constraints. The new entrants are aghast that they might be subjected
to CFTC jurisdiction and regulation if they create their own electronic exchanges. Thus we have been treated to a bizarre spectacle as every segment
of the derivatives industry tries to explain why its proposed or projected
exchange is not really an exchange and should not be treated like the CME,
CBOT, or NYMEX.

Technology alters reality far quicker than any regulator can respond.
Blackbird, the derivatives trading platform operated by Derivatives Net,
Inc., is the most visible of this recent trend. Blackbird appears to be an
electronic multilateral transaction execution facility for swaps and other
financial instruments. Each member's bids and offers are live and available to
every other participant that passes the automatic credit screen. The contracts
traded are highly standardized. No legislation or regulation seems to exempt
Blackbird from registration; yet it has apparently gone live. Reports are that
it offers trading facilities for swaps, Forward Rate Agreements and other
futures-like derivatives. Its members include many of the same major dealers
that use traditional exchange markets with its array of financial futures. The
essential difference between the two is that futures exchanges are subject to
regulation and oversight and acknowledge important public responsibilities
while Blackbird operates with no constraint.

The efforts of new exchange entrants to avoid a consistent, logical definition of exchanges that would subject them to CFTC jurisdiction have been
matched only by the efforts of SEC regulated securities exchanges to keep
futures markets from competing in turf they have reserved for themselves.
Seventeen years ago, the Shad-Johnson Accord resolved a jurisdictional conflict between the SEC and the CFTC. It was not intended as a permanent
barrier to innovation and growth. Stock index futures, invented on futures
exchanges, have matured into vital financial management tools that enable
pension funds, investment companies and others to manage their risk of
adverse stock price movements. The options markets and the swaps dealers

offer customers risk management tools and investment alternatives involving both sector indexes and single stock derivatives. Futures exchanges have been frozen out.

Under current law, public customers who want to trade a future on an equity need to go over-the-counter or do a synthetic future through the facilities of an option exchange. A synthetic future requires two transactions at twice the commission and four times the cost of a simple future to achieve an identical result.[1] The SEC and their option exchanges are intent upon denying their customers the freedom to trade a single futures contract on a narrow index or an individual equity. The reasons advanced against reform of Shad-Johnson disguise competitive and/or political concerns. Today, Shad-Johnson is being used as a weapon against competition. The SEC, through statutory misinterpretation and, what the 7th Circuit Court of Appeals in *Board of Trade v. Securities and Exchange Commission*, No. 98-2923 (August 10, 1999) has found to be at best "arbitrary and capricious," and at worst "suspect" application of its powers, has denied futures exchanges the right to trade futures on stock indexes that reflect price movements in substantial market sectors. The court of appeals found that: "The stock exchanges prefer less competition; but if competition breaks out they prefer to trade the instruments themselves. . . . The Securities and Exchange Commission, which regulates stock markets, has sided with its clients." Congress should lift the single stock futures ban and allow the marketplace to decide whether these instruments would be useful new risk management tools.

Thus, traditional U.S. exchanges are being squeezed by the combination of their own immobility, internal establishment pressures, technological advances, and U.S. regulatory inertia. Further, while the SEC and its clients are fighting to constrain the ability of U.S. exchanges to trade equity derivatives, foreign exchanges and the OTC market are eager to fill that gap. Foreign exchanges are pouring into the U.S., but no guarantee of reciprocity has been extracted that would permit U.S. exchanges equivalent treatment in foreign jurisdictions. Also lost in the current legislative stampede to give the OTC markets total freedom to act as an exchange without the burdens of a regulated exchange, is the underlying value of clearing houses of the traditional futures markets. Their proved ability at risk management have served this nation well for over a century without the public ever being victimized because of a defaulting broker. The Federal Reserve never had to step in and help bail us out. The new game plan with its "pick-the-regulator-of-your-choice," will clearly be more competitive and open. However, in diminishing the strength of CFTC-ordained clearing houses, the question begged is to what extent this introduces the specter of unbridled systemic risk. Only the next Long Term Capital Management debacle will provide the answer.

The foregoing realities are driving nearly every traditional exchange to consider a transformation of its structure.[2] For centuries financial exchanges have been member-owned organizations. But nearly all of them are considering a change from a non-profit, member-owned structure to a for-profit entity with publicly traded stock. The shift toward electronic trading of stocks, futures, and options changes not only the manner of how these instruments are traded but also the organization, governance, and finances of the exchanges on which they are traded. At the Chicago Merc this transformation is nearly completed.

The fundamental reasons for this evolution are threefold: 1) Technology is expensive. Large sums of money are necessary to transform the trading floor into an electronic state-of-the-art trading system, money that is mostly available in public equity markets; 2) Competition has become fierce and promises to get fiercer. Electronic Communication Networks (ECNs), and a growing number of electronic exchanges, as previously noted, have created a competitive environment which demands efficient decision-making processes. Rules, procedures, and decisions based on an archaic system of floor politics, committees, and establishment controls, cannot compete in today's world where decisions demand instant recognition and must be based solely on competitive considerations. Only the lean and mean will survive; 3) Electronic trading leads to "disintermediation." With electronic trading, many of the middlemen essential to the operation of an exchange floor will play a much different role. Historically, intermediaries—brokerage firms, floor brokers, and market makers—owned seats on exchanges either to protect their competitive positions or as a source of specialized income. Electronic exchanges and the Internet change all that and will offer the marketplace to a much larger universe of participants many of whom will gain direct access, taking the place of the former intermediary whose function is bound to shift. Already futures traders have learned to trade by way of the screen. Electronic trading rooms may be the wave of the future.

Recently Banking Committee Chairman Phil Gramm issued an invitation to a May 8, 2000 hearing on the regulation of derivative markets and asked the key question that Congress and the regulators need to address, "What regulatory and market structures would enhance the value of our markets?" The Chicago Mercantile Exchange has offered testimony which provides much of the answer.

By way of historical context, the CME, in juxtaposition to other American markets and contrary to the broad brush of condemnation used in the *Chicago Tribune* editorial,[3] anticipated the impact of advances in information technology. In 1972, we initiated the idea of financial futures. A decade or so later, our Globex concept first introduced the world to the idea of electronic trading in futures. We spent years negotiating with foreign regulators to secure access to offshore markets. We spent tens of millions rewriting our clearing system, making it the standard for the industry. We consistently updated our contracts to reflect new competitive realities. We used technology to expand the capacity of our existing trading floor. Sadly, the CME too for a long time lost precious ground in a fierce tug-of-war between the certainty of an open-outcry past and the insecurity of a technological future. Nevertheless, about two years ago the process righted itself and we began reshaping the corporate structure of the Merc to a for-profit composition. We expect to be the first American exchange to achieve this objective.

In the regulatory realm, our goal was and remains equivalent regulatory treatment for functionally equivalent execution facilities, clearinghouses and intermediaries. U.S. regulated futures exchanges suffer compared to offshore competitors and the domestic OTC market. Overly detailed regulation of futures exchanges increases direct costs and time to market of innovative products. We support relief for the OTC market, we support opening our markets to foreign competitors, but we cannot support a package that gives relief to one segment of the derivative market at the expense of domestic exchanges. We have proposed a holistic approach to regulatory reform that will bring legal certainty to the OTC market, relief to exchange markets and resolve the Shad-Johnson restriction.

But the hour is late. If the clock strikes midnight before the futures markets of Chicago—the very entities that created financial futures—do not complete their modernization agenda or are not allowed to compete equally with every other derivatives counterpart, whether foreign or domestic, then the *Chicago Tribune* will indeed be proven right.[4] I pray not.

CHAPTER 20

Merton Miller, 1923–2000

I t was love at first sight—I'm not speaking of Merton Miller's love affair with Katherine; that is a private matter that needs no public review. I am speaking of Merton Miller's love affair with financial futures.

Indeed, from the moment back in May of 1972 when financial futures were launched with the opening of the International Monetary Market, the IMM, to the day he left the Merc's boardroom for the ultimate futures market in the great beyond, Merton Miller remained passionately in love with our markets. So enamored was he with the IMM that in 1986 he unabashedly nominated financial futures as "the most significant financial innovation of the last twenty years."

He was fond of saying that if one of Rip Van Winkle's descendants fell asleep in 1970 and awoke two decades later, he would not be able to grasp what had happened in financial markets. In Merton's words: "So rapid has been the pace of innovation in financial instruments over the past 20 years that nothing could have prepared him to understand the myriad of innovations, from eurodollars to swaptions." Merton embraced these instruments as if they were members of his personal family. In a sense they were.

All the more reason Merton found it so exasperating that someone had to come to their defense. "Futures markets get no respect," he would say in Rodney Dangerfield fashion, and proceeded to do battle for their honor. This became his mission, his personal crusade, his academic assignment, his raison d'etre.

He even found it objectionable that our markets were called derivatives. "What are we, second-class citizens?" he would ask rhetorically. "Why are we not considered the real markets?" he demanded. Then he would use one of his homegrown analogies to emphasize the point: "Like maybe the derivatives market is a parasite market, living off the prices in the cash market, like ivy on an oak tree, sucking out its vital juice and undermining

Memorial Service, University of Chicago–Rockefeller Chapel, October 14, 2000.

its strength." *Stuff and nonsense*, he would say with a wave of the hand, leaving no room for doubt. "Our markets have succeeded because they provide a valuable service cheaper than its competition."

Notorious for speaking his mind, Merton personified intellectual honesty. No matter what the issue, no matter what the politics, no matter who the players, no matter how complex the subject matter, Merton Miller told it as it was. Whether the matter was philosophical or academic, whether it pertained to the private sector or public, whether it was about an entity as amorphous as a government agency or as specific as its chairman, let the chips fall as they may, let the feathers be ruffled as they might, other considerations be damned, the truth will be stated. When others might attempt to be diplomatic, to find words that would assuage an opposing view, if in doing so it caused a compromise to the underlying truth, Merton Miller would have none of it.

When the spate of so-called derivatives disasters shook up the corporate world several years ago—be it Procter & Gamble, Metallgesellschaft, Orange County, or Barings Bank—Merton held fast to the underlying reality: "These were swaps," he reminded the corporate world. "You entered into them voluntarily." Then, using one of his irrepressible analogies, he would drive the point home—I can still hear the echo of his words: "A swap is not a robbery, guys! It's not like someone stuck a gun into your ribs and asked for your wallet."

One of Merton's defining moments occurred in the aftermath of the 1987 Stock Market Crash—during a time that could have meant a death knell to futures. As he saw it, it was a battle between New York against Chicago. And above all else, Merton was a supreme Chicago patriot—and not just for the Chicago Bears. It was then that some of the most powerful forces in the financial establishment were joined by some of the most influential members of the media and gained the attention of some of the most prominent officials of government in their attempt to place blame for the crash on Chicago's futures markets. Merton Miller's credentials and uncompromising logic stood in their way.

The most contentious issue of that day was volatility. Index futures were accused of causing volatility in the equities markets, thereby driving away the small investor. Merton took to this challenge with gusto. Imitating the rhetoric of a former well-known mayor of Chicago, he mimicked, "I am going to deny those allegations and defy the allegators." Then Merton would ask in all innocence: "Are we academics like that fabled soldier during a parade who believed that everyone was out of step but him? Arrogant as it may seem," he would reply, "I will argue here that we academics are not out of step. It is the public and some parts of the financial press that are out of step on this issue."

At one point in the fracas, when Merton was asked by the press when he would stop fighting Treasury Secretary Nicholas Brady's demand for margin control over futures, Merton replied, *Never!* Then, as if thinking it over, he would quip: "But I will make the Secretary a deal: If he will resign, I will too." When Brady didn't, Merton initiated a campaign to find an ambassadorship for the secretary.

Nor was Merton afraid to take on the traders or heavyweights within our futures industry. Time and again he openly lambasted those CME board members who would resist the advancement of technology. He also minced no words in placing most of the blame on the Chicago Board of Trade for dragging its feet in the creation of a Common Clearing entity among the Chicago exchanges. And as for the overcrowded conditions in the pits, he had a simple solution: "Auction it off." Let each parcel of pit space go to the highest bidder instead of traders getting it for free. Somehow, our traders didn't appreciate this aspect of free enterprise.

But Merton reserved his most stinging invectives on regulatory authority, specifically for the CFTC. During a memorable moment, one that captured Merton's shy and retiring nature, he said to the chairperson of our agency who was on a fact-finding tour of the Merc, "Madam chairman, now hear this: the CFTC is an anachronism—a classic example of an agency that never had an economic purpose." It left the chairperson momentarily speechless.

Indeed, he compared financial regulation with that of being a dermatologist. As Merton saw it, dermatology was by far the best medical specialty; the patients never die, but they never get well either. Similarly, the mission for regulators, he would say, was never to kill the industry they regulate but never to have it get well either.

Often referring to the CFTC as Keystone Cops, he would tell the Merc board that as long as the agency was around, "the industry's operating costs will continue to be higher, its size smaller and it growth rate lower." A most comforting thought.

And in case we didn't fully get the picture, Merton underscored his message with a story that compared the CFTC to a referee at a boxing match. It seems that a prizefighter was taking a terrible pounding from his opponent, but when he finally staggered back to his corner at the end of the round, his manager encouraged him by saying, "Don't worry, he hasn't laid a glove on you." At which point the fighter gasped, "Well, then keep an eye on the referee because somebody is sure beating the hell out of me." It was vintage Merton Miller.

Thus, for futures markets, the loss of Merton Miller is immeasurable. Who will replace his wit, his candor, his earthy analogies? And who in academia will mount the barricades in the next attack? Not only have our markets lost its most authoritative voice, we lost our academic seer, our intellectual Muhammad Ali, our Horatio at the Gate, our Émile Zola, our Clarence Darrow.

Farewell, old friend, we will miss you dearly.

CHAPTER 21

Buy a Call on the Snake

Traditional Exchanges in an E-Commerce World

C an traditional futures exchanges survive in the e-commerce structure of
the twenty-first century? It is a question of some significance to nearly
everyone at this conference—or should be.

There are those who will be quick to tell you, no! The role of the
traditional exchange, they will say, is finished. *Kaput!* The myriad of transformations that have revolutionized the financial services arena over the
past two decades have not only terminated the need of traditional trading
floors but have even abrogated the functional necessity of a central transaction system. No more need to wait an hour or so for an execution report
from the soybean pit. No more need to pay exorbitant brokerage fees. No
more need to hope that the broker read your order correctly, that he didn't
hesitate, that he didn't lose it in his deck, that he didn't favor a friend before
acting for you, that the crowd didn't front-run your order. And no more
need to hope that the trade didn't result in an out-trade. The celebrated role
these exchanges played in the financial landscape of the twentieth century,
they say, has no place in the twenty-first.

In truth, these doomsayers make a formidable case. Some of their arguments are right on. Surely much of the past structure is indefensible. But
I for one am not prepared to throw in the towel just yet.

Let me begin by stating that the markets of futures and options have
been around for a very long time. I mean a *very long* time. I don't pretend
to know what part futures played in the Creation, but it is reasonable to
assume they had some role. Surely the Almighty or someone preparing for
the big bang must have contemplated hedging the bet. I realize, of course,

Conference, International Association of Financial Engineers, Nice, France, July 2,
2001.

that, according to Stephen Hawking, under the conditions existing before
the big bang all the laws of science, and therefore all ability to predict the
future, break down. But when you think about it, such chaos is a perfect
setting for futures. John Meriwether will always give you a price. I mean,
what if the first three seconds didn't quite go the way Einstein said they did?
Wouldn't it have been neat to have in your back pocket an option on, say,
an *Alternative Universe Swap*?

Speaking of options, I cannot substantiate the theory that before Eve
entered the Garden of Eden, she bought a call on the snake. But I agree
it makes sense. After all, this was before the Kama Sutra was published,
and Adam was totally without prior experience. According to one school
of thought, Eve acted on the advice of Myron Scholes. This clearly changes
the date of the Black–Scholes Model. It obviously also changes the age of
Myron Scholes. He won't exactly admit it, but he has intimated that it was
an American-type option. This made it much more challenging for Adam.
After all, in such matters, after the . . . expiration . . . the option is really quite
worthless.

Of what I am quite certain, is that the first recorded futures trade was
made in biblical times by Joseph. He and his brothers knocked it around for
a while, and it was 8 to 4 in favor of saving the Pharaoh's administration.
Joseph was chosen to convince the Egyptian monarch about putting on
some buy hedges in grains. Some say Joseph was the last central banker
to get it right. It of course saved the Land of Egypt from the coming seven
years of lean. Centuries later, Israel called in the debt, and it resulted in the
Camp David Accord between Anwar Sadat and Menachem Begin.

It is also historically correct that ancient Phoenicians, Greeks, and Romans extended Joseph's idea, taking it to another level. They began trading
options against the cargoes of incoming and outgoing ships. However, with
primitive vessels and no way to predict the weather, it was a very dicey
proposition—something like selling Treasuries to hedge junk bond exposure. Anyway, the actual earliest source of modern futures exchanges were
the seasonal merchant fairs during the tenth and twelfth centuries in places
like Brussels and Madrid. Of course, many of the merchants were attracted
to the festivities surrounding these events. Vast quantities of wine and spirits were consumed. Little wonder that liquidity has been the hallmark of
centralized markets ever since.

The first formalized concept of futures delivery can be traced to these
trade fairs. It took the form of an agreement between fair merchants for
the future delivery of merchandise at a forthcoming fair. In time, the merchants developed commonsense rules pertaining to trade which eventually
transformed itself into the Merchant's Code and for centuries was regarded
as the official set of equitable practices of trade. The idea of using common sense as the foundation for best practices lasted until 1933, when the

concept was summarily rejected by the newly formed Securities and Exchange Commission.

Japan was the first country to formalize the futures exchange. To be exact, the house of a wealthy rice merchant named Yodoya, in Osaka, in the year of 1650 is recorded as being the first stationary meeting place for merchants where they would gather to exchange and negotiate their "rice tickets." These were, in fact, negotiable warehouse receipts representing either rice already grown and stored or rice to be produced for future delivery. Rumor has it, though, that this great invention was banished from the Rising Sun for the next 200 years because the Emperor of Japan got caught in a short squeeze.

It was not until 1826 in England, and 1867 in the United States, that the traditional futures market was established. In the U.S., Chicago was the natural locale as it represented the great railroad center for products grown in the West to be moved to the population centers in the East. It proved to be a huge commercial success for the city. Carl Sandburg even wrote a poem about it. Trouble was, years later, when Chicago's alderman Paddy Bauler proclaimed that "Chicago wasn't ready for reform," the Chicago exchanges took it as gospel.

Forgive me if I dare to mention that throughout its formal history, traditional futures were based on agricultural products. It wasn't until 1972 when some wild-eyed mischief maker, without credentials, without permission from Arthur Levitt or even one New York banker, explained to a bunch of hog traders in Chicago that the Swiss franc *was not* some kind of foreign hot dog. The shock sent the traders into turmoil and resulted in a primordial financial soup on the floor of the Chicago Mercantile Exchange. Years later, their cousins—euphemistically known as financial engineers, but regarded in some circles as financial equivalents of Osama bin Laden—fed the concoction to their hungry computers and the rest is history. The age of derivatives sprang to life which today boasts of $90 trillion in outstanding contracts. Of course, somewhere along the way, Fisher Black and Myron Scholes showed up again and spoiled all the fun by explaining what we were doing and why. Let me say that there are experts—knowledgeable in the field of finance and astronomy—who believe that, as a consequence, distant galaxies are moving more rapidly away from us.

The point of this review is to show that, from their birth, the genetic code of futures markets made them both dynamic and resilient. While everything about them changed, while detractors accused them of everything from the Black Plague to the 1987 stock crash, and protagonists claimed that they were instrumental in lowering the cost of capital, raising the standard of living—and, some even say, a sensible substitute for violent crime—one thing remained constant: They provided liquid pools of buyers and sellers in the management of risk. Still, any comparison of futures exchanges in the twenty-first century with the one in the past is like comparing the Model T Ford to the Lamborghini Diablo. Both vehicles had four wheels, but that is about where the comparison ends.

While the confrontation between technological advancements that permeated the marketplace and traditional open-outcry methodologies has been brewing for over a decade, the immediate catalyst of the war that unfolded was the 1998 SEC promulgation allowing alternative trading systems. The ruling came in the nick of time to satisfy the federal mandate that every agency must do something worthwhile at least *once* every century. Status quo was forever changed. It caused a swarm of electronic communications networks, so-called ECNs, to be created. ECNs can and do encroach the traditional turf of exchanges and represent the greatest threat in the battle for transactional dominance.

Their general catchall definition is that they are transaction mechanisms developed independently from the established marketplaces like the NYSE, NASDAQ, Chicago Mercantile Exchange, Chicago Board of Trade, Chicago Board Options Exchange, and so on, and designed to match buyers and sellers on an agency basis. Some are designed for equities, some for cash, others for futures and OTC derivatives. They can also be grouped into market types: interest rates, credit instruments, foreign exchange, energy, weather, metals, chemicals, and even hedge funds to name a few.

There are different types of business models among ECNs. Most of them end up serving different client needs, but their most significant difference is that some are destination networks, which are principally execution systems, others are simply routing mechanisms. In addition, there are also crossing networks; hybrid models of electronic order routing and trade execution; smart-order-routing facilities; and noncontinuous automated call auction models. Each of these designs either has unique features that serve a specific array of clients or has built-in order flow from the systems users. There are literally hundreds, perhaps thousands, of them, and their sheer number makes one suspect of the genre. It is inevitable that many of them face the same dismal fate of a multitude of B2Bs and "dot-coms" that sprang up during the height of the Internet bubble—when even street people had their own web site. Still, those providing the greatest value added will flourish.

Mostly, traditional exchanges have only themselves to blame for their vulnerable condition—this is especially true in the case of futures exchanges. They will argue, and it is true, they were trapped in an antiquated thicket of federal regulatory requirements and prohibitions which had failed to keep pace with the competitive effects of globalization and technology. These conditions served to handcuff American exchanges and invite entities, both foreign and domestic, not so constrained, to create competitive transaction forums that were more efficient and more responsive to current needs. But that excuse *alone* won't hunt. It is not the first or last time that governmental interference or ineptitude stood in the way of the private sector. Rather than find remedies to overcome or ameliorate these constraints, the exchanges for the most part were satisfied to remain in a semicomatose state. Fat and lazy, controlled by establishment forces that, to paraphrase historian Barbara Tuchman, "refused to alter any of their cozy pre-arrangements," the exchanges remained adamantly committed to a way of life that ignored most of what happened in the last decade of the twentieth century. Status quo at all costs was their mantra. And although reality has now penetrated the four walls of open outcry, the foregoing was the setting for the current battle between alternative trading systems and the exchanges.

At the core of the technological revolution lies the capacity to collect orders, transmit them, and execute them in nanoseconds. This capability became a natural partner to the overriding goal of the modern trading era: *investment performance.* Survival and success will go to that market structure that provides the participant with the best chance of reaching this objective. All else is secondary.

In the past, U.S. market structures—generally composed of exchanges and broker-dealers—have catered to the needs of institutional and retail investors by focusing on centralization of trading activity. In that fashion, buyer and seller interaction is maximized. They acted as the fairs of a bygone era. However, the explosion of ECNs has led to the potential for the undoing of centralization. These issues have resulted in a debate whether it is feasible or not, good or bad, and who wins or loses. Then again, perhaps the market will evolve so that any one ECN, or a combine of them, become the equivalent of a centralized market. The success of traditional exchanges is materially dependent on the outcome of this debate.

At the heart of investment performance are two elements that are in the control of the participant: (1) trading costs and (2) the venue for "best execution." So the tug-of-war is whether a centralized marketplace can do better than the ECN in achieving the best price at the lowest cost. On one side is the contention that centralization is necessary for order-competition—in other words, to achieve the best price. On the other side is the contention that fragmentation maximizes venue competition—in other words, it offers competitive efficiencies to achieve the best "all-in" cost.

There are yet two additional considerations in this contest which are paramount: *liquidity* and *clearing.* Liquidity as a mandatory element for success is a given. Not to put too fine a point on it, liquidity is to markets what pitching is to baseball. No matter what else you have, without liquidity you don't win the pennant. The ability to clear, process, and settle transactions is, in my view, of similar significance. To stay viable in an e-commerce world, a transaction system must provide this competence or partner with someone that can.

In comparing who offers the most of what, I will simply state that with respect to liquidity, there is no contest. Traditional futures exchanges have it. It is, as I said, their hallmark. Can this hurdle be overcome by ECNs? Yes, it has happened—Eurex's wresting of the Bund contract from LIFFE is the clearest example of such a case—but it is a rare event and doesn't come easy. Especially not if an exchange is alert to the threat and takes the indicated measures. Consider, the Open Interest in Eurodollars at the CME—a good measure of liquidity—stands at 4,430,000 contracts, or $4.4 trillion. The Open Interest in Eurodollar options is even bigger, and the combined average daily volume of this futures instrument is nearly 700,000 contracts, or $900 billion. In similar fashion, clearing and processing on a multilateral basis has historically been the strong suit of traditional exchanges. This is not a skill ECNs are born with. Indeed, existing clearing organizations, sensing an opening in the battle, are stretching their reach to provide greater value to member firms and even extending their clearing services beyond the traditional markets.

I have characterized the battle as between ECNs and traditional exchanges, specifically futures exchanges. However, it must be understood that many of these platforms were created in conjunction with traditional broker-dealers and nearly all are owned by consortia of market participants, many of which are broker-dealers. For instance, BrokerTec Global represents an electronic interdealer trading platform backed by a consortium of 14 of the most powerful institutional firms—ABN Amro, Lehman Brothers, Merrill Lynch, Morgan Stanley, UBS Warburg, Credit Suisse, Banco Santander, S.A. Barclays, Deutsche Bank, Dresdner Bank, Goldman Sachs, J.P. Morgan, Salomon Smith Barney, and Greenwich Capital. BrokerTec recently received CFTC approval as a futures exchange. It will offer a single, fully electronic platform that aims to trade cash and traditional futures contracts, and claims that it will do it cheaper. One cannot dismiss this type of competitor lightly.

Still, I cannot yet accept the prediction for the end to traditional futures exchanges. Perhaps the best way to explain why is to examine what I view as a telltale test case. I am referring to the ECN known as Blackbird Holdings, Inc.—named after the world's fastest aircraft developed by the U.S. Air Force. Founded in 1996, Blackbird was the world's first interdealer electronic trading system for privately negotiated over-the-counter futures, including interest rate swaps and forward rate agreements. The ECN was no neophyte; its strategic partners included Garban and Reuters. Following its launch in 1999, Blackbird gained a great deal of well-deserved notoriety since it offered an efficient screen-based alternative to the current interdealer voice broker services. In plain language, Blackbird epitomized the competitive threat that traditional futures exchanges faced from sophisticated ECNs that could replicate the trading floor.

Nevertheless, a few years after its launch, Blackbird approached the Chicago Mercantile Exchange to join forces. It resulted in a historic trading initiative which linked the Merc's Globex2 electronic platform with Blackbird's electronic system. The initiative enabled Blackbird to effectively link its system with the centralized marketplace. The dealers, Blackbird stated, will benefit by being able to trade seamlessly through one screen. To put it another way, Blackbird decided that rather than do battle with the centralized market, it was a better strategy to ally with it.

Similar evidence of which way the wind is blowing can be found by examining what has happened so far in the American equities markets. In a word, it's a yawn. So far, the listed markets, particularly at the NYSE and other equities exchanges, have been nearly untouched by ECNs. On top of that, NASDAQ is launching the so-called Super-Montage which is intended to transform NASDAQ from a fragmented network of market makers and ECNs to a more centralized exchange in order to gain more of the benefits of centralized liquidity. Further, the Chicago Board Options Exchange has maintained its dominance in equity options. And across the street, the Chicago Mercantile Exchange is experiencing record volume and has reached number-one status on the American continent for the first time in its 100-year history.

These are all strong signals that traditional exchanges, once energized, can successfully compete. Because of their centralized structure, their historically impressive liquidity pools, their time-tested capability to clear and settle transactions, and the fact that perhaps they woke up in time, they have, in my view, the long end of the odds in the struggle to remain dominant.

Of course, the debate is far from over. Continued dominance by exchanges or even their survival is not without a set of provisos: Their metamorphoses must be quick and radical. They will have to look dramatically different from even the most streamlined entity of present day. They will have to become public companies. They will have to be predominantly, if not exclusively, *electronic*. They will have to be efficient, sophisticated, and cost conscious. They will have to make technology a primary asset of their infrastructure. They will have to replicate many features of today's ECNs, innovate with new products and product lines, and adopt strategies to expand their distribution on a global basis. They will have to deal in instruments encompassing the entire gamut of business needs and provide a panoply of services covering every facet of risk management. Their driving mission must be the augmentation of investment performance. In short, they must morph into an amalgamation of what they were and what they never were expected to be.

Some exchanges that were not up to this task have already vanished; others are being thrust to the sidelines. For those that survive there is bound to be massive consolidation. Way down the road, I would venture that there is room for two, maybe three, mega-futures-exchange networks operating on a global basis. While there may always be regional exchanges serving a local clientele, they will be irrelevant unless they are tied to a global network. There is also little doubt that the ongoing trend of blurring distinctions between the instruments of futures and securities continues so that in not too far a distant future, securities and futures exchanges may also integrate. The recent joint venture in single stock futures between the CME and CBOE is a step in that direction. Some day there may even be only one market regulator.

Above all, traditional exchanges to succeed in an e-commerce world must overpower what Milton Friedman calls "the tyranny of the status quo." In simple terms, they must stand up to the internal opposition of their establishment. If they resist change, if they fear innovation, if they cling to past arrangements, then Alderman Paddy Bauler's admonition against reform will be their legacy.

The jury is still out. My advice is to heed Myron Scholes—*buy a call on the snake!* Thank you.

CHAPTER 22

Transformation of Futures Exchanges

A llow me to briefly examine the transformation occurring on futures exchanges and the effects of September 11, 2001. The issues center around the pace of their evolution and give rise to several interconnected questions. When will open outcry be totally replaced by electronic trade? Is there a continued necessity for a centralized transaction system in an e-commerce world? And is there a use for the traditional trading floor in an age of electronic automation?

The confrontation between traditional open-outcry methodologies and technological advancements that permeated the marketplace has been brewing for over a decade. But the immediate catalyst of the war that unfolded was the 1998 SEC promulgation allowing alternative trading systems. It caused a swarm of electronic communications networks, so-called ECNs, to be created. ECNs can and do encroach the traditional turf of exchanges and represent the greatest threat in the battle for transactional dominance.

There are different types of business models among ECNs. Most of them end up serving different client needs, but their most significant difference is that some are destination networks, which are principally execution systems, and others are simply routing mechanisms. There are literally hundreds of them, and their sheer number makes one suspect of the genre. It is inevitable that many of them face the same dismal fate of a multitude of B2Bs and "dot-coms" that sprang up during the height of the Internet bubble. Still, those providing the greatest value added will flourish.

While to a large degree the battle is between ECNs and traditional exchanges—specifically futures exchanges—it must be understood that many of these platforms were created in conjunction with traditional broker-dealers and nearly all are owned by consortia of market participants, many

Unpublished comments edited for *The New Economy*, January 2002.

of which are broker-dealers. At the heart of the tug-of-war are three basic issues: (1) Where is liquidity best achieved? (2) Where can a participant receive secure processing, clearing, and banking facilities for the transaction? and (3) In what forum will a participant achieve the best price at the lowest cost? The transaction system that provides the best combination of answers to these three propositions will dominate.

That liquidity is a mandatory element for success of any transaction system is a given. Without it there is no market. One needs not dwell on this point; examples of failed systems because of a lack of liquidity are legion. In comparing who offers the most of what, I will simply state that with respect to liquidity, there is no contest. It is the hallmark of traditional futures exchanges. Can this hurdle be overcome by ECNs? Yes, it has happened—Eurex's wresting of the Bund contract from LIFFE is the clearest example of such a case—but it is a rare event and doesn't come easy. Especially not if an exchange is alert to the threat and takes the indicated measures.

This brings us to the ability to clear, process, and settle transactions. To stay viable in an e-commerce world, a transaction system must provide this capability or partner with someone that can. Again, clearing, processing, and banking on a multilateral basis has historically been the strong suit of traditional exchanges. This is not a skill ECNs are born with. Indeed, existing clearing organizations, sensing an opening in the battle, are stretching their reach to provide greater value to member firms and even extending their clearing services beyond the traditional markets.

Finally, can a centralized marketplace do better than the ECN in achieving the best price at the lowest cost? On one side is the contention that centralization is necessary for order competition—in other words, to achieve the best price. Again, this would point to the centralized marketplace which maximizes order flow. On the other side is the contention that fragmentation maximizes venue competition—in other words, it offers competitive efficiencies to achieve the best "all-in" cost.

Long before the terrorist attacks, there was mounting acceptance by users that centralized exchanges provide the best combination of the necessary three requirements: liquidity, clearing, and best execution at the lowest cost. Since September 11 this view has been greatly enhanced by a coincidental consequence of the attacks. More than ever, users want to take fewer chances. There is much less tolerance for experimentation. "Carry out my business on a forum that has withstood the test of time, that has established expertise, and that has unquestionable financial integrity" is the message we are getting. That message was certainly fortified—by an order of magnitude—as a consequence of the recent Enron experience. Indeed, EnronOnline seemed to epitomize a successful ECN providing worldwide energy and related financial trading facilities. Its sudden failure sent a troubling signal to the trading community about the reliability of a private ECN, even one as large as Enron seemed to be.

Moreover, because a sophisticated application programming interface (API) serves to mask the geographical location of both the matching engine as well as the clearing facility, the technological revolution actually favors centralized exchanges. By virtue of an API, every broker-dealer can plug into any sophisticated transaction system it chooses as well as clear its trade at the clearing facility of its choice. This gives the traditional exchanges a huge leg up.

We are then left with the questions of electronic versus open-outcry trade and the continued necessity of the traditional trading floor. To me it has been clear for a very long time that with the coming of the technological revolution, screen-based trading will overtake the traditional pit-trading environment. It is axiomatic. At the core of the technological revolution lies the capacity to collect orders, transmit them, and execute them in nanoseconds. Technology provides speed, efficiency, and lower costs.

It was that belief that led us at the Chicago Mercantile Exchange to propose Globex way back in 1987 before any other futures exchange in the world considered making such a revolutionary proposal. Since then, of course, the world has embraced the concept of electronic trade. In Europe there are no open-outcry exchanges left to speak of; in Asia this trend is recognized as well. In the U.S. the pace toward a full electronic replacement has been much slower. But with September 11 and the danger of a trading disruption that can incapacitate a trading floor—such as happened for the first time in its history of the NYSE—the pace toward electronic transaction systems is bound to accelerate.

The issues are complex. American futures exchanges have a long history of successful open-outcry trading. Our floor trading community still represents a majority of our ownership. Thus, the livelihood of our owners is to a large degree dependent on a floor-based system. At the CME we have spent a good deal of time educating our members. They have learned to accept the reality that some day the floor will cease to function. But we have agreed with them that the exact date is uncertain. Instead, we have struck a bargain with the floor members. While we have no doubt that ultimately electronics and automation will prevail to the exclusion of the trading pit, we will let the market itself determine the exact date for this transformation. Without a doubt, September 11 has quickened this metamorphosis. In the meantime the CME operates in dual fashion. We maintain our trading floor and continue to expand the capabilities of Globex in order to provide the best electronic system possible.

I would also argue that when open outcry goes, so will the purpose of the trading floor as we have come to know it. But in my view, the trading floor can be transformed into an important resource of a centralized exchange. It should become an "Electronic Arcade." To understand the rationale behind this thought, one must understand that a trading floor was always more than simply the place where a transaction occurred. It was a gathering place for traders where new ideas could germinate from old ones. It is precisely the reason that giant trading floors at banks and investment houses exist. While the trades their employees make may be executed strictly in a technological fashion, the traders shout at each other, and information as well as ideas are easily passed.. There are private electronic trading rooms springing up throughout the marketplace. A large electronic trading arena sponsored by a centralized exchange can be an important addition in the evolution toward automation.

The good news is that for futures markets, there is one unchanging constant: *Uncertainty lies at their very foundation.* Case in point, the volume statistics at the Chicago Mercantile Exchange. Since the first of the Federal Reserve reductions in the federal funds rates that began in January of this year, the CME continued to achieve record volumes. So much is therefore clear: The management of risk is the bedrock of futures exchanges. The prospect of any economic dislocation, the potential for any change in value or price, the expectation of any alteration in economic policies or behavior, whether it be the result of international upheaval or the consequence of domestic disruption in business flows, are the natural drivers of transaction volume on futures exchanges. The events of September 11 served to underscore this truth.

CHAPTER 23

Our Middle Name

C arl Sandburg gave us definition:

"Hog Butcher for the World,
Tool maker, Stacker of Wheat,
Player with Railroads and the Nation's Freight Handler;
Stormy, husky, brawling,
City of the Big Shoulders."

And this is how it evolved:
In the 60's we were called hustlers—
Bamboozling the last dime from widows and orphans;
Proprietors in a stacked game of corner the market;
And yet we grew!
In the 70's we were called arrogant impostors—
Pretending to be relations to the holy temples of finance;
Stealing the rightful markets of New York and London;
And yet we grew!
In the 80's we were called lucky—
Beneficiaries of the inflationary aberrations of the 1970s;
Catering to speculators, volatility and index arbitrage;
And yet we grew!
In the 90's we were called obsolete—
Archaic mechanisms of a bygone era;
Inefficient relics that could not compete with ECN technology;
And yet we grew!

Federal Reserve Bank, Roundtable on the Institutional Structure of Financial Markets, Chicago, Illinois, February 15, 2002.

For necessity had recast Sandburg's definition:
Risk Capital for the World,
Innovator, Conceiver of Markets,
Player with Concepts and the Nation's Futures,
Stormy, husky, brawling,
City of the Big Shoulders.

Carl Sandburg's recast definition became our new heritage, our new legacy. It brought us new fame, new image, new industries, new jobs, new banks, new strength, a new future. It protected us, rebuffing our competitors and rejecting our antagonists decade after decade. But our legacy is as tenuous as it is precious. Evolution is an unceasing taskmaster and the imperatives of the twenty-first century make new demands: modern technologies, demutualization, efficiency. So the old question resurfaces: *Can we again meet the challenge of change and yet protect our hard-earned franchise?*

The answer lies in understanding the three pillars of our legacy: financial integrity, liquidity, and innovation. Lose any one of them and you lose everything. It is a risky business.

Financial Integrity

Let me be blunt: *Metaphorically speaking, Enron would not have happened in Chicago.* Neither would Long Term Capital Markets, nor the most recent fiasco at the Allied Irish Bank. Of course, I am referring to their trading in over-the-counter (OTC) derivatives. For in the structures of Chicago exchanges, or, for that matter, at any centralized traditional exchange— whether in their boisterous open-outcry pits or in the cyberspace of their electronic screens—where trillions of dollars are transacted daily then cleared and settled by their clearinghouses, futures markets flourish within as safe a financial design as the human mind can devise.

At the core of these mechanisms lie some meticulously fashioned and highly sophisticated operations. Mechanisms that represent the very essence of their default-free success. Unlike Enron—a darling of the so-called "New Economy"—the combination of these interwoven components represent a marvel of human thought and time-tested experience. Call it the old-fashioned way, if you will. To be specific:

The neutrality of their clearinghouses
Their system of multilateral clearing and settlement
    —providing a central counterparty guarantee to every transaction
    —eliminating counterparty credit risk
Their daily mark-to-market disciplines
    —eliminating accumulation of debt

Their daily margining demands
Their full disclosure standards
Their transaction transparency
Their audit trail regimen
Their financial surveillance procedures
Their regulatory requirements

—Leo Melamed

I have no hesitation in saying that these components epitomize financial safety and transaction transparency—Enron represented their opposite. Gretchen Morgenson of the *New York Times* correctly called Enron "a master of obfuscation." Even more damning was Jerry Taylor, the director of the Cato Institute: "Enron," he said, "was an enemy, not an ally, of free markets. Enron was more interested in rigging the marketplace with rules and regulations to advantage itself at the expense of competitors and consumers than in making money the old fashioned way." To put it another way, while Enron correctly believed that energy could and should be traded like stocks, bonds, and futures, it wanted to conduct its transactions in an opaque manner, devoid of disclosure, conducive to conflicts of interest, and driven primarily by greed, ambition and arrogance.

No bilateral system, no matter the parties involved, can hope to match the financial integrity and transparency of a multilateral counterparty clearing facility composed of the above-enumerated strictures—safer yet if the facility is integrated with its trading engine so that at all times it has the pulse of the entire marketplace. For instance, at the Chicago Mercantile Exchange, the number-one U.S. futures exchange, about $1.5 billion in settlement payments are made daily. We manage $30 billion in collateral deposits. On September 17, we had pays and collects of $6 billion—without a hiccup. Instead, Enron was a counterparty to every transaction it executed—no trade intermediation occurred. In other words, every trade on EnronOnline depended on Enron's creditworthiness. If you don't understand what that means, ask the people who are left holding the bag.

Liquidity

Let me be brief: *Without it there is no market*. It represents the constant flow of bids and offers to the market, thereby liquefying the price-discovery process. It allows every participant to assume or eliminate market exposure quickly and at a fair cost. But liquidity is as elusive as it is vital. Examples of failed systems by virtue of a lack of liquidity are legion.

On the other hand, "If you got it, flaunt it." That motto is nowhere more applicable than to the liquidity at traditional futures exchanges. It is their hallmark—their genetic code. While everything about them changed—while detractors and demagogues accused them of everything from the Black Plague to the 1987 Stock Crash, one thing remained constant: Futures exchanges are by far the best in providing liquid pools of buyers and sellers for the management of risk. During world upheavals, this becomes their most coveted asset.

Look at the hundreds of millions of annual transactions at the CBOE. Look at the CBOT's 30-year bond contract with its $23 billion in daily notional value or its note contract averaging nearly $11 billion a day in turnover value. Look at the NYMEX with its average daily volume of 466,000 contracts. Look at the CME Eurodollar market. Consider, the average daily volume in that instrument alone (futures and options) is about 1,200,000 contracts, or $1.2 trillion every day. And unlike at Enron, our traders never have to pretend that they are busy.

Innovation

Let me be explicit: If financial integrity is the heart of our futures exchanges, if liquidity is the blood that flows through its veins, then innovation is its soul—*its middle name.*

Innovation, the willingness to try something new, the genius to invent, the nerve to confront what Milton Friedman calls the "Tyranny of the Status Quo," the audacity to take a risk, the courage to fail is what separates the commonplace from the phenomenal, the mundane from the divine, the past from the future. In markets it is the difference between failure and success. Without a soul, the market, like with every human endeavor, will soon expire.

That Chicago is the risk capital of the world is predominantly the result of its middle name. Other market forums can and have achieved financial integrity, other market arenas can and have achieved liquidity, but what sets this city's futures markets apart from everyone else is an abundance of all three components. Indeed, emulating the Chicago Nobel laureate tradition of Milton Friedman, George J. Stigler, Merton M. Miller, Gary Becker, Myron Scholes, and a host of others, Chicago's innovative soul is quite unique. Beginning in the 1850s with the inauguration of futures markets in the U.S., to the 1960s break from storable products, to the 1970s revolutionary introduction of financial instruments and the development of security options contracts, to the 1980s debut of cash settlement and the conceptualization of Globex, to the 1990s inception of electronic mini-contracts, Chicago markets have consistently been the incubator of innovation.

Indeed, Chicago's innovations in foreign exchange, interest rates, security options, and equity index futures were not only the model copied by every center of trade the world over, it served as a mechanism that in the words of Alan Greenspan *"has undoubtedly improved national productivity growth and standards of living."*

But past accomplishments do not by themselves guarantee future success. My fear is that in the process of modernizing and demutualizing, *which we must,* we neglect the principles on which we are founded—especially our middle name. As we become like corporate America, as we worry about quarterly results, as we concern ourselves with shareholder values, as we rush to give our clients what they seek, will our past continue to be prelude? *Will we remain the risk capital for the world? The innovator, conceiver of markets?* Or will we fail because we forgot that our legacy depended *not* on one or another of its embedded components but on all three? There is a real and present danger that we become transaction processing plants without a soul. It is a model with an immediate allure, but one that spells eventual ruin.

As our own history has proven, the inventor owns the market. A postulate easy to grasp but very hard to achieve. It is a goal that must resonate through every fiber of the institution—a most ephemeral ambition. *And, lest we forget, the marrow of our past innovative success has been our floor community.* As we prepare to meet current competition, as we evolve to become efficient, can we preserve the resource they constitute? Can we retain the intrinsic shareholder value they represent? While it is certain that an electronic future is our destiny, have we charted the correct course for its evolution? Let me be clear: While it is mandatory to create the best electronic system that can be devised, while we must advance its use and effectiveness, the market, and only the market, can dictate the timing of floor transference.

Innovation is also costly and includes risk of failure. Failure is counterproductive to the bottom line. Innovation is often also counterintuitive to what clients seek. Indeed, clients do not always know what they need. Were futures in foreign exchange, or Eurodollars, or bonds invented because of client demand? Were the energy contracts launched by the NYMEX in response to a demand from the energy industry? Not even close! By definition, innovation means to give birth to something of which clients know nothing. It means to prepare for contingencies not always visible. It means to create new clientele. It means to predict what our clients will need some day in the future.

The Business of Risk

To succeed, not only must we resist the temptation to serve solely immediate demands, we must be wary of what our competition wants us to become. There is a current philosophy in some competitive quarters that exchanges and clearinghouses should *not* be vertically integrated. That they should be run as separate entities—and operate as utilities. Were that to happen, it could prove fatal.

Who are these competitive quarters and what is their motivation? Mostly they are large intermediaries. Their avowed purpose in promoting the idea of transaction and clearing utilities is to lower costs to their customers. It is no more than a ruse. Werner Seifert, chair of Management Board of the Deutsche Terminbörse AG, the world's largest futures exchange, calls it a "red herring." Seifert understands as we do that their real motivation is to control their customer's' order flow. They want to internalize their dealings, take the markets upstairs, and exploit the profit from the bid/ask spreads. In doing so, they will no doubt make lots of money, but there will be at least two fundamental casualties in their wake.

The first will be in the transparency implicit in the exchange-transaction process, one that is vital to the world and its regulators. Need we explain the inherent dangers in the loss of transparency in financial transactions? Need we revisit the causes of the Enron debacle? If you want a glimpse of where lack of full disclosure can lead, you need look no further than current reports of ambiguous accounting procedures—reaching levels of abuse that often bordered on fraud. As a trio of erudite *Wall Street Journal* reporters (John R. Emshwiller, Anita Raghavan, and Jathon Sapsford) recently pointed out, "Some of the world's leading banks and brokerage firms provided Enron with crucial help in creating the intricate and misleading financial structure that fueled the energy trader's impressive rise." Forgive me for underscoring that some of these same folks are the ones advocating that we become utilities, and have organized their own exchange where the transaction process has little if any transparency. Now, that's what I call *Chutzpah!*

The second casualty will be that of innovation. Does anyone here remember the last innovation produced by a utility? Hardly, unless you count pre-demutualized futures exchanges—but we were unusual under any definition. Again, Werner Seifert states the proposition well: "The entire value-added chain of securities processing from the initial matching of trades and the determination of prices to the final steps in clearing and settlement has to work with extremely high reliability. . . . [O]nly vertically integrated organizations can combine innovation with the level of reliability that customers require."

To a degree, of course, this debate is an offshoot of the ongoing competitive conflict between centralized exchanges and ECNs. The fact that exchanges are regulated is only part of the issue. Who provides the most efficient forum, the highest liquidity, the best price at the cheapest cost, are the critical considerations? Well, the winner of that debate can be determined only by the ultimate arbiter—the marketplace itself. And although the jury is still out, there has already been some indication which way the verdict is leaning. Countless of would-be-competitive ECNs that were launched with great hoopla during the B2B bubble now find themselves in the historical scrap heap. Indeed, long before the terrorist attacks, there was growing recognition by participants that centralized exchanges provided the best combination of the ingredients necessary for safety and liquidity—just check our volume statistics. Since September 11, there is even less tolerance for experimentation. "Stick with the tried and true" is the message we are hearing. That theme is amplified—by an order of magnitude—with the Enron experience.

So call us hustlers or arrogant imposters; call us lucky or even obsolete; call us what you like. We will remain the risk capital for the world, the innovator and conceiver of markets, so long as we remember the principles upon which our legacy was built.

CHAPTER 24

CME Center for Innovation

Allow me to begin by expressing my pride on the Merc's inaugural of this center as well as its establishment of the Fred Arditti Innovation Award. The center will serve as a fertile forum from which will sprout ideas and ideals. The Arditti Innovation Award is a just tribute to someone within our family who served this institution with intellect, love, and integrity. Someone who is my close personal friend and colleague and with whom I have had the privilege to work in joy these many past years. Congratulations on both events.

"Without innovation art is a corpse," the great Winston Churchill once said. He might have been talking about almost everything—especially in matters of business—especially in matters of financial markets—especially in matters of futures exchanges.

According to Nobel laureate William Sharpe, "More than most sciences, economics not only analyzes reality, it also alters it. Theory leads to empiricism which changes behavior. Nowhere is this more evident than in financial economics."

Clearly, the past three decades were marked by unprecedented innovation in financial markets—their cumulative result represented in every real sense a financial revolution. The Chicago Mercantile Exchange, more than any other futures market, was both at the forefront of this revolution as well as able to capitalize on its rewards. The Chicago Mercantile Exchange, once the house that pork bellies built, is today the house that innovation built.

I will not belabor these proceedings to repeat the well-known history of the great innovations ushered forth or adopted by our exchange. They have been well documented and are the currency which gives us, more than most, the legitimacy to launch a Center for Innovation. Rather, at this celebration, allow me to make two observations about innovation that relate to the state of our industry, to our exchange, and to this evening: One is obvious, the other, maybe not.

CME Center for Innovation, Fred Arditti Innovation Award, Chicago, June 19, 2003.

First, the obvious: Simply stated, the motivation to innovate is inexorably intertwined with an incentive to receive a reward, monetary or otherwise. Ask any company in business. Ask Intel, or Allstate, or Pfizer, or General Motors, or Wal-Mart, and you will get the same emphatic response: We innovate to create new avenues of business, to gain an edge an competition, to achieve a greater share of a given market, in other words, to enhance shareholder value. Even in the academic world, where one might argue that motivation to innovate stems from a compulsion based on pure intellectual pursuit rather than tangible consequence, the reward of being in the forefront is as much the imperative as is accretion to the bottom line in business. Ask any aspiring theorist whether the prize of being first is not among the most driving forces in his or her intellectual quest.

Although this truth is axiomatic, unexpectedly, it has recently generated a bit of nonsensical controversy in our industry. There are some within our industry who question this obvious maxim. They suggest that futures exchanges give up the fruit of their innovations in favor of a rather discredited precept—one that smacks of socialism: *To share our wealth by giving up the exclusivity prize of clearing*.

Let me be explicit: The transactions the CME clears are a direct consequence of the innovations our exchange undertook, the intellectual capital we invested, the time we devoted, and the money we spent on research, development, education, and marketing. All of which begot us the crown jewel of the marketplace—liquidity. Without liquidity there is no market. Liquidity is that illusive Holy Grail that is awarded in those rare instances when an idea hits pay dirt. It is the market's way, if you will, of awarding the innovator a patent. And while this liquidity patent is limited—because little prevents anyone else from copying the idea—it nevertheless becomes nearly impossible to replicate. The monetary consequence of liquidity is of course clearing of the resulting transactions. At the CME, 80 percent of its revenue is generated from the clearing of transactions. Simply stated, removal of the exclusivity of clearing will result in the death knell to the motivation to innovate. And without innovation there will be no Chicago Mercantile Exchange.

Which brings me to the second point. During the past decades, at the zenith of our innovative process, the Merc operated within what Henry Chesbrough of the Harvard Business School identifies as the paradigm of "closed innovation." We were not alone. Indeed, it was the standard approach in business everywhere. Companies generated their ideas internally, financed them, marketed them, and supported them. It was an architecture that counseled a self-reliant approach to innovation. You hire the most talented people, you set in motion a race to be first to devise new products, you sponsor the internal research and development, then you market them before anyone else, and when possible you own the resulting intellectual property. It was a successful architecture for most of the twentieth century. It was an approach particularly well suited for futures markets, given the fact that we had spawned a brand-new market vista, given that it offered a vast range of virgin territory with untried product possibilities, given the intense competition requiring the utmost secrecy, given the race to be first, and given the fact that whoever was first "owned" the market.

But what was true for most of the twentieth century is not necessarily the case for the twenty-first. Indeed, in many industries, the very innovations successfully fostered through the closed innovation architecture resulted in fundamental changes which made the old way of doing things problematic. As Chesbrough points out, in the last century many leading companies held knowledge monopolies; they led their industry and indeed the world in the critical discoveries that supported their industry. Bell Labs was the premier example of such a research laboratory. Other examples of research-based companies include DuPont, Merck, IBM, GE, AT&T, and others that performed most of the research in their respective industries and did it internally.

Today these knowledge monopolies have been broken up. The distribution of knowledge has spilled out. The genie, so to speak, is out of the bottle. Information technology, a consequential innovation of closed inno vation, was a primary force in changing the innovation architecture. The growing mobility of experienced personnel made ideas nearly impossible to maintain in secret. Important pools of knowledge began to be distributed among many avenues, companies, customers, universities, industry consortia, and start-ups. But while innovation could no longer be supported by the old closed model, the maxim that *companies that don't innovate die* remained intact. Newcomers like Microsoft, Sun, Oracle, Cisco, and others grew up and succeeded by conducting little or no basic research of their own, yet found the means to garner the innovative fuel with which to succeed. The newcomers simply adopted what Chesbrough called open innovation. The new architecture invited and created avenues for ideas to flow from external sources. The newcomers used these external ideas to combine with internal ones in order to advance their innovative result. It worked. Existing companies that adapted to open innovation processes continued to survive; those that didn't perished.

Sometime during the latter part of the twentieth century, we at the CME similarly sensed the need to adjust to the new reality. Competition from foreign and over-the-counter markets became intense. The globalized marketplace induced the incubation of new ideas in far-flung arenas to which the CME often had little access. Demands for new products sprang up in spheres with which the Merc had little direct relation. The pace of change and the consequential market alterations were often difficult to decipher—unless, that is, one maintained a standing army of idea detectives on guard around the world and around the clock. Still, for us the altered innovation architecture was fairly easy to accommodate. The Merc was fortunate to have an extended family, a large and diverse group of members and member firms that by themselves or through their customers represented a legion of users and potential users—in other words, an army of idea detectives. It only required the relatively simple task of establishing a channel for such information to readily flow to our data banks. We made such a channel available. Our members gained access to its board and management.

However, the new innovation architecture requires more, and the CME is prepared to respond. We recently initiated the creation of a Competitive Markets Advisory Council. Chaired by Nobel laureate Myron Scholes, and offering me the privilege of acting as vice chairman, CMAC will invite to its domain some outstanding academicians, market practitioners, thought leaders, and other professionals who will afford our exchange the precious opportunity to gain from their knowledge and insights in our quest to discuss competitive challenges and formulate new ideas for market implementation.

Finally, tonight we celebrate the inauguration of still another dimension of the new architecture. The CME Innovation Center and the Fred Arditti Innovation Award will invite and embrace ideas from which can spring new products, applications, and markets. While these consequences will not always be directly related to our industry, or always result in a revolutionary change, I predict they will more often than not stimulate our internal think-tank processes and either directly or indirectly bring us the coveted prize of innovation.

Thus, open architecture of innovation must become and remain the signal component of our existence. In that fashion, and only in that fashion, can we assure that innovation continues to thrive in the house that innovation built.

CHAPTER 25

Remarks at the Celebration of the Chinese-Language Publication of *Escape to the Futures*

Allow me to begin by stating how honored I am to be at this celebration and the fact that the Shanghai Securities Newspaper Publishing House undertook to publish a translation of my memoirs, *Escape to the Futures*. Notably, this is the second language that my memoirs have been so honored, the first translation being into Japanese.

The Chinese-language translation could not have been possible without the special efforts of my friends Yang Ke; Chen Hen; Jiang Yang, CEO of Shanghai Futures Exchange; as well as the chairwoman, Madam Wang Li-Hua of the SHFE. I am deeply indebted to Yang Ke for his talent and translation skills in making this publication possible.

* * *

I was a child barely seven years old when World War II broke out and ensnared me in its iron grasp. I was destined to be a victim of the Nazi juggernaut, as were the 6 million other Jews in Europe, including 1.5 million children, who perished at their hands. Fortunately, fate had another mission for me. Clearly, my escape was due to providential intervention. But perhaps the biggest part was due to the brilliance of my father and mother, who miraculously found a way to save themselves and their only child from the ovens of Auschwitz and Treblinka.

Shanghai, May 28, 2004.

215

My escape to freedom in 1939 spanned two years, three continents, and six languages as my parents with me at their side outwitted the German Gestapo and the Russian KGB. To attempt now to describe that journey in detail would take days—to say the least—far more time than this celebration will allow. Suffice it to say that the journey, which took the three of us from Poland, through Lithuania, through all of Russia, across the Siberian steppes, to Japan, and eventually to the United States of America, is a story that could make a good Hollywood adventure movie. However, at the time it was anything but thrilling. Every step we took was fraught with danger, every step could have been our last. I believe my father had to make perhaps a thousand decisions, each one being the difference between life and death—and he made every one of them correctly.

So I found myself in Chicago as a young boy with my whole life in front of me. I chose the profession of law but very soon found myself fascinated by the world of futures markets. Ultimately, I decided that my future was in futures. Not knowing whether I would succeed or not, I took the risk. In a way that decision epitomized the essence of my being—a willingness to take risk. But I must say that my rise to the top of the complex futures world is a tribute to the beauty of America. Here I was, a refugee, without money, without clout, without connections, without family, and yet America gave me the opportunity to use my imagination and talent to lead the Chicago Mercantile Exchange, and, in doing so, some would say, I not only brought the CME from a pork belly exchange to a world-class financial institution, but revolutionized the markets worldwide.

Escape to the Futures is the story of how some of this came about. Let me dwell only on one or two salient aspect of that story. It is important to understand at the outset that in 1967, when I was first elected to the board of directors of the Chicago Merc, the exchange was a rather secondary, even meaningless institution that dealt in butter and eggs. It had a terrible reputation, it had antiquated rules—some would say it had no rules—it allowed underhanded schemes and chicanery to exist in the conduct of its affairs. It might be of special interest to all ladies in the audience that my first action on the board was to propose and enact a rule that removed an old prohibition that discriminated against women becoming members of the CME or even work on its floor. I am very proud of this achievement because the CME was one of the first exchanges in the U.S. to adopt this policy. I say "work on its floor" because in those days, all futures markets in the U.S. were by open outcry—where its members would gather in a ring, which we called a pit, and shout out their orders in auction style to buy and sell. Today, of course, although we still have some markets that are conducted through open outcry, 50 percent of the business is conducted through Globex, our electronic transaction system that was conceived in 1987. And of course we are a global institution with 99 percent of our transactions in financial instruments.

But I am getting ahead of the story. When I was elected CME chairman in 1969, my first order of business was to reorganize the structure of the exchange. I created a legal department, an economics department, as well as a rule enforcement department. Rule enforcement, as I said, was a brand-new undertaking at the Merc and to make it work we needed a modern rule book. This was a process that took the next year and a half and resulted in the framework of a book of rules for trading in futures that is still the foundation of our present exchange and the model for the rest of the world.

Once we had rules, and the ability to ensure their enforcement, I looked at our product line. Our origin, as you know, was in butter and eggs, but both of those markets had long lost their attraction. The production of butter and eggs had changed dramatically over the years, and with that change so did the need for futures markets in those products. We were now a "meat" exchange—pork bellies, cattle, and hogs. And although we had great hopes for these products, I realized that a successful exchange cannot rely on one product line. To be successful, I believed, an exchange had to diversify. So I began a search for new and different products. I tried everything, potatoes, shrimp, apples, chickens, and even turkeys. None of them worked.

I must now digress again and tell you a little more about my travels as we were escaping from the horrors of the Holocaust. Every time we crossed a border, my father, who was a teacher, would sit me down and explain how the money changed with the different government. First we had zlotes in Poland, then we had lit in Lithuania, then rubles in Russia, yen in Japan, and finally dollars in America. My father was careful to explain that the value of each of these currencies was different and that their value kept changing. It was my first lesson in economics, and it made a great impression on me as a child.

Later in life, when I was already chairman of the CME, I was reading book after book on economics. I was especially attracted to the writings and teachings of a well-known economist at the University of Chicago, the now world-famous Nobel laureate, Milton Friedman. His ideas about free markets resonated in my mind, and I became an avid advocate of this philosophy. The late 1960s and early 1970s, you may recall, was a time of great change in world markets. The economies of those countries that had been destroyed during the war—England, Germany, and Japan—had been totally rebuilt and were now entering into a new competitive world structure. The system of fixed exchange rates—the so-called Bretton Woods Agreement instituted in 1945 after the war—where all currencies were valued on the basis of the value of the American dollar was by then outdated. The first infant sounds of globalization were beginning to be heard. New technologies were allowing information to flow around the world at a speed that was previously impossible. Where it used to take days if not weeks to learn of a new action by, say, the government of Japan that affected the value of the yen relative to the dollar, now that information was available in minutes. Today, of course, that information is instantaneous around the world. So the change in value of a currency could no longer wait until the ministers of finance met once a year to officially proclaim a changed value in a given currency. Value change was impacted by the speed of information.

During those days, Milton Friedman was advocating the idea that currency should float. In other words, he was saying that Bretton Woods was an antiquated idea that could no longer serve the modern marketplace. I believed him, and all of a sudden the currency lessons I experienced firsthand as a child came to my mind. I started to think, Here I was, chairman of a futures exchange in Chicago looking to diversify the products of the Chicago Mercantile Exchange. What if Milton Friedman is right and the currencies of the world floated and changed their values every day instead of maintaining a fixed value? *Wouldn't that require a futures market in currencies?*

It was an epiphany. I became obsessed with the idea. Wouldn't that be a great market? A market in currency where commercial users as well as speculators could send their orders to buy and sell. A marketplace that would give the world a place to hedge their foreign currency exposure. A place to manage the risk of finance.

I could think about nothing else day or night. But at the same time I realized that the idea was revolutionary. Futures markets were exclusively used in agriculture: rice, soybeans, wheat, eggs, butter, cattle. For the thousands of years of futures markets, why, I wondered, had no one ever tried to use them for financial instruments? Maybe, I thought, futures markets would not work in finance. Perhaps, I said to myself—because I am not an economist by profession—I don't fully understand some underlying principles involved. Surely someone else would have tried it if it were possible to trade a financial instrument in a futures market. Am I therefore about to make a foolish mistake? Am I about to lead the Chicago Mercantile Exchange into a path of ridicule? One that might bring ruin to the institution? The idea would not let me rest and the worry would not let me sleep.

Finally, I decided there was only one way I could answer the dilemma. I had to ask Milton Friedman what he thought about my idea. Could a futures market support financial products? Could a market in foreign currency work? Was such a market a good thing for the world?

I met with the great man in November of 1971 and posed to him the question. He did not hesitate with the answer. "What a wonderful idea," he said. "The new world will need a futures market in currency."

I was ecstatic. Here was the great man of the University of Chicago, *the Deng Xiao Peng, but of global economics,* saying to me that the concept of a currency futures market was a wonderful idea. That financial instruments can be applied to futures markets. That such a market was needed. However, fearing that no one would believe me, I asked him if he would put his answer in writing. He smiled and responded that he was a capitalist. I said, "How much?" He said for $7,500 he would write a feasibility paper on the subject. I accepted the offer.

Of course, for the idea to work, currency values would have to float. Little did we know how quickly that would happen. A month later U.S. President Nixon closed the gold window and the Bretton Woods system of fixed exchange rates was forever gone. The world of finance was never again the same. At the CME I moved quickly. Sensing that I needed a specialized market for instruments of finance, I organized a financial division called the International Monetary Market—the IMM. It was designed to trade only financial instruments. It opened its doors on May 16, 1972. The first instrument was currency futures.

Of course, opening the doors on financial futures is one thing. Getting the world to accept the idea was quite another. I quickly learned how skeptical the world was about the idea. How much the world distrusted futures—especially in Chicago—especially at the Chicago Mercantile Exchange. As Mr. Donohue, the CME CEO, said this morning, "We faced skepticism and, indeed, criticism." The idea was labeled unnecessary, dangerous, and tantamount to gambling. It took years of work, years of education, hundreds, maybe thousands, of speeches and lectures, a nearly Herculean effort by myself and many people at the CME. Of course, the support of Nobel laureate Milton Friedman and later Merton Miller and Myron Scholes was most helpful.

Eventually, the idea took root, so much so that it was copied in every corner of the globe. From Moscow to Singapore, from Chicago to Shanghai, from London to Mumbai—to manage modern financial risks, the marketplace needed exchange-traded financial futures and over-the-counter (OTC) derivatives. Their economic function to provide a mechanism to manage inherent business risks in a globalized world was universally accepted and developed not only on centralized world exchanges but in over-the-counter markets as well. As a consequence, capital markets have been strengthened, national productively has improved, and standards of living have grown. In 1986, Nobel laureate Merton Miller bestowed upon the IMM of the CME the greatest honor: He called the invention of financial futures *the greatest innovation in business of the past twenty years.*

Make no mistake about it! In our global market environment—driven by constant and changing market risks, instantaneous information flows, and sophisticated technology—futures markets and OTC derivatives are essential instruments of finance. And for emerging economies that represent the ocean of the future, they are indispensable tools in the development of free and efficient capital markets.

To learn how all of that happened, I guess you will have read *Escape to the Futures*. Thank you.

CHAPTER 26

Knowledge Tag

Congratulations! You have arrived at a signal turning point in your life's journey. A milestone you have lost sleep over, sweated for, prayed for—and in some cases beat all the odds.

It's big! How big? Well, not to get overly metaphysical, it is a moment that more than anything symbolizes the difference between mankind and our counterparts in the animal kingdom. Other animals must learn everything anew from birth; humans have the capacity to record what they have learned and pass it on.

In other words, today's commencement exercises, in a very real sense, symbolize the moment at which the cumulative knowledge of all preceding human generations has been passed on to you. *That's scary big.*

When you think about it in this fashion, graduation is like a giant game of tag. Except now you are *it*. And you will remain *it* until you pass it on to the next generation.

But there is this one little hitch in the knowledge game of tag that I better tell you about. You cannot simply pass on the knowledge you received. We would still be using stone tools if that were the case. Before you can tag the next generation, you are required to give them *more* than you received. This may be the reason that these are called *commencement* exercises. They represent the beginning of your race in Knowledge Tag. Until then you remain *it*.

The good news is that it is a team effort. You are not alone. To win in Knowledge Tag, you have every member of your graduating class on your team pulling in the same direction. More than that, every member of *every* graduating class. More than that, every member of your generation.

The bad news is that it is a team effort. Don't look around you now, but some members of your generation will do diddley squat. That means the burden on each of you is to pick up their slack. And there is more bad

Commencement Address, DePaul University, June 12, 2005, Allstate Arena.

news: *You are late in the game.* It would be a cinch if you were starting from scratch; if no one had yet invented, say, fire, or the wheel. But no such luck.

I mean, you will get no credit for discovering what Aristotle already taught us, or what Galileo observed, or Darwin defined, or Newton uncovered, or the zillion ways Einstein enlightened the world.

And you will also not be given credit for those things in life which are the hallmark of today's civilization. According to Dave Barry, beer is the greatest invention in history—but beer has been around since 6000 B.C. By the way, Barry concedes, the wheel was a fine invention too, but as he points out, "the wheel does not go nearly as well with pizza." Anyway, we've had soap since the time of the Phoenicians, dentures since 700 B.C., and the button about the same time—although I question that fact since there is no record of a buttonhole until the thirteenth century.

What I am trying to say: You are *very* late in this game. Good old Conrad Gesner gave us a pencil way back in 1565, shoelaces have been around since 1790, we have had toilet paper since 1857, chewing gum since 1870, and by the way, the movie *There's Something About Mary* would never have been made if the zipper hadn't been invented back in 1893. And if you are thinking of a two-wheeler, forget about it, the bicycle is 200 years old. Even foodstuff like the potato chips or Jell-O are over 100 years old.

And I must tell you that the century we just left took a lot of stuff off the table. I mean, some nifty stuff like the teddy bear, born in 1902, and crayons the very next year, and cellophane in 1911. Then 1913 gave us two blockbusters: the crossword puzzle and the brassiere—though I fail to see the connection. This led directly to the discovery of lipstick in 1915, Kleenex in 1924, and the really big one: Scotch tape, in 1930.

And even though your generation was close to some really cool stuff—unlike in Horseshoes, in Knowledge Tag, close doesn't count. I know you represent the College of Commerce and the Kellstadt Graduate School of Business, but if you're into transportation, too late, Carl Magee unveiled the parking meter in 1932. Or if your calling is real estate, Charles Darrow beat you by inventing Monopoly in 1934. If fashion is your fancy, you are also very late, the bikini was exposed in 1946, which led directly to disposable diapers four years later. If sports is your pleasure, *fuhgeddaboudit,* Astro Turf was created in 1965. If its information technology, sorry, Post-it notes appeared in the mid-1970s. Oh yes, if finance is your bag, sorry again, some immigrant kid invented financial futures back in 1972. And if your specialty is human relations, I hate to break it to you, but you missed out on Prozac and Viagra.

You also missed all the easy stuff like the alphabet, the airplane, air-conditioning, the atomic bomb, the combustion engine, the credit card, gun powder, the lightbulb, the locomotive, the personal computer, the radio, the reaper, the steamboat, the telephone, television, and we all know that Al Gore beat everyone to the invention of the Internet.

Still, I do have some good news. For one thing, the Commissioner of U.S. Patents, Charles H. Duell, was just a wee bit off the mark when in 1899 he declared that "everything that can be invented has been invented." Ever say something really, really stupid?

But most important, you are in America.

According to the *Encyclopaedia Britannica*'s classification of the 321 world's great ideas and inventions, better than 50 percent were conceived in the U.S. In other words, while Americans may be losing jobs in manufacturing, and may be outsourcing services to foreign domiciles, we remain number one in ideas, inventions, and innovations. Bet that really frosts the French. In other words, we Americans are way ahead in Knowledge Tag. And that is your edge.

More than any other nation on this globe, Americans are free to think, to experiment, to innovate. It is no accident. In his book *Free to Choose*, Milton Friedman asserts that the story of the United States is a story of two interdependent miracles: an economic miracle and a political miracle. Each miracle resulted from a separate set of revolutionary ideas—both sets of ideas, by a curious coincidence, were formulated in the same year, 1776.

One set of ideas was embodied in Adam Smith's *The Wealth of Nations*, which established that an economic system could succeed only in an environment which allowed the freedom of individuals to pursue their own objectives. The second set of ideas, drafted by Thomas Jefferson, was embodied in the Declaration of Independence. It proclaimed the entitlement of some self-evident truths among which are life, liberty, and the pursuit of happiness.

During the two centuries following their introduction, when these two ideals were applied to a people with an immigrant ancestry, of a multicultural heritage, and a multiracial composition, they produced an unimaginable result. They became a lightning rod for ideas. They created a crucible for innovation. They combined to become the decisive driver of progress in science, technology, and economic development. Is not this diversity the essence of DePaul University as well? Our fundamental ideals, our way of life, our pluralistic society—one of a kind on the face of the Earth and unique to the history of mankind—produces an environment that invites thought. It is the winning formula in Knowledge Tag.

Aren't you the lucky ones. To be here in this country, at the start of a new century, at the start of a new millennium, and commencing the knowledge game of tag.

Ladies and gentlemen, start your engines.

CHAPTER 27

CME Fred Arditti Award

This award is more meaningful to me than any others I have ever received. It recognizes innovation and bears the name of Fred Arditti. In 1980 I had the good fortune to bring Fred Arditti to the CME. He was much more to me than a superb economist and innovator. To say that we became close friends does not begin to explain the bond between us. From the very first day, there was a chemistry, a trust, an intellectual love affair that never wavered and lasted until his death. He was the only sounding board I ever needed. The only opinion I valued more than my own. While his tenure at the Merc was intermittent, at no juncture, in the many difficult twists and turns of CME history, was it ever necessary to bring him up to speed. From near or far, he instinctively understood, and always, always provided inspiration, encouragement, and advice. It is a unique privilege to accept an award bearing Fred Arditti's name.

The American philosopher and historian Thomas Samuel Kuhn argued that scientific change occurs through "revolutions" in which one idea is overtaken by another. These revolutions can be triggered by conceptual breakthroughs, such as the invention of calculus which allowed the laws of motion to be formulated, or by technological breakthroughs, such as the construction of the first telescope which overturned Aristotle's postulate of a finite, spherical universe, with the earth at its center.

Historically, such revolutions occur many decades if not centuries apart. Futures markets, or what are today loosely referred to as derivatives markets, have in the short span of 30 years experienced both a conceptual revolution as well as a technological one. As remarkable as that may be, we "ain't seen nothing yet." While the full potential of both revolutions is far from exhausted, I believe futures markets have the unique opportunity of capitalizing on yet another revolution in the making.

CME Fred Arditti Innovation Award to Leo Melamed, April 20, 2006, Four Seasons Hotel, Chicago.

Few would argue with the fact that the launch of financial futures in 1972 was a conceptual revolution. It proved that the traditional idea about use of futures markets in risk management of physical commodities was applicable to finance. In the decade that followed the currency launch, this revolution was validated by the successful launch of interest rate futures in 1976 and stock index futures six years later. Nearly all successful financial contracts that followed at the CME and elsewhere were built on this foundation. Presently, the enormous potential of CME's reach into yet-untested arenas makes it clear that the building blocks of our conceptual breakthrough have not reached their limitation.

At about the same time as this conceptual revolution began, another revolution was brewing: computer technology. It started to seriously flex its muscles in the early 1980s and ultimately, as we all know, influenced every aspect of life. In financial markets computer technology gave birth to the idea of electronic transaction systems. At the CME this culminated in 1987 with the Globex idea. In the following decade, electronic trading platforms were launched by every futures exchange in the world. The technological breakthrough produced the remarkable consequences futures markets are currently experiencing: global distribution, speed of execution, growth of transactional volume, and computerized algorithmic applications.

Allow me very briefly to put the effect of these two revolutions into perspective: In 1971, the year just prior to the launch of the International Monetary Market, the IMM, there were 14.6 million contracts traded on U.S. futures exchanges—there were no futures exchanges of consequence outside the U.S. Last year's total global volume reached nearly 10 billion contracts, of which 3.5 billion transactions occurred on U.S. futures exchanges. There are some 35 futures exchanges in foreign domiciles today.

At the CME, in 1971 we had a whopping operating budget of $3,158,590. Our pretax income was all of $192,945. Fast-forward to 2005: CME expenses were $412 million and our net income was $307 million—that's more than $1 million per business day. Even more striking is the volume comparison. In 1971 CME transaction volume was 3.2 million contracts. That number in 2005 is over 1 billion contracts. I will let Myron Scholes figure out what percentage of growth this represents. But whatever it is, I doubt if there is any other institution in the world that can equal, let alone surpass, this record. It represented a notional value of $638 trillion.

The two revolutionary transformations in our markets were coincident with a much broader trend, one that in my mind exemplifies the twentieth century. I have often spoken of the fact that, during the last century, the scientific world moved from the big to the little, from the vast to the infinitesimal. From General Relativity to quantum physics, from individual cells to gene engineering.

Physics dominated the first half of the century. The first understanding of the atom was simply as a solid central nucleus surrounded by tiny electrons. With new technology came a much clearer understanding of the complexity of the atom with its subatomic particles of electrons, protons, and neutrons and a nucleus containing intricate combinations of quarks. Physicists had decoded nature's age-old secrets, bestowing upon the world perhaps the single greatest achievement of the human mind—the atomic theory and quantum mechanics. In the second half of the century, biology took center stage. Technological advancements taught us that cells, originally thought to be simple repositories of chemicals, are more like high-tech factories in which complex chemical reactions produce substances that travel via networks of fibers. In short, parallel advances in physics, biology, and other sciences made it possible to probe the fundamental components of nature.

In financial markets, the evolution from the big to the little was strikingly similar. Just as in physical science technology brought us to subatomic particles, just as in biological science technology brought us to molecules, so in investment science technology brought us to the basic components of financial risk. The most complicated risk management structure—from alimony to Z-bonds—could suddenly be broken down into its fundamental components. Financial engineers disaggregated, repackaged, and redistributed risks and their corresponding rewards, exchanging one set of risks and rewards for another that responded better to an investor's preferences. Financial futures and OTC derivatives became the financial counterparts to particle physics and molecular biology. Charles Sanford, the former chairman of Bankers Trust, dubbed it "particle finance." One might even say that the Scottish-cloned sheep "Dolly" was the biological equivalent to a "new issue swap."

The process is far from over. Just as futures markets are still expanding the boundaries of the conceptual revolution, so are our markets far from exhausting the potential of the technological revolution. The new technologies offer us the ability to consider risk management applications never before attempted on a global, national, and individual level. For instance, we have the potential to devise instruments dealing with global warming, long-range economic trends, or geographic transformations; we can design instruments for managing the national budget, trade deficits, or foreign currency reserves; we can provide risk management tools for health coverage, Social Security, or retirement. I could go on and on.

It is of course impossible to predict the future. Nor can anyone even predict the next invention or innovation of consequence. Nor its effect on growth of futures markets or the CME. For instance, there was no one anywhere in the world who predicted the effects of the Internet on commerce and trade, and that was only a decade ago. It is particularly foolish to make a prediction at the beginning of a new century when it may yet be decades before the innovation that will define it has occurred. Remember, it wasn't until the middle of the nineteenth century that Karl Marx published the *Communist Manifesto*, which served to dominate political thought in much of Europe and Asia for most of the twentieth century. Or remember that the lynchpin of the technological revolution, one that gave rise to the computer and all that followed, did not occur until December 23, 1947, smack dab in the middle of the twentieth century, when John Bardeen, Walter Brattain, and William Shockley invented the transistor. We are not even a full six years into the twenty-first century.

Still, some things seem clear. The technological revolution has speeded up and computer technology is on the threshold of yet another break-through. Computer scientists believe that in the next decade or two, a scientific revolution of similar proportions to the last one will be unleashed. Recently, some 34 of the world's leading biologists, physicists, chemists, Earth, and computer scientists spent some eight months trying to under-stand how future developments in computer science might influence life as a whole. Their report concluded that computing no longer merely helps scientists with their work. Instead, its concepts, tools, and theorems have become integrated into the fabric of science itself. Computers will soon play a role in formulating scientific hypotheses, designing and running experi-ments to test them, then analyzing and interpreting the results. It would represent a paradigm shift in scientific methodology.

Others believe that millions or billions of tiny computers will be embed-ded into the fabric of the real world. Twenty-four hours a day, year in, year out, nanocomputers will be measuring the effects of everything—from an ecosystem, to private sector interactions, to the human condition. The con-sequential results could then automatically be applied to risk management instruments dealing with employment, inflation, productivity, gross national product, federal legislation, or personal health. The list is endless. It would represent a utopian nirvana for financial engineers.

The impact on our markets from this technological revolution is impos-sible to fathom. Nor is it for us tonight to attempt a moral judgment on the radical consequences of these changes. Suffice it to say, it would represent a condition beyond Aldous Huxley's *Brave New World*. Or as Ralph Cramden might say to Ed Norton, "I don't even know what I am talking about."

Thank you.

CHAPTER 28

Math Is in Our Futures

It has to be obvious even to the most casual observer: Math is in our futures.

I mean, right from the beginning in 1898, when we were but the Chicago Butter & Egg Board on Fulton Street, we were inundated with numbers and math. Throughout our early checkered history there were grades, weights, and packaging requirements. For instance, you had to know that a carload of eggs amounted to 750 cases or 22,500 dozen, or that frozen eggs equaled 36,000 pounds packed in 1,200, 30-pound cans; or butter, 40,000 pounds, and so on.

And these specifications were rigorously enforced by the USDA. I mean, one pound or one dozen short and your delivery could be rejected. You might even end up in jail. Unless of course the inspector's wife or her cousin was by sheer happenstance on your payroll. And if she wasn't and your name was Sam Schneider, you might stand at the top of the steps and throw the inspector down the stairs rather than let him up into your egg-breaking plant, since you knew his math wasn't up to the rigors of inspection.

Then there were price fluctuations and their monetary equivalents that you had to know: Shell eggs fluctuated at 5/100 cents per dozen, which was equal to $11.25 based on a carload; pork bellies, as well as turkeys, hams, frozen eggs, and boneless beef, fluctuated at 2.5 cents of a dollar, which was $9.00 per carload, and so on. And, because of the frenzied conditions in the pit, no calculators were allowed—although smoking was permitted since that was a requirement of membership.

Then there were trading limits you had to know, above or below which you could not trade. Except, of course, on the last two days of the delivery month, which had no limit. This was a necessary exception so that the

CME-MSRI Prize in Innovative Quantitative Applications, CME Center for Innovation, September 21, 2006.

futures and cash prices could converge at maturity. It also served to allow corners and squeezes to reach the full measure of their ill-begotten potential.

This was when corners were rather the norm—often with participation of the board of directors during the so-called "No Math Too Dreadful" era. Once the board invoked the so-called "Math Exception Conjecture," which allowed onions to go up to a price that rivaled gold and then to come crashing down to below the value of the burlap bags in which they were delivered. This of course resulted in the "Futures Mathematics Prohibition Act" of 1958—which effectively banned onions from futures trade forever. Alas, elected officials are not known for their math skills.

When we launched the currency market in 1972, a revolutionary new set of math and numbers entered our world. Suddenly, a carload—yes, to this day we continue to call them carloads—contained a whole bunch of deutschmarks, or yen instead of frozen eggs or eviscerated turkeys, and was worth some $80,000 dollars, a far cry from the numbers the Fulton Street gang was used to. Of course, it took a while for our customers to understand that when we told them we were now dealing in Swiss francs, we did not mean foreign hot dogs. And in the very beginning, the mathematics for our futures prices was based on yet another conjecture. Since no one on the floor was certain of the cash market price in FX, we operated on what was called the "Whatever Morrie Levy Thinks" conjecture.

And again you had to worry about a brand-new set of statistics: Weather, for instance, a highly important variable for chickens and cattle, was replaced by such things as interest rates, inflation, and foreign reserves. A few years later, foreign currency itself morphed into Treasury bills, Eurodollars, and stock indexes, bringing us yet another new math—discount rates, money supply, budget deficits. Then came still another revolution—options. This gadget replaced some of our traditional math verbiage with fancy words: For instance, spoilage became something called time-decay; what we knew as limit down or limit up became volatility; and the CME Pricing Committee was replaced by something called Black-Scholes. Fortunately our traders learned fast—they were, after all, mathematicians at heart.

So if anyone asks why in the world did the Chicago Mercantile Exchange team up with the Mathematical Sciences Research Institute to create a prize for the innovation of mathematical, statistical, or computational methods in the study and behavior of markets, the answer is not simply because President George H. Bush put math on the national agenda for improvement; not simply because U.S. students are ranked fifteenth in eighth-grade math, behind the Slovak Republic; not even because it was the only way to get Myron Scholes to stop nagging about it; but because mathematics, futures, and options are all intertwined. In fact, no one knows for certain which came first.

From the beginning, mathematics arose out of the need to do calculations relating to commerce and taxation. Isn't commerce the very province of futures? And as far as taxation goes, where do you think the tax straddle was invented?

Math arises wherever there are difficult problems that involve quantity, structure, space, or change. That's exactly what futures and options are for.

The great Hermann Hess told us, "For mathematicians there is no reality, no good and evil, no time, no yesterday, no tomorrow, nothing but an eternal, shallow, mathematical present." That's pretty much how our traders feel about futures!

Math, according to Bertrand Russell, is the subject "in which we never know what we are talking about, nor whether what we are saying is true." That's a darn good description of futures and options. And Albert Einstein told us that he didn't believe in mathematics. Funny, that's exactly what Warren Buffett recently said about derivatives!

Anyway, let me cut to the chase. Twenty years ago, a little-known conversation took place on the floor of the Merc that is the consequential nexus for today's event. The conversation was classified by the Intelligence Division of the Commodity Futures Trading Commission—it's a well-kept secret, but they have one—and embargoed until this very day. It was a conversation between Joe Siegel, a superb pork belly spreader, and Joe Fox, a hog broker whose family lineage dates back to the founders of the Chicago Mercantile Exchange. Alas, both Joes have moved on to the big trading ring in the sky.

They were as different as day and night. One, the son of an Orthodox rabbi, had been a Talmudic student. One month shy of becoming an ordained rabbi, his brother, Sam, convinced him to try his hand in commodities. It turned out Joe had a rare mathematical gift that enabled him to mentally juggle a spreading regime involving four or five different commodities in six or seven different delivery months. He was said to possess three-dimensional proficiency. The other, a German, was one of the nine Fox brothers of the famous Fox Deluxe Foods family that for years dominated exchange politics. Joe Fox did not trade for his own account but as a broker he held thousands of orders in his hand. And it was rumored he knew by heart every price and amount of every order in his deck. Needless to say, the two Joes were friends and, as members of this arcane profession, could peer into the future. That common bond resulted in the following conversation in December of 1986:

"You know what happened today, Joe?" said one Joe to the other Joe.

"Tell me."

"I know for a fact that today, the board of governors approved Mclamed's black box."

"Black box?" questioned the second Joe.

"You know, a machine for electronic trade."

"Oh my God!" exclaimed Joe. "That could be catastrophic."

"Yes," the first Joe agreed, "it is bound to bring on algorithmic trading!"

"Much worse," said the second Joe, "it will prove that if any loop in a certain kind of three-dimensional space can be shrunk to a point, without ripping or tearing either the loop or the space, then the space is equivalent to a sphere."

"You mean," said the first Joe, "that anything without holes has to be a sphere!"

"Exactly," responded the second Joe, "like a three-way butterfly spread between pork bellies, hogs, and the Mexican peso."

There was a momentary silence until the first Joe whispered, "My Lord, it's the end of our world."

Reading the handwriting on the wall, the two Joes instantly knew that electronic trade would bring on a whole new paradigm of computer applications: things like black box trading, quant trading, programmed trading, and even someday white box trading—systems that may yet disintermediate the human trader entirely. They knew that while in the beginning, our Globex gadget would be only for after-hours trading, it wouldn't be long before the damn thing would invade their trading day. Because one thing would morph into another and then another. First, the Globex machine would simply export our trading pits to the far corners of the world. Then they would trade side-by-side with open outcry. Then the Merc would allow an open API and it was "Katy, bar the door."

The two Joes understood that eventually financial engineers would build programmable electronic machines that could perform high-speed mathematical or logical operations that assemble, store, correlate, or otherwise process information. That ultimately automated trading strategies could be devised to exploit microtrends in price movements to make a profit faster and better than even they could. That automated strategies could cover the gamut from simple techniques that break down the size of orders for execution, to the very sophisticated mathematical trading models that anticipate volume curves, react dynamically to complex signals, and trade with stealth to minimize impact.

There was no getting away from it. The two Joes knew that it did not really matter who won the philosophical debate as to whether mathematics is created, as in art—or discovered, as in science. Once the Chicago Mercantile Exchange performed the marriage of its markets to an electronic venue, the wizardry of mathematicians and financial engineers would deliver us to the Promised Land.

And there, they expected, Grisha Perelman would be waiting. Thank you.

CHAPTER 29

If It's Good Enough for Milton

Although I did not know it at the time, my first introduction to Milton Friedman occurred in 1940 when I was but seven years old. We were on the first leg of our escape from the Nazis at the outset of World War II and arrived from Bialystok, the city of my birth, to Vilna—that's Vilnius, for those who don't know the Yiddish name of this venerable Lithuanian city. My father, who was first and foremost a mathematics teacher, sat me down to provide my first lesson in economics. The circumstances made the moment historic and memorable. Years later I had the privilege of relating this story to Milton and Rose.

In one hand my father held up a Polish zloty, in the other a Lithuanian lit. "Do you know what these are?" he asked.

"Money," I answered, proud to show off my deep understanding of such matters.

"Yes," he agreed. "And do you know how much each of them is worth?"

I shrugged my shoulders, having exhausted my expertise in high finance.

My father then carefully explained that the value of those two units of currency could be determined only by what they can buy in the marketplace. What followed was my first exposure to the logic of Milton Friedman. I learned that while the official rate of exchange between the zloty and the lit was one for one, in fact it would take two zlotys to buy a loaf of bread but only one lit. "The government's official rate doesn't mean a thing," my father admonished.

It was the start of our two-year odyssey, as my parents with me at their side miraculously outwitted the Gestapo and KGB in a danger-filled escapade that spanned three continents, six languages, Japan, and happily concluded in the United States. The lessons in Milton Friedman's free market economics continued as we chased around the world, and as the lit changed

The Milton Friedman Commemoration, University of Chicago Rockefeller Chapel, January 29, 2007.

to a ruble, the ruble to a yen, and finally a yen to a dollar. It left an indelible impression, one that resonated some 30 years later when I became chairman of the Chicago Mercantile Exchange.

In 1970, the world was still chained to the failing fixed exchange rate regime agreed to in 1945 at Bretton Woods in the mountains of New Hampshire. Thereafter, foreign exchange trading was allowed only at the officially established rate of exchange. An individual, regardless of his standing, wealth, or businesses, was barred from participation. In a well-publicized story, when Milton Friedman attempted to go short the British pound, a bank refused him the right to do so on the basis that "Friedman did not have the necessary commercial interest to deal in foreign exchange."

As chairman of the CME, I was acutely aware that the idea of a futures market in currency, where everyone has sufficient commercial interest, was sheer heresy, akin to suggesting monotheism to a pagan. Knowledgeable people implored that the CME reject such a nonsensical idea. Most of our board of directors warned that futures markets were suited for traditional agricultural products and little else. The orthodox financial community was also vehemently opposed. At best we were considered an "unwelcome" and very distant relative of the mainline financial family. Futures markets, they predicted, would never be utilized for the sophisticated needs of world banks and commercial enterprises. Besides, Chicago was the wrong place. That was the habitat of Al Capone. Matters of finance belonged in the holy centers of finance—London and New York.

It is nearly impossible today to understand or visualize the world before Milton Friedman's ideas revolutionized the planet and became orthodoxy. What is self-evident today was heretical then. Much of the world was still suffering the pains of command economics. The Iron Curtain was still intact. The Berlin Wall had not yet fallen. The dollar did not freely fluctuate. "Free to Choose" had not yet become the road map for the international marketplace.

There was another overriding issue which plagued me then. How could I, a lawyer turned trader cum financial innovator, really be certain that foreign currency instruments could succeed within the strictures designed for soybeans and eggs? Perhaps there was some fundamental economic reason why no one had before successfully applied financial instruments to futures. Indeed, on the eve of our currency launch, a prominent New York banker stated: "It's ludicrous to think that foreign exchange can be entrusted to a bunch of pork belly crapshooters." Who could I turn to for advice? Who could overcome the weighty objections by so many? Who could give me courage to proceed?

For me there was but one person in the whole world capable of settling the issue. By 1970, I had become a committed and ardent disciple in the army that was forming around Milton Friedman's ideas. He had become our hero, our teacher, our mentor. I even had the temerity to sneak into his lectures at the U. of C., although I was not a student, to listen to the great man expound on the free market. What I heard made my spirits soar. Here was the voice of supreme economic authority saying that the system of fixed exchange rates was wrong. That it was time for its demise. Here was the fount of economic logic and vision saying that what I experienced as a child was true: That real value could be determined only by the free flow of supply and demand in an open competitive marketplace—perhaps, I mused, a marketplace like a futures exchange.

Suddenly, the inevitable came to pass—the stresses resulting from the dysfunctional fixed exchange rate system was more than the U.S. could bear. On August 15, 1971, President Nixon canceled the Bretton Woods Agreement and dropped the U.S. dollar convertibility to gold. It was what Milton Friedman had advised Nixon to do from the beginning. For the world it unleashed a financial tsunami whose reverberations would be felt a decade later. For me it represented the moment of truth.

We met for lunch on Saturday, November 13, 1971, at the New York Waldorf-Astoria.

I began by asking that he promise not to laugh. (At the time I had no understanding of what Alan Greenspan has described as Milton Friedman's utter disregard to status.) I held my breath as I put forth the idea of a futures market in foreign currency. The great man did not hesitate.

"It's a wonderful idea," he said emphatically. "You must do it!"

Elated, I pursued, "Is there any reason foreign currency might not work in futures markets?"

"None I can think of," he replied.

For a moment his words hung in the air.

When my voice returned, I said, "No one will believe you said that."

Milton chuckled. "Sure they will."

"No," I boldly said. "I need it in writing."

He smiled. "Are you suggesting that I write a paper on the need for a futures currency market?"

I nodded.

"You know I am a capitalist?" Milton ventured.

We shook hands and settled on the amount of $7,500 for a feasibility study on "The Need for a Futures Market in Currencies."

A friendship and bond was formed that lasted a lifetime.

Within a month, I held in my hand the Holy Grail for the Chicago Mercantile Exchange. The most influential economic mind of the twentieth century provided the CME with the intellectual foundation upon which to build its financial futures superstructure. He said all he needed to in 11 pages.

The rest, as they say, is history. On May 16, 1972, the IMM, the financial division established by the CME, ushered in the modern era of financial futures. Coincidentally, the following year, the Black-Scholes model provided the foundation for exchange-traded equity options. Both events occurred in Chicago. During the first decade of its existence, the IMM initiated a series of innovations in foreign exchange, interest rates, and equity indices. In 1986, precisely 14 years after the IMM's inception, Nobel laureate in economics Merton H. Miller declared financial futures as "the most significant financial innovation of the last twenty years."

Sure we were lucky. Sure our timing was great. Sure the idea was invincible. But the major difference was the paper written by Milton Friedman. It was the equivalent to an unvanquishable secret weapon. With it in hand, we crisscrossed the nation innumerable times, visited every nation on the planet, addressed audiences large and small, faced government officials, bank presidents, corporate treasurers, and the brokerage community and convinced them that a market in currency futures—a market in financial instruments—was an idea whose time had come.

It was magical. For when we said the IMM was a great idea, the world yawned or laughed. When we told them Milton Friedman said so, the world took notice. When we were told fixed exchange rates were coming back, we responded, Friedman said they are not! When we were told Chicago is the wrong place, we responded, Friedman is a Chicagoan! When we were told that we were crazy, we responded, Friedman is one of us! And each and every time, his name made the difference!

Throughout the years, this magic escalated. As his "*Capitalism and Freedom*" became the watchword for economic philosophy, as his logic on behalf of individual choice, free markets, and personal responsibility gained adherents, as his beliefs in individual liberty infused freedom around the globe, his name assumed near-mythical proportions.

Presidents, finance ministers, central bankers, businessmen who would otherwise not have given us the time of day, or allowed us near their door, because of his name, opened the door for us. In the winter of 1975, Alan Greenspan instantly embraced our next iteration, Treasury bill futures. He had read Friedman's currency paper. When the CFTC required U.S. Treasury approval for the T-bill contract, at my behest, Milton Friedman telephoned William Simon, the secretary of the treasury. Our contract was approved the same day. Milton Friedman rang the opening bell in January of 1976.

But perhaps the reaction of George P. Shultz is emblematic of the value of Milton Friedman's paper and tells the whole story. Shultz was the first American government official I visited after the launch of the IMM's currency market. He had just been appointed secretary of the treasury. Secretary

Shultz had no way of knowing that this was my first visit to Washington, DC, or that my knees were shaking as I entered his imposing office. Wisely, I had sent Milton's feasibility paper to the secretary before I arrived. There was very little conversation between us. Shultz listened to my explanation, smiled, and with a wave of the hand said, "Listen, Mr. Melamed. If it's good enough for Milton, it is good enough for me."

CHAPTER 30

Education

The Only Thing that Never Fails

*A*ristotle *told us that the fate of empires depends on the education of its youth.*

In ancient Greece, education for free men was a matter of studying Homer, mathematics, music, and gymnastics. Higher education was carried on by the Sophists and philosophers. Hebrews left education to its Talmudic scholars and rabbis. In medieval Western Europe, education was also typically a charge of the church. With the Renaissance, education in classics and mathematics became widespread. After the Reformation, both Protestant and Roman Catholic groups began to offer formal education to more people, and there was a great increase in the number of private and public schools.

American education developed from European intellectual traditions transmitted to the New World. Throughout the 13 colonies, the English language, laws, and customs came to define colonial educational practice. The first American formal schools appeared in the 1630s. The Boston Latin School, established in 1635, is considered the first town-supported school with a continuous history. In 1647, Massachusetts enacted a law requiring every town of at least 50 households to hire a teacher for reading and writing; those of 100 or more were required to establish and operate a grammar school.

Americans have always had a passion for higher education. Harvard College came first in 1636, William and Mary of Virginia followed in 1693, Yale in 1701, and Princeton in 1746. America's institutions of higher education are today accepted as the best in the world. Through a combination of growth, pluralism, and competition, our colleges and universities

---

The Scopus Award, Hebrew University, The Fairmont Hotel, Chicago, Illinois, June 18, 2007.

provide the widest access to postsecondary education anywhere on the globe. Indeed, recent international studies have concluded that 17 of the top 20 universities in the world are American.

It is said that education is the process, either formal or informal, that shapes the potential of a maturing organism.

It was 1939, the world was on fire, but my parents, consummate teachers both, never lost sight of their priorities. Although we were chased by the Gestapo and the KGB, my father sat me down one day to lecture.

In one hand, he held up a Polish zloty, in the other a Lithuanian lit.

"Do you know what these are?" he asked.

"Money," I answered, proud to show off my deep understanding of such matters.

"Yes," he agreed. "And do you know how much each of them is worth?"

I shrugged my shoulders, having exhausted my expertise in high finance.

My father then carefully explained that the value of those two units of currency could be determined only by what they can buy in the marketplace. What followed was my first exposure to the logic of Milton Friedman. I learned that while the official rate of exchange between the zloty and the lit was one for one, in fact it would take two zlotys to buy a loaf of bread but only one lit. "The government's official rate doesn't mean a thing," my father admonished. "Real value can only be determined in the marketplace."

These lessons in Milton Friedman's free market economics left an indelible impression as we chased around the world, and as the lit changed to a ruble, the ruble to a yen, and finally a yen to a dollar.

In the mid-1950s, when this young law student, futures trader cum financial engineer was captured by the tumult and dazzle of the floor at the Chicago Mercantile Exchange, his font of knowledge were the grizzled old-timers on the Exchange floor who sometimes would take pity on the wide-eyed youngster thirsting for every smidgen of information and offer some of their precious wisdom. Their lore was thoroughly appreciated. There was virtually nothing of any academic substance about the markets of futures available anywhere. It was still some 15 years before Thomas Hieronymus of the University of Illinois would publish his *Economics of Futures Trading*, the 1971 seminal work on our markets—a work that quickly became the bible of futures trade and established the author as the high priest of futures.

As Professor Hieronymus stated at the time, the arcane world of futures was "little known and less understood." For the very first time, someone with his academic authority defined a futures contract, explained the need for price discovery, the role of speculation, the mechanics of hedging, the value of risk management, as well as the architecture of a future's exchange, its unique operation, singular terminology, and its historical development.

Nelson Mandela lectured that education is the most powerful weapon with which to change the world.

The Chicago Mercantile Exchange today is well known as the house that innovation built. Its original logo, "The Exchange of Ideas," was as much a catchy phrase as a defining statement. However, far less known is the fact that among its greatest achievements is the Exchange's commitment to advancing market education. Beginning in the early 1970s and continuing throughout its three-decade rise in the financial world, the CME was a leading force, if not *the* leading force, in advancing academic education, courses, textbooks, studies, learning centers, workshops, and symposia in the field of futures options—and most recently on behalf of the advancement of electronic trade.

It was the first exchange to promote a center for futures education in partnership with the Comex at Columbia University, a prize at the University of Chicago to recognize outstanding scholarship by a business school professor, and to sponsor chairs for the study of futures at both Chicago and Northwestern universities. Nothing—neither success nor change in leadership—has altered or diminished this mission. In 2003, it founded the CME Center for Innovation. Among its accomplishments is the establishment of the Fred Arditti Innovation Award to individuals who have made significant conceptual or practical contributions to commerce or markets. The center also teamed up with the Mathematical Sciences Research Institute (MSRI) to create a prize for the innovation of mathematical, statistical, or computational methods in the study and behavior of markets.

Two years ago, the CME Trust—which originated in 1969 for customer protection—was converted to the CME Charitable Trust with a primary goal of promoting, teaching, and learning about financial markets. In 2006, toward that goal, the trust distributed grants in excess of $10 million, the greatest portion to universities and colleges in the Chicago area. Last week, the trustees announced an additional $1.75 million in grant commitments to Loyola University, University of Illinois at Chicago, and Erikson Institute of Chicago for early childhood education.

Albert Einstein believed that the supreme art of the teacher is to awaken joy in creative expression and knowledge.

It would be impossible to attempt to enumerate the number of books, textbooks, magazines, journals, and periodicals about financial futures and derivatives that permeate today's economic fabric, not to mention the daily coverage of these markets in the electronic and printed media. Suffice it to say that last week on my visit to the Shanghai campus of China Foreign Exchange Trading System (CFETS), with which the CME forged a historic agreement, I was escorted to its library, which boasted no less than 1,000 books, all in English, on the subject of financial futures and derivatives.

Futures and derivatives courses and MBA programs today exist at American universities too numerous to mention, including those at the top of the U.S. academic ladder, such as Harvard, Stanford, Pennsylvania, Cornell, Dartmouth, DePaul, Duke, MIT, Illinois, UIC, Loyola, University of Chicago, and Northwestern, as well as at relatively unknown academic institutions across the breadth of this country, from the likes of Emmanuel College in Boston, to Mills College in Oakland, California. Similarly, courses in futures and financial derivatives are available in universities throughout the world, including Singapore, India, Thailand, Spain, Great Britain, France, just to name but a few. And soon at Peking and Hebrew universities.

Indeed, the markets of futures have come a long way from the days of Thomas Hieronymus.

Clearly innovation has been the key to our achievements, but only because of our equal partnership with education. In no small measure, this success is due to a host of prestigious innovators and teachers, such as Milton Friedman, Merton Miller, Gary Becker, William Sharpe, Bob Merton, and Myron Scholes, to mention only those who have received the Nobel Prize for their academic contribution to our markets.

"The best thing for being sad," said Merlin, in T.H. White's The Once and Future King, *"is to learn something. That's the only thing that never fails. You may grow old and trembling in your anatomies, you may lie awake at night listening to the disorder of your veins, you may miss your only love, you may see the world about you devastated by evil lunatics, or know your honor trampled in the sewers of baser minds. There is only one thing for it then—to learn. Learn why the world wags and what wags it. That is the only thing which the mind can never exhaust, never alienate, never be tortured by, never fear or distrust, and never dream of regretting. Learning is the only thing for you. Look what a lot of things there are to learn."*

CHAPTER 31

The Boy of Steel

The following is a true story. It happened in Poland just outside of Wilno directly after the war. The great Jewish poet Avrom Sutzkover, a Holocaust survivor from the Wilno Ghetto, encountered a young boy hurrying toward him along a desolate and war-torn path. As the boy, perhaps 13 or 14, approached the poet, he occasionally looked behind him as if he was afraid of being chased. Deathly thin, carrying a bundle in one hand, and wearing rags that did not cover his exposed ribs, the boy stopped in front of Sutzkover. He explained he was not from those parts and asked for directions to a school in Wilno he had heard about. Sutzkover obliged. As they parted Sutzkover shouted to the boy, "And you, young man, where are you from?"

The boy stopped, becoming very still, as if the world had suddenly ceased turning. He faced the poet, his eyes began to shine a bluish gold, a smile formed on the corners of his lips, and his voice assumed a certain boldness.

"From where am I, you want to know? Sir, I am from steel."

We are gathered here today to pay tribute to that boy of steel. In four small words, he captured the resilience, the durability, the strength and defiance of the Jewish people. We are gathered here to guarantee that the significance of his words live on forever.

I have a special affinity to that boy. I was seven years old when the war broke out. We lived in Bialystok, Poland's second largest city, where 60 percent of the residents were Jews. You have all heard of Bialystok. Some famous people were born there, including Icchok Shamir, the former prime minister of Israel. It is also the place from where Jewish bakers invented what is today known as the bialy.

Our life was normal. That is until September 1, 1939, just as I was about to enter first grade. Then the world turned upside down and would never be the same. Captured by the Nazis, our fate would be the same as that

---

USHMM Luncheon, Chicago, November 3, 2008.

of 6 million Jews of which one and a half million were children like me, trapped in the inhuman grip of the German Wehrmacht.

But I was one of the fortunate. Because of my father's brilliance, determination, and foresight, because of my mother's perseverance and courage, they plucked us out of the fire, literally in the middle of one night. Thus began a dash for freedom, across borders, on foot, by train, and by junk boat as my parents outwitted the Gestapo and the KGB day after day, week after week. An escape that had the benefit of one of the world's most righteous human beings, Chiune Sugihara, the Japanese Consul General in Lithuania, who issued 3,000 life-saving visas to Japan. An odyssey that took two years, across Lithuania, the Soviet Union, and all of Siberia, across the Sea of Japan to the city of Kobe. Then in a stroke of amazing luck we were permitted passage to the United States, just a few months ahead of Pearl Harbor.

Yes, I have a personal affinity for that boy of steel. For whatever act of fate, I too became a survivor, but with a huge difference—unlike him, I do not have the numbers on my arm. The rest of my family was not that lucky.

Bialystok had one additional distinction, its Great Synagogue. Designed in 1908 by a renowned architect, Shlome Jakow Rabinowicz, the Great Synagogue's dome exhibited a Byzantine architecture that was famous throughout Europe. On July 3, 1941, the Nazis rounded up about 800 Jews from the surrounding neighborhood, including both my grandmothers, my father's sister, and all my cousins, herded them into the synagogue at gunpoint, locked all the doors and windows—saturated the outside walls with gasoline, and torched it. It was an early omen of things to come. The remaining Jewish citizens of Bialystok, along with 90 percent of the Jews of Poland and two-thirds of the Jews of Europe, were murdered in the gas chambers.

Fate does not explain its rationale. Fate had chosen to save me from the Holocaust and bring me to this exalted land of liberty. To grow up as an American and live in freedom. To participate in its opportunity and reach the level of my own capabilities. And to be here today to tell my story.

Oh, and to do one more thing: to tell you about the boy of steel. Because his story is the story of the Jewish people—it is why we are still here—and it must be understood, embraced, and repeated by everyone in this room.

For he is the symbol of our existence.

For his survival personifies the survival of the Jewish nation.

For his memory embodies the memory of the six million who perished.

For his courage represents the courage of all survivors and all the Ghetto fighters.

For his spirit is the foundation for the United States Holocaust Memorial Museum.

That's right. The United States Holocaust Museum, a bipartisan American effort—a proud achievement were it merely a monument in our nation's capital paying homage to the victims—victims of the most heinous crime in the annals of human history. What Winston Churchill described as so evil that it is a crime without a name. But the museum is much more. It is a statement of our survival. It is a precious living beacon from which emanates a warning to those who would deny or forget the history it depicts. It is a holy communion—whether Jew or Christian, white or black—a commitment of every living being—to remember that it happened and that it can happen again. It enshrines the eternal voice of the boy of steel.

Within its walls, at the epicenter of its structure, sits the museum's Committee of Conscience. It is the world's early warning system—a canary in the mine shaft—to sound the alarm, marshaling mankind's collective conscience, whenever or wherever the seeds of genocide are detected. As it did in Kosovo, as it did in Rwanda. For no other voice on this planet has the moral weight of the Holocaust Museum when it comes to racial hatred, bigotry, or ethnic annihilation. The Committee of Conscience embodies our sacred commitment of Never Again.

This message has particular relevance in today's moment of international turmoil. For it is during times of economic stress and uncertainty that bigotry and hatred become embolden and raise their ugly head. In the 1940s, the Jews were the cause of all evil. During 9/11, the Jews caused the attack on the Twin Towers. Today we hear the president of Iran tell the members of the United Nations—to overwhelming applause—that it was Jews that caused the current financial crisis. Check the Internet and you will see and hear countless echoes of similar vile hatred—directed at Jews. Those sentiments today represent a clear and present danger. It is precisely at moments such as these that our united commitment becomes critical. The United States Holocaust Memorial Museum is a unique fortress against the enemies of humanity and tolerance. It is our sacred and personal responsibility to keep it safe and indestructible.

It is in that context that I now ask for your full support to the United States Holocaust Memorial Museum.

CHAPTER 32

CME

The House that Innovation Built

We are here to celebrate innovation and honor the contribution of a great innovator, the Mayor of the City of New York, Michael Bloomberg. It is most appropriate that we do so here and that we do so at this moment in American history.

That we do so here, because the CME Group was built on innovation. Innovation is our existence, our raison d'être, our very being. Scratch beneath our surface and you will find it flowing in our veins; go deeper and you will find it in our genes; and if you psychoanalyze us, you will find that we harbor the crazy notion that maybe we invented it.

It has been said many times: The timing for the launch of financial futures at the IMM in 1972 could not have been more perfect. It was conceived as the world left the gold standard in favor of the information standard. It coincided with new technologies that were making it possible for news to travel at the speed of light. And the U.S. had the so-called "first-mover advantage." For the next three decades Americans dominated the world's capital markets, dwarfing everyone around. In financial futures, the CME together with the CBOT and NYMEX became the catalyst for the development of CBOE stock options, OTC instruments, the concept of financial risk management, and spawned financial futures exchanges in every corner of the globe. In securities, the New York Stock Exchange and the NASDAQ, as well as other American exchanges grew without equal—deeper, and more liquid than anywhere else.

Nobel laureate in economics Merton Miller liked to say the period between the mid-1960s and mid-1980s was singular. In his view, no other 20-year period in recorded American history witnessed even a tenth of the financial innovation of those two decades. Tonight's award winner

---

Fred Arditti Innovation Award Honoring Michael Bloomberg, April 23, 2008, Chicago.

exemplifies that conclusion. In 1981, at the same moment we at the IMM launched our Eurodollar contract under the guidance of Fred Arditti, the instrument that forever changed risk management of interest rates, Michael Bloomberg recognized that the traditional global approach to financial information was too slow and too arbitrary for the coming era. The information company he launched offered cutting-edge technology to bring transparency and scope of information that forever changed the speed, delivery, and efficiency of the financial world.

Both Merton Miller and Michael Bloomberg must have had a sense of the revolutionary advances in technology that were to follow. Indeed, Michael Bloomberg was among the first to understand the impact of the digital communications revolution. Advances that profoundly influenced the conduct of markets and exchanges, resulting in increased competition, global distribution, electronic trade, expansion of transaction volume, and unceasing waves of continuous innovation.

That we do so at this moment in history, because so much is heard these days about the downfall of America, about all that it is wrong, how we have fallen in the eyes of the rest of the world. No doubt there is room for criticism. Surely our nation is not without its faults. But let us keep everything in perspective.

In the history of mankind, there are as many different innovations as there are stars in the sky. They vary from the ridiculous to the momentous, from the innocuous to the historic, from the transitory to the permanent. The twentieth century probably witnessed more discoveries and innovations than were recorded from the beginning of our species. There is no reason to suspect that the twenty-first century will be bashful in this regard.

However, according to the *Encyclopaedia Britannica*'s classification of the world's great ideas and inventions, through the end of the twentieth century, better than 50 percent were conceived in the U.S. In fact, stimulated and fueled by the American industrial revolution, the number of patents issued to American inventors increased dramatically during the nineteenth and twentieth centuries, resulting in millions more than all foreign patents combined. These have immeasurably improved the world's standard of living and linked the U.S. globally across all physical and cultural divides.

No, I am not talking about the invention of fire, the wheel, or the printing press. I am talking about some fairly significant breakthroughs on which modern civilization stands. Things like the electric lightbulb, the phonograph, motion pictures, the electronic computer, the transistor, air-conditioning, the airplane, the telephone, and the credit card to name but a few. And, of course, there is the Internet.

And I while I am at it, how about some really, really neat items without which, I daresay, life would not be what it is. Things like: chewing gum, potato chips, toilet paper, scotch tape, duct tape, the zipper, the brassiere, the disposable razor, Kleenex, Post-it notes, Prozac, Viagra, the list goes on and on.

In other words, while Americans may be losing jobs in manufacturing and may be outsourcing services to foreign domiciles, we remain number one in ideas, inventions, and innovations. It is no accident. Milton Friedman explained the reason time and time again. The story of the United States is a story of two interdependent miracles: an economic miracle and a political miracle. Each miracle resulted from a separate set of revolutionary ideas—both sets of ideas, as we know, by a curious coincidence, were formulated in the same year, 1776.

We all know this history, but it bears repeating. One set of ideas was embodied in Adam Smith's *The Wealth of Nations*, which established that an economic system could succeed only in an environment which allowed the freedom of individuals to pursue their own objectives. No other nation on earth has understood and applied this principle better than the people of the United States. The second set of ideas, drafted by Thomas Jefferson, was embodied in the Declaration of Independence. It proclaimed the entitlement of some self-evident truths among which are life, liberty, and the pursuit of happiness. Although it took a civil war to completely execute that resolve, our nation became the first in history to be established on the principle that every person is entitled to pursue his own values.

More than any other nation on this globe, Americans are free to think, to experiment, to tinker, to innovate. Our pluralistic society based on fundamental human freedoms—one of a kind on the face of the earth and unique to the history of civilization—produced an environment that invites ideas. Thus, when these two ideals were applied during the two centuries following their introduction to a people with an immigrant ancestry, of a multicultural heritage and a multiracial composition, they produced an unimaginable and incomparable result. Contrary to the beliefs of some of our politicians and media commentators, they became a lightning rod for innovation. They created a crucible for experimentation. They combined to become the decisive driver of progress in science, technology, and economic development.

But time marched on. The industrial world has caught up with us. Suddenly we find that the American first-mover advantage has diminished. The growth track the U.S. maintained in the decades after the onset of globalization has been steadily leveling off, while the growth track of other nations has ramped up. Suddenly the U.S., its commercial enterprises, and its exchanges are facing serious competition from other capital markets. There is no one to blame for this reality. We were excellent teachers, and our students learned well. Nor can it be fixed with populist demagoguery or by advocating a protectionist agenda. In the globalized marketplace of today, such remedies would be devastating to both U.S. capital markets and the American standard of living.

The solution will be found first by recognizing that we have entered a new era in the global marketplace. All major capital markets have modern trading capabilities, competent securities and futures exchanges, and cutting-edge technology. In addition, we are beginning to feel the competitive pinch from the two Asian giants, China and India. To remain competitive in the twenty-first century, the U.S. must accept the fact that American businesses now face competitors from across the ocean rather than from across the street or across the river. The new paradigm necessitates continued innovation, reduction of burdensome compliance costs, containment of baseless litigation, and maintenance of open markets for goods. Beyond that, we must redouble our efforts to sustain our academic excellence—the very feature that had so much to do with our first-mover advantage.

But more than anything else, to keep things in perspective, we must recognize that the extraordinary strengths that brought us to the pinnacle of innovation are still in place. They have not changed, nor must they ever be allowed to diminish. Our constitutional and cultural birthright that allows and encourages Americans to think freely, experiment, research, and create represents a priceless legacy—an endowment of phenomenal potency with which we can face our competitive tomorrow.

This Center for Innovation will continue to celebrate the fulfillment of these triumphs.

CHAPTER 33

The Law of Selective Gravity

There is no way to sugarcoat it: Current economic conditions have the earmarks not only of a severe U.S. recession but—dare I say it—the potential of a global depression. That is about as dire as it can get. However, for me, as tragic and ominous as that prospect may be, it does not represent the worst consequence of today's global economic conditions. I fear the Law of Selective Gravity—a cousin of one of Murphy's Laws—which postulates: *"An object will fall so far as to do the most damage."*

As the world knows, a couple of weeks ago, Treasury Secretary Henry Paulson asked Congress to approve a $700 billion rescue of the banking industry. Without this sudden, massive infusion of federal cash, we were told, economic disaster loomed. Prompt approval, on the other hand, would assure the solvency of the financial sector, thaw frozen credit flows, and give investors a badly needed dose of confidence. Faced with the prospect of rising unemployment, a plunging stock market, and the inability of corporate America to borrow, Congress approved a revised package on Friday, October 3, 2008. This gave investors the weekend to contemplate the economic value of the federal action. Were it able to inspire some confidence and halt for a moment or two the bloodletting, one might be a bit more charitable in assessing the panic-driven action by the captains of American capitalism. On Monday, the stock market plunged into an abyss and the turmoil spread to Europe, Asia, and South America. The plan which Secretary Paulson and Fed chairman Bernanke told us we must approve to prevent a market crash did nothing of the sort. The market crashed. Now the plan is for government to rescue the banks with direct capital investment, whether they want it or not. Did you ever think that maybe the market doesn't want any more of government plans?

But don't miss the point. I am not lamenting the fact that the desperate plan did not have an immediate medicinal effect—in all reasonableness, the Troubled Asset Relief Program (TARP) will take time to take effect.

Financial Innovation Conference, Vanderbilt University, October 16, 2008, Nashville.

But what I am lamenting is the fact the executive branch of an American administration was so desperate that it proposed a rescue operation of gargantuan proportion which gave it unlimited power, with minimal oversight, little accountability, no recourse, and no judicial review. I am lamenting the mind-set that would devise such a plan—surely its blueprint had a Venezuelan origin. A plan that Steve Chapman of the *Chicago Tribune* described as "giving the executive branch powers that a Russian czar would envy."[1]

I am lamenting the fact that hardly anyone paid the slightest attention to a warning by a group of 122 economists, including at least two Nobel laureates, who stated:

> *If the plan is enacted, its effects will be with us for a generation. For all their recent troubles, America's dynamic and innovative private capital markets have brought the nation unparalleled prosperity. Fundamentally weakening those markets in order to calm short-run disruptions is desperately short-sighted.*[2]

I am lamenting that U.S. government officials were in such a state of panic that they abandoned market solutions in favor of third-world sorcery like blaming speculators and banning short selling. I am lamenting the fact that all the world's capitalists have turned to the government for salvation. I am lamenting the fact that federally inspired rescue operations were so quick to surrender the fundamental free market principle that mistakes by the private sector must be borne by the people who made them. As Thomas Donlan of *Barron's* remarked, "The U.S. and Europe are racing down the trail marked by such economic leaders as Mexico, Argentina and Russia."[3] Or as Yale's Professor Jonathan Macey put it: "Officials at the Federal Reserve, the Securities and Exchange Commission and the Treasury Department are to blame for publicly losing confidence in the very economic system they are supposed to protect."[4]

Above all, what I am lamenting is *the real cost* of these operations and not in terms of billions of dollars to American taxpayers. I am lamenting the fact that the Law of Selective Gravity will result in the unthinkable—a renunciation of the free market. With that,—America will lose its most precious asset, the ability to innovate.

This is not some fantasy of a hysterical pessimist with a propensity for paranoid prophesies. The developing underlying blame—within the walls of Capital Hill, Wall Street, and Main Street—is that the economic disaster is the result of a laissez-faire deregulatory mentality. *Greed on Wall Street* has become the conventional theme of both presidential candidates. In the public vernacular that is shorthand for *the free market*. "I was a free market guy, but no more" is a common refrain heard from ordinary folks on the streets of America. Its damning echo is resonating throughout the pages of American newspapers, radio talk shows, and TV programs.

And it is a message roundly applauded by every enemy of freedom on the planet.

This is not to suggest that the financial system is not in trouble. Or that some form of federal action was unwarranted. Nor is this an attempt to absolve the private sector from blame. Surely greed played a major role in what happened. Clearly financial institutions, in their rush for greater immediate returns irrespective of consequential long-term risks, were guilty of irresponsible behavior or worse. As Randal Forsyth of *Barron's* suggested, OTC structured investment vehicles became the financial equivalents to steroids. Regulatory reform, as suggested by former SEC chairman Arthur Levitt Jr., is necessary pertaining to lending practices, licensing standards, oversight of mortgage brokers, capital requirements for monoline insurers, and transparency in the sale of OTC derivatives so that risks associated within all forms of structured investment vehicles will be fully disclosed.[5] Similarly, as Nobel laureate Gary Becker recommended, there is a need for increased capital requirements relative to assets of banks in order to prevent the highly leveraged ratio of assets to capital in financial institutions.[6]

But while endorsing regulatory reform, allow me also to draw attention to one place where, in stark contrast to the turmoil of recent events, the market system operated flawlessly. I speak of futures markets, an indispensable component of the global marketplace. While their growth in the last decade was substantially less than in OTC derivatives, last year the CME Clearing House cleared more than 2 billion futures contracts, representing more than $1 quadrillion in value. Which begs the question, how did exchange traded futures perform during these unprecedented turbulent conditions? The answer is clear: *Flawlessly.* No defaults, no failures, no federal bailouts. The futures market model is a poster child for the free market and innovation: price transparency, liquidity, central counterparty clearing, twice-daily mark to market, zero debt system, and regulatory oversight.

Two examples: On March 14, 2008, the last day before Bear Stearns was acquired by J.P. Morgan Chase, Bear held $761 billion in notional value in open futures contracts for customer and house accounts at the CME. All positions were paid for and settled. Impressive, yes? Then how about this: On Friday, September 12, 2008—the last weekday before Lehman Brothers filed for bankruptcy—their total notional value of customer and house positions at CME was $1.15 trillion. No defaults, no failures, no federal bailouts. Unabated, futures markets continue to perform their essential functions: to create a venue for price discovery, permit low cost hedging of risk, and to innovate.

But here is the rub: The free market model cannot function when it is directed or, better still, misdirected by the heavy hand of governmental

edict. No matter how one views what happened, no matter of what political persuasion, much if not most of its causation has a governmental
origin. First, because during the past decade the world became awash with
liquidity. Low interest rates engineered by world central bankers caused
interest rates, especially in the U.S., to fall to the lowest level in a generation. The consequential cheap money when combined with loan syndi-
cation and securitization produced some highly unintended consequences.
A mortgage-lending boom ensued, and bankers found ever more clever
ways to repackage trillions of dollars in loans. Professor Bob Shiller of Yale
summed it up this way: "The housing bubble is the core reason for the
collapsing house of cards we are seeing in financial markets in the U.S. and
around the world."

This leads us to the second and most egregious culprit of the financial
collapse: two government-sponsored enterprises, Fannie Mae and Freddie
Mac. They were viewed in the marketplace, correctly as it turns out, as
government-backed buyers. These two GSEs were on an affordable-housing
mission, becoming the largest buyers of subprime mortgages between 2004
and 2007 with a total exposure exceeding $1 trillion. It was a mission
supported and backed by elected congressional officials who presented
themselves as champions of affordable housing.[7] It fostered what Princeton's Professor Burton Malkial described as the so-called NINJA loans to
borrowers—no income, no job, and no assets—and poisoned the global
financial system. "The Fannie-Freddie bailout," wrote the *Wall Street Journal*, "is one of the great political scandals of our age. Officials at the Federal
Reserve warned about it for years, only to be ignored by both parties on
Capitol Hill."[8]

In other words, it was a rigged game. The dictates of the free markets
are always stymied by a monopoly, a cartel, or the actions of government.
It would be a tragic misdirect and a perverted leap of logic if the conditions
that caused the global meltdown, the transgressions that occurred within
the private sector, or the regulatory reforms that are required were blamed
on the precepts that made this nation so great. More than any other nation
on this globe, Americans are free to think, to experiment, to innovate. It is
a legacy of the free market. A story of two miracles: an economic miracle
and a political miracle. Its application by a people with an immigrant ancestry, of a multicultural heritage, and a multiracial composition, produced
an unimaginable result. It became a lightning rod for ideas. It created a crucible for innovation. It combined to become the decisive driver of progress
in science, technology, and economic development.

I pray that my fear is misplaced—but Murphy's Law demands that I
sound the alarm.

CHAPTER 34

The Gray Swan

Some people in the financial world claim that the global meltdown that has occurred in financial markets is an example of a Black Swan event—random and unexpected. In other words, it was an occurrence that so deviated beyond what is normally expected that it was extremely difficult to predict.

The black swan, of course, is a large waterbird, *Cygnus astratus,* and is common in the wetlands of southwestern and eastern Australia. It is the official state emblem of Western Australia and is depicted on its flag. But the history of this rare bird is steeped in myth. It was first described in 82 A.D. by the Roman satirist Juvenal who used the term "black swan" to depict a creature that did not exist. Aristotle used examples of white and black swans to distinguish reality from the improbable. Thus, for most of history the black swan lived as an allegory for something that did not exist. That myth was exploded in 1790 when the black swan was discovered by English naturalist John Latham. It suddenly proved the existence of the improbable. That revelation gave rise to some deep philosophical discourse. As Nassim Nicholas Taleb explains in his brilliant bestselling 2007 book *The Black Swan,* the belief "all swans are white," is based on the limits of our experience. In other words, some occurrences are unpredictable because they deviate so far beyond what we can expect.

Was this the case with the causes of the current financial crisis? Was it a black swan event? I have my doubts. Sad to say, in my opinion, much of it was predictable. To put it another way, I will argue that the financial meltdown was a "Gray Swan" event.

Let's begin by stating that the primary underlying factor for the boom and bust that occurred was easy money. During the past decade central bankers allowed the financial world to become awash with liquidity. This was true for Europe, Asia, and certainly for the U.S. The American Federal Reserve held its target interest rate, especially, from June 2003 to June 2004

Presented at Peking University, Beijing, China, April 12, 2009.

at one percent, well below historical levels and guidelines. Easy money led to global excesses and a pyramid of debt. In my opinion, it was the root cause of most of the problems.

Second, because easy money means low interest rate structures, there was a global pursuit by investors—businesses, banks, financial firms, and individuals—to find means to enhance their returns. That is a predictable consequence. It is also no secret that by definition higher returns means higher risk. One modern-day approach to achieve a higher return was through over-the-counter (OTC) derivatives. Beginning in about 1988, investment banks found ways to repackage trillions of dollars in loans, selling them off in slivers to investors around the world. It began with the introduction of a financial derivative known as a collateralized debt obligation (CDO), or structured investment vehicle (SIV). The value and payments of these asset-backed securities were derived from a portfolio of underlying assets that were packed into the instrument: for example, corporate bonds, emerging market bonds, asset-backed securities, subprime and other mortgage-backed securities, REITs, bank loans, and student loans. There was little regulatory oversight. During the next decade and a half, CDOs and SIVs became the fastest growing sector of the asset-backed synthetic securities market and were sold to investors over-the-counter. The greater the risk pieces of a CDO or SIV, the greater returns to their investors. Rating agencies would rate the tranches being sold without fully understanding the totality of the risks involved. It was a recipe for disaster.

Here, I must digress. When talking about the derivatives markets it is imperative to understand the difference between OTC-traded derivatives and exchange-traded futures which are sometimes also referred to as derivatives. The two instruments of finance are galaxies apart and must not be confused.

- First and foremost, OTC markets do not have the protective components of the futures exchanges, namely: daily mark-to-the-market value adjustments, margin deposits, price and position limits.
- In the OTC markets it is up to the banks to set the reserves for their open positions while at futures exchanges margin requirements are set by an independent entity—the clearinghouse.
- OTC markets do not have the guaranty of a central counterparty clearing system (CCP).
- The hallmarks of exchange-traded instruments are their disclosure and transparency procedures.
- In the OTC market the original contract remains in place, sometimes for many years, increasing the total size of the market, even where an economically offsetting transaction is in place. Not so in futures where an offsetting position eliminates the original contracts and the obligation they represent.

- The OTC market greatly overshadows the exchange traded market, something on the order of five times as large.
- The OTC markets generally lacked the regulatory control of federal authorities to which futures and options exchanges are subject under the Commodity Futures Trading Commission (CFTC).

These differences are dramatic. While nothing is perfect and no one can foresee all eventualities, the structure and procedures at regulated futures exchanges represent a time-tested mechanism—the very essence of their default-free success. On regulated exchanges, not only are there daily clearing mechanisms, there can be no doubt about the integrity of their daily settlement procedures. On the other hand, in the OTC derivatives market, values are often measured on the basis of the original model when the instrument was created. Rating agencies make a value determination at that time. Over time, without some form of an updating mechanism, these valuations can become stale or meaningless.

Consider: In stark contrast to the turmoil of recent events, the CME clearinghouse has operated for more than 100 years without failure. Consider, during the current unprecedented financial crisis, as marquee names of finance such as Bear Stearns, Lehman Brothers, Merrill Lynch, and Bank of America failed or trembled, the CME performed its operational functions without a disruption. No failures, no federal bailouts. As I stated, OTC derivatives and exchange traded financial futures are galaxies different.

That is not to say, that OTC derivatives are to be banned or feared. That would be unthinkable. For the vast majority of financial managers, whether OTC or exchange traded, these risk management tools work exceptionally well. It is estimated that over 90 percent of the world's 500 largest companies—domestic and international banks, public and private pension funds, investment companies, mutual funds, hedge funds, energy providers, asset and liability managers, mortgage companies, swap dealers, and insurance companies—use OTC derivatives to help manage their business exposure. Nor could it be different in today's complex and interdependent financial world. Indeed, if OTC derivatives application were suddenly not available in business today, they would have to be invented. Without them, it would be like going back to the Stone Age. Still, the lessons learned must be applied. It is imperative that OTC derivatives have a measure of regulation, transparency, and disclosure of attendant risks.

The third consequence stemming from easy money was unconscionable leverage that occurred throughout the world within some financial enterprises, mainly investment banks and hedge funds. In the U.S., the government played a central role. In 2004 the Securities Exchange Commission (SEC) removed the historical ratio limit between debt to assets of about 12 to 1 and allowed it to go over 40 to 1. I don't think I need explain the nature of risk and debt created by this eventuality. Again it was predictable.

Fourth, mortgage refinancing combined with subprime lending. Low rates and adjustable rate mortgages (ARM) created a huge refinancing industry. It spread like wildfire and resulted in a housing bubble. Subprime mortgages were like gasoline to the eventual housing fire. Such lending practices were based on the philosophy that everyone should own a home. A worthy goal, but highly unrealistic. In other words, not everyone can afford the mortgage payments. While residential values kept rising, as they did until they peaked in mid 2006, it didn't seem to matter whether the new owner could afford the home or not. The owner was always able to refinance at a higher home evaluation. It substantially reduced the equity in home ownership, raising the risk to the overall housing market. When the boom ended home prices fell and mortgage payments could not be met by thousands upon thousands of homeowners, we experienced a rash of defaults and foreclosures. The crashing housing market became a primary cause of the recession we presently are enduring. Again, this was predictable.

Fifth, an adjunct to the subprime lending were the Federal National Mortgage Association, (Fannie Mae) and the Federal Home Mortgage Corporation (Freddie Mac). The government mission of these U.S. government sponsored enterprises (GSE) created in 1968, was to keep mortgage interest rates low in order to increase their support for affordable housing. Again a worthy goal. In the past several years, these two GSEs were sometimes encouraged by the U.S. Congress to continue to buy the subprime mortgage-backed securities. It created a global market for subprime debt which gave rise to a false sense of security and resulted in the toxic assets that U.S. government is now bailing out.

Sixth, the doctrine of "Too Big to Fail," was in my opinion mishandled. In theory of course, in a free market system, failure by any enterprise is an acceptable part of the bargain. Government should never intervene to save a failing company. Let the investor lose his investment when he has invested poorly or negligently. Bankruptcy is the solution in "normal" circumstances. A special methodology should be available for failure in "unusual" circumstances. But as we know, what is acceptable policy in theory is not always acceptable in practice. When government concludes that there exists the danger of systemic risk, in other words—when the entire economic system could unravel as a result of failure of one giant enterprise—then government may feel beholden to intervene. This has happened throughout world history. A word of caution, however: When government concludes there is a need for intervention, it better be quite certain that a) there is in fact the danger of systemic failure, and b) the rules for intervention are clearly defined.

In the case of Bear Stearns, the American government judged that the company was too big to fail. However, a few months later, in the case of

Lehman Brothers, it judged the opposite. Then, in the case of the American International Group (AIG), it reversed direction again. I was never convinced that Bear Stearns was too big to fail, nor was I ever convinced that Lehman Brothers was not. I became convinced, however, that there was never a bright line for the rules under which government will or will not intervene. The market cannot handle uncertainty. Our undefined policy caused the stock market to lose faith. That too was predictable.

And finally, seventh, greed. Some commercial banks, investment banks, hedge funds, and other financial institutions took advantage of the lack of regulation, and lax rules. In a rush for better returns they abandoned good business practices and allowed risk to become excessively underpriced. There was a breakdown of proper risk management controls as greed replaced common sense. Thus, although most of the causes of the financial failure were government inspired, greed in the private sector was a cause factor as well. But greed is a human frailty and predictable.

There you have it. Clearly, there was no single culprit. While there are other causes, the foregoing seven sins, in my opinion, were primary. Yes, there was lack of regulation; yes, there was failure of regulation; yes, there was greed in the private sector; and yes, there were misjudgments made by a host of government officials throughout the world. But surely the blame is not with the free market system. It represents the best economic model ever devised by mankind. These same or similar failures and many more have occurred under every economic model and under every type of government regime. Indeed, while the free market system is not free from failings, in the history of civilization no other system has produced so much good for mankind nor resulted in a higher standard of living for world populations. It represents the only answer in the globalized world of today, the only system that will encourage innovation and guarantee individual freedom.

Still, there are lessons we have learned. I will simply enumerate the most telling: First and foremost, capital requirement for financial institutions must be raised. Second, leverage must be contained so that enterprises cannot become too big to fail. Third, there must be regulatory oversight in OTC transactions. Finally, on a voluntary basis, central counterparty clearing for credit and OTC derivatives must be encouraged. A CCP clearing model, in my opinion would substantially reduce the probability that the failure of a significant participant in the markets would lead to a systemic failure or require government bailout.

But, of course, that is not the point of these remarks. My sole purpose here today was to examine the cause and effect of the actions which produced the current global crisis, and to suggest that in my opinion they were all pretty well predictable. In other words, they were not black swan events. Probably they were more like gray swans—and avoidable.

PART III

Appendixes

The Third Milestone

Financial futures have occasioned two milestones in their short history, both of a revolutionary nature. It is not without a measure of some pride that I point out that both milestones occurred on the floor of the Chicago Mercantile Exchange.

The first one, of course, was the creation of financial futures themselves. The departure by traditional futures from their century old agricultural base and entrance into the world of finance dramatically changed their direction and history. By definition, no financial futures history could have ensued without its conceptual inception.

It is clear today that the revolutionary concept sponsored by the CME 17 years ago was destined to change the world of finance and become an indispensable risk management tool the world over. Indeed, the invention of financial futures has been hailed by Merton H. Miller, Ph.D., Professor of Banking and Finance, University of Chicago, as "the most significant financial innovation of the last twenty years."

Alas, hardly anyone recognized that event as significant back in 1972. Indeed, hardly anyone believed it to be of any consequence at all, and few gave it any chance of success. Pundits and critics mocked the idea, regarding it as no more than a joke or, at best, a quixotic impossible dream. Some simply thought it ludicrous that a "bunch of pork belly crapshooters" would dare to contemplate treading on the hallowed ground of foreign exchange.

But succeed we did. The reason? Quite simple! Victor Hugo explained it when he told us that no general was smart enough and no army strong enough to suppress an idea whose time had come.

The second milestone came nine years later: cash settlement. In 1981, the Merc's Eurodollar contract became the first to settle by way of payment in cash rather than by delivery of the instrument itself. Once financial futures shed the requirement of physical delivery, the curtain was opened to instruments and concepts that were previously unthinkable. Cash settlement represented the gateway to index products and seemingly limitless potential.

Today, financial futures are poised at the threshold of their third mile-stone. Not surprisingly, the CME is again leading the way. I speak, of course, of Globex (formerly PMT), the automated global transaction system of the CME and Reuters Holdings PLC. As was the case with the first two mile-stones, the third one has generated a good deal of discussion and even controversy. For all the milestones have a single common denominator—they each represent a dramatic departure from status quo.

The third milestone represents a move toward automation in the trans-action process. It thus touches the very nerve center of status quo in our industry and has incurred the criticism of those who would oppose any movement toward change that involves automation or adoption of techno-logical advancements. To them, such reforms advance the black box and hasten the end of "open outcry."

The unequivocal truth, though, is that the world of futures is dynamic and continuously evolving. Complacency is the enemy; innovation and change are at the very heart of our success. As our markets' applicability extended to new products, new techniques, and new users, as our markets became the standard tools for risk management, the changes we engendered were dramatic and revolutionary.

Open Outcry

In 1977, I authored an article on the mechanics of a commodity futures exchange for the *Hofstra University Law Review*. In it, I concluded that an automated transaction process *cannot* supplant the trading floor or the open-outcry system.

While that assertion was made with respect to a world quite different from the one today, Globex does not run contrary to this view. Globex is not specifically designed to replace the present transaction process but, rather, to enhance it. Nor did my conclusions of a decade ago intimate that our industry should ever be precluded from experimenting with change. Indeed, we must continually evaluate the state of our industry in light of current demands and competitive pressures on our markets, and in recog-nition of the effects of scientific and technological changes in the world around us.

There is no doubt that throughout our dramatic metamorphosis and expansion, one thing has remained constant: In the United States, open outcry has been the liquidity engine for our success. This remains the case. The CME, like all other American exchanges, has a continuing commitment to the preservation of this transaction process.

However, the CME also believes that to blindly assume that open outcry is the perfect system for all time is to be lulled into a false sense of security and forgo any opportunities to strengthen or advance our way of doing business. Such a policy would be both foolish and dangerous and could lead to disaster. While we must always respect our heritage, we must never let ourselves be held back by its limitations. We must recognize the greater truth, that those who ignore or fear to embrace reality will quickly become history.

Therein, of course, lies the rub.

Historian Barbara Tuchman succinctly told us that "men will not believe what does not fit in with their plans or suit their prearrangements." Walter Wriston, the former chairman of Citicorp, is more explicit: "When major tides of change wash over the world," he tells us, "power structures almost inevitably reject the notion that the world really is changing, and they cling to their old beliefs."

The change that has washed over our end of the world is the telecommunications revolution. It is, by now, a cliché to explain that sophisticated satellites, microchips, and fiber optics changed the world from a confederation of autonomous financial markets into one continuous marketplace. We need no reminder that there is no longer a distinct division of the three major time zones—Europe, North America, and the Far East. No longer are there three separate markets operating independently of external pressures, maintaining their own unique market centers, product lines, trading hours, and clientele.

Today, we know all too well that users of every market come from around the globe because news is distributed instantaneously across all time zones. When such informational flows dictate market action, financial managers no longer wait for local markets to open before responding.

The old order offered our financial markets a geographical security blanket that kept them relatively free from the dangers of international competition. That order is history. Globalization, caused by the telecommunications revolution, has ushered in the information standard. Every financial market is now a potential competitor of the other.

Globex recognizes and embodies that change. Globex symbolizes the technological revolution that has engulfed every walk of life—none more than ours. Globex embraces reality and shakes the very foundations of complacency about us. And Globex will change our industry forever and what's more, extend its life.

Two additional observations:

First, successful open outcry is a predominantly American phenomenon. With few exceptions, other world centers have not long had this tradition nor much success with its application. As a consequence, many non-U.S. centers have, from the outset, opted for either a partially or totally automated execution system.

Second, while the futures market pits remain the single most important source of present-day liquidity, they are no longer the only source. Today, there exists an army of upstairs traders whose trading methodology is not dependent upon eye-to-eye pit contact but rather on two technological instruments: the computer screen and the telephone. Using these instruments, upstairs traders buy and sell in rapid fashion throughout the day—similar to pit traders—and provide a continuous flow of orders to the market. These traders thus represent a liquidity source virtually nonexistent a decade ago. While they will not, in the near future, replace the liquidity source of pit traders, there is no denying that they represent a growing universe with no visible limitation on its expansion. Globex should present no problem for the upstairs trader.

The Wave of the Future

The CME perceived the globalization reality when, four years ago, it instituted the mutual offset link with the Singapore International Monetary Exchange (SIMEX). It was the first successful attempt to link the trading capability of two different markets in two different time zones. It served as a model for others to follow and took the world one step closer to a global market. What's more, this experiment provided the CME with invaluable expertise and living proof for everyone that world markets can be safely and efficiently linked.

It also led us to the next logical evolutionary step. Globex combines elements of electronic linkage and integrates them with the open-outcry system. In effect, it draws the best from the present and marries it to the technology of the future.

It is critical to understand this point. We did not set out to re-create open outcry—we sought a way to secure it, a way to marry it to the technology of the future, a way to extend its market day; but not to re-create it. While we recognized the value of open outcry and the liquidity it generates, we sought to do better. We recognized the inadequacies of open outcry—its inherent unfairness. We knew that an automated system provided us an opportunity to do away with those inadequacies—an opportunity to make the system more fair.

At the same time, Globex represents a giant step toward unification of the separate world financial centers. Globex will offer the world a transaction capability that is as advanced as the imagination will allow and as far-reaching as the future itself; a transaction capability that will allow the products of all the world's great exchanges on the same system—on the same screen—to be utilized by everyone around the clock. The very words are breathtaking.

We envision a global, interactive, shared system for futures and options. A system whereby no partner exchange will relinquish its autonomy; whereby every partner exchange will continue to clear and guarantee its own products; and whereby the rules of the respective governments will continue in force, as before. Yes, we envision a transaction structure for the ultimate unification of the world's separate marketplaces. That is the essence of Globex.

Yes, Globex is a major departure from status quo. Thus, it has drawn heavy criticism from those who would benefit by status quo, from those who fear change, as well as those who recognize the competitive edge the new system will offer our institution. Those are some of the very reasons the CME conceived Globex.

Of course, there are no guarantees. There are many hurdles to overcome—some of them in the government domain. Unfortunately, our own government officials often fail to appreciate the prophet in their own backyard. All too often, American innovations are ignored or repressed by virtue of shallow reasoning or bureaucratic red tape. Such examples are too numerous to mention. We trust, however, that will not be the case with Globex. That in this instance, U.S. federal officials will recognize that Globex is the trailblazer, the model for all to follow; and, that it is a product of American ingenuity to be assisted and encouraged.

Again Wriston says it well. "If today's leaders in government and business fail to recognize that the world has changed, they will follow into oblivion a long list of leaders who have made similar mistakes. Those who can understand and master change will be tomorrow's winners."

The first two milestones the CME engendered offer unequivocal proof that our institution does understand change; that we are both willing and capable of embracing the realities it represents. The third milestone carries forward this tradition in a grand fashion.

Source: 1988 CME Annual Report.

Letter to Milton Friedman

CHICAGO MERCANTILE EXCHANGE

Leo Melamed
Chairman, Executive Committee
and Special Counsel to the Board

March 5, 1989

Professor Milton Friedman
Senior Research Fellow
Hoover Institution
Stanford University
Stanford, CA 94305

Dear Milton:

I apologize for the delay in responding to your letter of January 5, 1989. Unfortunately, the demands on my time have been more excessive than usual.

I thoroughly agree with you that American Jews should be more interested in strengthening Israel in ways other than giving money. I also agree that the Israeli government has too much power and authority. Thus, I cannot help but believe that the Israel Center for Social and Economic Progress can be a very worthwhile organization. Nevertheless, as will become obvious to you from the following, it is impossible for me to undertake involvement in this project at this time. I do promise to revisit this topic as soon as the demands on my time have been sufficiently reduced.

What is occupying my attention outside the normal time demands is a thing called Globex, perhaps I have already mentioned this before. In my opinion, Globex is about to change the way the world markets work. What

I have helped devise and launch is an electronic trading system for futures and options that will operate virtually around the clock.

As you know, as a result of the telecommunications revolution which occurred during the last decade or so, geographical distinctions for markets no longer exist. We live by virtue of an (information standard,) whereby money managers no longer reserve investment decisions until local markets open. Rather, all major financial centers have become part of a single global market. While everyone gives lip service to the foregoing, few understand its implications.

In my opinion, unless the markets in the U.S. recognize the meaning of this reality, unless they respond to the opportunities and competitive dangers it represents, they stand to lose their business to those foreign competitive financial centers that do. As you well know, given present technological competence, capital flows have no geographical or political allegiance.

In recognition of this truth, several years ago I conceived an idea that has given me no rest. I went to Reuters Holdings PLC and proposed an alliance to build with the Merc a global electronic transaction system called Globex. Reuters agreed, and since then, I have had time for little else. The idea is so powerful that, in my opinion, it will become the standard transaction system for all futures and options business, and, most likely, the model system for securities and all other market sectors, as well.

Proof of its power can be found in the fact that 88 percent of our membership approved the concept, even though its central premise—automation—represents the greatest danger to open outcry, from which they all make a living. Further proof is found in the fact that three fiercely competitive futures exchanges, the New York Mercantile Exchange (NYMEX), the Sydney Futures Exchange (SFE), and the Marché à Terme International de France (MATIF) have already become CME partners in the project. And, more exchanges are coming. When we are finished, the CME will be the central cog in a global system that will dominate futures and options trade for the forseeable future—and who knows were that will lead.

Anyway, it is literally the most exciting thing I have undertaken since the IMM, and well worth my while. I enclose copies of some further thoughts on the subject and a general booklet. Be glad to tell you more as we progress.

My best to Rose.

Very truly yours,

Leo Melamed

It's Time for a Change

Open Positions

The Newsletter of the Chicago Mercantile Exchange Equity Owners' Association

Vol. 1, Issue 9   December 15, 1996

It's Time for a Change

The election is approaching. A certain friend of ours, when he campaigns, often asks, "Are you better off now than you were two years ago?" This is a particularly pertinent question to those equity owners whose living is made every day on the floor of our Exchange. It applies to others in matters of lease prices, transaction volume and the cost of doing business at the CME. We advise taking a moment to ponder this question before you decide who deserves your vote.

There are more important considerations that should play a part in your decision, many of which we have uncovered and discussed in our past newsletters. You should be as troubled as we are regarding:

1. That our budget has been a matter of secrecy (since the EOA focused attention on this issue the policy has been marginally changed. We may now inspect some additional details of the budget, however, if we do, we are prohibited from describing what we find to you).
2. That the CME is the high cost producer among Chicago exchanges (operating expenses/contracts cleared) by almost a 40 percent margin.

3. That a $1,000,000 sale of real estate in the Eurodollar pit has been allowed to stand.
4. That our present Board is responsible for the dilution of CME, IMM and IOM seat values owing to a poorly structured idea misnamed "GEM."
5. The $1,000,000 donation to the Lyric Opera.

Then you share our firm opinion that It's time for a Change!

We ask that you vote for the candidates we support. They are intelligent, successful, experienced members, energetic and dedicated to the Chicago Mercantile Exchange. They have pledged their support for the EOA platform: A platform not constructed of political ideologies nor one with hidden personal financial motivations, but one that is grounded in practical and ethical considerations that should be at the heart of governance of the CME.

Change can sometimes be a fearful proposition. A fictional character, vain and selfish, asks the question, "Do I dare disturb the Universe?" We are traders. Traders cannot be successful without courage. It may appear safer to vote the status quo, but remember that we live in a democratic society. We pride ourselves on the smooth nature of our transitions. When George Bush was relieved of his duties four years before he intended, the American people decided it was time for a change. A smooth transition of power took place on Inauguration Day, 1992, as he handed the reins of power to the former governor of Arkansas.

Corporate transitions are similar. A CEO's tenure is often limited by contract or mandatory retirement (akin to term limits for a U.S. President). Timely leadership changes strengthen an institution. So does an infusion of different expertise, talent and levels of interest and intellect that combine to positively impact the culture of the institution.

When leadership becomes entrenched, an institution reflects not only the strengths of its leadership, but also its weaknesses. Those weaknesses are especially glaring when business conditions deteriorate and can no longer mask them. Change at the Chicago Mercantile Exchange is nothing we need to fear. Change will enable us to leap forward to a more dynamic future.

It's Time for a Change!

Equity Owners' Advisory Council

Richard Ford
Steve Goodman
Joe Gressel
Don Karel
Sheldon Langer
Kirk Malcolm

George Segal
Leon Shender   IOM Candidate
Bill Shepard   IMM Candidate
Howard Siegel
Joel Stender   CME Candidate

1997 CME Equity Owners' Association Election Platform

1. **Conflict of Interest:** A director or candidate for director must disclose
   all current or intended business investments which seek to profit from
   CME related business. He must recuse himself from voting on all issues
   in which he has a related interest.
2. **Open the Budget:** The complete line-item detail of the Exchange budget, including total remuneration and pension benefits of staff and
   elected officials through the level of vice-president, should be available to all equity owners.
3. **Accountability:** The Board of Directors should publish specific financial and business development goals and objectives for each year.
4. **Integrity of Membership Value:** CME pit location is not individually
   owned and cannot be sold.
5. **Disclosure:** The individual voting record of each Board member should
   be published.
6. **Contributions:** Cumulative contributions exceeding $10,000 to a single
   or related organization within a 24-month period must be disclosed.
   A CME Board member or staff executive having a present, proposed
   or subsequent Board position with any organization receiving a CME
   contribution, must disclose that position to the membership.

The Equity Owners' Association requests your support for the following
independent candidates. These candidates have jointly agreed to support
the above mentioned 1997 election platform.

CME CANDIDATES

Bob Haworth (BUCK)   Past independent order-filler in currencies and Eurodollars. Presently independent trader in back month Eurodollars. Certified
Public Accountant formerly head of CME audit staff. Number one priority is
restoring a sense of unity among the members.

Irwin Rosen (Irv)   Local hog and hog belly trader for 26 years. Attorney who
has championed member rights in numerous compliance proceedings. Irwin
is a potential Board member who will not be reluctant to speak his mind.

William Salatich (Sal)   Independent 21-year equity owner, order-filler in the Feeder Cattle pit. He states he has no favors to pay and none to collect. His motivation to become a director is to seek the best path for our future. Bill will speak his mind and has demonstrated in various committees the ability to be creative and productive.

Joel Stender (Joel)   Independent local trader for 21 years. Co-founder of the CME Equity Owners' Association and editor of EOA newsletter, "Open Positions." Believes that it's time to revolutionize the management and leadership of the CME. Stagnant growth, declining membership values, possible conflicts of interest and questionable vision have burdened the CME franchise. Will provide a fresh approach by experienced, energetic new eyes.

Paul Nelson (IA)   Long-time FCM employee and manager of CME operations for Iowa Grain. Regular participant on numerous committees. Independent personable thinker who will have a clear voice on important Exchange matters.

Tom Bentley (TAB)   Straightforward creative thinker. Not afraid to speak his mind. Concerned about staff productivity. Questions whether the Exchange is getting the appropriate bang for our 150 million bucks.

IMM CANDIDATES

William Shepard (Bill)   One of the most experienced members at the Chicago Mercantile Exchange. May hold the record for length and breath of committee participation. IMM member since May, 1973; CME member since September, 1973; IOM charter member. FCM since 1984, clearing local, commercial, and institutional business. Co-founder of the CME Equity Owners' Association.

Ron Sippel (SIP)   Fourteen-year back month Eurodollar local. Primary concern is representing equity and fairness issues, especially as they pertain to getting business into the pit. Will be an articulate local's advocate on the Board.

Don Lanphere(DJ)   Second-generation equity owner. Has spent last ten years fighting to maintain independent order-filling business. Prides himself on ability to appropriately distribute trades to both locals and institutions. Believes new business should be directed to IMM products, not the GEM.

YRA Harris (YRA)   Second-generation, long-time currency trader. Extensive global cash currency market contacts. Experience runs the gamut from arbitrage to order-filling to proprietary and fund trading.

IOM CANDIDATES

Leon Shender   Second-generation CME member. Independent order-filler and trader in equity quadrant. A peace maker who is able to smooth disputes in tense situations. Long-time Exchange committee contributor and Co-founder of the CME Equity Owners' Association.

You must vote for 2 candidates or your ballot will be invalid. The EOA suggests that you cast your second IOM vote for your choice of either Sonny Hersh or James Stavros.

Seymour I. Sonny Hersh (SNY)   Has been equity owner for many years. Believes Board accountability the most important issue. Active participant in the committee process. Presently serving on 17 committees.

Anthony James Stavros (IRS) By petition   Independent S&P local representing the next generation of CME leadership. Spearheaded a petition to use existing technology to make live bond quotes equally available to all S&P pit members.

The CME Equity Owners' Association recommends the following candidates for election to the 1997 Board of Directors. It's Time for a Change!

Chicago Mercantile Exchange Sample Ballot—CME Division
Vote for exactly 6 candidates

X	**Bob Haworth (BUCK)**
	Jack Sandner (JFS)
X	**Irwin Rosen (IRV)**
	Don Nadick (DON)
	Lou Schwartz (SWZ)
X	**Bill Salatich (SAL)**
X	**Joel Stender (JOEL)**
	Phil Glass (GLASS)
X	**Paul Nelson (IA)**
	Terrence Duffy (TDA)
X	**Tom Bentley (TAB)**
	Phil Karafotas (KARE)

Chicago Mercantile Exchange Sample Ballot—IMM Division
Vote for exactly 4 candidates

X   **Bill Shepard (BILL)**
    James Oliff (FILO)
X   **Ron Sippel (SIP)**
    Pat Mulchrone (PJM)
    Dennis Duffey (DPD)
X   **Don Lanphere (DJ)**
X   **Yra Harris (YRA)**
    David Silverman (DIS)

Chicago Mercantile Exchange Sample Ballot—IOM Division
Vote for exactly 2 candidates

Michael Dowd (FOC)   **You must vote for 2 candidates.**
Seymour I. "Sonny" Hersh (SNY)   **The EOA recommends your 2nd**
Gary Kattler (GKK)   **IOM vote be given to either**
X   **Leon Shender (JAZZ)**   **Sonny Hersh or Jim Stavros.**
Anthony James Stavros (IRS) By petition

Originally published in *Open Positions*, the newsletter of the Chicago Mercantile Exchange Equity Owners' Association (Volume 1, Issue 9, December 15, 1996).

A Brief Who's Who of the Members of the Equity Owners' Association

Richard Ford—Born in the Bronx, NY; received a Bachelor in Arts in English Literature at Ohio Wesleyan University; became an IMM member in 1985.

Howard Garber—Graduated the University of Wisconsin in 1971; received an MBA from University of Chicago; joined CME in 1976.

Steve Goodman—University of Illinois graduate in 1982 with a Bachelor's in Finance; came to the floor as a runner in 1977; became an IMM member in 1981.

Joel Gressel—Graduated Ohio State University with a degree in Agricultural Economics; became a member of the CME in 1976 and moved to Chicago to trade in lumber in 1981.

Don Karel—A Chicagoan by birth with a Bachelor of Arts from the University of Illinois; joined the IMM in 1975.

Sheldon Langer—A Chicagoan by birth; graduated Roosevelt University in June 1969 with a BSBA in Accounting; came to the CME in 1974.

Kirk Malcolm—Born in Gilmore City, Iowa; graduated from Iowa State University as an Industrial Engineer; received an MBA from University of Chicago; joined the IMM in 1973; became a partner of Shepard International in 1984.

George Segal—A New Yorker by birth; received a BA from City College of New York and MBA from the University of Michigan; became a member of the CME in 1971; worked as an account executive at Bache & Co and a vice president at E.F. Hutton & Co.

Aryeh (Leon) Shender—A Chicagoan by birth; attended Beloit, Roosevelt, and Southern Illinois universities; became an IMM member in 1976; became a member of the board in 1997.

Bill Shepard—Attended the University of Oklahoma; came to the CME in 1971 to join the launch of the IMM; became a member of the board in 1997.

Howard Siegel—A University of Wisconsin graduate; came to the CME in 1977.

Joel Stender—A Chicagoan by birth; received a BA from the University of Wisconsin and an MBA from Wharton School of Finance; joined the IMM in 1975; became a board member in 1997.

As described to author by each EOA member.

A Merged Future for Two Exchanges?

A recent recommendation by a Chicago Board of Trade task force that the exchange consider merging with the rival Chicago Mercantile Exchange has produced a loud chorus of derision and doubt.

Traders, former exchange officials and the chairman of the Merc pooh-poohed the idea, which has been floated at various times for more than a decade and has never gotten anywhere.

Short of a serious financial crisis, many sneered, the two exchanges are too different to ever get together. "It'll never happen in our lifetimes," said one trader after another.

But as part of a long-term strategy to keep the exchanges viable and competitive, merger should not be dismissed out of hand. In fact, the Board of Trade deserves credit for reopening and elevating the debate on how to maintain the future strength of the two exchanges, preserve jobs and keep Chicago as the global center of risk management.

It's true that many of the ideas now resurfacing have been quickly shot down in the past, but times have changed. Both exchanges suffered declining trading volume and seat prices last year. They continue to face rising costs and increased competition from foreign exchanges in London, Paris, and elsewhere, as well as from customized, off-exchange deals.

In an increasingly hostile business environment, the CBOT task force tried to look ahead and make recommendations on how to cut costs and increase revenues. The single biggest thing that could be done to reduce costs, it said, would be to merge with the Merc.

Such a marriage would create an institution "truly worthy of world-wide competition." The mega-exchange would have slightly higher annual revenues of $336 million and nearly $33 million in lower costs.

Realistically, such a merger may be several years away, but that doesn't mean serious talks on cooperation and cost-cutting shouldn't begin now. In fact, the effort may never produce a full union of the exchanges, but there are beneficial intermediate steps, including combining clearing operations.

Patrick Arbor, Board of Trade chairman, is expected to appoint a committee soon to study the task-force recommendations. This panel should include leaders and innovators from the two exchanges, and it must be chaired by a strong, respected individual. Leo Melamed, chairman emeritus of the Merc and the man credited with shaping the modern futures markets, would be perfect for the job.

It's only prudent to put egos and differences aside and plan now for long-term survival and prosperity.

Originally published in the *Chicago Tribune*, January 15, 1996.

The Merc Fights for Self-Regulation

Leo Melamed, architect of Chicago's financial futures market, is an outspoken champion of self-regulation, and it's easy to see why. With Melamed as its chief policymaker, the Chicago Mercantile Exchange has been a consistent industry leader in new products and services while remaining largely free of heavy government interference.

But Melamed knows that self-regulation is a right that can disappear rapidly if an institution doesn't act responsibly. Faced with increasing global competition and a government investigation of industry trading practices, he's fighting hard to preserve that right.

A committee of Merc leaders and industry experts, formed shortly after the federal investigation of the Merc and the Chicago Board of Trade was disclosed by The Tribune in mid-January, has proposed tougher trading rules and penalties. If adopted by the Merc's board of governors and the federal Commodities Futures Trading Commission, they would fundamentally change the way Chicago's futures markets operate. They would eliminate many opportunities for fraud and abuse and deter cheating by imposing harsh fines.

One far-reaching proposal calls for banning most traders from doing business for themselves at the same time they are handling orders for customers. This "dual trading" would be allowed only in a small number of lightly traded commodities. The committee also wants to restrict broker associations or rings, add surveillance staff, appoint non-exchange members to disciplinary committees and suspend a member for six months after a major rules violation. A second offense would result in lifetime expulsion from the exchange.

Merc officials claim some of these changes were in the works before the federal probe was revealed, but the package is clearly a response. It's also a genuine effort to restore public confidence in one of Chicago's most important financial markets by limiting both the possibilities and perception of abuses.

Critics may argue that the Merc is doing too little, too late. But the exchange constantly must balance its duty to keep its own house in order with its need to provide liquid and efficient markets.

Congress should realize that the futures industry has prospered under self-regulation. Even under the cloud of the FBI sting, Merc volume is up 34 percent this year and membership values are at record amounts. If the investigation reveals abuses not covered by these rule changes, further adjustments can be made.

Meantime, lawmakers should not add burdensome regulations that will drive up the cost of trading futures in America and force a successful U.S. industry to yield to foreign competition.

Originally published in the *Chicago Tribune,* April 26, 1989.

Dear Equity Owner

Open Positions

The Newsletter of the Chicago Mercantile Exchange Equity Owners' Association

Vol. 1, Issue 5   June/July 1996

Leo Melamed, under whose leadership financial futures were invented, who led the Merc in the creation of the IMM, the IOM, Globex and much more, participated in a frank discussion on the future of electronic trading. These are a few of the highlights.

Q: The original vision of Globex was of a central hub around which exchanges worldwide would revolve for after-hours trading. We, as members, approved what we thought would be our electronic franchise. The ball has been dropped. Multiple systems now trade on various exchanges. Given this new reality, what is the future of Globex?

A: Globex, from its inception, represented both a specific instrument as well as a general concept. We believed that the instrument called Globex, built on the joint foundation of the Merc and the CBOT, would preserve Chicago's role as the world's risk management center. While the instrument itself has been damaged, the overall concept is alive and well. Indeed, the concept of electronic trade—embodied in Globex—has been embraced by all exchanges worldwide and is clearly the gateway to the future.

Q: The Merc and the CBOT already tried this once and failed. Why do you feel a sense of optimism in going forward with them again?

A: The truth is that we almost didn't fail, we were on the threshold of great success. Since then, the world learned that we were on the right track. Today most futures market members and participants agree that electronic markets are the wave of the future. This can be evidenced from the many pages of electronic trade on the screens—EBS, Dealing 2002, Globex, Project A, Nasdaq, etc. Electronic trade is an accepted fact of life. Indeed, today both the FCM and local communities recognize that this is not an idea to be feared, but a reality to be embraced.

Q: Electronic markets certainly do exist, but that is not stopping the CBOT from entering onto a mutual offset agreement with LIFFE. Do you believe that the CBOT and the Merc are moving in the same direction?

A: Certainly, After all, the Merc has mutual offset with the SIMEX, why shouldn't the CBOT have the right to experiment with a similar idea. As they have learned, it will not be easy to implement because MOS is a very complex concept. In the long run, the efficiencies of electronic trading are cearly favorable to mutual offset. I think most exchanges understand this.

       It is also important to understand that our two exchanges are no longer all that different. While it's true that at one time the heritage of the CME and the CBOT was different, today only one culture exists. This commonality between our members will assist any future negotiations.

Q: You previously stated that the trading community has less trepidation of electronic technology today, yet we hear concerns voiced that pit-trading will become extinct and traders and order fillers will be displaced. How do you answer that?

A: The fear must be overcome. And that is precisely the role of our leaders: to provide an equitable and visionary transference of our members' expertise so that no member completely loses his franchise. This may not be easy, but it can be done. It should be emphasized that if this metamorphosis is not undertaken, we, as exchanges, may face the very real possibility of extinction.

       Remember that control of the electronic system is in our hands and allows us to maintain the current pit-traded products during regular trading hours. This provides us with an opportunity to consider new derivative products for listing on an electronic system, an enormous benefit which allows for more products to be tested—and at a much reduced cost—than in a pit environment.

       In addition, I would advocate placing terminals throughout the trading floor to encourage local and broker participation and familiarity. Traders would soon learn how to trade on the screen. Brokers could develop a customer base for whom they would act on the screen, a relationship similar to that between the floor brokers at New York futures exchanges and their customers.

Q: Having exported Chicago-style futures to the world, do we still have the synergy to again lead the way?

A: Both the CBOT and Merc together still have a good chance to make Chicago the center of electronic futures trading and to maintain our role as the risk management center of the world. Between our two exchanges, we have the talent and the markets. This concept Globex spawned is embraced by our two exchanges, our FCM community, and most participants. It doesn't matter whether the specific instrument we end up using is Globex or some other electronic system. What matters is that we accept the reality of what lies ahead and work together towards its implementation. As in many things—and particularly with respect to electronic trade—our two exchanges are much stronger together than as separate entities.

Originally published in *Open Positions*, the newsletter of the Chicago Mercantile Exchange Equity Owners' Association (Volume 1, Issue 5, June/July 1996).

Equity Owners' Association Status Report

Open Positions

The Newsletter of the Chicago Mercantile Exchange Equity Owners' Association

Vol. 1, Issue 2   February 26, 1996

Introduction

The Equity Owners' Association was formed to be a catalyst for creativity and vision as much as to challenge perceived inequities and inferior business practices. Our goal is to improve business prospects for our equity members. Thank you to the hundreds of members who have responded and particularly to those of you who have contributed to this effort. We are an army of talented, thinking, hard working partners in a business that genuinely needs everything we can contribute. We cannot be ignored.

Today, we have an opportunity to constructively influence our own destiny. The EOA has identified numerous crucial areas of concern. This status report on our initiatives explains where we are concentrating our effort, evaluates our progress, identifies stumbling blocks and suggests our future course.

The mission of the Chicago Mercantile Exchange is to provide an arena for locals to make markets, order fillers to fill orders, and FCMs to bring their customers' business. The EOA supports the imposition of strict accountability standards that measure how well our leaders fulfill their responsibility to maintain the vitality of our marketplace.

CME leadership must respond positively to our initiative because our strength comes from the entire membership and cannot be denied. They must capitalize on our initiative, strengthen the infrastructure of our marketplace and rejuvenate the CME for its equity members and for our future.

Membership Response to Post Card Survey Regarding Exploring Cooperation with the CBOT

The results of this informal opinion poll were slightly greater than 4:1 in favor of exploring the possibilities. Just under 400 responses were received.

Equity Owners' Association
Status Report
February 26, 1996

Issues and Projects Raised in Meetings with Jack Sandner and Present Status:

7-Point Currency Initiative
1. **Ten Percent Variable Operating Expense Reduction**—Initially, this concept was "not well received." We were informed that a contingency plan does exist for a reduced volume environment. The EOA believes every successful global business is liposuctioning fat to improve operating efficiency and competitiveness. Some elements of the "un-level playing field" are temporarily out of our control. Making our business more cost-effective and efficient, especially when our competition increasingly becomes a computer, is squarely within the grasp of our management.
2. **CTA Incentive Plan**—The idea of encouraging CTA business with "an appropriate" incentive such as membership credits, received a positive reception from the CTAs and Pool Operators we polled. The CME should sponsor an annual CTA and Pool Operator Conference to explore issues important to this significant customer class.
3. **Overnight Trading Session**—The EOA believes that we must offer our customers efficient, viable market access around-the-clock. The choice of an overnight (1:00 A.M. to 6:00 A.M.) trading session for currencies and Eurodollars, or the successful implementation of the recently approved Exchange backed arb support for Globex, would meet this requirement. Jack was receptive to an overnight session and the ability to potentially lease an overnight trading right, but cautioned that an indication of

support must be demonstrated. The major hurdle to an overnight session is providing adequate liquidity. This is an important issue in currencies during the day and an obviously greater challenge at night.

4. **Exchange-Backed Arb Support for Globex**—This proposal has now been approved by our Board. In our January 30th meeting with Jack, we stressed our greatest possible concern regarding those charged with the responsibility for this program. Impeccable reputations without conflicts of interest are absolutely essential qualities for participants. In follow-up discussions with staff, the EOA was assured that only demonstrated arbitrage professionals would be carefully and prudently considered. We will carefully monitor this process because its successful implementation is critical. Our currency quadrant will certainly benefit from direct Globex access for the CTA community.

5. **Internet Link to Trading Pits**—Prior to the formation of the EOA, this proposal was turned down when introduced to the Communications and Technology Committee. The matter was recently discussed with Jack and reintroduced to the Communications Committee. The coordinated input of technology expert, John Gelderman, together with staff and new committee support, overcame the original lack of enthusiasm. Systems expert, Mike Kelly, is working on linking Tops with Cubs. A pilot implementation for small orders is planned for lead month Euros in April.

The Internet link has progressed two steps closer to reality. The Technology Oversight Committee has approved a budget and an Inter net technology specialist has been hired. Business issues dealing with security, credit controls and price quote availability will be addressed to the appropriate committees. Mike Kelly is targeting a first version to be available by June with a working connection available in six months.

6. **Reduce Equity Member clearing fees**—The EOA approach to EFPs is to raise the price to $10 to $12.50 and to coordinate this with the CTA incentive plan. The plan offers a financial incentive for CTAs to execute their business in our pits and not incur the EFP fee at all. EFP revenue may still rise allowing a reduction in equity member clearing fees.

The EOA was recently asked whether we are advocating raising the fees of the group we are trying so hard to attract. Every CTA who signs on to our incentive plan will be totally relieved of EFP fees on Exchange and Globex executed business. One activity we do intend to stop is the abuse of our reputation by allowing EFPs to facilitate certain non-competitive transactions.

7. **High Profile Congressional Consultant**—to fight un-level playing field between the highly regulated futures markets and our less regulated inter-bank competitors—Jack turned the EOA down cold on this

issue. His justification was that we've tried Congressional consultants before, but found them "not cost-effective." He stated that he would love to do this job himself, but there is not sufficient time.

The EOA suggests that Jack find time for this critical issue. Yes, this is a difficult assignment. Yes, the banking industry has a well-financed lobby. Yes, banks own many memberships on our exchange, but this is what the challenge of leadership is all about. Jack demonstrated his effectiveness in Washington with Leo Melamed during the S&P crisis and in other instances. The currency situation is as important a core issue to our exchange as the S&Ps. We must resolve to win this battle.

This challenge is worthy of one of our silver bullets. Sitting close at hand is our Chairman Emeritus, Leo Melamed. Perhaps Leo could be charged with leading this difficult and delicate assignment.

Broker Association Control of Trading Groups

The EOA rejected the Board's annual meeting response that the Compliance Department conducted the most exhaustive investigation ever, but found no evidence of impropriety. We sought, and have been given a commitment, that actual P&S results of members within these groups will be compared to members outside the groups. One hundred members' statements will be compared over a 6-month-period evaluating the quality of trades, especially during active market periods (such as following the release of economic reports). The results are promised by March 15. To assure confidentiality, only a summary will be revealed to the EOA.

GEM Participation in Member Retention Program

EOA successfully argued that the GEM division should be removed from this program.

GEM Structure

Our discussion with Jack began with total disagreement regarding the existence of any problems. He later acknowledged that a successful GEM could re-distribute equity from the existing divisions. We argued that there is no reasonable means for most equity owners to hedge. Jack agreed that two EOA representatives should meet with his best GEM experts and resolve concerns on behalf of equity owners. On February 14, we were advised that Jack's representatives would be Scott Gordon and Jim Oliff, plus a member of staff. At the initial meeting, the Board representatives acknowledged that they possessed no authority and would only report their results to the

Executive Committee. At this meeting, your EOA representatives presented our concerns. The EOA and Board representatives agreed to consider strategies to maintain the potential of the GEM contracts without the dilution of the present GEM structure.

It is important to recall that the Board promised to take steps to avoid dilution, but membership prices have not been a comforting barometer of their safeguards. A large number of memberships were liquidated in a short time, but this does not tell the whole story. First, CME membership prices had fallen over $200,000 from their peak before Refco began selling memberships in earnest on 8-24-95. During the next 3 months, Refco liquidated 24 memberships. 9-CMEs were sold from $715K down to $615K, 4-IMMs from $705K down to $581K and 11-IOMs from $300K down to $255K. 18 full CBOT memberships were also sold. Their prices ranged from $625K down to $525K. The most recent membership prices as of February 26 were: CME: $550K, IMM: $522K, IOM: $224.5K and CBOT: $625K. CME membership prices have remained soft while CBOT memberships have fully recovered.

Do not misunderstand. This is not about membership values, but about what these values represent. Membership prices have always fluctuated up and down. When they peaked, there were several banks bidding for memberships at one time. Prices went too high. When a seller hit the market hard, prices fell. We don't like it, but we understand it. Our concern is that the market perceived the GEM as having substantial dilution potential, and re valued our equity accordingly. The steps taken by the Board to avoid dilution have obviously been insufficient. **We cannot allow any further dilution at the CME.**

Since publication of Steve Goodman's letter in *Open Positions* last month, the EOA has received a litany of complaints from the membership. Most of these revolve around the dilutive effects of the GEM. Many members voicing objections previously voted in favor of creating the Division. They want to know why so many important issues were not addressed by the Board.

The following are EOA suggestions for correcting the structural defects of the GEM. Implementing these improvements will insure that the builders of the CME divisions will share in the potential of GEM products, and not have their equity re-distributed.

A. Implement a one-year moratorium on all CME, IMM, or IOM lessees' switching to the GEM Division. This rule should be extended to preclude an equity owner from leasing out his CME, IMM, or IOM membership and leasing a GEM. The object is to stop interdivisional price compacting, or the GEM addition will continue to dilute. We cannot tolerate any further dilution of our equity in any form. The responsibility of our leadership is to our existing members even while new growth strategies are forged for the future.

B. The rationale for the establishment of the GEM division was to provide a lower-cost entry for young traders who would provide support for fledgling new contracts. No fee-splitting arrangements should be allowed to impair the economics of either the emerging traders, or their contracts. In other words, no broker groups should be allowed to adversely influence the fragile new ecosystem by splitting fees, or expenses, while using GEM memberships.

C. Another safeguard recognizes that fifty original memberships were sold to "only the most deserving emerging market participants" at a substantial discount. These members must be held accountable to use their memberships for the purpose for which they were intended. They must either personally trade in a GEM pit; route proprietary orders to the GEM pits; or send customer orders into the GEM in some appropriate quantity. In the absence of fulfilling these requirements, they misrepresent the intention of the GEM membership. In these cases, noncompliant members should have their investment returned and the membership re-issued.

50% Limit on Broker-to-Broker Trades

An unexpected dividend issued from our February 8th meeting. A proposal to place a 50% limit on broker-to-broker trades was offered by our Chairman. We all agreed this would go a long way toward curing many of the "accessibility to order" problems encountered every day in our pits. We will pursue and promote Jack's idea.

Membership Rental Pool

An EOA representative has been assigned to the Leasing Committee to work with Chairman, Lou Schwartz, to develop a rental pool plan.

Precious Metals Contract Proposal

On January 1, 1975, gold ownership and trading were legalized in the United States. Four exchanges vied for dominance at the start of trading. Ultimately, only two remained viable. One was the IMM. For the next eight years, the CME was synonymous with gold trading. For a long time it was our leader in volume and open interest. Cyclical economic and tax changes sapped gold's volatility and the marketplace could not support trading on two exchanges.

For the first time since 1987, a window of opportunity exists for the return of precious metals trading on our exchange. We suggest a unique trading vehicle that again gives the IMM a niche. The idea is an <u>actual</u> delivery combination contract, comprised of a one-kilo bar of gold (32.15 oz.) a 1000 oz. bar of silver and a 50 oz. bar of platinum. The total value of the contract is less than $40,000 at today's prices and would constitute an ideal diversified investment in precious metals. Three metals could be traded with only one commission. Companion contracts exist on other exchanges, offering flexibility, should an investor desire to sell or hedge a portion of his holding. We think that this is an idea for the balance of the 90s and into the next century.

Summary

This summarizes what the EOA has been involved in. The challenges we face did not develop overnight just as they will not be cured overnight. Maintain a positive attitude. As traders we have all weathered tough situations. Our problems are serious, but we will prevail. We are in time and right is on our side.

Send the EOA your constructive ideas to improve our business and our exchange. We will not successfully achieve every initiative, but we are helping focus attention on important areas. If you have remained in the background because you perceived that a closed shop existed, it's time to tear off the shutters. If you haven't indicated your support for the Equity Owners' Association, now is the time to send in your suggested contribution of $125. Your contribution will fund the administrative costs of the EOA and allow us to keep you up-to-date on our progress.

Sincerely yours,

Equity Owners Association Advisory Council
Richard Ford, Steve Goodman, Joe Gressel, Don Karel, Sheldon Langer, Kirk Malcolm, Leon Shender, Bill Shepard, and Joel Stender

Originally published February 26, 1996.

Creating a New Alliance—Why Here and Now?

Newsletter of   Volume 1, Number 1 Sept./Oct. 1996

The National Alliance of Futures and Options Brokers

The National Alliance of Futures and Options Brokers
CME Center/30 S. Wacker Dr./P.O. Box 13/Chicago, IL 60606
Tel: (312) 836-4244

One month ago a few members of the Chicago Mercantile Exchange came together to form *The National Alliance of Futures and Options Brokers.* Two weeks after the formation was announced, the number of members had grown to more than 200 and continues to grow. We recognize the importance of coming together to address critical issues of mutual concern.

We welcome the participation of all members on all exchanges, regardless of their current role in the market.

Over the past year, there has been a calculated dissemination of misstatements regarding floor brokers and floor broker associations. First it was just murmurs, rumor and innuendo, later repeated in a privately published newsletter sent to members. More recently, these unattributed attacks have found their way into the news media.

We will not speculate on who is behind the attacks or their true agenda. Clearly, it is the effort of a few who prefer to ignore the facts, disseminate misinformation and are seriously attempting to disturb the unity of the Exchange.

It is important to know that the forming of the Alliance is not part of a "counter attack." We know that putting individual interests above those of the institution of which we are each a part, is short sighted at best.

Our objective is to end the divisiveness among members, believing that such divisiveness serves no one's interests.

We don't have to agree about everything. When we disagree, however, we need to work it out in a professional manner, for the good of our customers and the Exchange. Public attacks, while they may be politically appealing, are counter-productive. Attacks place labels on our membership, when we all have one goal: to produce a better form of price discovery for the public. Our challenges are to move the Exchange forward; to create opportunities and products that global and domestic customers need for risk management and asset allocation; to provide a liquid market; to be cost-effective and competitive; and to use technology, order entry systems and the Internet as tools to accomplish these ends.

Over the coming months, we will address a number of challenges and will suggest ways to meet these challenges. We invite all members to use this space to comment and offer constructive ideas and suggestions.

A major challenge facing us today is in the area of technology. The Exchange's recent letter to the membership with respect to its efforts and initiatives on technology should be welcomed by all of us. The Exchange has made great strides in developing new technology (TOPS/CUBS) to automate the order entry and execution process consistent with open outcry. We welcome the Exchange's promise to demonstrate this new technology and to openly discuss its vision for our technological future. Once that vision is shared, it is time for us to embrace technology, not to fear it. Now it is up to us.

None of us welcome changes in our business methods. Innovation can be painful, uncomfortable and costly. To remain competitive and preserve open outcry, we must be receptive to innovation, not ignore it. That is our challenge.

We have been asked if the Alliance will be a "permanent" organization and the answer is a definite *yes*.

We will work to assist committees and the Exchange itself in a positive and constructive way, without attacking or tearing down the very institution to which we are so dedicated, deeply committed and invested in every sense of the word.

The Exchange has come a long way, yet we believe that our best days are still ahead. In rough markets, the need is greater to commit our energy and resources to creating opportunity.

We invite those in all quarters of the exchange community to join with us in working together to maintain the integrity of our markets.

For more information or to become a part of the National Alliance of Futures and Options Brokers, call us at 312/836-4244.

Whose Problem Is It?

An industry leader claims that open outcry is an anachronism—that the exchanges must look for—other opportunities for their members. That's somebody else's problem.

A critic of the Chicago Board of Trade expansion project calls the new addition an "albatross" that will be the death knell to the Exchange for not recognizing the floor is an "outdated" pricing product. But that's the CBOT's problem.

A piece in the *London Financial Times* argues that despite the safety of the NYMEX clearing house and the "transparency and openness" of its copper prices, copper traders should look to the London Metal Exchange and OTC markets where there is *less* regulation, *fewer* customer safeguards and *more* privacy. That's New York's problem.

A CFTC official argues open outcry must be more severely regulated, even if costs of such regulation drive customers away from the markets. That's everyone's problem.

The National Alliance of Futures and Options Brokers is about *voice*— one very loud voice—that permits no challenge to go unanswered and speaks for our entire community.

Therein lies the rub: We seem to have forgotten that we are, indeed, one community.

As entrepreneurs, we value our independence and rely on the exchanges to provide the marketplace in which we can earn our living. Exchanges, however, cannot always speak for us. They have their own agendas and their own priorities.

Occasionally, we recognize that we and the person standing next to us have a common interest. Still, locals view the marketplace as an opportunity to make a living, but resent order fillers and FCMs for placing demands on their market making function. Independent floor brokers feel a kinship with other independents, but distrust broker associations, floor traders and FCMs, believing they threaten their ability to function. FCMs consider the floor a costly necessity and believe order fillers and locals limit profit opportunity.

Our voice will only be heard if we recognize that we are larger than our individual interests. Our voice and our process goes beyond exchange borders. The volume of our collective voice can only be heard when we recognize that we are each a vital part of the process and that our shared interests outweigh our differences.

Our common goal is to provide the public with the best form of price discovery and price integrity: FCMs who bring the customers to the marketplace; floor brokers who represent customer's interests with integrity and professionalism; and locals who provide the necessary liquidity and price competition, making the market perform better than a silent, private market.

We must each appreciate the others' vital contributions to the process. We must also provide a means to vent our differences amongst ourselves; insure that all market participants have equal access to the price discovery process; embrace those changes that enhance order delivery and price reporting; and insure and enforce a standard of professional conduct that is beyond reproach.

We must use our voice *whenever, wherever*, and *however* open outcry is challenged. We must use our voices not *at* one another, but *for* one another. And now is a good time to start.

Setting the Record Straight

Today anyone seems to be able to accuse anyone else of just about *anything*—regardless of how baseless or damaging the accusation—and just walk away.

For example, in a recent memo distributed to members on the floor, two issues were raised in a clear attempt to create tension among CME members. One was committee composition and the other was broker-to-broker trading. Here is what was said and here is the truth:

Misstatement: Most important committees do not adequately represent locals.

The Truth: An Exchange examination of committee composition disclosed that locals are well-represented on all committees, including pit committees.

Misstatement: The CBOT local-to-broker trading ratio is nearly double that of the CME.

The Truth: An Exchange analysis done in cooperation with the CBOT showed the local-to-broker ratio to be virtually the same.

Misstatement: The LIFFE local-to-broker trade ratio is significantly higher than the CME.

The Truth: An Exchange review of this ratio with LIFFE showed CME local-to-broker trading to be significantly higher than at LIFFE.

Misstatement: Broker-to-broker trading at the CME occurs all too frequently to the exclusion of independent traders.

The Truth: An Exchange examination showed that, excluding local-to-local trading, locals trade opposite more than 50% of all trades in currencies; 60% in Eurodollars; and 65% in S&Ps. Customer-to-customer trading in these markets is no more than 17%.

A recent memo from the Ad Hoc Committee to Review Trading Floor Issues also attempted to correct these misstatements. The Committee, which itself is comprised of eight floor brokers, eleven locals and five firm representatives, was formed "for the purpose of assuring that all market participants have equal access to our markets."

With respect to the issue of committee composition, the Committee concluded that "An examination of committee composition, including pit committee composition, demonstrates that locals, brokers and firms are well-represented." With respect to trading by locals, it concluded that a "review of trading statistics in conjunction with those exchanges disclosed that broker-to-local trading is significantly higher at the CME than LIFFE and virtually identical to the CBOT."

Nevertheless, we call upon the Exchange to regularly review trading statistics on an individual basis to ensure that all members have equal access to our markets. Likewise, we call upon the Ad Hoc Committee to address ways to encourage those appointed to committees to attend their scheduled meetings.

Originally published in The National Alliance of Futures and Options Brokers' newsletter 1, No. 1 (September/October 1996).

Chairman Emeritus Remarks

I am honored to once again find myself at the boardroom table of the Chicago Mercantile Exchange. It has been six years since I last sat here—in a similar post—with a similar mission. To his credit, Jack Sandner has offered his hand of cooperation and I have gladly accepted it. As correctly portrayed by last Sunday's *Tribune* article, I seek to provide a unifying element to this Exchange, an exchange that has a very diverse membership, often divided and sometimes dissatisfied. Jack and I worked in harmony for many years and I'm certain we can do so again.

Nevertheless, I believe it's imperative to reflect on why I am here and what caused my return. Indeed, it would be disingenuous of me and foolish for anyone in this room to believe it is business as usual. The Merc election last month was anything but ordinary. Fully 50 percent of those elected by the membership as directors have never before served. Five directors of the Merc board who served for many years were defeated and a sixth chose not to run, no doubt because he would not have been reelected. Some of the directors defeated were for years high-ranking officers of the Exchange. Such results do not represent ordinary occurrences. Indeed, in the history of the Merc, to my recollection, the last election represents an unprecedented event.

To put it another way, if this were a national election and 50 percent of those elected by the American public replaced incumbents, it would be viewed as nothing short of revolutionary. And not only is our Exchange a microcosm of the country, it is the epitome of a democratic institution. Right or wrong, our electorate has spoken. Right or wrong, whether anyone in this room likes it or not, the membership of this Exchange has dramatically voted for change. And in a democracy, the word of the electorate is final.

Indeed, whether you agree or not, whether it is true or not, and whether we like it or not, a majority of our membership seem dissatisfied. There is a feeling that the Merc has lost its momentum. That our traditional role as a leader in the industry has been usurped by other exchanges. That our future is not as certain as it was. That some of our markets are broken;

that they are in need of repair. The members seem to be saying that our Exchange has lost its sense of priority: that we seem to be more concerned with celebrations, with appearances, with photo opportunities, with civic and political involvements, than we are about the primary business of the Exchange—our markets. There is a view that the Merc's budget and expenditures reflect this incorrect set of priorities. These feelings have given rise to internal strife, to bickering, to finger pointing and acrimony. Membership organizations cannot move forward when there is internal divisiveness.

The effects of these perceptions were reflected in the last election, bringing new faces to this room and me back to the table. Unfortunately, I have no magic bullets or magic solutions, nor does, to my knowledge, any one of the new board members. But they do have ideas and they are willing to work. I personally hope to provide new thoughts and a new direction. Hopefully, I can help reprioritize the Merc so that its primary focus is on the markets, on technology, on clearing capability, on new ideas. Moreover, I am certain that the new board members are welcomed by everyone on the board. From what I have witnessed, the board directors have accepted the clear message from our membership and are ready to begin this task. Jack and I have taken the lead in this respect. Indeed, we intend to show the board and our membership that we can work as a unified team and provide the leadership necessary to effectively respond to our membership. I look forward to working with all of you.

———————

Board of Governors Meeting, Wednesday, February 5, 1997.

Open Letter to the Members of the Chicago Mercantile Exchange

June 16, 1997

Dear Member:

Upon returning to the CME Board in February after five years' absence, I vowed to once again openly offer my thoughts to the membership at important junctures or as critical issues evolve. I have attempted to accomplish this through members meetings and letters such as this to the membership-at-large. Because the Merc recently experienced a rare competitive loss in the licensing of the Dow Jones Industrial Average, it is appropriate to express my feelings on the subject as well as to offer my thoughts about our state of affairs

Let me be frank and to the point. I am neither heartbroken nor despaired. To be sure, it would have been grand to have been awarded this license. Our neighbors down the street are to be congratulated for having begun their efforts long before the CME and having persevered. But to paraphrase an old saying "one contract does not an exchange make." The Merc is built on a rock solid foundation of contract diversity which is the envy of every futures exchange the world over. Distinct contracts in agriculture, currency, interest rates, and equity index markets have given the CME a success factor second to none and a potential impossible to duplicate.

But it is the Merc's future that attracts me most. The world is changing and with this change comes enormous opportunity. We must not and will not fail to seize the moment. While it would be imprudent to be specific in this letter, I can state with assurance that the CME has an array of plans in the works that will place us at the forefront of futures markets well into the 21st century. Our focus is both national and global. The plans are multifold, exciting, and bold. The overall strategy includes both dramatic innovations of major proportion as well as minor changes aimed at improving existing market conditions. In the coming weeks and months, the specifics will become known and submitted to respective committees. Suffice it to say, it is a strategy designed to serve every arena of our institution—from agriculture to finance—and calculated to make our equity index sector the showcase of equity markets. I am confident and exhilarated by what I know to be in the works.

Of equal importance is that the Merc finds itself in a most envious fiscal position. We are financially strong, unencumbered by debt, and are completing a top to bottom budget review. Do not underestimate this advantage. It will enable us to capitalize on every market opportunity during the coming years with the explicit ability to outdistance our competition. Our board is highly dedicated, motivated to expansion, and ready to innovate. The Merc's president and senior staff are esteemed professionals and eminently expert. There is a sense of reinvigorated momentum and purpose. Together, the board, its leaders, and staff have rolled up their collective sleeves and are prepared to capture the future.

To say much more is unnecessary; I will save it for other occasions. I invite all members to join me in preparing for the next dramatic chapter in the history of the Merc—an experience well worth your while!

Very truly yours,

Leo Melamed

A Return to the Table

When I returned to the boardroom table in January after nearly six years' absence from Merc affairs, I did so primarily at the urging of a multitude of members who had, from time to time, come to my office to express concern for the future of the Merc and to urge that I return to leadership and lend a hand. Ultimately, events led me back. The Merc, after all, is my first love.

At the time of my return, there were those who feared there would be acrimony between Jack Sandner and me; that this acrimony would translate into an open animosity that would create disunity among the membership and stymie the board's ability to move forward. I am here to tell you those fears were unfounded. None of that materialized. Indeed, one can make the case that the professional working relationship developed between Jack and me over many years of working together served as a bridge to our reunification of purpose in 1997. I am here to say we accomplished a great deal during this year, and Jack and I worked in harmony toward those accomplishments. While there were differences between us, we bridged those differences and joined hands for the betterment of this institution and its membership. I commend Jack for this. And while there will be more formal occasions to do this, I wish to take this opportunity—as he nears the end of this latest round in his many terms as chairman—to publicly acknowledge him to the membership and thank him for his years of dedicated service.

Clearly, the pivotal reason for my decision to return to the table was my increasing concern over the changes that had occurred to the financial fabric of the world and their impact on futures markets. I spoke of those concerns in my 1995 address entitled "Wakeup Call," presented at the annual meeting of the International Association of Financial Engineers:

> We are at an unprecedented moment in the evolution of finance and markets. . . . At an unbelievable pace that continues to accelerate, technology has produced, and continues to produce, fundamental changes that reverberate through every facet of our civilization, but nowhere

more than in financial markets where the transformations have been
spectacular, global, and absolute. . . . [In financial markets] we are nego-
tiating an unknown expanse between a world we knew and the one we
know not. We are on a gigantic bridge between past political arrange-
ments, past economic orders, past technical capabilities, past market
applications, and a new reality. . . . One can no more deny the fact that
technology has and will continue to engulf every aspect of financial
markets than one can restrict the use of derivatives in the management
of risk. . . . Those who dare ignore this reality face extinction.

But beyond the challenges technology poses for our markets, I was
equally conscious that we were facing increasing competition from domestic
as well as foreign forces. And some of these competitors were gaining the
upper hand. Not only were other exchanges threatening our turf, but the
OTC markets had learned to duplicate what we invented and could create
synthetic substitutes in the cash market that were often as good as—and
sometimes better than—what futures could provide. I recognized that this
threat to our marketplace was not going to disappear and in time would
become even more intense.

In short, I was concerned. I knew that while there was still time to meet
the challenges that faced us, time was running out. While it was not too
late, it was late in the day. And while far from having all the answers, I was
persuaded to assist in the process. Make no mistake, in battle—and we are
in battle—another soldier at the front is always welcome.

The previous brief description of the problems facing futures markets
provides ample testimony that the challenges are formidable and the solutions difficult. But lest anyone despair, allow me to set the record straight:
The Merc has always been best when it is challenged. Our membership is
toughest when it is under attack. Indeed, during the last three decades,
our institution has faced the onslaught of many competitors—from other
exchanges, the private sector, and from government. On each occasion we
have reached deep within to find the right answer, the right defense, and
the right strategy. I have little doubt that we can continue to do it in the
future.

For example, take the E-Mini contract. This is exactly what I'm talking
about. When we lost the Dow index to the CBOT, there was a sense of
defeat on our floor. It represented a tough loss to our membership, no
doubt about it. But in my letter to the members on June 16, 1997, I said,

Let me be frank and to the point. I am neither heart-broken nor de-
spaired. To be sure, it would have been grand to have been awarded
this license. . . . But to paraphrase an old saying, "one contract does not
an exchange make." The Merc is built on a rock solid foundation of

contract diversity which is the envy of every futures exchange the world over. . . . But it is the Merc's future that attracts me most. The world is changing and with this change comes enormous opportunity. We must not and will not fail to seize the moment.

And, in fact, the Merc did seize the moment. While we could have sulked and licked our wounds, we instead took a losing situation and turned it into a big winner. We reached into the deep resources of Merc courage and innovation and produced an idea that so far has stolen the show from the Board of Trade. Not only did we in just three months put together the necessary technology to launch a new electronic product—my hat is off to Don Serpico and our MIS Department. Not only did we launch a public relations campaign that has won us rave revues—my hat is off to Marshall Stein and Ellen Reznick, from staff, and the Merc Marketing Department. We put the new contract on a 24-hour window, attracted a universe of retail users that never before dealt in futures, provided a market for many of our members who otherwise had trouble participating in equity futures, provided another avenue of potential income for our brokers, and stole the thunder from the CBOT. Sure, ultimately the Dow will be a successful contract, but so far it must have been a big disappointment, much more so if you consider what the CBOT paid for it plus the cost of marketing. No doubt it put the CBOT in hock for years and years to come. And lo and behold, the unexpected and even unthinkable has happened . . . there are days that our E-Mini volume beats the Dow.

And this is long before we have reached the Internet, and long, long before we have achieved our full potential with retail users worldwide. And all the while, the E-Mini has taken no business from our main S&P contract, in fact you can make the case that it adds to it. And while I am on this subject, allow me to do this risky thing, there were many who put their shoulder to wheel of this success, but there were those whose names I want to give mention—Bill Shepard and Barry Lind. They stood tall at my side throughout the difficult process.

The E-Mini is an example of what I meant when I stated that the Merc is best when challenged. But, of course it doesn't end there. The E-Mini is just one step in the right direction. But it counts because success is the culmination of a series of steps. And one success begets another. The Merc was not built in one day, nor on one successful contract. It took several decades and many contracts. And the turnaround in our fortunes will also occur over time and within a menu of many steps we have already taken and those we have yet to take.

Of course, instead of joining hands and moving forward step by step, we can turn our back to the reality of today's difficult demands. We can bicker amongst ourselves, spend valuable time on the inconsequential, divert our attention from the substantive, write nasty letters about each other, make unrealistic demands, dream about the past, hope for status quo, and create a disunity among our membership. This would be exactly what our competitors would applaud. It is a path destined to certain failure.

For our only salvation is to realize that times have changed and will never again be the same. Our only salvation lies in recognition that the path to success will sometimes be painful, it will contain elements that will not be loved by everyone, there will be sacrifices to be made, there will be difficult adjustments, and it will not be a straight path to the finish line. But we can persevere! And the process has begun.

- For instance, we are the only futures exchange that had the guts to put itself on a solid financial footing, not because we were forced by circumstances, but because we had the foresight to do so. Special thanks to Merc treasurer Tom Kloet and the Merc's chief of operations, Jerry Beyer. This move will yet pay us enormous dividends in the years to come. In comparison, the exchange down the street has spent itself into humongous debt which will shackle its ability to compete for a long, long time. And not only did we cut $17 million from our budget, we returned a lion's share of it to the membership.
- For instance, we have moved forward on GFX, which has already proven to be a huge success. It was a risky move. Few exchanges have created an arbitrage unit to compete for CTAs in currency business. Indeed, the GFX gave the Merc a weapon with which to compete against the EFP business that has been stealing our currency transactions. And GFX has shown great promise. For the period January through October, 1997, Globex currency volume is up 110 percent over the same period last year. That is to GFX's credit, and little else. Allow me to mention some of the people instrumental in this success, David Silverman, who chaired the effort, Sherwin Kite, and Kim Hough, and from Merc staff, Steve Heller, Mike Dengis, and, of course, the president of our clearing house, Kate Meyer. And don't forget the guys in the trading room itself.
- For instance, we initiated a *Technological Emancipation* which allowed our membership to bring technological innovations to our floors; innovations that will permit everyone to be more efficient and cost effective; innovations whose dividends have yet to arrive. My congratulations to Jeff Silverman, who chaired technological oversight.
- For instance, we had the courage to split the multiplier of the S&P contract, a decision that is bound to bring additional transaction volume and liquidity to S&P traders, brokers, and our FCM community. My hat is off to Jack Bouroudjian who led the fight on their behalf.
- For instance, thanks largely to the efforts of Bob Prosi, our agricultural division has a new sector in Cheddar Cheese Block futures. Nothing

to sneer at when you consider the potential. Cheese futures has the backing of the U.S. dairy industry and represents a $10 billion a year enterprise.

- For instance, we had the political will and intellect to stand tall on common clearing and put a realistic offer on the table to move the process forward.
- For instance, we have protected our markets with respect to new federal legislation and stopped OTC forces from making new inroads to our business.
- For instance, the Merc recently negotiated a deal with the MATIF and DTB that will place Globex on the same electronic network as the Europeans, in their quest to dominate financial markets on their continent. This puts the Merc way ahead of all its American competitors and provides our contracts the ability to expand their universe of users during the European time zone. All of which will pay us enormous dividend in the years ahead.
- For instance, we have initiated efforts to bring the Treasury cash market to our Eurodollar pit. Although most of this effort is still totally under wraps, I will give you this update: Even as I contemplated returning to the Merc boardroom, I discussed with Fred Arditti the possibility of his return with me as chief of product development. Fred is the one economist who I trust in the intellectual battle for market turf that we must face. He came aboard. And one of the critical issues we discussed from the beginning was the ability of Merc members to use the interest rate cash markets to compete with their OTC counterparts. Even as we discussed this innovation, Scott Gordon was thinking along similar lines and independently holding discussions with members of the Eurodollar pit. My salutations to Scott for his forward thinking. These separate actions have been joined and we have moved forward with this major innovation. Our Treasury Facility Committee is holding court and discussions are in the works. If we bring this effort to fruition, it will represent a major breakthrough and a sea change in our competitive battle with the OTC interest rate markets.

The foregoing are just some of the steps already taken in our journey back to the top of the mountain. There are many more to be made. But I will say no more at this time for it would be downright foolish to publicly discuss our strategy in any further detail. Suffice it to say, some will be dramatic, some inconspicuous. Some will be obvious, some deeply hidden from view. Some will be easy, some tortuous. Some popular, some not.

Our mission is to preserve our franchise. I repeat, *to preserve our franchise*. A franchise that we must keep intact as we cross the bridge to the new financial frontier I earlier described. A franchise that represents the values of our memberships; that represents member opportunity; that represents income for our members. Yes, that means that we have to turn our membership from market makers and brokers into market masters. Masters of the risk management universe in forwards, futures, and options.

And I know we can do it! But it will require three certain ingredients: First, a strong and united membership that will put aside all forms of nonsensical bickering; second, a bold and committed board of directors and professional staff; third, and most important, a membership that understands the need to take risks and is willing to leave status quo behind whenever the demands of innovation call for it.

Let me leave you with this first thought: Right now our membership prices have fallen to a low not seen in recent years. And maybe because of mergers and other factors the prices may fall somewhat lower. But remember, membership values are not a leading indicator; they are a lagging indicator. You need only to look at historical fact to know that truth. In 1994, when membership prices hit their historical high, they were certainly not a leading indicator. Nor now when they are down do they indicate their values of the future. In my way of thinking, if you the members and our professional staff provide the three ingredients I suggested, then the Merc membership offers the best value of any membership in the world. In my way of thinking, our future is well worth fighting for. I am glad to be back.

Thank you.

Chicago Mercantile Exchange Annual Members' Meeting, The Renaissance Chicago Hotel, Thursday, October 30, 1997.

James J. McNulty Joins CME as President and Chief Executive Officer

To All Members:

It gives me great pleasure to inform you that James J. McNulty will join the Exchange as President and Chief Executive Officer, effective February 7.

I told you at our Annual Members' Meeting that the candidate unanimously selected by our Board Search Committee has a thorough understanding of derivatives, technology and the global financial services land scape, has managed organizations through change and will provide us with the creative vision and strong leadership needed to propel us forward at Internet speed.

Jim has outstanding credentials as an experienced and knowledgeable global financial markets professional who has creatively applied technology to the financial risk management business. His in-depth knowledge of our business and the technology that drives it, his more than 25 years of diverse trading and management experience, and his leadership skills are exactly what the CME needs going forward to ensure that we are the premier marketplace of the 21st century.

As a Managing Director for the international investment banking firm Warburg Dillon Read, Jim is Co-head of the Corporate Analysis and Structuring Team within the firm's Corporate Finance Division. He made his mark as a general partner of Chicago-based O'Connor & Associates, one of the world's leading futures and options trading organizations which most of you know was recognized as a pioneer in applying sophisticated risk management technology and quantitative techniques to securities, futures and options markets. He then brought that expertise and cutting-edge approach to Swiss Bank Corporation (now UBS AG) and its investment banking arm, Warburg Dillon Read, after SBC purchased several O'Connor businesses.

Jim frequently lectures to top executives of major corporations on the topics of shareholder value creation, cost of capital, capital structure and dividend policy. As a member of Warburg Dillon Read's Corporate Finance Technology Committee, he recently designed and launched a global Corporate Finance Web portal incorporating more than 20 product and sector Web sites. Attached is a news release with more details about Jim's impressive background.

As you know, the Exchange is at a cross-roads, and we must continue to turn the challenges we face into opportunities in order to secure our global leadership position. I am very enthusiastic about the partnership I will have with Jim as we strive to do just that.

I want to express my sincere appreciation for the countless hours of hard work and dedication of the Board's Search Committee, which in addition to me included Terry Duffy, Jim Oliff, Marty Gepsman, Tom Kloet, Leo Melamed, Jack Sandner, Verne Sedlacek, and David Pryde. Our deliberate and thoughtful search process through which we selected Jim will produce great benefits in the future as we gain from his talents and experience.

Please join me in welcoming Jim to the Merc family.

SCOTT

CME Names McNulty New President and CEO

CHICAGO, January 18, 2000—The Chicago Mercantile Exchange (CME) has named James J. McNulty President and Chief Executive Officer, Chairman Scott Gordon announced today. The appointment is effective February 7.

McNulty, 48, has more than 25 years of exchange and over-the-counter experience in global financial markets. He will assume the CME's top staff position after serving as Managing Director for the international investment banking firm, Warburg Dillon Read, where he also is Co-head of the firm's Corporate Analysis and Structuring Team within its Corporate Finance Division. Warburg Dillon Read is a division of UBS AG, one of the world's leading financial institutions ranking among the top five banks worldwide by market capitalization.

"Jim brings outstanding credentials to the helm of the Merc at this critical juncture in our history," said CME Chairman Scott Gordon. "His comprehensive understanding of our markets, his creative applications of technology to derivatives trading, and his strong leadership skills make him uniquely qualified for this position. We set our standards very high when we embarked on this search, and Jim is exactly the right person to carry us forward. I look forward to working with him closely as we continue to pursue our strategic goals."

An experienced international banker, McNulty is a fourth generation Chicagoan who served as a general partner with O'Connor & Associates. One of the world's leading futures and options trading organizations, Chicago-based O'Connor was widely recognized as a pioneer in applying sophisticated risk management technology and quantitative techniques to the securities, futures and options markets. In 1992, Swiss Bank Corporation (SBC) purchased several O'Connor businesses, integrating them into its global Capital Markets and Treasury organization. UBS AG was formed from the merger of the banking groups of Swiss Bank Corporation and Union Bank of Switzerland (UBS) in 1998.

"Traditional financial markets are at a strategic inflection point," said McNulty. "The winners will be defined by how they apply new technologies and globalize their business the most efficiently. The CME members and staff have consistently been agents of change in the financial markets, and I am excited to take the exchange through the next phase of its evolution."

A member of Warburg Dillon Read's Corporate Finance Technology Committee, McNulty recently designed and launched a global Corporate Finance Web portal incorporating more than 20 sector and product Web sites. At SBC, he was responsible for designing a number of the risk management advisor tools which the firm used to advise multinational corporations and investment managers.

Prior to his current responsibilities at Warburg Dillon Read, McNulty was Co-head of Emerging Market Equities and served as investment banker for a number of U.S. and Mexican corporations. He founded SBC's Mexican Equity Derivative alliance with Banamex and its affiliates. He was previously North American Head of Interest Rate Corporate Coverage, Global Manager of the Structured Transactions Group and founder of the Risk Management Advisor Program for SBC.

From 1984 to 1987, McNulty was the founder and President of Hayes & Griffith Futures, Inc. He was also a director of Intermarket Publishing Corporation. He has held foreign exchange management positions with the Harris Bank and served as Citibank's Treasurer in Mexico City in the early 1980s. *Euromoney Currency Reports* named McNulty the top foreign exchange forecaster in 1982 and in 1983.

Throughout the course of his career, McNulty has traded or supervised trading in virtually all of the financial futures and options at the Chicago Mercantile Exchange.

McNulty is a popular international public speaker to top executives of major corporations on the topics of shareholder value creation, cost of capital, capital structure and dividend policy. Said John Dugan, formerly Chief Executive Officer for SBC in the Americas and Managing Partner of O'Connor & Associates: "You cannot be in the same room with Jim without feeling excited about the future and glad to be alive."

McNulty earned a bachelor's degree in liberal arts and sciences from the University of Illinois in Chicago, and a master's degree in Anglo-Irish studies from University College Dublin in Ireland. His wife, Jamie K. Thorsen, is Executive Managing Director and Global Head of Foreign Exchange at the Bank of Montreal. They reside in the Chicago area with their two sons.

The Chicago Mercantile Exchange is a global marketplace trading futures and options on futures on agricultural commodities, foreign currencies, interest rates and stock indexes, as well as weather-related products.

Chicago Mercantile Exchange Holdings Inc. Board Elects Officers

News release from Apri 24, 2002.

CHICAGO, April 24, 2002—The Board of Directors of Chicago Mercantile Exchange Holdings Inc. (CME Holdings) and its subsidiary, Chicago Mercantile Exchange Inc. (CME) elected a new Chairman this afternoon. Terrence A. Duffy, previously Vice Chairman, was elected Chairman of the Board during the Board's annual organizational meeting. His term as Chairman, succeeding Scott Gordon, is effective immediately.

In addition, the Board today appointed James J. McNulty, CME Holdings' President and Chief Executive Officer, to a newly created directorship which was authorized by shareholders at CME Holdings' annual meeting on Wednesday, April 17. At that time, shareholders also elected 10 directors to two-year terms expiring in 2004. This election was the second step in a two-step process to streamline governance and reduce the size of the company's Board from 39 to 20 positions.

At today's organizational meeting, the Board also elected the following officers, who will hold their positions on the Boards of CME Holdings and CME for a one-year term (through the April 2003 election):

Vice Chairman:	James E. Oliff
Second Vice Chairman:	William R. Shepard
Secretary:	Martin J. Gepsman
Treasurer:	Patrick B. Lynch

In addition, Chairman Emeritus Leo Melamed will continue to serve as Senior Policy Advisor and former CME Chairman John F. (Jack) Sandner will continue as Special Policy Advisor.

"I am honored by the responsibility with which the Board has entrusted me," said Duffy. "As a member of the Board for the past seven years, I have been fortunate to be involved in helping to guide the strategy that has made

CME the largest futures exchange in the United States. I am committed to working with our Board and management team to ensure that we continue to embrace change for the benefit of our shareholders, members, employees and customers. Scott has done an outstanding job in leading the exchange over the past four years."

"I'm looking forward to working with Terry as he leads the CME Board with the experience, energy and determination that he has applied over two decades of trading and many years of service as Vice Chairman on CME's Board," said McNulty. "Terry has demonstrated strong leadership skills in working with legislators to establish a fair regulatory environment for the U.S. futures industry."

Terrence A. Duffy, 43, is a floor broker and trader and has been President of TDA Trading, Inc. since 1981. He has been Vice Chairman of the Board of CME Holdings Inc. since its formation in August 2001 and of the Board of CME since 1998. He has been a CME member since 1981 and a Board member since 1995. As the company's Vice Chairman, Duffy most recently served on the executive, compensation, nominating, strategic planning and regulatory oversight committees. This year, he was appointed by President Bush to serve on a National Saver Summit on Retirement Savings. He studied business administration at the University of Wisconsin-Whitewater from 1976 to 1980. Duffy is married and resides in Lemont, Ill.

James E. Oliff, 53, has served as Second Vice Chairman of the Board of CME Holdings Inc. since its formation in August 2001 and of the Board of CME since 1998. He has been a director of CME since 1994. He previously served on the CME Board from 1982 to 1992. He is President and Chief Executive Officer of FFast Trade U.S., LLC, and Chief Operating Officer of FFastFill, Inc. In addition, Oliff is Executive Director of International Futures and Options Associates, the largest floor broker association at CME. Oliff earned a bachelor of arts degree from Brandeis University, Waltham, Mass., and J.D. from Northwestern University School of Law in Evanston, Ill. A resident of Deerfield, Ill., he is married with three children.

William R. Shepard, 55, has been a director of CME Holdings since its formation in August 2001 and a director of CME since 1997. A CME member for more than 28 years, he is founder and President of Shepard International, Inc., a futures commission merchant, since 1984.

Martin J. Gepsman, 49, has served as Secretary of the Board of CME Holdings Inc. since its formation in August 2001 and of the Board of CME since 1998. He has been a director of CME since 1994. A member of the Index and Option Market since 1985, Gepsman is an independent floor broker and trader. He received a bachelor of arts degree in French and German and an MBA in Finance and Marketing from Indiana University.

Patrick B. Lynch, 36, has been a director of CME Holdings since its formation in August 2001 and a director of CME since 2000. He has been a member of CME for more than 12 years and an independent floor trader since 1990. He earned a bachelor's degree in Finance from Michigan State University, East Lansing, Mich. A resident of LaGrange, Ill., he is married with three children.

The other members of the Board are:

- Timothy R. Brennan, Executive Vice President, RB&H Financial Services, L.P.
- John W. Croghan, Director, Republic Services, Inc. and Schwarz Paper Co.
- Daniel R. Glickman, Partner, Akin, Gump, Strauss, Hauer & Feld
- Scott Gordon, President, Chief Operating Officer and director, Tokyo-Mitsubishi Futures (USA), Inc.
- Yra G. Harris, independent floor trader
- Bruce F. Johnson, President, Packers Trading Company
- Gary M. Katler, Head of the Professional Trading Group, Fimat USA
- John D. Newhouse, President, John F. Newhouse & Co.
- William G. Salatich, independent floor broker and trader
- Myron S. Scholes, Chairman, Oak Hill Platinum Partners; Managing Partner, Oak Hill Capital Management; 1997 Nobel Laureate in Economics
- Verne O. Sedlacek, Executive Vice President and Chief Operating Officer, Commonfund Group
- Howard J. Siegel, floor trader

Chicago Mercantile Exchange Holdings Inc. is the parent company of Chicago Mercantile Exchange Inc. (www.cme.com), the largest futures exchange in the United States based on trading volume, open interest and notional value. As an international marketplace, CME brings together buyers and sellers on its trading floors and Globex around-the-clock electronic trading platform. CME offers futures contracts and options on futures primarily in four product areas: interest rates, stock indexes, foreign exchange and commodities. CME traded 411.7 million futures and options on futures contracts in 2001, with an underlying value of $293.9 trillion. The exchange moves about $1.5 billion per day in settlement payments and manages $28.2 billion in collateral deposits.

Letter to Audit Committee from Scott Gordon

Released March 20, 2002.

As we prepare for our possible IPO it is necessary to apply wherever possible the principles of corporate governance found in the "best practices" of public companies. This will allow our shareholders, members, potential investors, employees, and the public at large to clearly understand and support the Exchange. With less than one month before our Annual Shareholders' meeting, and in light of the present environment of increased scrutiny of for-profit companies, I would like to highlight several outstanding issues that need to be resolved as soon as possible for us to continue to make progress on this front.

With respect to the work of the Audit Committee I understand that among the issues you are analyzing are several that involve corporate governance (e.g., the need for committee charters, including decision rights and responsibilities) as well as how to determine and resolve conflicts of interest regarding topics brought to committees and the Board. Given our unique nature as the first major U.S. exchange to demutualize, and the two-year transition envisioned in the original S-4 registration statement, the nuances associated with some of these issues could not have been anticipated prior to now. Nonetheless, they are of paramount importance today, and the Board needs the benefit of analysis by your Committee and outside counsel in order to determine the best course of action to be taken by the Exchange. I encourage you to proceed without delay.

As to issues within the purview of the Compensation Committee (on which I serve), there has been much discussion and analysis over the past year regarding how best to compensate Board members, many of whom dedicate countless hours in assisting the Board and management. For the most part, the Committee's work in the area of determining fair and equitable cash compensation paid to Directors has been completed, and the Board last year adopted the Committee's recommendations on several key items. Left to be determined at a later date was how to compensate Board members elected by the Board as Advisors.

On this point I would ask the Compensation Committee to consider the advisability of compensating Board Advisors in a manner different from other Board members.

The Board and/or management can and should engage experts and pay for advice rendered, but I believe that Board Advisors should not be paid an additional stipend. One either serves as a Board member, or as a paid outside consultant. Our present practice of paying Board Advisors an additional stipend might have served the Exchange well as a membership organization, but needs to be reexamined in light of our desire to emulate the best practices of public companies.

As with my encouragement to the Audit Committee, I ask the Compensation Committee to analyze this issue expeditiously in order that the Board is in a position to make a proper determination as soon as possible.

I am confident the Exchange will be stronger based on the informed actions the Board takes on the above matters.

APPENDIX 19A

Futures' Future Isn't in Chicago

U pon his departure after nearly two decades as president of the Chicago Board of Trade, Thomas Donovan called it an honor to lead a world-class institution like the CBOT and "to help shape its destiny for the future."

Just what that destiny is remains a mystery.

Donovan had become a polarizing figure at the CBOT, it is true. But it is not at all clear that the powerful forces obsessed with his departure, including Chairman David Brennan, have a clue as to what to do now with this deeply riven, 152-year-old Chicago institution.

Its membership structure makes rapid and drastic change—essential though it is—virtually impossible. It is burdened with debt from a new $182 million trading floor for its cherished "open outcry" trading method that has become an expensive albatross in an electronic world. And, frankly, it is running out of time.

"Who would want to become mayor of Beirut?" asked former CBOT Chairman Les Rosenthal. Indeed.

There was a time when Chicago and futures trading were synonymous around the world. Between them, the CBOT and its LaSalle Street archrival, the Chicago Mercantile Exchange, ruled the roost. That is no longer true. Anyone looking at the future of futures at the dawn of the 21st Century must look east—across the Atlantic Ocean—to Eurex, the Frankfurt-based electronic marketplace created by a merger of the German and Swiss derivatives exchanges.

In volume, the upstart Eurex surpassed the CBOT last year to become the world's largest futures exchange. Eurex provides cost-efficient, one-stop shopping for futures and options trading in an electronic age and its volume is surging. Last October, after a fractious on-again, off-again courtship, the CBOT signed an alliance with Eurex.

How did this come to be, that the once-mighty Chicago exchanges are now scrambling to catch up in a market they created?

Perhaps no amount of savvy leadership could have slowed the technological juggernaut that is threatening the future of this industry in Chicago.

The CBOT and the Merc are facing intense competition, both from electronic exchanges at home and abroad and from the burgeoning off-exchange custom derivatives business that is not subject to regulation.

But in the years when Chicago still controlled this market, leaders at both the Merc and CBOT—driven by personality clashes and a deep mistrust for each other—botched opportunity after opportunity to combine forces to ensure the franchise.

As recently as 1998, common trade-clearing for both exchanges was proposed—again. But this effort, which would have cut the exchanges' costs and thereby made trading cheaper and more competitive for customers, foundered like all the others before it.

Both are continuing to proceed separately into a very uncertain future. The Merc is farther along the road to remaking itself and thus, is in better shape than the CBOT, to be sure.

But there's little doubt about who is winning the battle for the future. Sadly, it isn't LaSalle Street.

Notes

Chapter 1: Countdown to Liftoff

1. Currently Scott Gordon is the CEO of Rosenthal Collins Group, a global futures clearing firm.
2. My hiatus lasted but six years. In 1997, upon election as its Senior Policy Advisor with a permanent seat on the board, I returned to active leadership of the CME. As the saying goes in Jewish: "Man thinks and God winks."
3. I served as chairman of CME from 1969 to 1973 and as founding chairman of the International Monetary Market (IMM) from its creation in 1972 until its merger with its CME parent in 1976 when I was elected as the first chairman of the combined CME exchange. In 1977, after I declined to continue as chairman, the board of directors created the post of "Special Counsel to the CME board," a new office intended to retain my role as chief policy maker and implicit leader of the Exchange. In 1985, as the CME became more international, my title was amended to "Chairman of the Executive Committee," a position that officially made me Executive Chairman of the CME, irrespective of the fact that there was also a CME board chairman—the Executive Committee included all the board officers, including the elected CME chairman. I remained in this post until my "retirement" in 1991. In 1997, I returned to CME leadership as Chairman Emeritus and Senior Policy Advisor.
4. By coincidence, 1996 was also the year that *Escape to the Futures*, my memoirs, were published by John Wiley & Sons. The book was reviewed in the *New York Times Book Review* by Martin Mayer.
5. The PMT proposal was approved by referendum of the CME membership on October 6, 1987.
6. Its permanent name, Globex, was adopted a few months later.
7. Leo Melamed, "Embracing Reality," 1987 CME Annual Report.
8. Asian markets operate, more or less, 12 hours ahead of the U.S. time zone. Their opening of business coincides with the American dinner hour. To bridge this time difference, rather than open a night market, the CME joined with the financial community in Singapore in 1984 to

create the Singapore International Monetary Exchange (SIMEX). Beverly Splane, CME's former executive vice president then on loan to the Singaporean group, was instrumental in devising the Merc's Mutual Offset System that made it possible for the CME's Eurodollar contract to be traded in both time zones.

9. Carol Jouzaitis, "Merc Plans Trading by Computer Exchange's Link-Up with Reuters is Alternative to Night Hours," *Chicago Tribune*, September 3, 1987.

10. Carol Jouzaitis, "Merc Members To Take Vote on 24-Hour Trading," *Chicago Tribune*, October 5, 1987.

11. SEC Exchange Act, Release No 12,159, 9 SEC Docket 76, March 2, 1976.

12. Their plan for the development of a national book system was submitted to the SEC's National Market Advisory Board in 1976.

13. At a conference at New York University in 1979, the executive vice president of the NYSE stated that automating the NYSE would cost as much as $30 million and rhetorically asked where the industry would ever find that much money.

14. April 1979 SEC Exchange Act Release No. 15,770. It permitted a trio of unconnected systems to be implemented.

15. Leo Melamed, *The Tenth Planet* (Chicago, Illinois: Bonus Books, 1987).

16. The 1986 Strategic Planning Committee: Leo Melamed, Chairman; Brian P. Monieson, Vice Chairman; John T. Geldermann, Philip L. Glass, M. Scott Gordon, Richard J. Kapsch, Larry B. Leonard, Barry J. Lind, Laurence M. Rosenberg, Louis G. Schwartz, Steven E. Wollack, Robert E. Zellner, and John F. Sandner (as an ex officio member).

17. Leo Melamed, *Escape to the Futures* (New York: John Wiley & Sons, 1996).

18. *Barron's* Special Edition on Global Markets, September 28, 1987.

19. The other notables to deliver a eulogy included Nobel laureate in economics Gary Becker; Czech Republic President Vaclav Klaus; University of Chicago president Robert Zimmer; Arnold Harberger, UCLA economics professor and distinguished professor emeritus at the University of Chicago; and Michael Walker, president of the Fraser Institute Foundation.

20. Melamed, "Embracing Reality."

Chapter 2: Globex

1. This ethnic distinction was mostly wrong. Both Exchange memberships were, over the years, fairly equally divided among Irish, Jewish, Italian, Polish, Greek, and other ethnic groups.

2. Daniel J. Roth, the current President and CEO of the NFA, has carried forward this outstanding tradition.

3. Over the span of nearly three decades (1970–2000), under my guidance, five CME members of the board maintained a continuous leadership role at the Exchange: Jack Sandner, John Gelderman, Larry Rosenbeg, Brian Monieson, and I.

4. It is instructive to note that at that time our demand to achieve the capacity of 30 transactions per second was considered by Reuters to be difficult and unnecessary. Today, Globex has reached a peak of 23,513 messages per second.

5. As indicated, the French Futures Exchange, Marché à Terme International de France (MATIF), was already aboard.

6. I had placed a buy order of 10 Japanese yen so far above the going cash market that it would be nearly impossible for anyone to beat me for this honor. The trade ended costing me several thousand dollars. Jim Krause eventually became the chief information technology officer and made Globex the present-day premier global futures and options electronic transaction system.

7. William B. Crawford Jr., "CBOT Says Goodbye to Globex," *Chicago Tribune*, April 16, 1994.

8. At the time of its final shutdown, August 25, 2000, Project A had generated only 4.4 percent of CBOT's volume.

9. "LIFFE Declines to Join Globex, Citing Excessive Restrictions," *Wall Street Journal Europe*, May 18, 1994.

10. Leo Melamed, op-ed piece submitted and withdrawn, "The Final Appeal," *Chicago Tribune*, April, 22, 1994.

11. Presented at the Annual Meeting of the International Association of Financial Engineers, November 9, 1995, New York. Published in the *Journal of Financial Engineering* (December 1995). The essay, "Wakeup Call," was also used as the epilogue in my publication of *Escape to the Futures* (New York: John Wiley & Sons, 1996).

Chapter 3: EOA

1. Bruce, Blythe, "CME Independent Traders Seek Greater Voice at Exchange," *The Dow Jones Capital Markets Report*, Telerate Systems, December 27, 1995.

2. Many observers blamed reduced volume, especially in the Eurodollar contract, on the fact that the U.S. Federal Reserve had kept interest rates constant for a long period of time. It was a valid observation.

3. Globex, born as PMT in 1987, was officially launched in 1991.

4. In December of 1996, T. Eric Kilcollin was named president and CEO, succeeding William Brodsky. Kilcollin joined the CME in 1981 and had been serving as executive vice president of business development.

5. The CME division, representing full rights in all the markets, the IMM division, representing the financial markets, and the IOM division, representing the index and options markets. This divisional structure is still in place for certain purposes.

6. In futures trading, the term "broker" may refer to one of several entities: (1) floor broker—a person who actually executes the trade in the trading pit or electronically; (2) account executive (AE), associated person (AP), or registered commodity representative (RCR)—the person who deals with customers at FCM offices; and (3) Futures Commission Merchant (FCM)—a firm or person engaged in executing orders to buy or sell futures contracts for customers. FCMs are often clearing members of the Exchange. In the context of the current discussion, I am referring principally to floor brokers. These brokers earned a fee for every trade they executed for customers—normally customers of clearing members.

7. Throughout these writings, the male gender is utilized for convenience and efficiency. The female gender is equally applicable unless otherwise indicated.

8. For a more comprehensive description of floor traders, their methodologies and value as market makers, see Leo Melamed, "The Technique of Spreading," 1977, at LeoMelamed.com.

9. Liquidity, simply defined, is the quantity of bids and offers flowing to the market. Thus, when a broker acted for his own account assuming the role of a trader, he theoretically became a factor in creating additional liquidity.

10. Michael Fritz, "Document Untangles Merc Web," *Crain's Chicago Business,* August 5, 1996.

11. To act on the floor as a trader or floor broker, all members had to be qualified (guaranteed) by a clearing firm. Clearing firms would charge a fee for this service, usually based on the transactions processed by the firm on behalf of the trader or broker.

12. Michael Fritz, "Pit Bull," *Crain's Chicago Business,* January 6, 1997.

13. For a complete description of the FBI sting and more, see Leo Melamed, *Escape to the Futures* (New York: John Wiley & Sons, 1996), memoirs that chronicle my early life, the initiation of financial futures, and my role in the development of the modern Chicago Mercantile Exchange.

14. Sallie Gaines and Carol Jouzaitis, "Broker Rings Legal—But Can Lead to Abuse," *Chicago Tribune,* January, 30, 1989.

15. On April 26, 1989, an editorial by the *Chicago Tribune* lauded the creation of the Blue Ribbon panel and its recommendations. Among

the sweeping recommendations were the ban on dual trading in all highly liquid contract months, some critical restrictions concerning broker groups, a "Top-Step rule" that prohibited brokers on the top step of the S&P pit from trading for their own account, strengthening of surveillance, and even video cameras in the pits.

16. Fritz, "Pit Bull."
17. George Gunset, "Powerhouse Merc Group Seeks Peace Broker Associations Band Together To Answer Critics," *Chicago Tribune*, August, 21, 1996.
18. On December 9, 1996, *Crain's Chicago*, Reuters, and Dow Jones Commodities Service all reported that CME chairman John F. Sandner sold his estimated 10 percent stake in International Futures & Options Associates (IOFA), the largest broker association at the exchange.
19. Fritz, "Pit Bull."

Chapter 4: E-Mini

1. George Gunset, "Melamed Returns to Power at the Merc," *Chicago Tribune*, January 23, 1997.
2. With the single exception of 1969 when I managed to unseat the majority of the entrenched board members, which led to my first stint as chairman.
3. Gunset, "Melamed Returns to Power at the Merc."
4. George Gunset, "Leo's Second Coming," *Chicago Tribune*, January 26, 1997.
5. Michael Fritz, "Merc Vote Shakes Up Exchange," *Crain's Chicago Business*, January 20, 1997.
6. Gunset, "Melamed Returns to Power at the Merc."
7. Gunset, "Leo's Second Coming."
8. The PMT project director was Kenneth Cone, a brilliant Stanford University–trained economist who had taught at the University of Chicago Business School and had worked as a consultant at Booz Allen Hamilton. Cone reported directly to Eric Kilcollin, CME's chief economist, who had encouraged me to appoint Cone for this undertaking.
9. In 1976, I recruited Beverly Splane to this CME post after she completed her official government assignment as the first executive director of the CFTC, in which job she created the initial organization and staffing of the new agency.
10. Fred Arditti, *Derivatives* (Boston: Harvard Business School Press, 1996).
11. Colleen Lazar is the Executive Director of the CME Center for Innovation.

12. This was the approximate contract valuation (beginning in October 1997) after the original size of the S&P 500 futures and options contract was split by decreasing its multiplier from $500 to $250.
13. Once listed on the screen, the E-Mini contract quickly also became the dominant after-hours S&P Globex instrument.
14. Dow Jones News Service, "CME E-Mini S&P Futures Break 10,000 Open Interest Mark," October 16, 1997.

Chapter 5: Strategic Commotion

1. CME rules limited chairmanship to three consecutive two-year terms.
2. The full Strategic Planning Committee was composed of senior board members: Jim Oliff, chairman; Yra Harris, vice chairman; Thomas Kloet, vice chairman; Bill Shepard, vice chairman; Tim Brennan, Scott Gordon, Robert Haworth, Bill Salatich, David Silverman, Jeffrey Silverman, Joel Stender; Leo Melamed, advisor; Jack Sandner, advisor. From CME management, Rick Kilcollin, Fred Arditti, David Emanuel, David Goone, Jerry Beyer, Jerry Salzman, Geoff Price.
3. Three months after the program's inception, the CBOT saw the light and signed an alliance for after-hours trading with the DTB.

Chapter 6: Global Competition

1. Edward Luce and Khozem Merchant, "Cantor Launches Electronic Trading for Bonds," *Financial Times*, July 2, 1999.
2. Susan Kelly, Reuters News, "U.S. Exchanges Embrace For-Profit Moves to Survive," August 10, 1999.
3. Ibid.
4. Steven Strahler, "Profit Motives: Pitfalls Ahead as Exchanges Eye 'Demutualization,'" *Crain's Chicago Business*, August 16, 1999.
5. Kelly, "U.S. Exchanges Embrace For-Profit Moves to Survive."
6. "CBOT board approves parallel electronic, pit trade," Reuters News, July 28, 1998.
7. David Goone, Product Marketing Senior Vice President, was given the difficult responsibility of phasing in side-by-side trading by providing up to 500 additional Globex terminals at select locations for locals to trade at as well as deployment of the new handheld technology.

Chapter 7: Demutualization

1. Visitors included: in 1977, Ernesto Zedillo, the president of Mexico; in 1980, Ronald Reagan, U.S. President; in 1985, Li Ziannian, president of

the Republic of China; in 1988, Robert J.L. Hawke, Prime Minister of Australia; in 1991, Mary Robinson, president of Ireland; in 1991, George H.W. Bush, U.S. President; in 1992, Mikhail Gorbachev, president of the Soviet Union; in 1998, Willian J. Clinton, U.S. President; in 1999 (in addition to the visit of Premier Zhu Rongji), Keizo Obuchi, prime minister of Japan; in 2001, George W. Bush, U.S. President; and in 2006, Richard B. Cheney, U.S. Vice President.

2. The Federal Election Campaign Act of 1971 (FECA, enacted February 7, 1972) is a U.S. federal law that increased disclosure of contributions for federal campaigns. It was amended in 1974 to place legal limits on the campaign contributions. The amendment also created the Federal Election Commission (FEC).

3. Originally known as the Commodity Futures Political Action Committee, it is known today as the combined CME/CBOT PAC.

4. Of equal importance in these efforts were the public relations personnel in Chicago. Of special note, Carol Sexton, director of Public Relations, Joan Bush, manager of Government Relations, and Colleen Lazar, director of Public Affairs. Printed brochures and material were organized courtesy of the very able hands of Betty Hanning, associate director of the Document Processing Center, and her staff.

5. The broker had been charged with rule violations and settled, without admitting or denying the charge, by paying a $225,000 fine and leaving the Exchange. Michael Fritz, "The World's Priciest Real Estate?", *Crain's Chicago Business,* May 20, 1996.

6. Suzanne Cosgrove, "US FIA-CME Chair Sees Technology, Regulation as Drivers in '99," Market News International, March 19, 1999.

7 "Chicago Mercantile, London Futures Exchanges To Form Partnership," Dow Jones Business News, August 5, 1999.

8. Ibid.

9. Market News International, "Eurex and CBOT Considering Resumption of Cooperation," May 19, 1999.

10. Richard Irving, "BrokerTec Woos Liffe For 'Ultimate Prize,'" *Financial News,* July 5, 1999.

11. Peter A. McKay, "Donovan Resigns His CBOT Position Following Period of Strained Relations," *Wall Street Journal*, April 17, 2000

12. *Banking Technology,* "A/c/e Keeps Clearing Switched Off," September 1, 2000.

13. Melissa Goldfine, "Clash of Cultures Brews Trouble for CBOT, Eurex," Reuters News, May 25, 2001.

14. *Financial Times*, "Companies & Finance International – Eurex, CBOT in Link-Up Dispute – News Digest," May 7, 2001.

15. Meredith Grossman Dubner and Marius Bosch, "Update 3- Eurex, CBOT Settle Dispute Over electronic Trading," Reuters News, July 11, 2002.

16. Euronext was created in 2000 from the merger of the Amsterdam, Brussels, and Paris stock exchanges. In 2001 and 2002, Euronext acquired the London International Futures and Options Exchange (LIFFE) and the Portuguese stock exchange, Bolsa de Valores de Lisboa e Porto (BLVP) to become Euronext Liffe.
17. Isabelle Clary, "CBOT Turns to LIFFE Platform; Eurex Targets U.S. Markets," *Securities Industry News,* January 13, 2003.
18. Strahler, "Profit Motives: Pitfalls Ahead as Exchanges Eye "Demutualization.'"
19. *Securities Week,* "CME Board Receives Demutualization Plan—Or Plans?" September 6, 1999.
20. Dave Carpenter, "'Open Outcry' to Stay When Chicago Merc Becomes For-Profit Business," Associated Press Newswires, November 3, 1999.
21. Ibid.
22. Peter McKay, "CME Overwhelmingly Supports For-Profit Plan," *Wall Street Journal*, June 7, 2000.

Chapter 8: Dot-Coming

1. In 2008, the Dow was down 34 percent, the steepest drop since 1931; the S&P 500 suffered a loss of 38.5 percent; and the NASDAQ Composite experienced a decline of 40.5 percent, the worst year since its inception in 1971.
2. Gregg Burns, a top *Sun-Times* reporter, after hearing a speech by Jim McNulty about his plans, once asked me whether it was possible for a futures exchange to make enough money to exist purely from clearing activities of the B2Bs. We both were amused by the notion.
3. Reputedly, some 40 candidates were interviewed.
4. The full search committee was never involved with the economic package that was ultimately negotiated with McNulty. That was carried out principally by Tom Kloet, who was CME Treasurer, with Jerry Salzman, our outside legal counsel. Jim McNulty made some very tough demands and in the end received pretty much what he wanted. Years later, Tom Kloet, an honest and straight-up guy, confided to me that after he told Scott Gordon that he and Jerry Salzman thought McNulty's demands were "over the top," Gordon told him to "just do it." Gordon had publicly promised the membership that the new CEO would soon be aboard. George Gunset of the *Chicago Tribune* reported on February 15, 2000, that McNulty would be paid a base salary of $1 million; an incentive bonus of $1.5 million or 10 percent of the new Merc's net income, whichever was less; a signing bonus; a lump sum of $2 million; a stock option that vest over four years, essentially

entitling him to 2.5 percent of the increase in the value of the new Merc from the starting valuation; and 2.5 percent of the increase in excess of 150 percent.

5. Chicago Mercantile Exchange, CheMatch.com Sign Exclusive Agreement to Jointly Develop Certain Chemical Futures, Options; Agreement Formalizes CME Entry into B2B Arena," Houston Business Wire Report, September 15, 2000.

6. Fischer Black passed away in 1995. The Nobel Prize is not given posthumously.

7. To my disappointment, as of May 2008, Myron Scholes no longer serves on the CME Board.

8. Myron Scholes's acceptance was predicated on the agreement that I would act as vice chairman of the CMAC.

9. CME Center for Innovation Web site www.cmegroup.com/cfi. The Fred Arditti Innovation Award winners include: William Sharpe (2005), Leo Melamed (2006), Eugene Fama (2007), and Michael R. Bloomberg (2008).

10. David Goone left the CME to become Senior Vice President, Chief Strategic Officer at the Atlanta-based Intercontinental Exchange (ICE). At ICE, under the leadership of its chairman and CEO, Jeffrey C. Sprecher, Goone became a vital force in advancing the exchange into a major player in the global futures arena.

11. By the "Perfect Storm" I believe McNulty meant the coming together of a series of fundamental changes brought about by the dot-com revolution to what he called the "eco-system" such as stock options, B2B and B2C opportunities, OTC clearing, and so forth.

Chapter 9: Cabal

1. Edward Lawler and Jay Conger, "Comment & Analysis-Building better boards – Personal View," *Financial Times*, April 1, 2002.

2. Gretchen Morgensen, "It's Time for Investors to Start Acting Like Owners," *New York Times*, March 24, 2002.

3. Peter McKay, "CME Overwhelmingly Supports For-Profit-Plan," *Wall Street Journal*, June 7, 2000.

4. Zahida Hafeez, "CME's Chairman Vote about Keeping Old Ties in the New World," Dow Jones Commodities Service, April 23, 2002.

5. David Greising, "Not the Time for a Legends' Match at Merc," *Chicago Tribune*, April 17, 2002.

6. The first board Steering Committee, appointed on May 1, 2002, included me as chairman; Bill Shepard as vice chairman; Terry Duffy, Jim McNulty, Craig Donohue, Marty Gepsman, Scott Gordon, Yra Harris, Pat

Lynch, Jim Oliff, and Jack Sandner. Committee membership fluctuated over time, but the committee was always composed of experienced senior members of the board and management. It is now known as the Strategic Steering Committee, and I am still its chairman.

7. The initial conversation between the two chairmen, as reported, really did occur at the fabled Chicago Gene and Georgetti's steakhouse, where many of us traders were frequent customers. On a separate occasion, Charlie Carey rounded up some influential CBOT traders, and asked me to do the same for the CME, for a dinner meeting between our two communities (at Sullivan's, another famous Chicago steakhouse) to begin establishing a "mind-set" of integration.

Chapter 10: Baptism by Fire

1. Video presented by Milton Friedman on the occasion of the thirtieth anniversary of the International Monetary Market, May 16, 2002.
2. Closing of the congratulatory message by Federal Reserve Board Chairman Alan Greenspan on the thirtieth anniversary of the International Monetary Market, May 16, 2002.
3. Mark Skertic, "Eurodollars to Trade Electronically on London International Exchange," *Chicago Tribune*, January 27, 2004.
4. David Roeder, "Eurex Chief Insists Exchange in U.S. For Long Haul; Shrugs Off Low Volumes Since Taking On CBOT," *Chicago Sun-Times*, April 23, 2004.
5. Kopin Tan, "European Invasion: New Electronic Exchange Takes on Chicago," *Barron's*, Market Week, September 22, 2003.
6. Ibid.
7. The German delegation included Dr. Hartmut Schwesinger, President, Frankfurt Economic Development; Mr. Rudolf Ferscha, CEO, Eurex Frankfurt AG; Dr. Burkhard Bastuck, Partner, Freshfields; Dr. Annette Messemer, head of Public Sector Group Germany, Investment Banking, JP Morgan Chase; Dr. Karin Zeni, Managing Director, Chamber of Commerce, Frankfurt; Mr. Michael Gallagher, Deutsche Bank; and several other officials from the city of Frankfurt.
8. Joseph Weber, "Eurex Blows Into Chicago: The Merc and CBOT Lobbied To Keep The Upstart Exchange Out of Their Turf. Now, With That Fight Lost, A Battle Royal is Set To Begin," *Business Week*, February 5, 2004.
9. Daniel P. Collins, "New platform for CBOT. (Out with the Old)," *Futures Magazine*, Cedar Falls, Iowa, vol. 32, issue 3, February 1, 2003.
10. Some observers have said that one of the CBOT's greatest sins was not owning its own clearing facility.

11. Joseph Weber, "Chicago Takes on Europe; A Newly Revitalized Chicago Board of Trade is Fending Off Eurex – For Now," *Business Week*, July 5, 2004.

12. Jeremy Grant, "Two U.S. Futures Exchanges Join Forces," *Financial Times*, April 16, 2003.

13. *Dow Jones Commodities Service*, "ODJ, CME, CBOT Reach Agreement On Clearing Services," April 16, 2003.

14. Ibid.

15. Ibid.

16. Grant, "Two U.S. Futures Exchanges Join Forces."

17. *Securities Week*, "While Focus is on Eurex, Liffe To Challenge CME In Eurodollar Futures," February 2, 2004.

18. Adam Bradbery, "Euronext Liffe Has Tough," *Dow Jones Capital Markets Report*, January 26, 2004.

19. Kristina Zurla, "Liffe to Unveil Eurodollar Futures, Setting Up a Battle With CME," *Wall Street Journal*, January 27, 2004.

20. *Securities Week*, "While Focus is on Eurex, Liffe To Challenge CME In Eurodollar Futures."

21. Isabelle Clary, "Donohue: Winner Does Take All," *Securities Industry News*, March 1, 2004.

22. There were 40 Eurodollar quarterly contracts listed for trade, representing 10 years of 90-day interest rates instruments.

23. Leo Melamed, *Escape to the Futures* (New York: John Wiley & Sons, 1996), page 87.

Chapter 18: There Are No Jews in Bialystok

1. F. Richard Ciccone, *Chicago and the American Century: The 100 Most Significant Chicagoans of the Twentieth Century* (Chicago: Contemporary Books, The Chicago Tribune Company, 1999).

2. Decades later, the fascist movement in Germany also used the name "bund," which means "league," in creating a Nazi organization with dramatically opposite objectives.

3. Miriam Weiner; *Jewish Roots in Poland* (New York: YIVO Institute for Jewish Research, 1997).

4. Ruth R. Wisse, *I. L. Peretz and the Making of Modern Jewish Culture* (Seattle: University of Washington Press, 1991).

5. Motl Zelmanowitcz, *Memories of the Bund, in Love and in Struggle* (New York: 1998).

6. On April 12, 1945, General Dwight D. Eisenhower, then commanding the Allied military forces in Europe, visited the Ohrdruf concentration camp. After viewing the evidence of atrocities, he wrote in a letter to

General George C. Marshall, dated April 15, 1945: "The things I saw beggar[ed] description....The visual evidence and the verbal testimony of starvation, cruelty and bestiality were ... overpowering....I made the visit deliberately in order to be in a position to give first-hand evidence of these things if ever, in the future, there develops a tendency to charge these allegations merely to 'propaganda.'" This letter is in the archives of the U.S. Holocaust Memorial Museum (hereinafter: USHMM).

7. The ZOB was made up of 22 fighting groups, mostly leaders and active members representing various points on the political spectrum. The groups ranged from the Orthodox religious organization Agudas Israel, through the Zionist parties Hechalutz groups, Poale-Zion Left, and Poale-Zion Right, to the Socialist Bund, and the newly created Ghetto branch of the Polish Workers' Party (PPR).

8. Quoted in "Resistance During the Holocaust," USHMM.

9. The armed revolt in Vilna took place in September 1943, under the command of Itzak Witenberg and, upon his death, under the command of 23-year-old Abba Kovner after the issuance of a manifesto by its Jewish Fighting Organization (the FPO), imploring the remaining 14,000 Jews to resist deportation. The most successful organized resistance was carried out by members of the underground in Minsk, who helped between 6,000 and 10,000 persons flee to the nearby forests. The Jews in Lachva, lacking guns, set fire to the ghetto and attacked Germans with axes, knives, iron bars, pitchforks, and clubs. Source: USHMM.

10. *The Holocaust Chronicle* (Publication International, Ltd., Louis Weber, CEO; 2000).

11. Vladka Meed, *On Both Sides of the Wall, Beit Lohamei Hagetaot and Hakibbutz,* (Hameuchad Publishing House, 1972).

12. The concentration camps in Poland where Jews perished were Auschwitz/Birkenau, Belzec, Chelmno, Gross-Rosen, Majdanek, Plaszow, Sobibor, Stutthof, and Treblinka. Source: USHMM.

13. Elie Wiesel, "Pilgrimage to the Kingdom of Night," *New York Times,* November 4, 1979.

14. Tomasz Wisniewski, *Jewish Bialystok* (Ipswich Press, 1998).

15. Ibid.

16. Ibid.

17. Mimi Sheraton, *The Bialy Eaters* (New York: Broadway Books/Random House, 2000).

Chapter 19: Chicago Futures in the Twenty-First Century

1. Salzman, "Unnatural Monopolies: The Aftermath of the Shad/Johnson Accord," *Derivatives Quarterly,* Summer 1999.

2. Craig Pirrong, "Electronic Exchanges Are Inevitable and Beneficial," *Securities Regulation*, vol. 22, no. 4, 1999.
3. Ibid.
4. Ibid.

Chapter 33: The Law of Selective Gravity

1. Steve Chapman, "The case against a federal bailout," *Chicago Tribune*, September 25, 2008.
2. Ibid.
3. Thomas Donlan, "Where Are All the Capitalists?" *Barron's*, October 13, 2008.
4. Jonathan Macey, "The Government is Contributing to the Panic," *Wall Street Journal*, October 11, 2008.
5. Arthur Levitt, Jr., "Regulatory Underkill," *Wall Street Journal*, March 21, 2008.
6. Gary S. Becker, "We're Not Headed for a Depression," *Wall Street Journal*, October 7, 2008.
7. Charles W. Calomiris and Peter J. Wallison, "Blame Fannie Mae and Congress for the Credit Mess," *Wall Street Journal*, September 23, 2008.
8. "Review & Outlook," *Wall Street Journal*, September 8, 2008.

About the Author

Leo Melamed is globally recognized as the founder of financial futures markets. At the close of 1999, Melamed was named by the former editor of the *Chicago Tribune* among the 10 most important Chicagoans in business of the twentieth century. *Chicago Magazine* included him among the century's top 100 Chicagoans. In 2003, *Pensions & Investments* included Mr. Melamed in the list of 30 individuals whose contribution "made the most dramatic difference" in the management of money during the last 100 years.

Leo Melamed's achievements exemplify the splendor of America. He was a Holocaust survivor who found safety in the United States during World War II. The story of his escape from Bialystok, Poland, where he was born, as he and his parents miraculously outwitted the Gestapo and KGB, is the stuff that Hollywood movies are made of. It was an odyssey that took two years, spanned three continents, seven languages, the Trans-Siberian railroad, Japan—courtesy of a life-saving transit visa from the Japanese Consul general to Lithuania, Chiune Sugihara—and happily concluded in the United States in 1941.

In 1972, as chairman of the Chicago Mercantile Exchange, Mr. Melamed launched currency futures with the creation of the International Monetary Market (IMM)—the world's first futures market for financial instruments. Twenty years after their inception, the 1992 Nobel laureate in Economics, Merton Miller, named financial futures as *"the most significant innovation in the past two decades."* In the years that followed, Mr. Melamed led the CME in the introduction of a diverse number of financial instruments, including Treasury bills in 1976, Eurodollars in 1981, and stock index futures in 1982. In 1987, Mr. Melamed spearheaded the introduction of Globex, the world's first futures electronic trading system, and became its founding chairman. The Chicago Mercantile Exchange, today known as the CME Group, is the world's premier futures market whose shares are publicly traded on the NYSE.

Mr. Melamed has written extensively on financial markets. His memoirs, *Escape to the Futures*, have been translated and published in Chinese and Japanese, as well as Korean. Mr. Melamed is the 2005 recipient of the prestigious Fred Arditti Innovation Award of the Chicago Mercantile Exchange. He holds an honorary degree in Doctor of Humane Letters from DePaul University, 2005; Doctor of Human Letters from Loyola University, 2000; Doctor of Letters, University of Illinois, 1999. He holds an honorary professorship at Renmin University, Beijing, China, and in 2007 was appointed honorary dean, Peking University. In 2008, Leo Melamed received the William F. Sharpe Lifetime Achievement Award and was the recipient of the Ellis Island Medal of Honor. He is an attorney by profession and an active futures trader. He is chairman and chief executive officer of Melamed & Associates, Inc., a global market consulting service.

Index